Passion and Play

Passion and Play
A Guide to Designing Sexual Content in Games

Michelle Clough

CRC Press
Taylor & Francis Group
Boca Raton London New York

CRC Press is an imprint of the
Taylor & Francis Group, an **informa** business

First Edition published 2022
by CRC Press
6000 Broken Sound Parkway NW, Suite 300, Boca Raton, FL 33487-2742

and by CRC Press
2 Park Square, Milton Park, Abingdon, Oxon, OX14 4RN

© 2022 Taylor & Francis Group, LLC

CRC Press is an imprint of Taylor & Francis Group, LLC

ISBN: 978-0-367-40550-2 (hbk)
ISBN: 978-0-367-40465-9 (pbk)
ISBN: 978-0-429-35665-0 (ebk)

DOI: 10.1201/9780429356650

Typeset in Minion
by codeMantra

To the loving memory of my Mom
and the loving presence of my Dad:
Thank you for supporting me,
for loving me,
and for being proud of me
(even if it's for having video game sex on the brain)
(kinda awkward)

Contents

Acknowledgments

This book would not have been possible without the support of many wonderful people, both in and out of the industry, who I want to thank:

- My fantastic editors with Taylor and Francis, Randi Cohen, Will Bateman, and Sherry Thomas, who helped wrangle this book into shape!

- My amazing and kind contributors: Souha Al-Samkari, Ashley Ruhl, Kris Wise, Antonin Fusco, Aubrey Jane Scott, Monica Fan, and Sharang Biswas. This book wouldn't be half the book it is without your wonderful contributions!

- Special thanks as well to Zsuzsa James, Naomi Clark, Kyle Machulis, and Arden Ripley for additional support for the book!

- Thank you to all the amazing voices, game developers, and game critics that have already been talking about sex in games; it's an honor to follow in your footsteps.

- Thank you to those who have made all the games this book covered; your work has made a real, lasting impression, and I hope I've done it all justice!

- My mentor, Toiya Kristen Finley, for taking a chance on me all those years ago and for being such a guiding star in my career and in my life. I can't tell you how lucky I feel to be able to call you a friend.

- My other mentor, Tom Abernathy, for providing me my very first opportunity to talk about these subjects at the GDC Narrative Summit. This would not have been possible without your faith in me, and I hope this book has lived up to that faith.

- Warm respect and thanks to Heidi McDonald; your work and writing on romance in games has been an inspiration and a beacon in my work, and your friendship means the world. I hope this book makes even a quarter as much positive impact as you have, my friend.

- My colleagues and fellow partners in Talespinners (Matt Gibbs, Chris Tihor, and Cash DeCuir) for kindly propping me up during the last month or two of writing, and helping reshuffle assignments to give me time to write!

- Countless non-industry friends who have held me together over the pandemic months, whether my regular gaming crew in Vancouver or my old *World of Warcraft* guild. Shout-out to Logan, Grace, Fred, Shih Oon, Mike, Frank, Jarinduva, Vite, Yukashani, and Victoria, and everyone else I somehow forgot!

- Special thanks to Elizabeth Pinsent for being an absolutely invaluable sounding board and for mopping me up every time I had a meltdown.

- My extended family for politely asking what I was writing about, and being equally polite when I told them. Believe me, I appreciated it!

- Thanks to my late mother, who always believed in me and knew I would succeed. I hope you're watching over me still, Mom…and that you averted your gaze when I had to write the really sexy bits in this book.

- And the biggest, warmest, most heartfelt thanks to my father, who is honestly one of the best human beings I've ever known, who's been a lifeline through the writing process, through the pandemic, through everything…who turned off his embarrassment long enough to read everything I wrote…and who loves me and supports me with his whole heart. I love you so, so much, Dad. This book exists because of you.

Author

Michelle Clough is a freelance game writer, editor, and narrative designer, as well as partner in the game narrative co-op Talespinners. As of writing, her credits include writing for *EverReach: Project Eden, Destruction All-Stars*, and the *Choices* mobile interactive story, *Open Hearts 3*, as well as editing for titles such as *Purrfect Date* and *Ageless*; of course, there are also plenty of projects still in development!

Michelle also co-founded the IGDA Romance and Sexuality Special Interest Group with Heidi McDonald and has been a major voice on sex, sex appeal, and sexuality in video games. Since 2014, she has spoken regularly at the Game Developers Conference on subjects such as male sexualization, healthy fanservice, sensuality in game writing and, of course, multiple sessions on how to write and design sex scenes, which formed the backbone of this book. She also runs regular PAX West panels on sex scenes in games and on sexy characters for non-straight male audiences.

A geeky fangirl through and through, Michelle likes to spend her spare time playing video games (shocker!) as well as swimming, playing board games, watching movies, reading romance novels, spending time with friends, and falling down the YouTube rabbit hole. A lover of smutty things and a diehard romantic, she looks forward to having more steamy romance games to play and is looking forward to making her own soon!

Introduction

IF YOU'RE PICKING THIS book up, chances are that, like me, you have some interest in the subject of sex in games, how it's done, and how it can be improved. Sex in games has come a long way since the porn games of the Atari era, or even the days of the Fox News *Mass Effect* moral panic. But there's still a lot more that can be improved, both in AAA space and in indie space, and a lot of it won't be without a lot of frank, awkward, and detailed discussions about what's working, what isn't, what's not even been *tried* yet...and what audiences we're *really* considering when we make this content.

That, in essence, is what inspired me to write this book, and even before that, what inspired me to talk about writing sex scenes in games at GDC, to host sex scene deep dives at PAX West, etc. I don't pretend to have all the answers, but I DO want to talk about sex in games on both a practical and a conceptual level, to critique video game sex scenes in more detailed terms than just "good vs. bad," or "tasteful/mature vs. sophomoric/titillating," and to provide visual and gameplay language for future games to tap into. I talk about this stuff because I want to see *more* sex in games, in varying narrative and design contexts and goals, more mature, nuanced depictions AND more fun wish-fulfillment – and above all, more sexual content for *everyone* to enjoy, not just the audiences currently served by mainstream game sex. This book is geared to guiding you in that direction, as well as preparing you for some of the challenges you'll face.

This book is divided into four rough sections:

- Part 1 is about **sex, games, and culture**, and how all three collide when it comes to sexual content in video games. It tackles issues like censorship, technical challenges, sales and marketing issues, and industry pushback. It also touches on the purpose of this book and what it does and *doesn't* do.

- Part 2 focuses on **sex and pre-production** – in other words, considering sexual content and dealing with sex in the very early stages of development. This can include anything from the initial decision whether or not to include sex, to working with your team to establish their comfort level and investment in your sexual content.

- Part 3 deals with **sex in the larger game structure**, and what its place is in the game as a whole. This covers considerations like character development and creation, the narrative impact of sex happening at certain story or game beats, and even how sex can be triggered by design concepts like "kindness coins" or quest completion.

- Lastly, Part 4 deals with **the craft of sex scenes** and provides more focused, detailed considerations of how to write, present, and design the actual moment or sequence when sex is happening, be it in cutscene form or gameplay.

Along the way, you'll see some examples from well-known AAA sex scenes, as well as some standout indies, to see the nuts and bolts of how they present certain content or how they execute certain moments. Just to be clear, though, *I am not speaking as a representative of any of the relevant companies or as a developer who has worked on these games.* For full disclosure, I did do some QA for *Mass Effect 3*, and several of my contributors are good friends and colleagues, but other than that, I am simply an enthusiastic observer of the games we'll discuss here.

I hope this book inspires you to talk more about sex in games and ask more questions on the subject, both of each other and of yourselves. Moreover, I hope it inspires you to make your own sexual content in your games, whether it's by following tried and true methods or coming up with brand-new ones! Keep reading, and you'll find a mix of inspirational ideas, guidance on best practices, and elements of sex scenes you might never have considered. I hope you find it useful!

Michelle

PART 1

Sex, Games, and Culture

CHAPTER 1

What This Book Is (And Isn't)

W HEN I BEGAN THIS project, my goal was to provide a comprehensive catch-all book for explaining literally *anything and everything* to do with sex and sex scenes in games, with foolproof instructions on how to do amazing, sexy, universally appealing sex scenes that would work in every single game possible, along with in-depth information for every single discipline involved that ensured that devs, together, would find The One Right Way to do sex scenes.

This bold ambition lasted all of about…oh…five minutes (Figure 1.1).

For one thing, the topic of sex in games is, like, big. Really big. You could write entire books about one single aspect of it, possibly aspects I haven't even thought of – anything from technical instructions on how to do kisses in the Unreal Engine to the queering of game mechanics in "non-sexual" indie games that are, in fact, Totally About Sex. If I wanted to cover every single possible angle and topic, it would take me upward of a decade

FIGURE 1.1   "Okay, I've gotten as far as writing 'sex scenes in games are…' and already I'm seeing problems." (Rido/Shutterstock.com)

DOI: 10.1201/9780429356650-2

to write this book, and it would be roughly the length of the entire series of *A Song of Ice and Fire*, but with even less end in sight, particularly with new sexy games coming out all the time. So sadly, as much as I wanted to cover every related topic in this book, there are going to be some…gaps (Figure 1.2).

For another, sex is…a subjective topic, to put it mildly. There IS no "one-size-fits-all" approach to sex among games because, well, there's no such thing for humanity in general! There's the obvious aspect of sexuality as a whole – queerness, heterosexuality, asexuality, and the infinite diversity within those. But even beyond that, sex can be very personal! What really appeals to one person might do nothing for another, and even disgust a third. That can extend to anything from one-night stands to certain sex acts, as well as how those things are depicted in media. Everyone has their own perspective on sex, and while some perspectives may be "wrong" in terms of harm or bias, there's no "right" perspective on sex so much as "right for that person." And while I have done my best to make this book accessible and useful for everyone, my approach is of course influenced by *my* perspective, and a privileged one at that (cis, straight, white, abled, etc.) So how could a single book, written from mostly a single perspective, offer The One Right Way to do sex scenes when there is no such thing?

The answer is that it doesn't – it doesn't even try. What this book WILL try to do is to give you the tools you need so that YOU can find The Right Way To Do Sex Scenes for YOUR Game.

So, before we get into the meat of the topic, I wanted to go over a little about what this book is (and is not) so that you, gentle reader, know what to expect in the pages ahead.

This book is…a flexible toolbox with both best practices and self-evaluation

I originally started talking about sex in games partly out of frustration that few people were discussing how to actually develop the craft behind them – when people did discuss sex scenes, it was in big generalities like "lots of sex scenes present sex as pure titillation"

FIGURE 1.2   Yeah, kinda like that. (Songdech Kothmongkol/Shutterstock.com)

or "we need more mature representations of sex." Fantastic, but what do those scenes actually look like, how are they made, and what is the impact of the creative choices made? This is something where the composition of a shot, the nature of a player interaction, or even the light that the artists use can heavily influence how the scene plays out and how the players interpret it. So why are we not talking about THAT? And if we do talk about that…maybe we can learn what to do – and what to avoid – in more sexual content in the future?

That, at its core, is the genesis of this book – to provide a framework of questions, details, and things to consider for game developers who might NOT have thought of these things before crafting a game with sex scenes or sexual content. By taking all the details that developers have to consider for non-sexual scenes – what's the impact of this light choice? How do we respect player agency? How much is too much dialogue? How does this work into the larger arc of the game? – and applying them specifically to sex and sexual themes, there is plenty to think about as you move forward on your sexy projects.

To that end, every chapter in this book will feature a "workshop questions" component at the end – a series of questions for you to apply the principles covered in that chapter, both in creating your own sexual game content and in analyzing how other games apply those principles.

My hope for this book is that those who read it will be introduced to aspects of sex scene creation they may never have considered before. More importantly, I want it to help readers and developers evaluate their own creations by asking and answering questions about how they approach this content, examining their larger themes and goals, and bringing a new level of attention and care to the details that make a scene come alive. Whether this book serves as simple inspiration or a framework to build on, its intent is to empower you to identify and build sex scenes in the way that best suits your needs.

In other words, the only person/people who can really know how to present sex in a way that matches your game and enhances it…are YOU and your team. You are the expert about your game, after all. This book is just here to help you apply that expertise to the fullest, and in ways you might not have considered.

That's not to say that you'll be thrown completely to the wolves, dear reader! This book does include plenty of suggestions of things to do (or things to avoid) as well as some best practices for presenting sex in games. However, these are intended to be fluid and flexible. If something in this book isn't working for you, I give full and hearty permission to throw it out and try something else…but my hope is that it will at least work as a starting point to make your job easier and your sex scenes hotter and more engaging.

This book is NOT…a set-in-stone list of dos and don'ts

However, if you purchased this book hoping for the perfect recipe that would solve sex scenes forever, I'm afraid this is where I must disappoint you. As discussed above, there is no One Right Way to do sex scenes because there is no One Right Way to have sex (besides, well, consensually). For every "don't," there's a player out there who would genuinely enjoy that thing; for every "do," there's someone who would find it boring or repulsive or just Not Their Thing.

Beyond the larger question of individual sexual preference, however, there's also the game-specific question of craft, execution, and even genre. What works for a sex scene is entirely dependent on the game you're making, whether it's gameplay, tone, or characters. Learning the perfect way to craft a romantic, tender, uplifting scene between two idealized fantasy heroes is great and all, but if you're making a grim and gritty modern shooter with a bleak outlook on humanity, that's not exactly going to fit unless it's in a very deliberate, carefully done way.

Actual execution, be it technical or creative, can also throw "dos" and "don'ts" out the window. We all know that, in game development, there are often massive gaps between the developers' vision and what they are finally able to put on the screen and in players' hands. Similarly, there are plenty of games (or other media) that, on paper, sound like a *terrible* idea, yet end up working with excellent execution. Sex scenes are no different; every "do" could be ruined by tech issues, bad writing, or just general bad execution, while for every "don't," you could probably find a game that actually manages to pull it off!

Again, that's not to say there won't be plenty of recommendations and advice in this book, both in terms of what to do or what to avoid. But again, none of this is set in stone, and if you genuinely believe that something I recommend against is the right call for your game, then have at it! Just be sure you've taken a careful, thoughtful look at *why* you're doing it; make sure you have a full understanding of what you are choosing to do and to present, and what its impact is. That, in the end, is the real goal of this book – to help you get that understanding.

This book is…a guide for presenting consensual, sex-positive depictions of sex in games

Sex positivity is a philosophy that recognizes sexuality of all forms as a natural, healthy part of human experience, as well as advocating for consent, sovereignty, and safer sex practices. This is not the same as saying "everything must be sex all the time!" or "everyone has to have lots of (casual) sex" or "people should be able to have sex without regard to their partners or people around them." Rather, it is understanding that people should be free to enjoy the sex (or lack thereof!) that appeals to them, as long as it's safe, consensual, and healthy – that it doesn't matter whether you've slept with one person, a thousand people, or no one at all, as long as you (and your partners) are content and respected.

This book aims to apply that philosophy to games, characters, and narratives – to present sexuality, sexual themes, and sexual scenes and moments as natural parts of the world and of the characters' lives, as opposed to something shocking or controversial or "dirty" (the sex-negative approach). This means resisting the urge to write off explicit sexual content as "pornographic" – not only is this inaccurate, but frankly, the idea that "pornographic=bad" is very sex-negative to begin with! A sex-positive approach to games also means being willing to treat sex frankly, openly, and without judgment. It means exploring ways to portray sex with maturity and nuance while also acknowledging that yes, sometimes we just like to have a hot sex scene with hot characters, and that's perfectly fine. It is an approach that embraces sexual pleasure, both that of the players and that of the characters, and treats designing and writing toward that pleasure with respect and consideration.

Note that this sex-positive approach does not mean that EVERY depiction of sex has to be glowingly positive. There is certainly narrative room to explore consensual sexual activity that is a bit more "negative" – cynical, unhealthy, or just not very pleasurable. This is, after all, part of how sex can play out in the real world. While a lot of the advice in this book is geared toward creating sex scenes that are hot and/or moving to the player, you'll find plenty of suggestions about how to explore more complicated sexual moments. The point is, whether your sexual scenes are passionately romantic, casually hot, or deeply cynical, you and your team should be open to exploring the full range of consensual sexuality, and comfortable considering how and why characters might pursue sex, want sex, or agree to sex, and how they express agency in exploring those aspects.

This book is NOT…to be used as a guide for depicting sexual violence in games

The material in this book is geared toward designing depictions of consensual sex, even in slightly "grimier" and more cynical situations. Those discussions do NOT cover depictions of sexual violence, such as sexual harassment, coercion, or rape. This book should in no way be used as guideposts for the creation of this sort of content, as many of the suggestions would lead to potentially harmful, triggering, or wildly inappropriate results in the context of sexual violence – for example, inadvertently eroticizing what is intended to be a heinous or horrific moment, and causing immediate distress and harm to people who have experienced this kind of violence.

Advice on how to portray these themes in game – and the much larger question of whether they SHOULD be portrayed in games, or what sorts of games should portray them, or for what reasons (e.g., nuanced and realistic portrayal vs. dark sexual fantasy) – is beyond the scope of this particular book, and to be honest, I am not the person to lead that conversation. It's a very difficult, potentially painful discussion in which the perspectives of survivors should be centered, listened to, and, where possible, acted on. There are other game critics and designers who have more experience and credentials and who have much better insight on the subject than I do. Thus, *my* focus will be on the safe and consensual.

The one piece of advice I would give for those who are intent on exploring sexual violence in a game, particularly those looking to handle it in a dramatic game (i.e., not a porn game*), is to proceed with EXTREME caution and hire a sensitivity reader from the very beginning. Listen to them if and when they point out harmful issues with the project, or content that could be exploitative. Also, be willing to ask yourself difficult questions: Is this content *necessary*? Is it serving an artistic purpose, or is it for shock value? Are you and/ or your team the right people to explore the topic? If you're not sure, seek guidance and do what you can to minimize harm…even if it means stepping back from the content entirely.

(* as for porn games and games intended as safe spaces to explore darker sexual fantasies…well, we'll get to that part in a bit…)

This book is…mostly focused on narrative-heavy games with major/minor sexual themes

In a shocking twist that surprises no one, a narrative designer/game writer has written a book that focuses a lot on how sex and sex scenes can be part of your game's narrative and writing (Figure 1.3).

That's not to say there won't be discussion of game design in relation to sex and how to explore sexuality in less traditional narrative – games like *Plug and Play*, *Luxuria Superbia*, and *Stick Shift* do fantastic jobs of exploring sex through symbolic imagery, surreal situations, or experimental gameplay. There will be sections of this book that cover more of the mechanical design of sex in games.

But for the most part, the focus of this book is on how sex is presented in more "traditional" narrative games, whether they be cutscene-heavy AAA adventures, indie RPGs, or visual novel dating simulators. In general, these games often incorporate sex and sexual relationships as subplots to a larger, non-sexual story arc, such as saving the world, overthrowing the evil overlord, and navigating college. As such, some of the advice will be geared toward this kind of model and taking the questions of pacing, narrative integration, and so on in relation to fitting sex and sexiness into a larger narrative arc.

(But never fear, sexy dating sim devs, there's plenty of discussion of games purely focused on navigating romantic and sexual relationships as well!)

In terms of illustrative examples and case studies in this book, most of them are taken from AAA games, as they're the ones most known and most accessible by the widest audience (via YouTube, cultural osmosis, etc.)[1] But this book is intended just as much for indie developers as for AAA, and there will be advice applicable to both as well as suggestions purely for smaller indie studios. Regardless of what type of game you're making, whether it's indie, mobile, or AAA, you should find useful info here.

This book is NOT...focused on pornographic, adult, or hentai games (though advice is still applicable!)

Having said that, this book *can* also be useful for those making explicitly pornographic games or hentai games (i.e., pornographic games either made in Japan or using anime/manga aesthetics). However, these genres are not this book's primary focus, for various reasons. One of which is...well, to be fair, it's not my area of expertise! But another is that porn games often have a very different "narrative" goal and intent than more mainstream

FIGURE 1.3 Try to contain your utter shock. (Suzanne Tucker/Shutterstock.com)

titles and thus may require some significantly different approaches than the ones outlined in this book. For example:

- Pacing can become a much different affair in something specifically geared to titillate or arouse above other narrative concerns. For example, a slow burning sexual tension that doesn't resolve until the end may work for lots of more mainstream game genres, or even some erotica games; however, it may be counterproductive in any porn game where the object is to "get to the sex" as quickly as possible. Similarly, the point where a sex scene has "gone on for too long" is very different between a porn game and, say, an RPG – which at some point must get back to, y'know, saving the world!

- The level of explicitness in the detail can also hit differently when a game is intended as pornographic. For example, in an M-rated game, certain descriptions or dialogue would likely be handled with a lighter touch, or wouldn't be included at all – moreover, those descriptions and dialogue would need to serve a purpose (usually a narrative one) other than just "be hot." Pornographic games don't have the same concerns regarding their rating, and "because it's hot" is enough reason to lay on the explicit detail.

- With some exceptions, pornographic games function primarily as wish-fulfillment and fantasy when it comes to sexual content, with little regard to reality; in contrast, while other games may have wish-fulfillment elements, they often also grapple with more nuanced, realistic explorations and portrayals of sex, which is what this book is geared toward helping with. Things that are "fine" in the personal fantasy/imaginary space of porn (e.g., more aggressive foreplay without explicit "check-ins" with a partner, or even darker, more taboo content) may not be so "fine" when part of a larger story about "real" people and their relationships. The recommendations in this book are geared more to the latter than to the former, so may not be appropriate for porn games that are purely sexual fantasy.

- Lastly, pornographic games often (though not always) take as much of a mechanical gameplay approach to sex as they do narrative; rather than focusing on character, story, or relationships, many focus purely on the gameplay verbs (e.g., grab, squeeze) or how the verbs can translate into direct sexual action (e.g., clearing a line in a puzzle game -> removing an article of clothing).

None of this is to say that this book is against pornographic or hentai games! They absolutely have their place and their audience, and if you are planning to create an adult game, great! Much of the advice in this book CAN be applied to those kinds of games, whether it's the benefits of sexual tension or the role of dialogue or even ideas of how to use game mechanics and design for erotic gameplay. It's just that this book is not specifically geared for porn, hentai, or other adult games, so please take this into consideration in regard to its design and narrative advice.

This book is…for diverse game developers wanting to make games for diverse audiences

One of the main reasons I began speaking about romance and sex in video games is to push for there to be MORE sex in games, but more specifically, more sex and sexual content that appeals to a wide variety of audiences, not just one or two. Sex positivity is for everyone, and this book is intended to help developers create great sexy content for diverse audiences – either by empowering members of those audiences to create, or by helping developers who aren't part of those groups to make better, more inclusive content.

Of course, making inclusive content isn't always all fun and games, and it's not to say that sex positivity means absolutely no critique! Part of applying this lens to sex scenes is recognizing where depictions of sex can, by accident or intent, uphold harmful attitudes toward sex or toward our fellow humans. As an example, you can absolutely reconcile the idea that "titillation can be okay and healthy!" with the need to challenge titillation that objectifies characters in sexist or racist ways – for example, calling out how female characters always get certain "sexy" angles in sex scenes while the male characters get none. This book aims to point out common issues and pitfalls to be aware of, while keeping the tone affirmative and positive.

As for this book reflecting a particular (straight-ish white female) perspective, I'm hoping that the results will still be useful and helpful to *everyone*, but of course, I have my own blind spots! I owe a huge debt of thanks to my amazing contributors, who bring some diverse and thought-provoking perspectives and insight to this book. And there are plenty of fantastic writers, critics, and developers out there – particularly queer, BIPOC, disabled, and/or sex worker voices – with their own views and insights about sex in games. Once you're done with this book, I hope you'll continue exploring the subject of sex in games and checking out what those other voices have added to the conversation. Brenda Romero, Naomi Clark, Robert Yang, Christine Love, Ana Valens, Patricia Hernandez, Nina Freeman, and Lindsay Grace are all great places to start, but you can find a plethora of other developers and critics on blogs, Twitter, and in game dev communities like the IGDA Romance and Sexuality SIG. The more voices you can hear on this, the better!

This book is NOT…for developers who actively want to make sexist, racist, or homophobic content.

I cannot fully express enough how much this book is NOT for you. Move along! (Figure 1.4). And lastly…

This book is NOT…the final word on sex in games.

This book is…a good place to start!

So…let's get started!

WORKSHOP QUESTIONS

Analysis: Choose one or two games that feature at least one sex scene (optional or otherwise) that you are familiar with. In future chapters, you'll be analyzing how the sex scene(s) in this game are designed, written, and presented to audiences, as well as some thought exercises on what some of the challenges or creative intents of the scene may have been.

FIGURE 1.4   Don't let the door hit you on your way out! (Dirima/Shutterstock.com)

Creative: Think of a game project you would like to undertake that could potentially have sex or sexual scenes as part of its narrative or user experience. This can be a hypothetical project, or it can be something you are planning to make soon or in the future. Over the course of the book, we will be workshopping the sexual themes, content, and scenes for this project so, if and when you begin work, you'll have a clear and detailed idea of your goals and approach for your sexy stuff!

NOTE

1   Also, if I was unable to gain permission for copyright and screenshot use by time of printing, at least you can all still easily follow along via YouTube or image searches!

CHAPTER 2

The Myths and "Myths" of Video Game Sex

Part of the problem with having serious and detailed discussions about sex in games is having to handle the weight of cultural assumptions and so-called truths about sex, both in general and in terms of video games specifically. A lot of these assumptions have little basis in reality, or are based on highly negative attitudes toward sex; others may have a grain of truth in them, but are too broadly applied or boiled down to simple good/bad binaries.

Here are some of the most common – and most creatively harmful – assumptions about sex in games that underlie many struggles and resistance that developers face when adding sex to their games. If you've been pitching your sex-related game idea at an industry mixer, chances are you've gotten one of these lines as a response, or at least a line that's hiding one of these at its core. And if you've said some variant of these, then never fear, read on and learn...

MYTH #1: SEX IS INAPPROPRIATE FOR VIDEO GAMES

Firstly, there are some people who would argue that sex shouldn't be in games at all, that video games should not be depicting sex in any form and that doing so is inappropriate to the point of being scandal. Think the outcry on Fox News over the Mass Effect sex scenes, in which the inclusion of tasteful, romantic scenes of intimacy triggered a frenzy of controversy and insistence that the game was interactive pornography which featured rape (it didn't) and full digital nudity (it didn't; characters were blurred, shadowed, or shown in close-ups), and that it was marketed to kids (it wasn't; it had a Mature ESRB rating and was not intended for audiences younger than 17).[1] While Fox News was rightly scorned and criticized at the time for its inaccurate reporting, it reflected a deep current of discomfort over the very idea of sex in games. Arguably, that current still runs today, both inside and outside of the industry, just buried a little deeper...but it's still there, ready to bubble up again, and sometimes in the most frustrating and annoying ways (Figure 2.1).

DOI: 10.1201/9780429356650-3

FIGURE 2.1 "I was all set to invest in your M-rated mutant bloodgore splatfest hack'n'slash but…you're planning to show people having sex? Well, I'm out…gotta think of the children." (Krakenimages.com/Shutterstock.com.)

This discomfort begs the key question: Why is it inappropriate to depict sex in video games but not, say, movies and books and art? Sure, some critics are so sex-negative or prudish that they'll criticize ANY media that depicts sex explicitly. But there are also critics who seem perfectly fine with sex in movies or books, but balk at video games.

This can often be an artifact of old beliefs that video games are "for kids" – that video games in general are always going to be played by minors and, thus, should not "expose them" to sex. This, of course, is a ridiculous and outdated attitude, considering the demographics of gaming. The vast majority of gamers are over 18, and the biggest demographic is 18–34, more than old enough to handle a little sex.[2] Games designed for those audiences are marketed to those audiences, not to children. On top of that, the entire point of rating systems like the ESRB and PEGI is to establish age ratings and mark certain games as inappropriate for children. So the pearl-clutching "think of the children" is, for starters, based on archaic and incorrect ideas of who our players actually are.

But deeper than that, there is an even larger issue: the double standards between violence and sex. In games and other media, there is the unspoken acceptance that violence is "okay" to show (to minors, to teenagers, heck to anybody!), but sex is not. This attitude is not unique to video games, but it has a deep impact on the medium in terms of how we design our games and what we are "allowed" to focus our creative attention on. No one thinks twice about making a game with intricate, dramatic mechanics for dealing violence; there are countless games built around complicated melee systems, visceral gunplay, or impressive blood physics as their gameplay selling points. But if someone were to design gameplay with the same level of detail and consideration for sex – touching minigames, sexual rhythm mechanics, or sweat physics – many critics would immediately write it off as a "porn game" and somewhat pathetic.

This double standard – where violence is an "appropriate" gameplay theme, but sex is not – cuts off multiple creative avenues where designers could explore sex as play, as mechanic, and as experience. It means sexual, erotic, or romantic narratives are not given the same opportunities to drive a game's story, compared to the more traditional narratives of violence, aggression, and conflict. But it doesn't have to be this way! If more developers were free to explore interesting design or stories with sex as a theme, without having to negotiate the baggage of negative judgment or assumptions about sex, the result could be new genres of exciting, thought-provoking games and experiences for players.

Speaking of negative judgments…

MYTH #2: SEX CHEAPENS THE STORY/GAMEPLAY/EXPERIENCE

A very common refrain from sex-negative critics and developers about having sex in games is some variant on the idea that adding or including sex makes a story cheap, tawdry, or somehow "lesser." You may have heard one or more of the following:

- Urgh, why do they need to add sex to everything nowadays?

- It's a good story – it didn't need the sex/romance!

- Why would you ruin a good relationship/narrative/game/etc. by adding sex to it?

- Why didn't they just tell an emotional story rather than trying to get people horny?

- I didn't *need* to show the characters having sex (with the subtext that the game or story is stronger by avoiding it)

- And the big kicker: Why does everything have to be about sex?

To the last, I pose a counterquestion – Why does everything have to be about revenge? Or familial love? Or the urge to explore? Or the desire to conquer, or saving the world, or human greed or *literally any and all other human emotions, experiences, and themes that games explore?* (Figure 2.2).

Sexual desire – or lust, horniness, passion, thirst, however you want to name it – is a common human emotion, the same as any other emotion – love, sadness, anger, curiosity, and so on. We admire games that inspire these other emotions in us! If a game makes us cry, that is often considered the highest compliment; same with games that make us laugh, or make us feel warm and cozy. Games that inspire sexual desire and emotions in us SHOULD be regarded with the same respect as inspiring sadness or rage or joy.

But surprise! They're not. In fact, not only is inspiring desire or lust not acknowledged as valid or respectable as other emotions, but it's seen as inherently cheapening or making a game less emotional, sincere, or meaningful. Again, it's the idea that something that evokes tears or laughter is a valid piece of art or media, while something that evokes lust or desire is only shallow and meaningless pornography.

We need to normalize the idea that sexual emotions are as valid, deep, and worthy of exploration as any other emotion games explore. We need to move away from the idea that

FIGURE 2.2   Fires of lust? Not worth talking about. Fires of BLOODlust? Worth 50 hours of gameplay, apparently. (Tithi Luadthong/Shutterstock.com.)

explicit sex somehow cheapens those other emotions or makes a game "lesser" in terms of meaning, impact, or "worthiness" in terms of art or experience. And most of all, we need to move toward a model in which sex is not seen as a value-detractor or something that "cheapens" a work, but instead as something that gives new dimension and context, even if the context is, "naked hot people are fun."

MYTH #3: SEX IN GAMES IS ALWAYS AWKWARD

Unlike previous myths, this one has a grain of truth to it, in that there are countless examples of sex scenes – particularly in AAA games – where the sex ends up as visually or narratively awkward. Some of it is struggles with uncanny valley – the weird "realistic unrealism" of many 3D characters – while some involve other technical issues – hands clipping through flesh, strange facial expressions or animation, and so on. There can also be a lot of narrative awkwardness, such as cheesy or unconvincing dialogue that ends up being more laughable than sexy. And let's not forget the occasional hilarious misstep in terms of sex minigames! Certainly, the history of sex in games is fraught with awkward moments (Figure 2.3).

However, the idea that sex will be (or MIGHT be) awkward is not a good reason to avoid depicting it entirely. For one, it ignores the fact that there are ways to mitigate awkwardness, or even avoid it entirely. If developers are aware of the limitations of their budget, scope, and tech, they can design sexual scenes and sequences in ways that don't result in awkwardness or uncanny valley. Similarly, game designers and writers can approach sexual content in a way that balances organic character work with the limitations of the engine and game. And if explicit 3D sex is going to look incredibly awkward, there are always ways to have an erotic scene without needing to show the details, such as fading to

FIGURE 2.3 "Oh crap, our hips clipped right through each other again!" (wavebreakmedia/Shutterstock.com.)

black or focusing on things that *won't* be awkward. Those are all more valid approaches than just saying, "nope, too awkward, don't even try."

On top of that, avoiding sex because of awkwardness passes up on the opportunity to actually improve and iterate on how we depict sex as a medium. Sex in video games, like the medium of video games, is somewhat in its infancy. Pornographic video games are only 40 years old, with the first example being *Softporn* for the Apple II in 1981; non-pornographic games with sex in them are an even more recent development. A lot of awkwardness in the medium can be boiled down to experimentation, of designers and developers trying to find new, game-specific ways to present these themes and experiences, and…well, sometimes failing at it. But that's more reason to keep experimenting and finding better ways to tangle with this subject matter, particularly as more diverse perspectives are brought to the table and as technology offers new solutions to old problems. Being willing to embrace awkwardness sincerely – or at least take the risk of causing it – can help us improve how the medium depicts sex.

MYTH #4: SEX IN GAMES IS TOTALLY UNNECESSARY AND/OR ONLY FOR TITILLATION

A particularly common myth is that the only reason designers would add sex into a game, or have a game with sexual themes, is for titillation, i.e., to provide players with tantalizing sexual content purely with the intent to arouse and turn on, rather than any larger artistic or narrative intent. This usually results in people responding to sexual content in games with an eyeroll and a comment about how it's all about "boobs boobs boobs," or about how the only reason to have a sex scene is to satisfy teenage horniness.

To be fair, there are some games that do use sex purely for titillating and arousal purposes. The obvious example would be pornographic games where the entire intent is to arouse and titillate – but there are also mainstream games (e.g., early God of War games) in which the sex scenes arguably do not contribute to the plot or theme and only serve as an arousing intermission. These scenes have earned criticism for taking a shallow or immature approach to sexual themes and visuals, and at least some of that criticism is legitimate and earned.

And yet, assuming sex can only serve to titillate ignores the countless other purposes sex can play, in both a ludic and narrative sense. Sex and all its concerns – the pursuit of sex, the whys of sex, the act of sex itself – can be huge and important aspects of daily life for many people and many cultures. So why would it not inform the fictional worlds, characters, and experiences that the developers are building? Why would we not want to use sex scenes as a tool to explore how fictional characters navigate their relationships, pursue their own interests, and exist in their bodies and their world? Sex in games can be used to develop relationships or characters, set an emotional mood, and even move the plot forward – all of which are more than just a simple turn-on!

We'll delve more into how sex in games can be used later, but there's a deeper assumption here that needs untangling…

MYTH #5: TITILLATION IS BAD!

This is the natural extension of the earlier point about sexual desire being disrespected and seen as "base" compared to other emotions. Somehow, finding something arousing and sexy is Bad, and you should feel Bad for being so perverted and gross as to find sex *fun* and *hot* and *arousing*. Serious Games (™) would never be so shallow and awful! If you're going to have sex, then it had better be extremely mature and respectable and very, very *tasteful*, without a hint of horny fanservice in it! By the act of showing naked people for hot, sexy reasons, you are showing yourself to be base and lewd and awful and gross…and god help you if you actually acknowledge that you WANT to see hot naked people! (Figure 2.4).

FIGURE 2.4 The face I make when I have to listen to this line of reasoning. (Lisa Charbonneau/ Shutterstock.com.)

Again, it comes back to the question of double standards about emotion. No one blinks an eye at the concept of people wanting to play games that make them cry, or make them think, or make them laugh. But people who want to play games that turn them on, that are *designed* to arouse them and excite them sexually? Oh, they're perverts. It's yet more sex-negative attitude, and there's no need for it. There is nothing inherently wrong or immoral in wanting to consume or create erotic media or media that has sexual content that *you* like. Our sexual desires (or lack thereof) are a healthy, natural part of us, and exploring and satisfying those desires should not be seen as some inherently degrading or morally negative act.

Having said that…

MYTH #5.5: TITILLATION IS ALWAYS GOOD, TOTALLY HARMLESS, NON-POLITICAL, ETC.

On the other side of the spectrum from "titillation is awful and morally wrong in all situations," there's its counterpart, "titillation is always completely healthy and totally harmless, and no one should ever criticize it ever." At this extreme, any sort of criticism proves that you're "sex-negative" or a "prude"; to be a sex-positive game developer means liking and approving of all sexual content regardless of what it is (Figure 2.5).

Not all titillation is created equal, and not all of it makes games better; some even makes them worse, particularly for marginalized players and developers. What counts as "good" and "bad" titillation can get murky, as there are multiple threads in play: sex positivity vs. negativity, sexism, over-sexualization, gender representation, sexuality, beauty standards, the role of sexual fantasy and judgment-free spaces, and so on. In a void, titillation is perfectly fine, but in the real world, it must be considered in the context of the larger social structures it plays into or reinforces: harmful thought patterns, stereotypes, lines of

FIGURE 2.5 Oh look, I make the same face when I have to listen to THIS line of reasoning. (Lisa Charbonneau/Shutterstock.com.)

privilege, objectification, othering, and so on. Not bothering to consider the impact these structures have, or the implicit messages that your titillation is sending, will result in heavy criticism from your players and the community at large – and that criticism will be all the heavier if the titillating content is just meaningless fluff on top of it.

For example, if you have a sex scene that just boils down to "boobs boobs boobs" and nothing else – no larger story, no character development, just BOOBS – then you open yourself up for legitimate criticism on several fronts:

- **The role of the sex scene and the titillation itself** – Is it enough to carry the scene or justify its existence?

- **The treatment of the female characters** – Are they being shown as active sexual agents, or are they just sexualized/objectified without regard for their character?

- **The fact that this is Yet Another Boobs Boobs Boobs Sex Scene (™) of an industry full of Boobs Boobs Boobs** – Is it right to be yet another game that focuses on attractive female characters to the exclusion of all else?

That last one brings us to another, extremely pernicious myth…

MYTH #6: ONLY STRAIGHT CIS MEN LIKE SEX OR WANT EXPLICIT SEX IN GAMES

Many times, in creation and discussions of sex scenes and sexual content for games, there's an underlying assumption that the target audience for these scenes – for any sort of sexual content at all, really – is straight cisgender male players who want titillating imagery of hot naked female characters. This casts the "defenders" of sex in games as, well, horny straight men, and the "critics" as non-straight men who engage with every sex scene with the lens of, "this was made to please straight men and no one else."

But in all this discourse, the desires – and masturbatory fantasies – of queer audiences and straight cisgender female audiences are curiously absent. At best, it's assumed that these groups just aren't interested in such things and are not the target market. At worst, it's assumed that they're actively against explicit sex in games, and that they're going to "come for" any game that dares to flash a naked boob. Reactionaries will whine about "feminists" and "SJWs" being "offended" by sex in games and demanding it to be removed. "Well-meaning" developers will remove sex scenes or sexual content and claim they did it to "appeal to women and diverse audiences." And behind it all is the overarching assumption that straight women and queer people just aren't interested in hot, explicit sex

If you will pardon the personal, non-formal response to this… (Figure 2.6).

AHAHAHAHAHAHAHAHAHAHAHAHAHAHAHAHAHAHAHAHAHAHAHAHAH AHAHAAAAAAAA!!!!!

Ahem.

The idea that straight women and queer people aren't actively interested in sexual content is _**ludicrous**_. Let's start small and look at just a few stats related to how well women, both straight and queer, engage with sexual content they enjoy:

FIGURE 2.6 *deep breath* AHAHAHAHAHAHAHAAAHAAHAHAHAHAHA! (Khosro/Shutterstock.com.)

- The 50 Shades of Grey trilogy, known for its explicit, kinky sex geared toward straight female readers, sold over 35 million copies.[3]

- The romance novel industry makes over 1 billion every year and makes up 23% of the fiction market.[4] Plenty of those books have *extremely* explicit sex in them, and the erotica subgenre contributes around 14% of sales as of 2016.[5]

- Google Analytics data for 2019 showed that one-third of Pornhub's audience is women.[6]

- On average, college age women think about sex over 18 times a day.[7]

- Women watch and enjoy shows with explicit sex like Outlander (64% female viewing audience, with 2.5 million tuning in weekly in 2015[8]) and Game of Thrones (2 million out of 4.8 million weekly viewers in 2013, a 42% viewership[9]), to name a few.

The message is clear: Women are really, really interested in hot sexual content. If you expand that to also include queer men and people of other gender identities, then you have a huge audience of people who are eager for sexual content in games (Figure 2.7).

We don't have to look far to see that eagerness in relation to the games we make; devoted and creative fandom communities have sprung up around games with sex scenes created with queer and straight female perspectives. BioWare has earned a lot of female and queer fans for their romantic and sexual content, particularly queer romances and straight female romances…and you'd better believe their fans have Thoughts (™) about those sex scenes! There are also legions of fan creators – fan artists, fanfiction writers, and modders – who create huge amounts of sexual fan content for games, sometimes for games that don't even have sex in them! Between all the erotic pinups of male characters and explicit, lovingly

FIGURE 2.7 I think this meme sums it up best. (Meme image created by author using Imgflip, "Distracted Girlfriend Meme Generator," accessed September 13, 2021, https://imgflip.com/memegenerator/118429510/Distracted-girlfriend.)

written sex scenes between main characters, it's impossible to justify the belief that "feminist SJWs are anti-sex" or that these audiences don't have a deep thirst for sex and sexy stuff in games.

That's not to say that any old sex scene will do, or that games don't sometimes frame sex in ways that alienate female and queer audiences in favor of a straight male gaze. But if and when those audiences complain, the takeaway should *never* be they aren't interested in sex or aren't worth making sex scenes for. Quite the opposite, sex scenes can and should be crafted with these other audiences in mind to make them more accessible, more erotic, and more exciting. If "sex sells," then the game industry needs to start selling it to players outside the limited demographics they've been catering to. Rather than treating sex as something only a horny straight guy will dig, consider having more sex that appeals to more people, that involves different characters, incorporates different ideas of what is sexy, and thinks more inclusively about who is playing with a big grin on their face.

Having said *all* of that, let's preemptively tackle another assumption that might mistakenly grow from this…

MYTH #6.5: *ALL* PEOPLE LIKE SEX AND SEX IN GAMES

So, you've internalized and embraced the idea that people of all genders and sexualities like sex and sexual content. Fantastic! But it's easy to make the shift from that to the idea that ALL people like sex and sexual content. This assumption is inaccurate and harmful, as it marginalized asexual people and people who, for whatever reason, just don't dig romantic or sexual content.

Asexuality is defined as a lack of sexual attraction to others, as well as low or absent interest in sexual activity; aromantic orientation is similar, but for romantic attraction and activity. It's important to note that asexuality is a spectrum with different expressions and different degrees. As such, not all asexuals or aromantics dislike sex scenes or sexual content in their games and media. In fact, some asexuals will happily enjoy pornographic games or create sexual stories – they enjoy sex in fiction, just not in real life.

However, it's worth remembering before you add sex to a game that there are asexuals who do not enjoy sexual themes and content, either due to discomfort or just a bored sense of, "oh, not this again." There are also allosexual people (people who experience more traditional sexual desire and attraction) who aren't comfortable with watching or playing through sexual content – or maybe even just specific types of sexual content. As a result, centering or featuring sex and sexuality in a game will, invariably, turn some players off.

That doesn't mean you shouldn't explore sex and sexuality through games – otherwise, this book wouldn't exist! But it should not be considered simply a "spice" to add to a game that will make it more palatable to all audiences. Just as game developers should respect their "horny" audiences (including queer and marginalized players), they should respect their disinterested audiences as well. That could involve giving players agency to choose whether or not to have sex or initiate sexual relationships and give them the option to experience the game in full without any extra romantic or sexual themes. And it's fine if the game requires sex (e.g., as part of a linear narrative or a core theme), just know that some of your audience might go, "thanks, not for me!" (Figure 2.8).

FIGURE 2.8 Not everyone enjoys sexual content, so keep this in mind when including it in your work. (brgfx/Shutterstock.com.)

CONCLUSION

Many of these myths about sex in games come back to an inherently sex-negative attitude – that sex, sexual themes, and interest in sex are fundamentally bad or lesser, that the only options are to either bury and avoid it, or to offer it up in a lewd, debased form for some hypothetical perverted straight male audience (i.e., "men are animals"). Challenging these assumptions about sex – both within the team and within yourself – will be vital in ensuring you approach sex in games with the same level of respect and comfort as any other ludic or narrative theme.

WORKSHOP QUESTIONS

Analysis: For the game you've picked to analyze, look at the 6+ myths and examine how the sex in the game contradicts (or possibly reinforces!) those myths.

- Was the sex appropriate for the game and content?

- Did it "cheapen" the story in some fashion, or did it enhance it?

- Was it awkward? In what ways? Could it be improved?

- How, if at all, does it approach titillation? Who is being titillated? What are the possible larger implications of how it titillates?

- Is the sex for "straight dudes," for a different audience, or for "everyone"? What makes you conclude that?

Creative: Similarly, apply these questions to the game + sex scenes you are planning to workshop and make. If it helps, imagine you are encountering developers, stakeholders, or people at industry mixers who hold some of these myths as beliefs. How do you discuss your project, or the theme of sex in games in general? Examples:

- This is why sex can be appropriate in games/in MY game in particular.

- This is how sex can/will enhance my game/games in general.

- Here's how I'm planning to avoid awkwardness and deliver a really well-executed scene (or: here's how I'm going to experiment and learn from the awkwardness).

- This is how my game handles titillation in relation to sex, and what it offers beyond titillation.

- This is how my game will cater and appeal to diverse audiences/why there should be more games with sex catering to those audiences.

If you're still not sure of the answers to some of these questions, no worries! Keep reading, and you may find at the end of the book you have much clearer ideas of what you're planning to do and how you will do it.

(Or, as an alternate workshop step: Imagine these hypothetical people who are resistant to the idea, then politely and respectfully tell them to go screw off; sometimes, you've got better things to do than educate!)

NOTES

1 "FOX NEWS *Mass Effect Sex* Debate," YouTube video, 6:45, "tsweeney79," January 21, 2008, https://www.youtube.com/watch?v=PKzF173GqTU.

2 According to statista.com, only 21% of video game players in the United States are younger than 18; the largest age demographic is 18–34. (Statista, "Distribution of video gamers in the United States in 2020, by age group," accessed August 8, 2021, https://www.statista.com/statistics/189582/age-of-us-video-game-players-since-2010/).

3 G. Aviles, *NBC News,* "'Fifty Shades of Grey' was the Best-Selling Book of the Decade," December 20, 2019, https://www.nbcnews.com/pop-culture/books/fifty-shades-grey-was-best-selling-book-decade-n1105731.

4 S. Leach, Glamour, "Romance Is a Billion-Dollar Literary Industry. So Why Is It Still So Overlooked?" December 2, 2019, https://www.glamour.com/story/romance-is-a-billion-dollar-industry.

5 R. Dalke, "The Business of Romance Novels in the U.S. and the World," accessed August 8, 2021, https://cpb-us-w2.wpmucdn.com/u.osu.edu/dist/6/17036/files/2016/04/The-Business-of-Romance-Novels-Presentation-1t534ld.pdf.

6 M. Castleman, *Psychology Today,* "This Is Why Many Woman Watch Porn," June 1, 2020, https://www.psychologytoday.com/ca/blog/all-about-sex/202006/is-why-many-women-watch-porn.

7 B. Mustanski, *Psychology Today,* "How Often Do Men and Women Think About Sex?" December 6, 2011, https://www.psychologytoday.com/ca/blog/the-sexual-continuum/201112/how-often-do-men-and-women-think-about-sex.

8 J. Nededog, Business Insider, "5 Reasons so Many Moms are Obsessed with Starz's Sexy New Historical Fantasy Show 'Outlander,'" May 7, 2015, https://www.businessinsider.com/starzs-outlander-mom-audience-2015-5.

9 A. Watercutter, Wired, "Yes, Women Really Do Like Game of Thrones (We Have Proof)," June 3, 2013, https://www.wired.com/2013/06/women-game-of-thrones/.

CHAPTER 3

Challenges Part 1

Censorship and Storefronts

Contributor: Kris Wise

S O IF SEX, SEXUALITY, and sex scenes are a fascinating well of potential characterization, thematic exploration, and fun titillation, why doesn't every game have them? (Figure 3.1).

Well, of course, sex scenes aren't always the right fit for every game due to pacing issues, tone, or just different focus. But moreover, sex scenes can also be hard to do *well*. On top of the usual difficulties with making ANY sort of video game content, there are unique difficulties and challenges in the mix, both technical and cultural. If you think it's a miracle we're able to make rocks and doors and combat AI, wait until you're trying to make realistic butts and convincing skin contact!

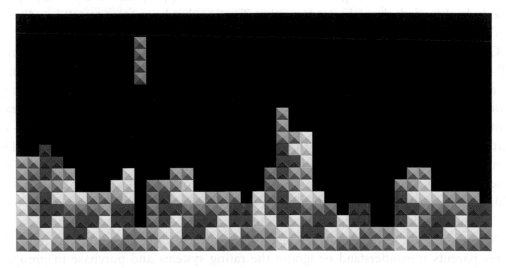

FIGURE 3.1 Yes, even this one! Look at that long, satisfying line piece sliding in there! (ace03/Shutterstock.com.)

DOI: 10.1201/9780429356650-4

These challenges ARE worth taking on, and surmounting them can create meaningful experiences and brand-new possibilities for gameplay and storytelling. But it's important to go in with eyes open as to what some of the pain points might be…hence this chapter and the next. This chapter will deal with the larger cultural issues in play that may affect your game development – censorship, obscenity laws, and storefront rules (or lack thereof). The next chapter will tackle more of the technical issues you may encounter.

CENSORSHIP, CONTROVERSY, AND RELATED ISSUES

The specters of censorship and controversy loom so heavily over the discourse over sex in games that they could have an entire chapter devoted to them; in fact, many of the other challenges we'll address have their roots in these. After all, how easy is it to be unrestrained and creative in exploring and presenting sex in games when you're constantly worried about whether you will even be "allowed" to put it in the end? When any and all sex scenes are at the risk of someone saying YOU CAN'T DO THAT – be it an industry organization, a publisher, a platform, or even a stakeholder – is it any wonder that many developers decide not to take the risk? Of course, it can still be a risk well worth taking – this book is geared toward encouraging more devs to take that risk! – but it's important to be aware of the restrictions and boundaries, even when they can be a little nebulous, and even when they're more social than legal.

For starters, including sex in your game – even if you're just mentioning it! Even if you're just lightly touching on sexual themes or having a very tasteful fade to black! – is one of the more surefire ways to earn a higher age rating with organizations like the ESRB, particularly in North America. As we discussed before, there are some heavy double standards around sex and violence in games, and which is "more appropriate" for young players; a bloody hack and slash might get by with a T rating, but have some tasteful nudity and you're often looking at a "mature" rating.

Getting a higher rating is not a death knell – most retail stores and game storefronts sell M-rated games, and many very popular games are M-rated, including titles with the dreaded Sexual Content™ in them. In some cases, that mature rating is exactly what you *want*. But if a rating system tends to hand out blanket "mature" ratings to any sexual content – if all games that include or address sex get painted with the same brush – that flattens the landscape and denies the nuance of how different games explore sex. Do a thoughtful and emotional lovemaking scene AND a raunchy, exploitative sequence both deserve the same rating of "mature"? What about an educational game for teenagers that addresses sex healthily and realistically; wouldn't a "mature" rating keep it out of the hands of the audience that needs it?

Nor is a mature rating a talisman against controversy either. For example, more than a few parents misunderstand or ignore the rating systems and purchase inappropriate games for their children – and of course, as far as those parents go, it's always the *sex* that's inappropriate for them, not the violence! But when they discover the error and that their children have been "exposed," many grow angry with the developers, and few are mollified by reminders that the game was clearly labeled for older audiences. In their eyes, it's not enough that there were warning labels to keep away from kids; these "dangerous" or "obscene" games shouldn't exist at all! And if their moral outrage starts getting traction in places like mass media, or even worse, the government or court systems, the results can be games like *Mass Effect* or *Grand Theft Auto* becoming lightning rods for controversy despite both games clearly indicating, "hey, this isn't for kids."

Of course, there are often even higher ratings than "Mature," ratings that come with much more major impact on the developers and game sales. For example, the highest rating the ESRB can give is the AO (Adults Only) rating, given to games with explicit sexual content (as well as particularly intense and extended depictions of torture and violence and real-world gambling); in Australia, similar content gets the R18+ rating. In those countries, fear and concern over selling those games in "the same places" that children may buy their games have led to a blanket ban on sales from retailers; you cannot "walk in" anywhere to buy them. The three console storefronts – Nintendo, Sony, and Microsoft – also do not allow any AO-rated games. This means that if you create a game with an AO rating – either deliberately or by getting slapped with the rating after the fact – you cannot sell your game on any consoles, hugely reducing the potential market for your game. Small wonder that most developers shy away from creating games with AO-level sexual themes and aim for the relatively "safer" M rating…when they're willing to keep the sexual themes at all!

(It's worth noting that the issues with ratings are more nebulous on the PC and mobile side, as many PC and mobile games don't *have* ratings. But we'll get into those in a bit…)

Beyond ratings, there is a new front where censorship and content restrictions can become a major issue: that of streaming and Let's Plays. Games can gain major boosts in popularity and sales by being featured by streamers, but due to the content guidelines of certain platforms, certain games with sexual content are barred from being streamed or shared to an audience. For example, Twitch, one of the most popular streaming platforms, has extremely strict guidelines about allowing almost any sexual content on stream. The rules state, "Games featuring nudity, pornography, sex, or sexual violence as a core focus or feature are entirely prohibited," and add that, for permitted games that include nudity or sexual content, "users may only spend as much time as is required to progress" (Figure 3.2).[1]

Note that the rules are unclear about how much sex or sexual content has to count as a "core focus or feature," resulting in, once again, an inconsistent and often arbitrary enforcement of the rule. This inconsistency was highlighted by Robert Yang when his games *Rinse and Repeat* and *Cobra Club*, both games dealing with explicit, thoughtful explorations of gay sex and nudity, both got banned for Twitch broadcast, while other AAA games with explicit sex scenes are allowed to be broadcast freely.[2] The implication is clear; unless you are creating sexual game content from the safety of a AAA studio and game, your game may fall under Twitch's axe and lose out on a potentially massive chunk of popular and critical attention. Luckily, other platforms do provide looser guidelines. Vimeo, for example, will "allow videos that depict sexuality that serve a clear creative, artistic, aesthetic, or narrative purpose,"[3] and YouTube similarly allows sex and nudity in the context of artistic content.[4] But even looser guidelines are not guarantees, and it's another layer of worry and effort for game creators to deal with in terms of whether their games will reach their audiences.

FIGURE 3.2 "Here's hoping I don't 'appreciate' Geralt's naked ass for five seconds longer than allowed!" (Parilov/Shutterstock.com.)

On top of all the market considerations, there is also the legal issue of obscenity laws to consider. That's not to say that games with sex are automatically obscene! After all, the laws are ostensibly crafted to target harmfully offensive material or material that harms minors...in *theory*. Unfortunately, the application of those laws can vary wildly, from lax to punishingly firm, and it's heavily dependent on individual judges and legislators. The situation was summed up best in 1964 when a Supreme Court Justice, Potter Stewart, called upon to define what counted as obscene material, simply said, "I know it when I see it."[5] In other words, the final word on obscenity vs. "worthy" material often lies not in a clear code, but in the personal judgment of those in power, a judgment that is presented as some sort of universal wisdom that anyone with common sense just "knows."

Even some of the "tests" for whether material is obscene or not can be extremely open to that individual interpretation. For example, the three-prong Miller test used in the United States to determine if material is "obscene" or not requires that the material (a) be prurient to "the average person," (b) depict sexual acts in an "offensive" way, and (c) have no artistic, political, or social merit.[6] But this raises the question: Who judges whether the acts are "offensive"? Who judges whether it has no artistic or social merit? Who is the "average person," and by the standards of which community? Will whoever judges this hold queer sexuality to different standards as heterosexuality? The arbitrariness of the decision and the judgment makes it difficult to anticipate how a game will be interpreted or whether it will fall foul of obscenity laws. And of course, if the people making those judgments are not familiar with games, adhere to conservative notions of sex, and/or are not part of marginalized sexualities or communities (e.g., queer), then developers suffer a greater risk of running afoul of "the rules" as interpreted by those people (Figure 3.3).

Working out censorship rules, controversy, and obscenity laws for one country is hard enough, but there's also the complication that comes with localizing for multiple

FIGURE 3.3 "I don't get it. Therefore, it MUST be obscene." (Anneka/Shutterstock.com.)

countries – every country has laws, attitudes toward sex, rating organizations, and rules as far as what is and isn't acceptable in terms of sex. Thus, it can make things very hard in terms of a "one-size-fits-all" approach and creating for one market may involve heavy editing for another. This is what happened with the French-developed game *Indigo Prophecy*, also known as *Fahrenheit*. Its European release included an interactive sex scene and only earned a 16+ rating in the United Kingdom and most European countries, reflecting more moderate attitudes toward sex. However, when localizing and releasing the game in the United States, developer Quantic Dream had to cut the scene entirely, or risk basically being banned for sale via the AO rating.[7] It's an added consideration that anyone wanting to release their games in multiple countries has to be aware of.

Of course, it's worth noting that, sadly, obscenity laws often disproportionately hit queer content – for example, insisting that a simple kiss between two characters of the same gender is "sexual" in the same way that a male/female explicit sex scene would be. In North America and Europe, the laws may purport *on paper* to treat all sexual content equally, but the lawmakers and gatekeepers often apply those laws much more harshly on queer content or queer creators. In other countries, there may be actual explicit laws about depicting queer sex or sexuality: For example, in 2013, Russia adopted an "anti-gay propaganda" law which banned anything that promoted "denial of traditional family values" or "non-traditional sexual relations."[8] Obviously, that would include any positive depictions of queer sex, but even simple kissing, hugging, and cuddling are still tied to the idea of "deviant" sexual relations and acts. China also applies strict restrictions to same-sex content in media, with even non-explicit queer sexuality often being looped in with "pornographic content" and subject to efforts to "clean up harmful and vulgar content" in an effort to "protect" young people.[9] In these countries and contexts, creating and selling a game with even minor G-rated queer content may get you labeled as "deviant porn."[10] You can imagine the reaction, then, to outright *explicit* queer sex...

Of course, that's no reason to shy away from queer content; arguably, it's a reason to double down and make MORE queer games, MORE queer sex, and challenge homophobic norms both domestically and internationally. But be warned that you may face pushback (from your team, publishers, stakeholders, etc.) who are focused on ensuring the game can still be sold and who may push to make that content optional, or drop it entirely. It's important to be ready to counter that pushback – to point out the importance of that content for the audiences you're trying to reach – but also to have a plan on how to proceed, even if it's, "so we won't localize to that country if it means compromising on our content."

Speaking of selling your game and finding your audiences…

FINDING A PLATFORM + MAKING YOUR MONEY (I.E., CENSORSHIP MARK 2)

Unless you are offering your game for free, you'll need to find a platform to sell it on, and that can often affect the actual game design (e.g., mobile design vs. console design vs. PC design). This is where our old friends censorship and content permissions rear their sex-averse heads again. As with streaming, AAA games have less to worry about nowadays; a blockbuster M-rated RPG or action game can feature explicit sex scenes while still getting onto big platforms without much pushback. But if you're an indie studio making an explicitly sexual game – or, sometimes, not even something THAT explicit – getting your game onto a storefront can be an uncertain, sometimes shockingly difficult prospect.

For one thing, the Adults Only rating ban on consoles and console markets means a lot of missing possibilities. Adult game designers have been unable (or understandably unwilling) to experiment with design or content in that space, such as exploring ways to use the proprietary elements of those consoles. We'll never see games that use Joy-Cons or PlayStation Moves in meaningful erotic ways – at least, not outside of small hacker and maker communities that experiment in jury-rigging them. On top of that, the main mobile game marketplaces – the Apple App Store and the Google Play Store – also bar "adult" games. While some enterprising developers have found routes around this – e.g., sideloading adult game apps outside of the app stores – it means that just putting up a sexual game in the store through regular means is impossible. Thus, the only market a hypothetical adult mobile game is likely to reach is a subsection of devoted, technically inclined enthusiasts (Figure 3.4).

There are more marketplaces on PC that allow for adult sexual content, such as Steam and itch.io. But there is starting to be some sinister pushback even in that space. As of the time of writing this chapter, the Epic vs. Apple court case has been playing out with a surprising but concerning twist: Apple is critiquing Epic for allowing "offensive and sexualized" games on its storefront. Epic does not allow adult games on the Epic Games Store, but it does offer an app for the itch.io game market, which DOES allow adult games. This was enough of a connection for Apple to accuse Epic of being "on the hook" for games "that are so offensive we cannot speak about them here," and asking if Epic supported "offensive and sexualized apps" to which Epic's general manager responded, "I don't support sexualized content of any sort." Itch.io's response to this controversy was mostly comedic (e.g., announcing that they would rename its "sensitive content" filter to "Unspeakable Games") but otherwise stood by their decision to platform and sell adult content.[11]

FIGURE 3.4 "At last, I can play adult games on my phone and Xbox! It only took an engineering degree, five hours of work, and 15 highly sketchy websites!" (FOTOSPLASH/Shutterstock.com.)

It should be noted that a good chunk of this resistance to adult content in storefronts is less to do with moralistic pearl-clutching (though that is part of it!) and more with larger financial concerns, particularly those to do with credit cards. Many of the large credit cards and their related institutions have been cracking down or keeping an extremely firm hand on allowing purchases related to sex, sex work, or any related adult content, not just in games but for multiple storefronts, markets, and other media.[12] Adult-only storefronts are often targeted (e.g., FetLife and OnlyFans), but more open storefronts are arguably targeted even more strongly. After all, credit cards do not want to be dealing with enraged parents, reversed charges, or legal action, so better to put pressure on storefronts to cut out that kind of content entirely. Game storefronts are vulnerable to this, particularly given the cultural baggage of "video games=kids" that we discussed earlier, and the hammer of the credit card companies could very easily fall on the places that sell games. It's not surprising, then, that many companies and storefronts would prefer to "play it safe" and be stringent about what adult content they allow, bury their adult content behind heavy filtering, or just ban adult games entirely.

"But that's fine," I hear you say, "none of that will be a problem for me! For one, I'm planning to release my game on Steam, which DOES explicitly allow adult content, so I'm okay there. And for another, it's NOT a pornographic adult game! It's just a game with some mature, sexy depictions of intimacy and sexuality, not a porno. So there won't be any trouble at all, right?" (Figure 3.5).

Firstly, Steam's acceptance of adult material is relatively new. The first uncensored adult game on an "Adults Only" filter was published on Steam as recently as 2018. And there have definitely been a lot of growing pains since, with examples of games being allowed, disallowed, banned, and unbanned, even games that aren't particularly explicit. Several

FIGURE 3.5   Oh, you sweet summer child. (FocusStocker/Shutterstock.com.)

FIGURE 3.6   Despite *Errant Kingdom* only featuring mild nudity and sexual content like this, Steam initially added severe age gating to the store page and was generally resistant to allowing Lunaris Games to sell without restriction. (Lunaris Games, *Errant Kingdom*, published by Lunaris Games, January 24, 2020.)

developers, including many queer developers like Lunaris Games, have had inconsistent experiences as recently as 2020, getting mixed messages on whether an age gate or Not Safe For Work filter was required while other, more explicit, non-queer adult games like *House Party* and *Custom Order Maid 3D2* having far fewer filtering requirements (Figure 3.6).[13] Lunaris Games' director, Kris Wise, is a contributor to this book and shared some further insight as to their experience.

SIDEBAR 3.1 – A NOT SO STEAM-Y EXPERIENCE (BY KRIS WISE)

At Lunaris Games, we rate our games as M17/18+, but none of our content is any more "explicit" than your typical BioWare game like Dragon Age or Mass Effect. While we do have mild nudity, swearing, violence, and suggestive sexual scenes/ writing, when we ran into issues with getting our game, *Errant Kingdom*, approved on Steam, they essentially launched us into a poorly managed back and forth that wasted our time and money and caused us to have to delay the release, all because they decided to interpret our game as something it wasn't.

It felt particularly pointed for us as a queer team making a queer game when you look at the content that *does* get approved on Steam without things such as the age gate that they sometimes tell developers to add to their pages. There are a host of incredibly explicit games that are apparently not beholden to the same rules that Steam often tries to inflict upon smaller developers like ourselves.

The forced "Adults Only" age gate that they initially added without our agreement during review would essentially greatly reduce our games visibility, and we really had to fight our case to get that, which is specifically crafted for games with explicit content, taken off. It's already difficult enough for indie devs, specifically marginalized ones, to get their game seen on Steam.

"But wait," I hear you pipe up again, "surely the issue is that these games went against the content rules of Steam! As long as I review those content rules carefully and check what is and isn't allowed, I should be fine. So where can I find that list of allowed and disallowed sexual content?"

If you find those rules, *please* let the rest of us know. We would *love* to see them.

Thus, we come to one of the biggest problems with many of the game platforms, particularly Steam and the Apple App Store, or any store which has content restrictions: The Unwritten Rules of What Is and Isn't Allowed. If these platforms provided a clear, codified rule set for sexual content and what they are willing to accept vs. reject (e.g., "partial nudity is fine, but no genitalia can be visible" or "sex scenes should only last for X number of seconds/long enough to further the plot" or "no bodily fluids allowed"), then developers would be aware of the platform's boundaries and be able to design within those boundaries. But surprise, there are no such rule sets available, nothing for developers to consult before or during development, no solid metrics they can refer to about what is and is not allowed.

Instead, the management and approval system of many of these platforms is, once more, "I know it when I see it" ("it" being "inappropriate sexual content") writ large – individual or groups of moderators and dev liaisons behind closed doors that look at the games in question and have the final decision on whether the game is "appropriate" or not. In many cases, this evaluation may only take place when the game is already in an advanced state of production, or even when it's finished…in other words, a little late to find out that the sexual content (or even *slightly risqué* content) that you've been working on for months is now getting your game barred from the storefront it's intended for (Figure 3.7).

FIGURE 3.7 "How dare you have nude Roman statues in your game set in Ancient Rome! For your crimes, you shall be BANISHED from the App Store!" (Oleg Senkov/Shutterstock.com.)

In theory, there are understandable reasons to make approvals based on human evaluation vs a strict set of rules. Sexual content in games is complex and almost impossible to quantify as "good" or "bad," and ideally, a human "gatekeeper" can provide useful feedback, guide good-faith developers, deal with bad-faith developers, and even advocate in terms of fighting for a particular title to get accepted. In practice, however, the process can be frustratingly opaque to developers and result in inconsistent and mysterious approvals, denials, and applications of what rules do exist. By fully embracing a "know it when you see it" protocol for approving games with no documented rules to refer to, the result is that games can be denied store access with no warning and sometimes with no specific, identifiable infraction. And without rules to refer to (i.e., "Oh, I see, we showed a nipple, and rule 3.4 says no visible nipples"), it makes it much harder to adjust the game appropriately (e.g., "We'll redo the scene without nipples") or to challenge the ruling (e.g., "If you take a look at the tape, you'll see that that was not a nipple, but just a shadow").

Leaving the decision purely in the hands of a single human gatekeeper (or group of gatekeepers) can also mean that it becomes, in a sense, purely subject to their whim(s), feelings, and even daily moods about sex, sex in games, and how the dev they're dealing with tackles sex in games. This can result in huge issues with consistency and dependability. If the success or failure of your game to be published on a platform comes down almost solely to which individual reviewer you're dealing with, that is A Problem™. It becomes a dice roll as

FIGURE 3.8 "I know that the other guy just approved Nude Wild Wet Beach Orgy Volleyball, but I'll be damned if I let this subtle and understated sexual fondling make it through on MY watch!" (Luis Molinero/Shutterstock.com.)

to whether your reviewer will be open and accepting or closed off and disapproving. And of course, it makes the platform's track record wildly inconsistent as every game ends up having a wildly different experience not only because of different content, but also because of different reviewers (Figure 3.8).

Other issues:

- Having multiple gatekeepers with multiple Opinions™ on sexual content means that even when things are going "well," they may not go well forever. You might have a developer relations representative, for example, who genuinely loves your game and believes in how it uses sexual content…but what do their bosses think? Or worse, what happens if they leave the company or project, and your new rep is a lot less enthusiastic?

- If the reviewers approach their work with "I know it when I see it" as their mantra for determining whether a game is appropriate or not, that begs the question: Can they clearly communicate what "it" is? Similar to the obscenity laws discussed earlier, where it's left unclear as to what counts as "artistic merit" and who determines that, not every reviewer is going to be able, or willing, to explain their objections in a useful way to their developers. Thus, many devs are stuck with stock rejections like "Your game does not meet our standards for sexual content" with no sense of which standards those are! When they press for actionable feedback, they may only get vague hints or impressions, if that.

- And of course, sadly, this is yet another place where biases and harmful attitudes like sexism and homophobia can come into play. The Lunaris Games example certainly raises eyebrows about how a tastefully sexy queer game that would earn an M-rating at worst somehow gets more pushback about its adult and NSFW filters than pornographic games featuring explicit straight sex or sexual content geared for straight men. Is it just bad luck that developers like Lunaris got reviewers who are just sex-negative in general? Or possible evidence of a trend where reviewers are comfortable with explicit sexual content for straight men but uncomfortable with even the suggestion of sexual content for other audiences? It suggests at best a mismanagement of who should review which games (e.g., are there enough marginalized, sex-positive voices at the reviewing table?) and, at worst, an open homophobic bias of what sex games are "worthy" to be sold on the storefront.

The good news is, there are still some storefronts with a much more accepting, open attitude to sexual content in games. Platforms like Steam, the Epic Game Store, and the Apple App Store are no longer the only options. While it may mean losing out on a wider user base, your user base and target audience may be more easily found elsewhere. If your goal is to put up something uncensored and explicit (particularly "adult") and you don't want to go through a rigorous approval process, some of the more well-known platform options are:

- **Itch.io** – An open platform that allows any and all developers to upload, host, and sell their games to audiences. It's known for allowing huge levels of freedom to the developers; there is no "approval" process, and any developer can simply upload a game to the storefront and set their own price. As such, it's very easy to create and sell games with sexual content. However, itch.io arguably struggles more with discoverability than Steam or other platforms. Steam, for example, is a well-known brand, and thus, more people shop there for their games or browse around; itch.io users, in contrast, tend to be looking for something very specific. The storefront is filled with so many independent games that it's even easier for your game to get "buried" in the landslide of content so that no one can "find" your game in the first place. More worryingly, the attention from the Apple vs. Epic case may result in the platform receiving more negative scrutiny for its permissiveness in regard to sex. And unlike larger platforms, it has way more to lose if the credit card companies come knocking.

- **Adult game platforms like Nutaku** – There are several web-based storefronts that do specialize in adult games, encouraging developers of explicit, pornographic games to publish on their platform and, in some cases, even convert non-adult games to an adult format! If you are creating that sort of sexual game content – particularly if your game is targeted at the hentai market or other straight male adult markets – those platforms might be perfect for you! However, it goes without saying that just because a game is sexual or sexy, or because it features explicit sex, that does not mean that it's porn. And if it's not porn, well...it probably doesn't belong on a porn site. For many games, even those with sex scenes or sexual intimacy, a platform like Nutaku is not the right match as the focus and tone are entirely inappropriate. And of course, many of the pornographic game platforms are heavily branded toward

FIGURE 3.9 A visual representation of 99% of the Nutaku user experience. (Image courtesy of Shutterstock; unpict/Shutterstock.com.)

particular demographics and thus can be pretty hostile in terms of first impressions for players outside their demographic. While companies like Nutaku are now seeking games with other kinds of sexual content (e.g., porn for queer audiences), the branding and artwork on their site can be a turnoff for those other audiences. And if you're aiming for those other audiences, what sorts of things are they going to have to click through to find you? (Figure 3.9).

Given the sheer weight of complexity in terms of choosing and negotiating storefronts, it's no wonder that many developers avoid sex entirely, or at the most stick with a more "tasteful" and "restrained" approach where the sex is a minor part of the larger game. Who wants to do that much work only to have it tossed at the last minute?

None of this chapter is intended to dissuade you from including sex in your game; in fact, my hope is that it will galvanize you to make your stand, create great sexual content, and push back against some of the larger cultural resistance against sex in games. But I also want to ensure that your game actually gets made, rather than getting blocked by censorship or storefront issues. So, if you are making a game with sexual content:

- Know what platforms you are planning to release to, and research their policies, both their stated and "unstated" ones. Reach out to other developers who have had dealings with the platform to learn more about their experiences, the reviewing structure, and what "unwritten" rules they may have come across.

- Identify games with a similar focus and/or content rating as yours and research their route to storefronts and sale. If possible, make contact with the developers to find out more about their experiences. Be ready to refer to these games if/when challenged; it can be a lot easier to communicate with reviewers on platforms like Steam if you can say, "Our game is about as explicit as [X game]" or "We're aiming for the same feel as [Y game]."

- Consider whether the sexual content is best served as an integral part of the base game, or whether it can work as a "Not Safe For Work" DLC add-on. Several games have been able to establish themselves in storefronts by keeping the base game at a lower rating (T or M) and either avoiding sex or fading to black when scenes get steamy; they then place the explicit content (nudity, sex, etc.) in a separate DLC add-on that is age-gated for adults only. This doesn't work for every game – some games NEED the sex as part of the base game – but it's worth considering if there's flexibility there.

Even if you're not making sexy games and having to deal with this personally, there are still things you can do to help make the larger culture better for these creators:

- Vote for progressive, sex-positive policies, representatives, and policymakers, particularly those who support sex work and adult content providers. Protest against sex-negative policies and business decisions both in and out of the gaming industry (e.g., OnlyFans recent and brief decision to excise sexual content, the even more recent change at Gamejolt in which games with sexual themes were removed from the marketplace). Normalize the cultural idea that sexual content is, well, normal!

- Use social media to signal boost and support developers creating sexual content in games, particularly queer and marginalized creators.

- Similarly, support and signal boost critique of sex negativity, gatekeeping, and double standards in storefront and platform policy. If your favorite developers are struggling to get their games approved for Steam, let Steam know you're not happy!

- Push back against sex-negative attitudes among your peers and platform holders. Challenge blanket assumptions and remind people that there is more to sexual games than hentai and porn (not that there's anything wrong with those either!)

WORKSHOP QUESTIONS

Analysis: For the game you've picked to analyze, answer the following questions:

- What rating does the game have, if any?
  - If it has been rated, compare its ratings across different regions (e.g., United States vs. Europe vs. Japan vs. etc. etc.). Would you say its rating is appropriate based on its level of sexual content?
  - If it has NOT been rated, what rating would you assign it based on your local rating board?

- What platforms was this game sold on? Were there any reports of struggles to get the game released on those platforms?

- In terms of how its sex scenes are presented, can you identify any elements that may be there for reasons of censorship or keeping the rating low (e.g., using modesty underwear during sex scenes vs. fully nude models)?

- Research to see if there were any controversies around the sexual content in the game, either before release, at release, or later.

Creative: Consider the game you're planning to make, and answer the following questions:

- What do you imagine as the ideal "rating" for your game to accurately convey the nature of the sexual content? Will you be planning to pursue an official rating with any game regulatory organizations?

- What platforms are you planning to release on? What are their policies in regard to games with sexual content? Are there similar games as yours on these platforms? Will players be able to find your game easily, or do you expect there to be filters in place?

- What scenes or content, if any, do you expect controversy about? What kind of controversy – among players, among media, or at a legal level? If appropriate, consider some possible responses for if challenges or controversies arrive; you are not bound to these responses and can craft a better one if the need arises, but it can be handy to have a rough idea of how you will defend your game and your creative choices on a publicity and a legal level.

NOTES

1 Twitch, "Nudity, Pornography, and Other Sexual Content," accessed August 14, 2021, https://www.twitch.tv/p/en/legal/community-guidelines/sexualcontent/.
2 R. Yang, "On My Games Being Twice Banned by Twitch," September 24, 2015, https://www.blog.radiator.debacle.us/2015/09/on-my-games-being-twice-banned-by-twitch.html.
3 Vimeo, "Vimeo Acceptable Use Community Guidelines," April 15, 2021, https://vimeo.com/help/guidelines.
4 YouTube, "Nudity & Sexual Content Policies," accessed August 14, 2021, https://support.google.com/youtube/answer/2802002#zippy=%2Ceducational-content.
5 FindLaw, "Movie Day at the Supreme Court or 'I Know It When I See It': A History of the Definition of Obscenity," April 26, 2016, https://corporate.findlaw.com/litigation-disputes/movie-day-at-the-supreme-court-or-i-know-it-when-i-see-it-a.html.
6 Ibid.
7 S. Morris, Outcyders, "Video Game Age Ratings Around the World: A Look at How Countries Rate Their Games," October 15, 2016, https://www.outcyders.net/article/video-game-age-ratings-around-world-a-look-at-how-countries-rate-their-games.
8 Human Rights Watch, "No Support: Russia's 'Gay Propaganda' Law Imperils LGBT Youth," December 11, 2018, https://www.hrw.org/report/2018/12/11/no-support/russias-gay-propaganda-law-imperils-lgbt-youth.

9 Graeme Reid, Human Rights Watch, "China's Pornography Laws Are a Backdoor for Censorship," November 29, 2018, https://www.hrw.org/news/2018/11/29/chinas-pornography-laws-are-backdoor-censorship.

10 Not that it won't get you the same label unofficially in Western countries like the States, mind you…

11 A Robertson, The Verge, "Apple Is Using Itch.io's 'Offensive and Sexualized' Games as a Cudgel Against Epic," May 7, 2021, https://www.theverge.com/2021/5/7/22425759/epic-apple-trial-app-store-itch-io-offensive-sexualized-unspeakable-games-day-5.

12 J. Malcolm, Electronic Frontier Foundation, "Payment Processors are Still Policing Your Sex Life, and the Latest Victim Is FetLife," March 15, 2017, https://www.eff.org/deeplinks/2017/03/payment-processors-are-still-policing-your-sex-life.

13 Valens, Daily Dot, "Queer Developer Blasts Steam Over 'Backwards' Adult Filter Review," Published January 16, 2020, updated May 19, 2021, https://www.dailydot.com/irl/steam-adult-content-queer-developer/.

CHAPTER 4

Challenges Part 2

The Terrors of Tech

I N THE PREVIOUS CHAPTER, we discussed the larger cultural barriers and concerns about including sex in games – censorship, obscenity laws, and storefront policies, etc. But I assume that, if you're reading this book, you're willing to push through all those external pressures and challenges to make the sexy game of your dreams. Hooray!

So it's all easy from here, right?

Well, sure…if you discount that whole "making a video game" thing.

Let's face it; making games is *hard*, regardless of whether sex even enters the picture. Depending on the engine you're using, the resources you're dealing with, the size of your team, and a million other factors, making a *door* open when a player touches it seems like a miracle. So if your goal is to make skin that flushes realistically (and erotically) when a player touches it…well, let's just say you're looking at a challenge. Both in terms of the tech and in terms of convincing your team that it's worth the effort (Figure 4.1).

Creating sex scenes in video games, particularly 3D video games, involves dealing with a lot of the regular challenges that all game creation goes through, but also involves some unique challenges due to the nature of sex and how it features humans (or non-humans) in more intimate, more exposed situations than most kinds of gameplay or even narrative cutscenes that we see. Still, these challenges aren't insurmountable, particularly if you have a big budget behind you…and even if you don't, there are still ways you can make fantastic sexual content in your game. It just helps to be aware of a few pitfalls starting out, either to conquer them or to plot a different route…so let's talk about them.

TECHNICAL BARRIERS AND CONSTRAINTS OF 3D GAME SEX

There are many, many technical challenges in creating satisfying, erotic sex scenes, arguably more challenges than other kinds of moments and story beats in a game. Part of the challenge is that, with sex, so much of the larger mood depends on getting the details right – not necessarily the mechanical details, but the sensory details that come from the

DOI: 10.1201/9780429356650-5

FIGURE 4.1 "Let's put it this way…I can either finish this level, or I can spend time building the Bedroom of Boink. I know which I'd rather do…" (DC Studio/Shutterstock.com.)

human (or inhuman?) experience. Think of how the skin might react to being touched, or the unique way a breath sounds against someone else's body, or the different way lips move against each other…all the little details that convey the idea of human flesh, of movement, of vitality. Unfortunately, a lot of them can be very difficult, time-consuming, or resource-intensive to include in a game. And while photorealism has become more of a reachable goal in recent years, that's mostly only for large companies with equally large budgets. For everyone else, at least everyone working in the 3D space, they and their character models are often stuck in what we call the uncanny valley, at least when it comes to sex (Figure 4.2).

The uncanny valley refers to a phenomenon with human-like artificial figures, be they robots or digital characters. It turns out that humans often feel deeply uncomfortable when presented with an artificial being that looks ALMOST perfectly human…except for something that's clearly "off" or unnatural.[1] This can be anything from a slight plasticky sheen on the skin to eyes that don't look real to a jerky, inhuman way of moving. There's a gap between our eyes telling us, "This looks like a human," and our mind telling us, "Wait, no it isn't," and it's this gap (the uncanny valley) that often causes cognitive dissonance and discomfort. And while this discomfort might be negligible in the context of regular gameplay and action, it often hits players particularly hard when it comes to sex scenes. Such scenes are often described, at best, like seeing plastic Barbie dolls make out…and at worst, as creepy to the point of killing any arousal the scene might otherwise cause.

In my opinion, this particular repulsion to the uncanny valley in 3D sex scenes is for several reasons:

- Sex represents a somewhat vulnerable state for most people, physically if not emotionally. We might be naked, or in close quarters, or in our private living spaces, or just in an awkward position (literally). In reality, sex is a very human experience and

FIGURE 4.2 No, not that valley! That valley looks actually fun to have sex in! (Denis Belitsky/Shutterstock.com.)

involves everything that goes into human bodies, warts and vulnerabilities and all. Thus, when presented with a character that is pinging our NOT HUMAN radar – unless they're *actually* not human, like an alien or fantasy race – we feel even more uncomfortable than we would in a less vulnerable situation. Even if we logically know these uncanny digital characters aren't going to terrorize us, our subconscious still connects "moment of vulnerability" with "looks like a human but something's WRONG" and gets "DANGER," or at the very least, "not making me feel reassured in my vulnerability."

- Similarly, sex between actual humans is not a particularly delicate or idealized act – it's pretty much one of the sweatiest, "flesh"-iest things you can do. So if we end up seeing a sexual scene taking place between two idealized, unreal beings who don't sweat or who don't move naturally, our brains immediately pick up the disconnect. It's a lot harder to hide strange model structure or movement with no clothes on, after all…

- Barring certain sexual positions and things like blindfolds and leather hoods, most real-life sex involves some sort of eye contact or looking at the partner's face. We can see the emotions of our partners play out in their eyes and facial expressions, and know that they're there and connected with us and with what's happening. But if game characters have no facial expressions – or facial expressions that seem inhuman – the lines of non-verbal communication are cut. And if the 3D characters have a vacant, blank stare, then it feels less like the sex is happening with a person and more with an empty shell, which is more than a little creepy (Figure 4.3).

FIGURE 4.3   Characters like this might be physically attractive, but notice the slightly unfocused and vacant eyes...and ask yourself if you'd want them staring up at you while you have sex? (Aitor Serra Martin/Shutterstock.com.)

It's worth noting that the uncanny valley effect hits harder the closer the character looks to a real human being – in other words, characters who aim for photorealism. The effect is much less noticeable in stylized 3D models – anime characters, for example, or more cartoonish or exaggerated designs. That's because there isn't the same cognitive dissonance as with more realistic models; our eyes and mind both immediately recognize, "Oh, wait, that's not human," and adjust accordingly. While not everyone may find anime or hyper-stylized characters to their tastes, it at least doesn't trigger the same "something's *wrong* with/about them!" instinctive response and thus is less likely to creep the player out or ruin their engagement with the sex scene. Another option for those working with 3D models but without a budget for full photorealism is to use camera tricks or other fixes to misdirect the player's attention away from the uncanny elements. It's hard to be creeped out by a vacant plasticky gaze if the character has their eyes closed...or if the camera is focused elsewhere!

On top of uncanny valley, there are other technical considerations unique to sex in 3D that are worth taking into account:

- **Extra asset creation** – In most games, your characters are going to want to take at least some of their clothes off when it comes to having sex. But in some cases, that means creating a unique, undressed character model specifically for the scene, which demands more time and effort from your art team, as well as raising the question... how "undressed" are you talking about?

  - Full nudity can be the right call for many projects, but it's also an almost sure-fire way to bump up your ratings, and you may risk publishers or storefronts requesting that it be censored. There may also be considerations as far as details for nipples, genitals, etc. – contributor Aubrey Scott has a particularly useful talk on these details in the context of character creation, but it's also useful information for anyone interested in rendering realistic nudity.[2] It may also be worth considering partial nudity or suggested nudity, where the player may not see any erogenous zones but can tell from context (e.g., a bare back) that they are fully naked.

- Another option is "modesty underwear," where characters wear underwear or smallclothes of some sort during intimate scenes, or any other scenarios where they might be undressed (e.g., sleeping, captured, and stripped of armor). These were once a very common feature in AAA games, particularly the *Mass Effect* series and the early *Dragon Age* games. Now, more companies are gravitating to actual nudity, at least for female characters (the male characters, it seems, still end up wearing underwear of some sort...I'm looking at you, *Witcher 3*!). Modesty underwear is a good way to make your scenes "acceptable" to a wide audience and – more importantly – any sex-negative gatekeepers like stakeholders or publishers who might balk at nudity. And for fades to black, it can be more than enough to convey the concept of a state of undress. However, in other circumstances, it can stand out like a sore thumb. For example, fading in AFTER the sex to find everyone still decorously dressed in underwear can be unintentionally funny, and if you're having sex in a location like, say, a shower or hot tub, the underwear may end up looking wildly out of place.

- Lastly, if ratings or scope is a major issue, you may decide not to bother with undressed character models at all, preferring instead to stick with the default clothed models. Like modesty underwear, this can work very well in the lead-up to sex (kissing, foreplay, etc.), up to a point – and for certain sex acts or positions, you can get away with clothing remaining on. But full clothing is even less flexible and believable than modesty underwear for most sex scenes, and players will be pressed to believe two lovers snuggling in bed in full armor or other equipment. If your team decides not to create original models for this, block out your sex scenes accordingly.

- **The difficulty of skin-to-skin contact** – Object collision is an entire THING in video games (even outside of sex) and a lot comes down to providing the illusion of touch or physical contact. With sex, that contact becomes the focus of the scene and thus can sometimes be harder to fool or fake...though definitely not impossible! On top of that, bodies can, well, "squish" during intimacy (e.g., breasts pressing against something, grabbing a handful of butt, and scratching one's back). 3D bodies do not, unless your team takes a lot of extra time and effort to render it properly. Is it worth focusing on that, possibly to the exclusion of other features? Will *not* doing it result in a more noticeable uncanny valley effect as players notice the lack of physical contact or the movement of flesh?

- Kissing is an important subset of this issue. Kissing close-up is a particularly difficult technique, particularly in sex scenes that feature lots of close-ups or shifting shots, or particularly deep and passionate kissing. How much effort can your cinematic or animation team spend on getting those heated, erotic kisses just right? Or is it better to frame the action in such a way that the kisses are never seen full-on?

- **Hair** – I think just by saying that word, I've caused all of my art and animation readers to put the book down and hyperventilate for several minutes. Hair is even more notorious than skin for being difficult to render, and even the simplest of hair interactions can be extremely challenging. Of course, sex is often full of hair interactions – hair pushed out of the way, hair splayed out on a pillow, long hair grabbed for leverage, hair getting damp with sweat, etc. etc. Is your team ready and willing to render these interactions?

- **Sweat and other fluids** – This is usually only a major concern for pornographic games, as many place heavy emphasis on sweaty bodies or sexual fluids as part of the action. However, other games may want to use some of these elements more subtly and in certain contexts. For example, how might you create a realistic, glistening sweat that's visually interesting without being over the top? If your characters are having sex in or near water, is there a sweet spot between the models being bone-dry or having a "slathered in Vaseline" look? If a character is moved to tears, how will those tears appear on the character's face? In the end, you and your team have to weigh the added realism vs. the added effort, as well as how these details may alter the mood of the scene (Figure 4.4).

FIGURE 4.4   And if you're not going to be including those details, you may need to rethink your steamy shower sex… (Photographee.eu/Shutterstock.com.)

- **Environments** – Can't forget that all this sex has to be happening somewhere! We'll be covering environment design in a future chapter, but there are also technical considerations to take into account here. For example, if there's a bed that the characters are going to have sex on, how do you make that bed look actually tactile and soft as opposed to just a hard rectangle? What about other assets in the room? Lighting? Do you have the bandwidth to create a specific location for the sex, or will you have to work around an existing location…and if so, are your locations appropriate for sex? Don't discount the difficulties of environment design on top of the character-focused challenges!

WHAT ABOUT 2D GAME SEX?

So, here's the good news! All of that incredibly difficult, time-consuming stuff we've just discussed is relatively specific to 3D games, 3D art, and 3D design. If you're making 2D games? Depending on your genre, your workflow, and your art style, you're likely to have a *much* easier time of things…though that doesn't mean there aren't still some stumbling blocks here as well, depending on your game (Figure 4.5).

2D games are almost universally less likely to struggle with issues of the uncanny valley. Their artwork is often stylized and "non-realistic" to begin with, so it doesn't trigger the discomfort in a player audience. And presenting sexual content is not inherently more difficult than presenting any other sort of content, at least not on a technical level. It's not like having characters come into sexual contact with each other opens a giant Pandora's box of

FIGURE 4.5 All the visual novel and retro RPG/platformer devs can take a deep breath and let it out. (fizkes/Shutterstock.com.)

extra technical challenges like 3D modeling and animation does. It does still mean creating more content, however, whether it's still images and CGs,[3] or whether it's extra sprite animations or characters, so scope can still be an issue for you and your team. Moreover, some 2D games can struggle to convey sex and sexuality in the constraints of their format, which is something your team may need to keep in mind if you are making a game in those particular genres.

Visual novels, in many ways, have the simplest technical task of integrating sex into the game. The majority of their presentation either comes through text or through still images and artwork, with little or no animation involved. Text, of course, is limited only by the character limits of the text window and the imagination, comfort level, and, ahem, "good taste" of the writer. Even in a game with extremely limited art assets – or even NO art assets! – text can be used to create a lengthy, fully detailed sex scene. Similarly, using CGs of sex scenes may involve a little work for the artist (i.e., making another CG on top of whatever others are needed for the project), but the level of technical difficulty in implementation remains the same as any other CG. And while two entwined bodies might be more of an artistic challenge than just one, there are plenty of artists very comfortable and very able to draw sexy still images of erotic content. Games like *Coming Out on Top*, *Cute Demon Crashers*, *Errant Kingdom*, and *Call Me Under* are able to use explicit (or not so explicit) drawn images with minor to major nudity and equally explicit text to create detailed sex scenes with minimal technical requirements (Figure 4.6).

FIGURE 4.6 Visual novels like *Call Me Under* can conjure up half-naked characters and plant erotic suggestions with just carefully chosen artwork and text, much the same as any other part of the visual novel experience. (Lunaris Games, *Call Me Under*, published by Lunaris Games, release date Q4 2021.)

There are also 2D games with animated sprites, such as platformers and RPGs. Depending on their design, they may have a harder time depicting sexual activity in an erotic, appealing way. This can be particularly true of games which use "chibi" stylization (i.e., draw characters in an exaggerated, stylized way that renders characters as short and "cute"). It can be more difficult to evoke sexual desire in players if the sprites look like children, or if they simply do not have enough body detail to visually parse what's happening ("is that her right arm, or her right boob?"). Sprite animation and poses can also be a challenge due to the limitations of the sprite in terms of detail, size, and number of frames of animation.

- If a game has very simple animations or dimensions (along the lines of, say, *Final Fantasy VI*), you may need to create an entirely new pose or "appearance" for sex (e.g., nudity). We can see examples of these in the indie RPG *Always Sometimes Monsters*, which features undressed character sprites seen lying in bed together. In these cases, the intent of the nudity and sex is usually not particularly arousing or titillating – as it's somewhat hard to get excited over two-inch tall bobbleheads! – but usually marks a particularly important story or character beat, hence the unique character sprites. You may need to also consider how characters might "transition" from default sprites to undressed sprites – depending on the accepted tropes and shorthand of your genre, it may be as simple as a quick spin in place and reappearing as the new naked sprite.

- If your game is elaborately animated (say, *Symphony of the Night*), and you intend to handle the sex in the game engine (as opposed to a CG or animated cutscene), then your team will need to handle the sprites' sex animations to the same degree of quality as every other animation in the game (jumping, running, attacking). Having these animations be of lower quality (e.g., fewer frames) than the other animations will stand out in a bad way; having them be HIGHER quality may result in your player base making certain assumptions about your "real" focus. So, when in doubt, aim for roughly similar detail, number of frames, etc., to remain consistent across the rest of the work. Many hentai and adult platformers can and do use these sorts of animations – whether they're actually "sexy" is a matter of taste, but they do prove it can be put into motion. But those are games where sex and sexuality are the focus and the main draw of the game, so they can devote full focus to the technical and artistic challenges of the relevant sprite animation. Non-pornographic platformers feature in-game sex significantly less...though that doesn't mean you can't give it a try... (Figure 4.7).

GAME CONTROLS, HAPTICS, TOUCHSCREENS, VR...

...you know what? I think we'd better stop here, or we're going to be here all day – each of these could easily be an ENTIRE chapter on their own. Suffice to say that even beyond the visuals of the game – be they 3D or 2D – there are still PLENTY of technical challenges to overcome in terms of gameplay, hardware, and the feedback it offers players (Figure 4.8).

FIGURE 4.7 Your character sprite sheets for *Orc Lover 2021* are probably going to have to get a bit weirder than this… (pzUH/Shutterstock.com.)

FIGURE 4.8 Can we make this kiss and this embrace feel real to the player with only some touch pads and some very enthusiastic rumble motors? (Dean Drobot/Shutterstock.com.)

CONCLUSION

Sex in games is not as easy as grabbing two actors, sticking them in a room with a script, then yelling "action"! There are a lot of moving parts to manage, and a lot of restrictions in terms of the tools you use and the time and budget you have to apply them. Then again, that's the case for all video game creation, so if you've already made that leap, the next leap to creating believable, meaningful sex in games is not the impossible step you might think. It just means thinking a little creatively, being aware of your limitations and their impact on what you're making, and using your tech restrictions as inspiration for finding unique and effective ways to explore sexuality.

WORKSHOP QUESTIONS

Analysis: Going back to the game you're analyzing, look at how it presents its sex scenes and sexual content and answer the following questions:

- Is the game 3D or 2D? How does it take advantage of its format best?

- What creative decisions, if any, do you think were made due to limitations of the tech? For example, are there particular camera angles, animations, etc., that are clearly there to compensate for other technical weaknesses?

- Are there any particular moments, visuals, or other elements that strike you as a failing in tech, art, or animation? How do they make you feel (e.g., amused? Taken out of the moment? Or just willing to ignore it?)?

- If the game you're analyzing is older, how do you think the same scene might be presented today?

Creative: Working with your team or by yourself, jot down the following information for your game:

- Whether your game is 2D or 3D, as well as what genre the game is (e.g., 3D RPG, 2D platformer, and visual novel)

- How you intend to present most of the sexual content (e.g., cutscenes, gameplay, CG stills, text, and in-game animations)

- What you and your team foresee being the biggest challenges and blockers to these presentations

- Your plans for dealing with these challenges (e.g., work to overcome them, or find ways to sidestep them and try another tack?), as well as possible backup plans if they end up interfering with your team's vision.

- A clear sense of you and your team's priority for this as related to the other content your team will be working on. Are you willing to scale back, say, combat animation in favor of your team devoting their time to realistic kissing animations?

Also, if you are working on a team, make sure to listen to ask your team for their input, and listen to their questions and concerns.

NOTES

1 J. Hsu, *Scientific American*, "Why 'Uncanny Valley' Human Look-Alikes Put Us on Edge," April 3, 2012, https://www.scientificamerican.com/article/why-uncanny-valley-human-look-alikes-put-us-on-edge/.

2 A. Scott, *GDC*, "Genderf*ck 2077," accessed September 4, 2021, https://www.gdcvault.com/play/1027180/Genderf-ck.

3 CGs, short for "computer graphics," are a visual novel term for a unique picture or still image used for special events or moments (such as having sex!), as opposed to regular sprite and background graphics.

PART 2

Sex and Pre-Production

CHAPTER 5

The Narrative Functions of Sex Scenes (And Why/ Why Not to Have Them)

S O, YOU WANT TO have a sex scene in your game? Great!
Why?

This is not a sex-negative gotcha question or demanding extra justification for including sex. In fact, it's asking for the same thing we demand of everything ELSE in our games: that it's there because it *needs* to be, because it serves a purpose, or because it makes the game better, not because "I just think it's neat" (Figure 5.1).

FIGURE 5.1   And no, "because I want to" doesn't count here… (Dean Drobot/Shutterstock.com.)

DOI: 10.1201/9780429356650-7

Part of game design, whether it's mechanics, level, or narrative, means constantly asking ourselves the question "why is this here?" or "why are we adding this?" It's part of how games avoid bloat, stay within scope, and keep their focus on the larger goal of the game. Sexual content is no different. Sex absolutely can and should fulfill important functions and purposes within the game, the same as any other narrative scene or gameplay element. And if it doesn't, then it should be treated the same as dialogue that goes nowhere, or superfluous game mechanics, or plot cul-de-sacs that end up dropping the characters right back where they started (Figure 5.2).

Ensuring every piece of content contributes to the whole is something that writers (whether writing for books, games, movies, or television) have to consider frequently, to the point where many writers have codified it into sets of rules. You can find multiple websites dedicated to laying out things like the 4 Purposes of Dialogue (or 5, depending on which writer you're asking!). Adapting and applying evaluations like these to sex scenes and sexual content provides a useful framework to consider what purpose or function that service provides. And while this is a narrative-specific approach, it can also be a handy gateway to considering larger gameplay questions: What functions in terms of mood and user experience does a particular sexual mechanic serve?

A video game narrative scene should do at least one of the following, ideally more than one:

- Establish character

- Develop a relationship

- Advance or reveal the plot (including exposition)

- Establish a mood or emotion

FIGURE 5.2   Snip snip... (nikolaborovic/Shutterstock.com.)

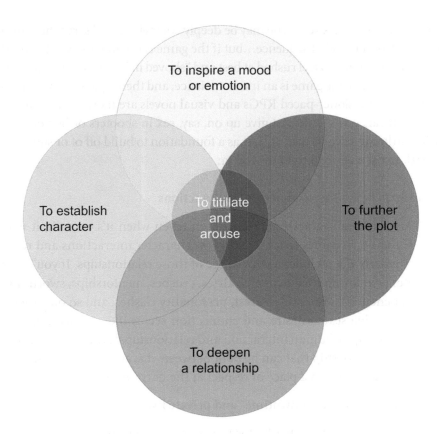

FIGURE 5.3   A Venn diagram of the four main functions of a sex scene (and the fifth "shadow" purpose).

And so it is with sex! Sex in games should be there to fulfill at least one of these functions. We'll look at how sex can fulfill all of these purposes in the chapter ahead.

"But wait," I hear you say, "what about the BIGGEST reason to have a sex scene? What about the main goal of surely every designer who ever suggested a sex scene, the main reason players are going to buy our game and consume this content…which is to see attractive characters having sex?" In other words, what about titillation? (Figure 5.3).

We'll get to that in a bit, but first, a quick thought or two about when and under what circumstances to use sex scenes to these four narrative purposes.

PURPOSE VS. PACING: WHEN IS A SEX SCENE NOT THE RIGHT CALL?

Sex scenes are great building blocks for emotional and narratively resonant scenes and should be treated the same as any other kind of scene or narrative element. However, that does not necessarily mean they are "right" for every game. One can have two kinds of equally great building blocks, but they're best suited for building different types of structures. Similarly, you can envision a sex scene that establishes mood and character, deepens relationships, and furthers the plot…and still doesn't quite "fit in" as well in, say, *Call of Duty*. What gives? Why is sex the right call for some games, and not for others?

Well, there are a lot of reasons, many of which are difficult (if not impossible) to quantify. But many of them relate to considerations of game genre, general tone, and, possibly most importantly of all, pacing. A sex scene may be deeply compelling and serve the same narrative functions as any other kind of sequence…but if the game is rushing too fast to give that scene room to breathe, it's going to feel rushed at best and "shoved in" at worst. Figuring out whether sex scenes fit the pace of the game is an inexact science, and there's plenty of wiggle room – for example, just because slower-paced RPGs and visual novels are more likely to have good sex scenes doesn't mean you should just give up on, say, sex in shooters or horror games! – but there's still a little advice to be had, at least as a foundation to build off of or subvert.

In general, sex scenes tend to fit in well in:

- Games with heavy focus on personal interactions

  - Given that sex is a personal interaction (even when it's casual!), it makes sense to feature it in games that are heavy on character interactions and relationships, particularly if it includes a wide range of those relationships. If you've already got content exploring friendships, rivalries, crushes, mentorships, sworn siblinghood, secret enemies, romantic interest, personality clashes, and so on…then failing to acknowledge sexual desire and connection seems like an incomplete picture of the full range of human interaction and relationships! And while sex isn't the only kind of relationship that can be built between characters, it's a perfectly valid one and should be given a place of respect at the narrative table.

- Game genres that offer "downtime" and private lives

  - This downtime can either be for the characters (taking a breather between missions), the players (same!), the narrative (moments of calm between major crises), or all of the above. The point being that, with some exceptions, sex scenes are best used in moments where the narrative has room to breathe and the characters have the actual *time* to engage in sex before the next crit path beat hits. Similarly, while it's certainly possible to have sex "on the job" or in the middle of a mission, the majority of sex scenes take place in the context of being "off the clock," of being part of the characters' private lives; so if a game provides room for those private lives, either in narrative or gameplay, sex can be a part of that game and story experience.

- Games that take place over longer periods of time (narrative or gameplay)

  - This one's a bit woollier, as you can certainly have sex with someone you just met or in a short window of time…but in general, sex scenes work best in games that take place over an unspecific but lengthy amount of time. This is why sex scenes often work so well in RPGs; to a certain extent, players can imagine sex happening on a scale that makes sense for their imagination, whether it's over several days or several months. Also, longer games tend to spread out their major sex-interrupting crises in ways that allow for that "downtime" discussed above. It's a lot easier to sneak in a quickie between "a demon's just appeared in our world" and "someone's blown up the palace" when there's at least a day or two between them!

On the flip side, it may be more difficult to integrate sex scenes with the following kinds of games, and you may be better off finding non-sexual ways to fulfill your gameplay and narrative needs:

- Games that are all "mission"

    - If every single story beat of your game focuses on being a soldier, or hero, or city planner, or [insert lofty combat/administration title here], with no time spent on quiet, private moments, chances are you're not going to have many story beats with room for sex or intimacy. This isn't to say that you can't have a game about, say, a character in the military and still feature sex! But there's a difference between a game which explores that military commander's social life, private life, and personality beyond the mission (say, for example, Commander Shepard in *Mass Effect*) and a game where the story is 100% focused on their combat role (e.g., most modern military shooters, games like *Warframe* and *Destiny*). This doesn't have to only be combat either; it could be city-building, cooking, space exploration, even just surviving a hostile environment. If it's taking up all of the core narrative or core gameplay loop, then best not to try awkwardly shoving in some sex on top of it if it doesn't match.

- Games that are frenetic/fast-paced/depend on big momentum

    - Quick! Shoot the thing! Now explode the thing! Now jump out of a spacecraft! Now run from zombies! No, we don't have time for sex! We gotta save the world! While it's true that sex itself can be pretty frantic and fast in some situations, there is still something to be said about pacing. It's an inexact art, but there are definitely some games where a sex scene, even a well-crafted and narratively deep one, will cause the momentum to screech to a halt. On a related note, abrupt shifts due to fast pace can also cause otherwise well-done sex scenes to come off weirdly.

- Games that don't offer sexual context

    - That sounds a bit weird, kind of like "a thing shaped like itself." But in fact, it's more of an expansion and conclusion on the previous points; if your game is exploring themes or stories in which, well, it doesn't really make "sense" for characters to have sex...then don't use sex as your storytelling tool. This could be something as simple as gameplay or story logistics – "hey, this horror game protagonist isn't exactly meeting anyone they want to bone, and they're too busy trying not to die!" But it can also relate to larger gameplay and narrative themes – "this game is about the gentle coziness of completely platonic friendships, and sex doesn't fit that context/ dynamic." In general, if it feels like too much of a stretch to include sex, then that's probably an accurate feeling, and you should look at other ways to tell your story.

But hey, you're making a game where you know sex will fit, and you're interested in knowing what thematic or narrative functions a sex scene can fulfill! Let's get back to the four main purposes for having a sex scene.

THE FIRST PURPOSE: ESTABLISHING A CHARACTER

There are many ways to establish who a character is and what makes them tick. The concept of an "establishing character moment" at the beginning of a story, a moment that immediately defines where a character is or where they start from, is so common that it has its own TV Tropes page.[1] Character exploration is then continued through gameplay and narrative scenes where the character says or does things that reveal more of who they really are.

Sex can absolutely be one of those revealing things. Every character has a sexual side – even if their side is, "absolutely no sex, please, thank you" – and being invited to witness them having sex or exploring sexual aspects of themselves is an invitation to get to know more of them. Sex can be a uniquely personal, vulnerable experience, and characters can reveal surprising aspects of themselves in the act, either deliberately or in a moment of uncontrollable emotion. Even if they keep their true selves hidden and closed off during sex, that choice in and of itself is another aspect of their character. Seeing a character like Kratos in *God of War* being stone-faced and disinterested during sex tells us a lot about the person he is, just as seeing BJ from *Wolfenstein* being thoughtful and emotional tells us a lot about him. One might also look at character revelations during sex and extrapolate them into larger insights into the character as a whole. For example, one of Kratos' first character moments in the first game establishes him as being somewhat callous and selfish in regard to sex with the courtesans in his bed; it's easy to make the connection between that and his general callous selfishness in the rest of his life.

It's worth noting that establishing a character through sex can have particular resonance in games with branching narrative and character choices, in that by choosing whether or not to have sex, or what the context of the sex is, *the players themselves* are establishing something about their player character! A version of Geralt in the Witcher series who only sleeps with Yennefer and no one else is a different Geralt from one who actively sleeps with every sex worker in every brothel in the game – and they are in turn different Geralts from one who never has sex with anyone, or a Geralt who sleeps with Triss, or a Geralt who tries to sleep with both Yennefer and Triss, etc. etc. etc. Even though Geralt is an established character, the choices of the player can allow them to role-play and build their own vision of this aspect of Geralt's life and sexuality – whether he's lustful, romantic, or disinterested, or whether he pursues sex as respite from his harsh life vs. for simple pleasure or connection, or even his views on monogamy vs. polyamory. Similarly, players may end up extrapolating additional meaning onto Geralt from these sexual interactions: Is he loyal to the end? Closed off? Disrespectful of his partners? Romantic? The player's sexual choices can give all of these questions more context and more gravity.

Of course, there is also the holy grail of narrative design for sex scenes: sex that *develops* a character even as it happens. This is rare in almost every medium – most "changes" in the middle of sex have to do with relationship dynamics, and any changes to the character tend to come out only before or after the sex. But in certain circumstances, the immediate experience of sex – of owning one's own pleasure and sexuality – can cause profound changes to a person even in the moment, where their evolution is visible even as they make love or have sex. One of the all-time best examples of this in non-game media is the sex scene between Khal Drogo and Daenerys Targaryen in season 1 episode 2 of *Game of Thrones*; while the sex certainly developed their relationship, it also marked a turning point in their separate character arcs and a radical, fundamental shift for both as individual personalities. One finds new appreciation for the strength of others, and for embracing new ideas and ways; the other takes control of her sexuality and finds confidence, power, and new determination. It's a crucial moment for both, and one can tell simply by looking at the way they have sex, at their expressions and body language, that neither of them will ever be the same again after their tryst.[2] Moments like these are what more games should be aiming for, particularly as technology and visual fidelity improve and allow for more nuanced body language, facial expressions, and movement. Imagine seeing an entire character arc – from nervousness to confidence, anguish to numbness, or slyness to surprised pleasure – flitting across their face as they make love.

Of course, a large part of what can be revealed or established about a character through sex revolves around how they treat their lover or sexual partner. Which brings us to the next purpose for having a sex scene…

THE SECOND PURPOSE: DEVELOPING A RELATIONSHIP

One of the most obvious functions sex can serve in a video game is in progressing a relationship (usually romantic) between two characters; it's also one of the most common examples of how sex is used. AAA franchises in particular are replete with examples of sex scenes which deepen or develop the relationship between the characters, usually either:

- As flirtatious relationships that become romantic or "upgrade" from flirtation by falling into bed together (e.g., Fenris/Hawke in *Dragon Age II*, BJ/Anya in *Wolfenstein*, Garrus/Shepard in *Mass Effect*). A related version of this is where two characters may be attracted to each other, have sex, and then choose (via player control) whether to progress the relationship into more serious territory or to keep things casual.

- As established romantic relationships that reach "a new level" in terms of romance, intimacy, or seriousness via sex (e.g., Tali/Shepard and Peebee/Ryder from *Mass Effect*) – sex is shown as a special event that deepens the romantic connection and the trust and emotion between the lovers. For example, in *Andromeda*, it's in the context of trusting, affectionate sex that Peebee feels safe enough first to suggest an asari melding, then to declare her love.

Of course, relationships don't have to be sexual to be romantic, and there are plenty of examples of game relationships that become deep and loving without any sex. Sexual scenes should not be considered the *only* way to deepen or alter a romantic relationship; however, they are a *good* way, one of several, and should be given equal value and attention to other non-sexual scenes and events. In other words, showing relationship progression without sex isn't necessarily "better" (save for asexual players), and showing it *with* sex isn't necessarily "lazy shorthand."

Likewise, relationships don't have to be romantic to be sexual. Character dynamics can evolve and change through sex in ways that don't lead to true love! Friends with benefits and casual encounters might develop a deeper friendship, or sarcastic banter, or a new knowledge of how each other ticks; they might like each other more OR less in the aftermath! Some sexual encounters might even damage or destroy the relationship between characters; for example, in Mass Effect 2, having sex with Jack right away damages her trust in Shepard, and she shuts down entirely around him after that. The point is, sexual interaction, whether healthy or unhealthy, casual or committed, is still an *interaction* between people. Like any character interaction, that always carries the potential for changing how they relate to each other and how they will interact in the future.

Player agency and branching narrative also offer unique possibilities here compared to other media. In games with branching narrative, choosing to have sex can be a way to shape a character's romantic and relationship dynamics with other characters, whether it's choosing who the PC hooks up with or pushing certain NPCs together. In games which focus on the social network around a player character, sex is one of many tools which players can use to explore and develop those relationships in the way they want.

THE THIRD PURPOSE: ADVANCE OR REVEAL THE PLOT

This is a relatively rarer purpose for sex scenes in games, partly due to it not always being directly connected or related to the larger story arc. Having sex doesn't usually connect directly with saving the world or stopping the bad guys! But just because sex scene plot progression is rarer doesn't mean it can't be done, or that it shouldn't be explored in new and interesting ways. We already have game stories that tackle the *aftermath* of sex – questlines to do with the consequences of infidelity, for example, or characters born from taboo or unique sexual unions. It's not too much of a stretch to imagine stories that show the sex in question and tackle the aftermath immediately.

Sex as plot progression can range from lavishly ludicrous epic silliness ("the only way to unlock the portal to the demon's dimension is through a sex ritual!") to the deadly serious dramatic storytelling ("These two characters giving into their mutual desires set off a chain reaction that kills several key figures in the story"). Games heavy in political intrigue are particularly fertile grounds for this kind of storytelling, as people's sexual acts (wanting and/or having sex with the wrong people, the right people, or not at all) can potentially have profound effects on the balance of power in the context of the game world. Consider how Henry VIII threw England into upheaval and created an entirely new religion just because he really, *really* wanted to have sex with Anne Boleyn; games could be equally fertile ground for this sort of grand-scale sexual plotting! Outside of political intrigue, stories that rely heavily on personal inter-dynamics and relationships can be massively shifted or pushed forward by sexual activity; in soap operas and games like them, entire arcs might be thrown into motion by an illicit, passionate sexual tryst.

And of course, don't discount the potential of speculative elements like magic or alien cultures. *Dragon Age: Origins* offers an example of an optional but major shift in plot due to sex; the player can either choose to sacrifice their life to kill the Archdemon, or have sex with Morrigan (personally or asking another Warden party member) to impregnate her with a child to absorb its life force. Choosing between sex and refusal has a massive impact on the game plot, fundamentally altering the potential future of Thedas, the arcs of future games, and the ending of *Origins* itself. If the player agrees, the Warden characters survive, the Archdemon's soul is recovered, and major plot arcs for *Dragon Age: Inquisition* are different.

On top of progressing a plot, a scene can also reveal more of the plot to the audience; rather than driving the story forward, it uncovers story that is already there and shares it with players. The most common form of this is sharing information, and of course exposition. Sex scenes can be used for this as well, but here, one should be careful about how and why to use sex in that capacity. There are certainly organic ways to have sex reveal new plot information; for example, you might set up two characters to be at each other's throats, make the player believe that they're dire enemies and working against each other, then... BOOM! A sex scene that puts not only their interactions, but their whole storyline and role in the plot in a new light ("Wait, but if they're lovers, that means she's...uh oh, we're in trouble!").

As for sharing information and exposition, this CAN be done gracefully and organically – for example, some sleepy pillow talk dropping some information about the world or story – but beware of the urge to "spice up" exposition with sex. This trope, also known as the dreaded "sexposition," has characters sharing information about the world/plot/etc., in the *middle* of sex; usually, the intent is to share "dry" information with the player or audience while keeping them interested with sexy content. This is...not a good approach, to put it mildly, and is usually criticized for laziness or using sex as "shock value" to keep eyes glued to the screen. Unless you have a really, REALLY good thematic reason for combining exposition with sex, it's usually better to put that exposition either before the clothes come off or afterward, during pillow talk or other times. We'll discuss this more in future chapters when we discuss dialogue in sex and how to construct "aftermath" or "afterglow" scenes.

THE FOURTH PURPOSE: ESTABLISHING A MOOD OR EMOTION RELATED TO THE NARRATIVE

Lastly, we have the somewhat hazy but vital goal of using a sex scene to establish an emotional baseline for a story beat. Sex can be an emotional experience, even if the emotion is just, "hey, this is fun!" In a well-done sex scene, general emotions become personal, and vice versa; the feelings exist not just between the characters involved, but permeate the scene and the experience the player has. For example, depending on the presentation of a scene, a desperate tryst in the middle of a world of horrors can express a state of quiet melancholy, or it could be something warm and life-affirming, or it could something harsh and brutal like the world it's set in. Sexual sequences can (and usually should) serve as an emotional beat that evokes a particular mood in the player. In games, one can go a step further and give the player agency over what kind of mood they're going to experience; perhaps they are the ones who can decide whether the sex they're having is something fun and cheerful vs. deep and serious!

Using sex to establish a mood is one of the easiest goals and purposes that a sex scene can accomplish, but it can be a hazy prospect; how to know when a scene is needed for conveying that emotion vs. when the scene is an unnecessary step? While sex is as good a method for conveying mood and emotion as any non-sexual scene, it may be worthwhile to evaluate your non-sexual scenes leading up to it to ensure that they're not *already* doing the heavy lifting of setting your mood. If you've already had twenty scenes that get across the message, "the mood is bleak," then you don't need to have a sex scene JUST to drive home, "yeah, the mood is bleak." Have a bleak sex scene, certainly, but incorporate other purposes as part of it.

Needless to say, it's also important to ensure the mood of the scene complements the game, the story beat, and the relationships involved! While contrasts can be very effective (e.g., a gentle, warm mood offsetting the harshness of the game world), such differences must be managed with care. Having an off-mood scene can result in players being put out, amused, or confused by the tonal shifts. Borrowing another example from *Dragon Age: Origins*, if you're having fun, no-strings-attached sex with an elven playboy assassin in the middle of living rough in a campsite, maybe transcendent choirs and deliberately exaggerated romantic emotion isn't quite the mood you want to be hitting?

THE SHADOW FIFTH PURPOSE: TITILLATION

We've discussed characters, relationships, plot, and mood: These are the four elements that every narrative element, from cutscenes to dialogue to flavor text, should be contributing toward, and as such, so should sex scenes and sexual content. Unsurprisingly, the goal is for a scene to serve as many of these goals as possible; ideally, the minimum should be at least two. The more narrative purpose a sex scene has, the greater its impact and the more reason to include it in the game.

But what about that not-so-silent fifth purpose for a sex scene, the purpose of titillating the players? Many sex scenes feature attractive characters and explicit sex purely to evoke sexual interest in the player. Some developers would consider that the only reason to have a sex scene; others are so against the concept of titillation that they would reject sex scenes entirely, or certainly any sex scenes that tended that way.

The question is complicated by a huge amount of historical baggage to do with whose titillation is traditionally aimed at. The vast majority of titillating content, particularly in AAA games, is geared toward straight male players. For many, the word "titillation" conjures a single image: conventionally attractive, naked, objectified female characters in sexual situations for the benefit of an appreciative, leering male gaze (and that leaves some – not all! – queer women disinterested). Understandably, if that is the ONLY kind of titillation one thinks of, one can see reasons to reject it.

Of course, titillation is more complex. For one, titillation does not have to be inherently exploitative or objectifying; a character can be presented as a fully realized human being with agency while STILL being arousing in terms of design or in the context of a sexual scene. Also, titillation can absolutely target other audiences with different kinds of content, with anything from sexualized depictions of male characters to non-traditionally sexy female characters to attractive genderqueer characters. One only has to see fan response to games like *Final Fantasy VII* and *Hades* to see that there is plenty of appreciation for titillating content for those characters and audiences. But does that mean titillation is okay?

Are some types "acceptable" and others not? Is it sex-positive to champion titillation, or upholding unhealthy attitudes toward sex?

It's a complicated question, but as far as this book is concerned, the answer is: **Titillation is not a bad goal, but it also cannot be the only goal** (Figure 5.4).

As discussed in an earlier chapter, lust and sexual desire are completely valid emotions to evoke, no different from any other emotion. Designers should not be shamed for hoping to inspire those feelings in their player audience, or for designing with that inspiration in mind. In a sense, titillation is only a hair's breadth away from falling under the umbrella of "establishing a mood or emotion," the emotion being desire in this case.

However, there is a small but critical difference that keeps them as separate goals: A sex scene should evoke emotions *specifically* related to the narrative and game itself. Titillation, though fun and potentially healthy, usually evokes emotions on a meta-level, outside of the story. The feelings in the player aren't about the narrative, but about their own response to the sexual imagery or content. As a result, a sex scene *only* made to titillate can result in feeling narratively or systemically hollow; it doesn't connect with or boost the extant narrative, or perform any of the key functions. Similarly, it does no good to start with titillation as the goal, but force other functions on the scene in an inorganic way. Players will notice if you're coming up with really weird plot reasons to get a character naked and orgasmic on the regular, and unless you're actively going for a more erotic or adult experience, the result is going to be lackluster and easily seen through by players.

But titillation still has a healthy, good place in sex scene creation. Titillation, or at least creating a scene with the goal of arousing and enticing the player, works best not as a singular goal, but as a complement to the four key goals and purposes of sex scenes. The language of sex appeal and titillation can be used to enhance, intensify, and highlight the narrative thrust of the scene, as well as adding further dimension and investment to character, mood, relationship, and story. For example, a good sex scene that focuses on characters and relationships might have the player excited that the couple in question *finally*

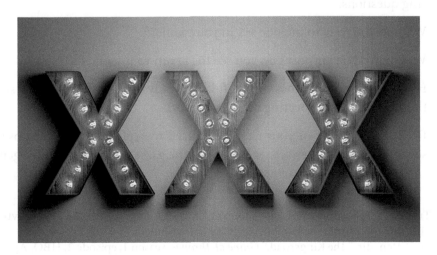

FIGURE 5.4 Unless you're doing porn or erotica games, of course. At which point, go nuts! (Patrick Krabeepetcharat/Shutterstock.com.)

got together; this excitement can be paired with the sexual excitement of seeing attractive, compelling characters get naked and be sexy and sexual. Sex appeal and titillation can be used thoughtfully, with attention to broad and diverse appeal, to reward player investment in the narrative, in the characters, and in the game itself.

In this way, sex scenes can be fully realized narrative beats…but that doesn't mean they can't still be hot as hell!

CONCLUSION

If you're considering including sex in your games and projects, make sure you know why – not because sex needs special justification, but because knowing the role and function your sexual content plays will make for more meaningful stories, more engaging gameplay, and more memorable sex!

WORKSHOP QUESTIONS

Analysis: For the game you've picked to analyze, which of the four major purposes – establishing character, developing relationships, furthering plot, or establishing mood – does its sex scene(s) serve? How many do they serve, and if there are more than one, do they all serve the same types? Once you've identified the base purpose(s) of the scene(s) in question, analyze exactly what they reveal and how they fulfill those purposes:

- What do they establish about the character?

- How does the relationship between sexual partners develop?

- What do we learn about the plot, or how does the plot move forward?

- What mood does the scene establish?

Creative: Consider your project and the sorts of sexual scenes you want to have, and answer the following questions:

- Why do you want to include sex in your game?

- What narrative purposes do you see the sex in your game fulfilling?

- How many purposes does the sex fulfill? If only one, are there ways to strengthen the scenes by incorporating other purposes?

- Does the structure of your game lend itself to exploring these purposes via sex scenes, or would other scenes better suit the game's pacing/structure/genre/etc.?

NOTES

1 TV Tropes, "Establishing Character Moment," accessed August 12, 2021, https://tvtropes.org/pmwiki/pmwiki.php/Main/EstablishingCharacterMoment.
2 T. Van Patten, dir. "The Kingsroad," *Game of Thrones*, season 1, episode 2, HBO, April 24, 2011.

CHAPTER 6

Considering Your Thirsty Audience

Diverse Desires vs. Target Demographics

O NE OF THE THINGS your team will be discussing very early in the game design process is your demographics, whether it's based on age, gender, or market competitors or comparison points. Whether it's "18–25-year-old young people" or "middle-aged women who read *Twilight*," having a particular image of who will play your game can be helpful if handled correctly. And if sex is going to be a part of your game, these demographic considerations can take on new weight, as well as adding sexual attraction to the list of considerations. After all, knowing who you are making these sex scenes for and what that audience actually enjoys is pretty useful to know (Figure 6.1).

Heavy reliance on demographic focus for sexual content has its pros and cons. On the one hand, it allows for a more focused, directed approach to sex, sex appeal, and sexual scenes when it is made for a specific audience, to say nothing of the greater ease of marketing. On the other hand, it can alienate other demographics who might also play your game and who are hungry for content. At best, it can be a simple failure to provide them with content geared for them; at worst, the content that IS there can repel or annoy them. Finding the right balance of catering to one demographic over many can be difficult, but the results can be creatively and socially rewarding, particularly depending on the genre.

Note: It is important, when designing sexual content "for" a particular demographic, to explicitly acknowledge and label what you are doing with your team; naming it aloud can force the team to address certain assumptions about that demographic, as well as inviting them to consider potential adjacent groups. Ideally, you and your team may figure out more specific descriptors for your target audience, as opposed to just a demographic. For example, if the target demographic is stated as "18–25-year-old young men" only for the development team to charge ahead with focusing on conventionally attractive female characters in chainmail bikinis and emphasizing the straight male gaze, it suggests blinkered

DOI: 10.1201/9780429356650-8

FIGURE 6.1 Reports just in! Customer satisfaction with the "likes hot shirtless guys having sex" demographic is at an all-time high! (Tirachard Kumtanom/Shutterstock.com.)

assumptions about that demographic; it ignores the many 18–25-year-old gay and queer men that are part of that group, to say nothing of straight men who might not like that particular kind of sexual content. In contrast, if the target demographic is specifically laid out as "young straight men, 18–25," or even more specific, "young straight men, 18–25, who like cheesecake-style sexual content," the team can focus on an audience while still being much more aware of the limits of that audience. In turn, by identifying your main target group, you can also get a clearer idea of who the players OUTSIDE of that group will be. If your primary market is a very specific X, who are your secondary markets? What will their experience be? What do you *want* it to be? And are there ways to make it more welcoming? (Figure 6.2).

So, when it comes to sex in games, when do you attempt to broaden beyond a target demographic, and when do you focus on delivering what your target demographic wants?

DIVERSIFYING BEYOND THE DEMOGRAPHIC

As a general rule of thumb, unless your game is explicitly a romance, erotica, or porn title for a specific audience, *you should make the sexual elements in your game as broadly appealing to a diverse audience as possible.* Why? Because while romance and sex games usually offer a specific romantic/sexual experience geared to a specific audience, other games – whether RPGs, match-3s, or FPS – have mechanics and stories that appeal to audiences of all kinds of sexualities and preferences. Even if a game genre tends to attract a certain demographic more than others, there will always be enthusiasts and players outside of that demographic, and as such it's worth making them feel welcome rather than ignored

FIGURE 6.2 "The chainmail bikinis did nothing for me. The chainmail Speedos, on the other hand…" (Cookie Studio/Shutterstock.com.)

or dismissed. That's why it's unwise to *only* have sexual content that's hyperfocused on the "main" demographic. It can be a clear signal to other groups that their tastes, interests, and comfort level around the sexual content isn't being considered…and if they're not respected here, where else might they encounter disrespect? That's not to say that sexual content in a game can't feature more of a particular perspective – either that of the main character or of the target demographic – but care should be taken to avoid making that perspective the exclusive, dominating one.

There are several strategies for avoiding this, but one good place to start is to present sex and sex appeal equally. Many games have a tendency to present certain classes or groups of characters – for example, certain genders, body types, etc. – as sexy or sexual without applying the same lens to other groups. When sex does happen, certain bodies are lingered over and presented as sexual, while others are not. Consider how your sexual content can be tweaked and framed in a way that presents *other* characters as attractive and sexual to a wider audience. It's a win–win scenario; the original target demographic still gets the sexual content they enjoy while other groups still have an enjoyable or appealing experience. We'll discuss this further in future chapters on gaze in games – on how the lens of "who is sexy vs. who is not" has a lot to do with who the game assumes is playing – but for now, keep in mind that presenting a broader range of characters as sexual and attractive can be a great way to get all *kinds* of people eager for your game!

(It should go without saying, of course, that delivering sexy or sexual content for other audiences outside one target demographic is much easier and more authentic when your team includes members of diverse sexualities and tastes! Rather than have to guess at "what do X group like," have X group at the table to weigh in and help guide the process.)

Example – The *Witcher* trilogy provides multiple opportunities for Geralt, the main character, to engage in sexual relationships with various female characters. In *The Witcher* and *The Witcher 2*, during these scenes, emphasis was mostly on the bodies and sexual attractiveness of the women. In the former, the sex scenes were marked with collectible cards featuring naked or underdressed women; in the latter, the camera during sex scene cinematics focused almost exclusively on the bodies and nudity of the female character, with very little intimate exploration of Geralt's body. Both games received criticism for this narrow focus, particularly from nonstraight male players. However, in *The Witcher 3*, there was a shift in focus; while female characters were still highlighted in sexual ways, Geralt was also similarly highlighted, with more erotic attention paid to his body via lack of clothing, lighting, camerawork, etc. As such, many male-attracted people found Geralt much more appealing on a sexual level and became fans of both the game and its sexual content.

The majority of games can benefit from a broader approach to sex and sex appeal, but what about those exceptions mentioned earlier, those of romance games and porn games? Are there situations where focusing on one demographic to the exclusion of others is the right thing to do?

DOUBLING DOWN ON A DEMOGRAPHIC

In the case of romance and porn games, the decision of "tight demographic focus" vs. "all inclusive broad appeal" is a little fuzzier than for other titles. There is 100% a strong argument to be made for creating all-inclusive romance and porn games that allow for the player to tailor their romantic and sexual experience to their preference. Queer games are often at the forefront of this, doing a fantastic job of creating sexual and romantic experiences that work regardless of player orientation. Games like *Errant Kingdom*, *Monster Prom*, *When the Night Comes*, and *Boyfriend Dungeon* all allow the player to choose their own gender identity and a love interest from a cast of varying genders. And it absolutely works!

But there is also still a place for romance and sex games that focus on more of a niche romantic and sexual experience and story, and that cater to a specific audience. Unlike other genres like RPGs and adventure games, there is an implicit assumption that the players are playing romance and sex games in order to…well, romance and have sex with characters who they find attractive, and to do it in ways they find appealing. The question is, do you aim to offer everyone a character or scenario they find appealing, or do you focus on one type of character/fantasy/sexuality/etc., and just knock it out of the park catering to that? It's important in this stage of preproduction for teams to decide which they are going for, so they know how best to direct their time and energy.

For example, if you are explicitly creating an erotic game that features lesbian sex scenes and lesbian romance intended for a lesbian audience, there is no obligation to spend extra development time and focus on making sexually attractive male characters, or including straight, gay, or other nonlesbian sex scenes. Nor do you have to focus that much on making the lesbian sex palatable or appealing to nonlesbian audiences if your target market is only lesbians. Deciding on that goal early in the development cycle will have a profound effect on the art pipeline, storytelling, game design, and other elements of the game, as much as aiming for a larger appeal. Regardless of the decision, ensure that the entire team is apprised of it and that everyone is clear both on the target and on how – or whether – to handle groups outside that target.

Of course, even if the design intends to target only one demographic, there is still plenty of opportunity for variation within that, such as different archetypes of love interests, different kinds or amounts of sexual content, etc. There is still plenty of room to aim at appealing to different players in different ways! While sex and romance games can rarely be all things to all people, a careful consideration and planning for what things you CAN be, and how well you can be them, will go a long way to creating a game that will resonate with your target demographic, and possibly beyond if you so choose.

Example – *Coming Out On Top* makes no bones about the fact it is a sexy romance game about conventionally attractive gay men, and it rarely tries to be anything else. The cast is mostly male, and while there are a few sexual sequences involving women (e.g., one male character has a threesome with two female characters), it is almost a minor afterthought to the sheer volume of gay male sex and sex appeal offered by the other characters. Rather than allowing the player to choose the gender of their avatar, or to romance characters of all genders, *Coming Out* keeps a very tight and narrow focus on what it wants its players to experience: the story of a cis gay man romancing and having sex with other cis queer men, all of whom fulfill different character archetypes, fantasies, and so on. *Coming Out* is a complicated example – some players have critiqued its lack of diversity in race and body types, while others have questioned if the creator (a heterosexual woman) was the right person to create a game for or about queer men – but it has still found a strong fanbase among queer men, and you cannot fault it for not knowing what it is, what it wants to be, and who it wants to get into sexy sex scenes! (Figure 6.3).

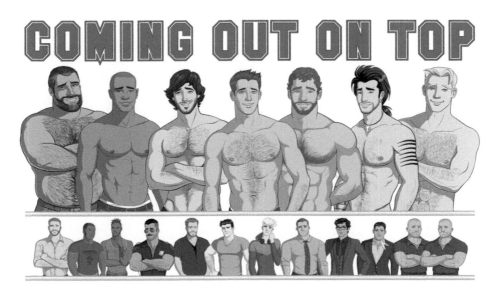

FIGURE 6.3 *Coming Out On Top* has a very narrow and specific target in terms of what genders it presents in sexual terms and what sorts of sexual relationships it portrays. It may not cater to people looking for male/female romances, but there's tons of male/male if that's your thing! (Obscurasoft, *Coming Out On Top*, December 10, 2014, https://obscurasoft.com/.)

CONCLUSION

Should your sex scenes be for a specific group, or should there be sex scenes for everyone? It's a tough question, and it depends heavily on the type of game you're making. For a dating sim or sex game, focusing your efforts on a particular character type, fantasy, or sexuality can be rewarding and allow you to craft a tailored sexual experience for your audience. But for other genres – or even for dating sims and sex games! – there's something great to be said for creating sexual content where *everyone* can find something to enjoy!

WORKSHOP QUESTIONS

Analysis: Consider the game you've been analyzing and how its sex scenes are presented. Can you guess what their target market/demographic might be, or if they even have one? Do the sex scenes reflect a focus on this target market, and if so, how? Do you think these scenes are also designed to cater to other audiences, and if so, how? To your knowledge, how well has this content been appreciated by players in and out of their target groups?

Creative: Is your game project aimed at a wide audience, or a narrow one? If a narrow one, how would you describe that audience? Will you include content to appeal to other audiences as well (and if so, how?) Or will you focus purely on generating sexual content for that smaller audience? What would that content look like?

CHAPTER 7

The Trifecta of Sexual Approach and Aesthetic

CONSIDER THE FOLLOWING HYPOTHETICAL situation:

A team is making a game about a dark, post-apocalyptic war that focuses on the difficult emotional journeys of the protagonist and the depravity humanity can sink to. In a game's design discussions, one member of the team suggests that the game could feature some explicit sexual scenes.

Immediately, another member disagrees. This game is supposed to be serious and emotional, they argue, not raunchy and titillating!

Across the table, another member of the team has a different perspective. Sex is soaring and ecstatic and full of joy. Wouldn't that be a palate cleanser from the unremitting grime and darkness of the world of this game?

Between them sits a third person scratching their head in confusion. What are the other two talking about? Sex isn't filthy and smutty OR exalted and dramatic, is it? It's just…a regular thing that lots of people do. What's the big deal either way?

Part of the difficulty in discussing sex in games – indeed, sex in any media – is that sex has different meanings to different people, resulting in the risk of people talking past each other like in our example. Some envision sex as something lustful and sordid, while others envision it as something sacred and joyous and still others envision it as something natural and every day. To be honest, all of them are right in certain contexts, and there are examples of all three kinds of sex in media, including games. The problem comes when, as part of talking at cross-purposes, your team has entirely different visions of "what sex means" and how it works within the overall tone of the work; if those perspectives and beliefs about sex aren't fully worked out early in the process, the resulting mismatch of tone can be disastrous.

So what IS sex, then? And how can it be so many different, oppositional things at once? (Figure 7.1).

DOI: 10.1201/9780429356650-9

FIGURE 7.1 That's us, asking the deep philosophical questions. (Richard Panasevich/ Shutterstock.com.)

Those questions are way bigger than the scope of this book, but for the purposes of a useful framework to think about game portrayals of sex, I propose that sex (or at least, how we present it) **is the ultimate mix of the sacred, the profane, and the mundane.** Our viewpoints and depictions of sex are part of a fluid, overlapping spectrum of all three philosophies and perspectives on sex, and on life in general! Understanding these approaches to sex – including how they can coexist and overlap – and mapping those approaches onto your design for sex scenes *and* your larger game narrative can do a lot to help keep the tone of the work consistent, to elevate the core themes of the game, and to say something about the world in which your characters are having sex.

Having an idea of the larger thematic and aesthetic core of your sex scenes is imperative to the early stages of the project – hence, why we're talking about it in THIS section. If you are planning a project with sex scenes, it's important to decide as early as possible how that sex will be presented, not only in terms of the individual characters and relationships but in terms of the larger themes, aesthetics, and tone of the encounter. Knowing that will help anchor and guide your project, as well as avoiding miscommunications and arguments like the one at the start of the chapter; your team will be in a better position to push in that direction via their art, audio, animation, design, and writing. On the other hand, if the vision for the sexual content is too muddled and complicated to communicate, or comes together too late in the project, or just doesn't really exist at all, then it's going to be that much harder to point the whole team in the same direction and to ensure the resulting sexual content is cohesive and tonally consistent. By adopting a simple framework based around three key themes and aesthetics – in this case, the sacred, the profane, and the mundane – your team can use clearer visual and thematic language to describe the sex in your game and to orient the team in a shared direction.

Note that in this case, the concepts of the sacred, the profane, and the mundane are NOT moral judgments, only as descriptors of particular **aesthetics, mood, and purpose**. Just because sex is "sacred" does not mean it is somehow "better" or more "moral"; similarly, "mundane" sex does not necessarily mean boring, and "profane" sex doesn't mean evil or sinful. Also, while some of the descriptors and iconography of sacred/profane/mundane may overlap with Western Christian iconography (e.g., references to choirs or devils, etc.), it is NOT meant to imply that those images and values are universally applicable! While this phrasing works for me – I'm a sucker for rhyming, if nothing else! – different cultures and traditions may use different iconography or models of sex, and you may find it more helpful to apply those lenses instead. In the end, this chapter is meant to offer a religion- /culture- /tradition-agnostic framework with which to analyze a game's approach to sex; if it's not working for you, feel free to dump what's not working and use the rest or come up with your own model!

THE SEX IN GAMES TRIFECTA MODEL

Rather than conceiving sex in games as on a linear value spectrum – for example, vanilla -> kinky, tasteful -> lewd, or even good -> bad – this three-way model focuses more on three different visual, narrative, and thematic ways that sex scenes can be presented, all while providing plenty of room to explore how those ways can overlap. Those three approaches can be roughly broken down as follows (Figure 7.2):

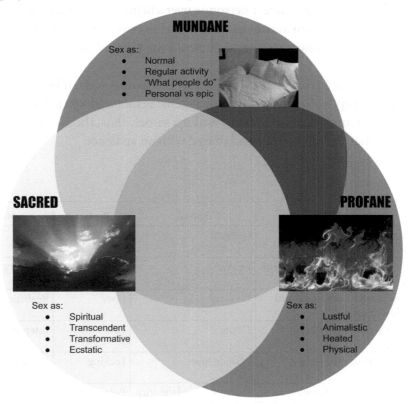

FIGURE 7.2 The Venn diagram (or "trifecta") of sacred, profane, and mundane sex. Note that, in reality, the "boundaries" between these three are much, MUCH fuzzier.

- **Sex as sacred** – sex as a transformative, spiritual experience of ecstasy and desire

- **Sex as profane** – sex as a physical, "animalistic" experience of heat, lust, and hunger

- **Sex as mundane** – sex as a common, everyday activity between two or more people, done for a variety of reasons

These approaches would seem to be antithetical to each other, but in fact, most sex scenes in games (or indeed most media) can be mapped out in the blurred space between them. There are sex scenes that blur the lines between sacred and mundane, mundane and profane, profane and sacred…and could even incorporate all three.

Each of the three aspects of sex tends to have certain tropes, aesthetics, and associations assigned to them, and while these should not be seen as prescriptive and set in stone, it's at least useful to know what the most common associations are, either to use as shorthand for yourself and your team or, alternatively, to have an idea of which associations you want to subvert and why (Figure 7.3).

Let's look a little closer at each of the three approaches to sex.

SEX AS SACRED: THE AGONY AND THE ECSTASY

In many cultures and traditions, the concept of "ecstasy" is actually a spiritual and religious one, referring to a moment where a person is overwhelmed by an intense, almost painful emotional experience, where awareness of the world is swept away in favor of altered and exalted state of consciousness, connected both to the self and to the cosmic forces of the universe (Figure 7.4).

Insert "sounds like a great orgasm" joke here. But joking aside, if both religion and sex share similar concepts of ecstasy, then it suggests sexual and spiritual experiences can absolutely be interconnected, or even one and the same…thus, the idea of "sacred sex" as a particular way that sex can be seen and shared with an audience.

	Sacred	Profane	Mundane
Most commonly associated sphere of experience	Spiritual	Physical	Mental
Most commonly associated descriptor of emotional state	Exalted	Debauched	Ordinary
Most commonly associated visual and narrative presentation	Idealized	Lewd	Realistic
Most commonly associated kind of sexual feeling	Desire	Lust	Interest
Most commonly associated verb(s) for sexual activity	Making love	Fucking	Having sex
Most likely media to find examples in	Romance novels/erotica	Pornography	Drama, literary fiction

FIGURE 7.3 The Most Common Associations with the Three Approaches to Sex. Note That These are Not Prescriptive or Set in Stone

FIGURE 7.4 …yeah, kind of like that. (Zelenov Iurii/Shutterstock.com.)

"Sacred" sex does not refer to a specific religious or theological definition; rather, it is sex presented as a transformative, transcendent, exalted experience that is as much or more spiritual and emotional as physical. If it's the kind of sex that people make comments about how the heavens opened, or the earth moved, or about sensations of "soaring" or "explosions of light" or so on – yeah, that kind. In this model, sex is not seen as something gross or base, but as something that elevates the participants; less "pleasures of the flesh" and more "pleasures of the soul." It's a deliberately idealized portrait of sex, with much of the real-world sweat and dirt smoothed away in favor of a carefully built aesthetic and emotional mood for the audience.

How is sacred sex usually portrayed in games?

- **Emphasis on heightened emotion, intensity, and drama** – Sacred sex focuses on emotional and mental state as part of the sexual act. The most common example of this is physical ecstasy, particularly in climax, and how the character has a dramatic and fundamental shift of mental process such as blocking out the physical world, being overwhelmed with sensation, rapturous focus on pleasure, and so on. Other examples of intensifying the drama and emotion include sweeping music and other audio cues, highly poetic or emotional dialogue, and characters being overwhelmed by emotions, sensations, or holistic desire (as opposed to physical lust).

- **Iconography and language related to height and divinity** – This can be using words like soaring, climbing, or flight, or can also refer to camera tricks and shots (e.g., the camera panning upward in a moment of ecstasy). Many Western games pair this with Christian iconography, such as heavenly clouds or sky, angels, or god rays, as well as audio cues like choirs, but imagery from other religious and cultural traditions can and should be explored as well.

- **Otherworldly, dreamlike, or mind-altering presentation** – Building on the concepts of "soaring" and "flight," a lot of sacred sex is presented in terms of a "magical" experience, one that is somehow above mere mortal encounters and into something otherworldly or supernatural. This connects with the mind-altering nature of this kind of sex; perceptions, awareness, or behavior shifts away from conscious reality and onto a more sensual or spiritual plane, where participants might close their eyes and throw their head back as a sign of abandoning oneself to sensation.

- **Intense emotional connection (usually)** – It is absolutely possible, and often very interesting, to explore sacred sex from the perspective of casual sex partners! But the emphasis on intense emotion and spirituality lends itself most easily to sex within explicitly romantic relationships. Similarly, the emphasis on drama means it works well as a transformation, twist, or climax in a romantic arc. This is the sort of sex where "I love you" can be easy to infer from the act, or to be murmured before, during, or after the sex. Sacred sex is presented as a melding not only of bodies, but of minds and hearts, even if it is just for the one encounter.

- **Abstraction and obscuring of the physical act** – While sacred sex does not deny the physical or shy away from depicting sex acts explicitly, it also does not necessarily explore the nitty-gritty details. This corresponds to its greater emphasis on the spiritual and emotional over the physical. There's less interest in the moment-to-moment animated bumping and rubbing and thrusting, and more interest in the high points, key moments, and crucial beats. As such, sacred sex often uses cinematic techniques like cross-fades, close-ups, slow motion, and dramatic montages to highlight those key moments, such as a particular touch or embrace, or an expression of ecstasy, or a final moment of climax.

There are several examples of sacred sex in games, particularly in those with a heavy emphasis on romance. The *Mass Effect* series in particular has several excellent examples, thanks to the in-world ability of the asari characters (see sidebar):

- In the sex scene with Liara at the end of *Mass Effect 3*, Liara emanates a swirling, glowing biotic field that fills the room and tinges the scene with a purple, "magical" light. The scene is shot in slow motion, and particular attention is paid to Liara's ecstatic, raptured expression during their embrace. Every movement is in deliberate slow motion, evoking an unreal, ethereal quality. The very last shot even shows Liara and Shepard entwined and apparently floating in mid-air in a dreamlike vision.

- In the sex scene between Peebee and Ryder in *Mass Effect: Andromeda*, on top of Peebee's trust and developing relationship with Ryder, she speaks of the sexual melding in intense, poetic terms ("Our bodies and minds weave together…become one.") The camera pays particular attention to Peebee's ecstasy and abandon before she engages in the meld. Within the meld, the two lovers are shown floating in midair in a misty nebula-like star field, staring into each other's eyes in a trance-like state; the player has the option to say, "I love you," and if they do so, both Ryder and Peebee say it as one. The meld ends, and both fall back on Ryder's bed.

In both cases, the scenes emphasize sexual ecstasy as a transformative, mind-altering state as well as one that promotes unique harmony and togetherness (a "meld"). Moments in which the lovers float in air, lost to the real world, and totally enraptured with each other emphasize the magical, dramatic, and intense connection, as well as how "beyond" normal sexual experience the encounters are. That, in the end, is the key to "sacred sex" – something beyond mere mortal experience, something that catapults the lovers into another realm of sensation and existence.

SIDEBAR 7.1 – SPECULATIVE SETTINGS AND SACRED SEX

It should be noted that fantasy and sci-fi settings offer some quite unique opportunities for presenting sacred sex – now all that "floating" or "explosions" or "melding of souls" can actually be quite literal! Characters can use magic, technology, or alien abilities to enhance sexual encounters and create a more transcendent, magical experience. One example is the floating sex scene between Syanna and Geralt in the *Blood and Wine* DLC for *The Witcher 3*; while neither party is emotionally close, the use of Syanna's magic results in a scene that feels dreamlike and ecstatic rather than merely physical.

Beyond that, a speculative setting offers opportunity for exploring new cultural norms for sex and spirituality. Perhaps a fantasy religion sees sex as *literally* sacred, incorporated as part of ritual or iconography. Or perhaps an alien race sees every sexual encounter as a solemn, moving meeting of minds, regardless of how deep the emotional relationship is otherwise. An example of the latter can be seen with the asari of the *Mass Effect* universe. Asari are a telekinetic and telepathic race of blue humanoids who engage in telepathic "melding" as part of the sexual act. This is initiated by them saying the words "Embrace eternity" as their eyes turn a solid black color. The language chosen emphasizes a spiritual, almost religious element to the psychic and sexual link.

SEX AS PROFANE: THE RAUNCHY ANIMAL WITHIN

While sacred sex rejects the idea of sex as merely "pleasures of the flesh," profane sex embraces that identity. If sacred sex is all heavenly choirs and artful, graceful shots of soaring spiritual ecstasy, then profane sex is debauchery and sweaty rutting in the shadows, enjoying and satisfying lust on a physical level.

Not that there's anything wrong with that! (Figure 7.5).

Profane sex is the term for sex that's presented in terms of physical, almost animalistic lust and sexual activity. There is little-to-no emphasis on the emotional connections or spiritual fulfillment of sex (though there can be, as we see when sacred/profane are blended in a scene). Rather, the thematic emphasis of the scene is on satisfying the body's sexual instincts and hunger, often in the most indulgent, over-the-top, orgiastic way possible. While mundane sex can be casual or lustful, profane sex is those lusts taken up to 11. It's sweaty, raunchy, and animalistic – and that's what makes it fun!

FIGURE 7.5   Talk about hungry for sex… (immfocus studio/Shutterstock.com.)

It's easy to fall into a stereotype that sacred sex=good and profane sex=bad, particularly as some of the more problematic sex scenes in games tend to fall toward that end of the spectrum. But the point is not that one is better or worse than the other, or even to position them in total opposition, but rather to better identify the contrasting aesthetics and approaches. Profane sex is not "bad" or "wrong," it is simply depicting sex and sexual themes in a raw, physical aspect.

Some common signatures of profane sex in video games are as follows:

- **Emphasis on the physical act and physical body** – While sacred sex focuses on key moments of eroticism and connection, profane sex usually lays it all out in filthy, fully animated glory. The camera rarely "cuts away" during profane sex, lingering instead on fully animated action. Similarly, the body is usually nude and shown in full detail, including some aspects of sex and arousal that are more "messy." Profane sex scenes in 3D often heavily feature sweat, not just as acknowledgement of "sweat happens" but as a highlighted aspect of the scene. In even more explicit games such as porn and hentai, there're also depictions of various sexual body fluids (including semen and vaginal fluid) as well as an abundance of drool.

- **Emphasis on insatiability and/or "performative" pleasure** – While sacred or mundane sex can be deeply pleasurable and evoke dramatic visual and vocal reactions, profane sex in games exaggerates those reactions up to 11. Rather than using them as a background element to build mood, profane sex shines the spotlight on them and makes them the costars of the performance, along with the sex itself. The most common form of this is loud, repeated, constant moaning, usually from a female character, building to even louder screams of ecstasy, as well as particularly lewd dirty talk. Profane sex also often focuses on facial expressions, particularly orgasmic expressions, less as ecstatic transcendence and more as exaggerated, semiperformative displays of physical pleasure. Many of these performative or physical reactions also highlight sexual insatiability – the physical and the mental state of needing sex immediately, or needing sexual fulfillment, being frantic, and loudly demanding to get it as fast/hard/deep/etc. as possible.

- **Body ecstasy vs. spiritual ecstasy** – Sacred sex portrays ecstasy as an almost religious experience, but there is no such idealization here; sexual ecstasy is portrayed as something more guttural, sweaty, and earthy compared to the more vaunted, elevated portrayals.

- **Iconography and language related to heat** – Many traditions connect physical desire with heat and fire, partially due to the heating of the body during arousal, but also in connection with the metaphor of being "consumed" by the fires of lust.

- **Emphasis on rawness, speed, and roughness** – Profane sex is not about trembling, worshipful touches or slow, tender lovemaking. It tends to showcase harsher, faster, more desperate, or enthusiastic activity. Sex is usually very active, fast, and filled with a lot of movement, and dialogue is likely to be rough, dirty, or to the point.

- **Less/no emphasis on emotional connection** – While a sacred/profane or mundane/profane scene can certainly have steamy profane sex occurring between lovers in love, a fully profane scene rarely has this aspect of connection, at least in the context of the sex. Many profane sex scenes take place between casual partners, or in some cases, outright enemies. The sex is often for the sake of its own enjoyment, rather than some deeper emotional relationship.

One can find many, many, MANY examples of profane sex in pornographic and hentai games; visiting adult game portals such as Nutaku will bring up several visual examples in just a few clicks. In AAA space, pure profane sex is a little harder to come by, though later we will see some examples of blending profane with mundane sex. But the AAA franchise that comes closest to pure profane sex is probably the *God of War* franchise, at least its earlier iterations. At least once per game, Kratos encounters nude or nearly nude women who are eager to have sex with him, or at the very least willing. Pressing a single button begins a sex scene that usually occurs off-screen, but features extremely loud and performative moans and cries of pleasure from the women, along with almost violent "shaking" from Kratos' thrusts. There is nothing spiritual, gentle, or romantic about the encounters (i.e., not sacred), but nor do they feel like "ordinary" sexual encounters (i.e., not mundane either); instead, they slot quite firmly into purely lustful fantasy scenarios that center around rough sex and uncontrolled lust. A few titles in the series offer even stronger examples of profane sex:

- In *God of War: Chains of Olympus*, Kratos breaks into a dungeon area to find two identical-looking young women trapped in a jail chamber. Despite their predicament, it's heavily implied that they're in the middle of having sex; both are topless and nearly naked, and they're posed in an intimate embrace. Apparently, they're so horny, not even being trapped and in danger can restrain their lust! They immediately offer sexual favors to Kratos ("Is there anything we can do to repay you?"). The player can then choose to interact with the two women, at which point Kratos kneels down and takes both women in his arms. The camera pans over to a bronze candleholder shaped like a woman holding the white wax candle (a phallic symbol). As Kratos and the women begin having sex, on top of the usual moaning and shaking, the candleholder shakes and shudders under the power and roughness of sexual activity. Of particular note is the way wax spatters and covers the bronze woman with white wax droplets; this evokes the image of seminal fluids spattering a woman. While the player never sees the actual sex acts themselves, the details emphasize themes of sexual insatiability (i.e., the two women's behavior) and sexual physicality (rough, active sex, body fluids, etc.) that is consistent with profane sex.

- In *Ghost of Sparta*, another sex scene takes place in which Kratos approaches a brothel and takes two courtesans to bed. Again, heavy emphasis is placed on the loud, performative pleasure of the women and the physicality of the scene; while the sex is not shown, the player can see the bed bouncing, shaking, and flying off the ground, all while the women moan ecstatically. Moreover, as the scene progresses, more and more female sex workers enter the room, regard the scene with excitement, and leap onto the bed to join the sex. Other women are shown writhing in arousal in the doorway. The scene plays as an over-the-top fantasy of sexual prowess, again with the emphasis on sexual insatiability from the female sex workers (and Kratos/the player as the only one able to satisfy their desires) and the raw physicality of the act.

- In *God of War III*, Kratos enters Aphrodite's room only to find her already in a sexual embrace with two of her handmaidens. When she notices Kratos, she dismisses them, then immediately invites Kratos to sleep with her. When he rebuffs her, she immediately starts complaining about it being too long since "a real man" came to her chambers, all while posing provocatively. Between her sexual escapades with her handmaidens and her complaint about not enough men, her sexual insatiability is front and center. This theme is echoed with her handmaidens themselves; as they watch Kratos and Aphrodite having sex, they grope each other and grow aroused to the point of jumping on each other in a frenzy of lust.

As mentioned above, the scenarios in these *God of War* games play out like fantasies as opposed to realistic encounters, and offer little sense of elevated emotion or connection between the participants. The details emphasize physicality, performance, and in some cases, the so-called dirty aspects of sex such as sweat and body fluids. Above all, they emphasize the lust of the participants (at least the female participants; Kratos is another matter, one we will discuss later). Despite some coyness about sex and explicitness (e.g., never showing the sex on screen), these details place God of War's scenes in the profane camp.

SIDEBAR 7.2 – SIN, KINK, AND THE KITCHEN SINK OF PROFANE SEX

Profane sex is an interesting and worthwhile thematic aspect of sex to explore, but there are ways in which certain presentations of profane sex can uphold negative, problematic, or harmful stereotypes. Developers wishing to explore or present profane sex as part of their game should be aware of those potential pitfalls so as to ensure their depictions of profane sex have all of the hotness and none of the harm.

- **Detach the concept of profane sex from "sin"** – While it can be useful to consider the aesthetics of profane sex vs. sacred, a clear line should be drawn about regarding profane sex as somehow inherently sinful, bad, or evil. Some "sinful" aesthetics and iconography can be interesting and fun (e.g., sexy demons and demonesses), but straying too far into the idea of raw animalistic sex as "sinful" is applying a strict, inaccurate, and sex-negative attitude to sex, that there is "good" sex and "bad" sex and that those who have "bad" sex are somehow morally degenerate.
- **Kink does not always mean profane sex** – The emphasis on rawness and roughness means many associate kink and kinky activities with profane sex. If characters pull out whips, handcuffs, or leather, many people immediately make the mental classification that the scene is profane. However, kink, like many kinds of sexual activity, is nuanced and a part of many people's sexual life, whether it's mundane, sacred, or profane.
- **Profane sex isn't just for cis (straight) men** – A lot of people assume that gender minorities like cis women, nonbinary, and trans people are only interested in sacred or mundane sex, and that profane sex is something only cis men appreciate. This, coupled with the dominance of straight male perspectives in games, results in a lot of profane game sex focusing on presenting titillating, sexualized, or objectified "hot women". If a male character is sexualized as part of profane sex, the assumption then is that it's still for cis men, only gay instead of straight. Of course, straight cis women and queer/trans people can be just as horny as anyone else, and developers showing profane sex would do well to create accordingly and acknowledge the raunchy sides of those audiences.
- **Avoid racist ideas of "savagery" in relation to profane sex** – Some developers associate "animalistic" concepts of sex and lust to extremely racist tropes about indigenous people or people of color being "uncivilized." As such, sex with these characters is often portrayed as profane to drive home their "savageness" – for example, the sex scene with Citra in *Far Cry 3*, which on top of being animated and sweaty is also shown in the context of a tribalistic blood ritual. While characters of all races are capable of some profane, sweaty rutting, depicting racial minorities *exclusively* in those terms has extremely problematic implications and plays into harmful stereotypes. Approach profane sex with extreme caution in such situations, hire sensitivity readers to review the material, and when in doubt, go for a more mundane approach.

SEX AS MUNDANE: BACK TO REALITY

Sacred sex and profane sex both function as different types of sexual fantasies – one idealized, one raunchy. But what if your game is less interested in fantasy and more interested in reality? What if you want to depict sex in the way that real people might have sex, or as something that's just a part of life, whether good or bad? Then, we're talking about the wide world of mundane sex and the various depictions within.

To describe sex as mundane does not mean that it's boring! The word "mundane" comes from the Latin word "mundus," meaning "world" – in this context, "mundane" means "of the world." It's a useful descriptor for presentations of sex that are grounded in portraying it as a normal, common part of daily life. If sacred sex is associated with divine ecstasy and profane sex is the "fun" kind of hell, then mundane sex has its feet squarely planted on Earth, in the real world. There's less emphasis on soaring exalted feelings or on fleshy "animal" lust. Sex is just a thing that people do, for an almost infinite array of reasons (Figure 7.6).

This, of course, means that unlike sacred and profane sex, the mood and type of sex in mundane depictions can be extremely diverse. Depictions can run the gamut from romantic, gentle sex, to meaningless casual fun, to passionate quickies, to empty, joyless coupling, and so on. Mundane sex can be dramatic, boring, special, ordinary, smooth, awkward, emotional, passionate, slow, meaningless, healthy, unhealthy, romantic, lustful, disinterested, and everything in between – as long as it feels like it reflects some aspect of how people in real life deal with sex and sexuality, it can count.

Of course, given the huge range of depictions and types, it's hard to give a list of hallmarks of mundane sex; no two scenes look alike! But as a rough guideline, mundane sex tends to have the following:

FIGURE 7.6   Just another ordinary thing to do in an ordinary bed… or wherever the urge takes you! (AimPix/Shutterstock.com.)

- **Sexual narrative drama as personal vs. world shaking** – Having sex can absolutely be a major moment in a character's life or story arc, or in their relationship with another character. But unlike sacred sex, this is not framed as something world-shaking or reality-altering; the gods aren't descending from on high to bless this moment! If there is a dramatic moment, it is framed in terms of a personal character moment or shift, not as the world shifting on its axis or the skies and seas parting to herald the event.

- **More flirtation and relaxed attitude** – While mutual consent and enthusiasm is important for sacred and profane sex as well, mundane sex often presents this in less dramatic, more relaxed ways. Characters often flirt with each other in the lead up to sex, or have conversations laden with heavy, mutually acknowledged subtext…or even text sometimes! Mundane sex is where you will often see characters smiling at each other and bantering, both clearly knowing where things are going to lead.

- **Realistic settings** – Mundane sex takes place in mundane places like bedrooms, kitchens, living rooms, showers, baths, barn lofts, motels, even alleyways, and quiet corners. Even in speculative settings, the places are recognizable and relatable as opposed to idealized or fantasized locations. If you're presenting a mundane sex scene, possibly rethink the impossibly giant boudoir with the enormous silk bed and the 50 million candles?

The examples of mundane sex in video games are almost too many to list and range the scale from deeply romantic to deeply cynical, and everything in between. A few well-known examples are as follows:

- The husband/wife team of Bayek and Aya in *Assassin's Creed Origins* are depicted as having an active, healthy, and mutually pleasurable sex life. Sex is shown, implied, or mentioned explicitly in many of their reunions, and they engage in easy, affectionate sexual banter and flirting, with body language that is comfortable and intimate. The depictions of their sexual encounters are depicted as emotionally intense and full of love, and some have shades of sacred sex, but it's clear that sex is part of their regular relationship.

- While the *Mass Effect* franchise offers several examples of "sacred" sexual encounters as already discussed, they also offer as many, if not more examples of mundane sexual relationships and encounters. Various romantic partners visit the player character's cabins with drinks and music to set the mood, or invite the player to quickies in the engine room, or even go through amusing research about the logistics of interspecies mating. Some lovers are emotional and vulnerable, while others are awkward and stuttering; in all cases, the sexual intimacy is depicted as relatable, mutually pleasurable, and completely normal, at least in the context of saving the galaxy! Outside of love interests, there are also multiple options for one-night stands with various characters, including more "casual" relationships with some of the romantic interests.

Most casual encounters are presented as fun, relaxed, and healthy ways for two adults to pass the time. However, the games also show more complicated and nuanced portrayals of mundane sex, including the consequences of pursuing sex without sufficient care for a partner. As discussed in an earlier chapter, leaping at the opportunity to have sex with Jack before establishing trust and respect results in some very negative – but realistic! – results in which she permanently loses trust in you.

- *Grand Theft Auto V* also depicts sex and sexuality as a "regular thing" that the characters do, but in a deliberately cynical, less positive light, one that matches the larger world perspective and the characters involved. There is little-to-no sense of mutual connection or affection in the sex scenes, or even mutual pleasure; in several scenes, one participant will be "hammering away" while the other is bored or detached, and neither party shows much arousal or signs of actually enjoying themselves. Sex is used as a storytelling tool to highlight the characters' narcissism and disconnection from their own desires as well as those of their partners. Instead of doing it for fun or pleasure, some use it to manipulate, some use it to establish dominance, and others use it as an escape from boredom, making it literally a "mundane" act. While the vision of sex *GTA V* paints is not always a pleasant one, it is one that reinforces the core themes of the game, as well as one that feels grounded in something resembling the real world.

THE TRIFECTA TOGETHER? OVERLAPPING THE THREE

By now, you may have gotten the hint that while these are useful classifications for depictions of sex, the boundaries between them are wildly fluid and overlapping. Combining sacred, profane, and mundane motifs can create a more holistic, nuanced portrait of sex. Sometimes, one is more dominant with small but meaningful hints of the others; in other cases, the three aspects are blended so thoroughly that it's hard to see where one ends and the other begins.

In other words, yes, it is completely possible to have a sex scene that is sacred, profane, and mundane all at once. And as an example of which, let's take a look at one of the sex scenes from *Wolfenstein: The New Order*.

The scene is a short one and features BJ and Anya having sex in a supply closet while their allies overhear them outside and react in annoyance. The space is tight, and the camera shows both lovers enthusiastically hammering away at each other and loudly grunting in rhythm. BJ murmurs that he wants to be like this with her, always, and Anya says they will…but their allies knock on the door and demand they finish up. Anya comments wryly that it won't be today.

Let's breakdown the scene's aspects via the sacred/profane/mundane triad:

- **Profane** – The sex is presented extremely physically and raw, with emphasis both on Anya's grunts and cries of pleasure and on the thrusting, rough sex. The reactions of their allies can be summed up as, "they're at it again?!" implying that the characters have already been showing a strong lustful dynamic that can't be resisted. The closeness of the space also suggests warmness and sweat, other common aspects of profane sex.

- **Sacred** – Despite all of the above, the scene also features the spiritual, connective aspect of sacred sex. BJ's words to Anya, while simple and in the throes of passion, are deeply poetic and heartfelt, as if simultaneously moved to speech but also unable to speak properly, and they paint a picture that is almost an otherworldly ideal of making love forever. The music during this confession is soft and uplifting, and the two characters maintain steady, deep eye contact, creating the impression that the rest of the world has faded away for them and that they are totally connected to each other.

- **Mundane** – You don't get much more mundane than a supply closet! The setting lends a strong real-world grounding to the scene, as does the presence of other people having comedic reactions to the loud sex. The setting of *Wolfenstein* and the Resistance also lends realistic context to the sexual encounter; in a small base of operations, space is at a premium, and with the constant threat of death, it's realistic to expect people to have sex as a life-affirming act (Figure 7.7).

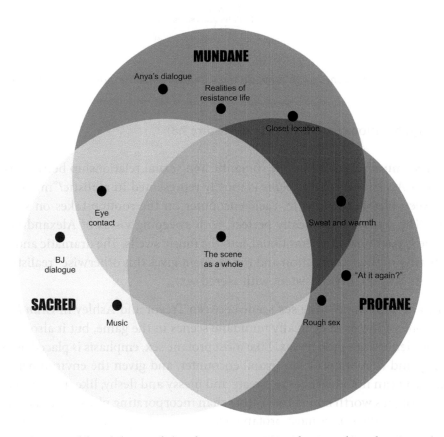

FIGURE 7.7 Suggested breakdown of the closet scene using the sacred/profane/mundane Venn diagram.

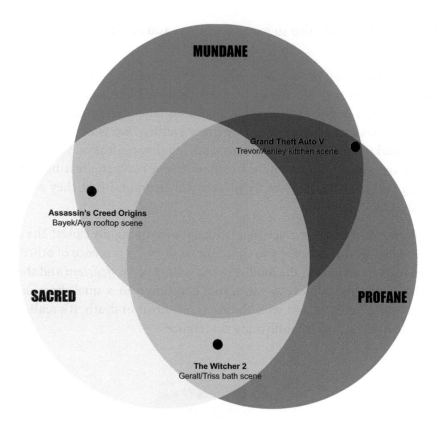

FIGURE 7.8 Other sex scenes plotted out on the sacred/profane/mundane Venn diagram.

Other combinations from other games (Figure 7.8):

- **Sacred/mundane** – While the romantic and sexual relationship between Bayek and Aya in *Assassin's Creed Origins* is mostly represented in realistic/"mundane" terms between husband and wife, their encounter on the rooftop takes on sacred qualities. The setting is idyllically perfect, with sweeping vistas of Alexandria. The dialogue is passionate and emotional, and the music swells. The dramatic and emotional intensity of their connection and the moment gives this otherwise "realistic" tryst an almost holy quality consistent with sacred sex.

- **Profane/mundane** – The sex scene between Trevor and Ashley in *Grand Theft Auto V* is one of the most cynically mundane scenes in the game, but it also incorporates some elements of profane sex. Like most profane sex, emphasis is placed on the physicality and roughness of the sexual encounter, and given the environment and context, you can imagine it being sweaty and messy and fleshy, like much profane sex is. However, it's worth noting that rather than incorporating pleasure and lustful excitement about the sex, as most profane sex does, this keeps the emotions "mundane" in the most extreme sense. There's no *heat* to the scene, no sexual need or hunger; the characters are depicted as almost going through the motions as something to do.

- **Sacred/profane** – The sex scene between Triss and Geralt in *The Witcher 2* offers a lot of sacred imagery and mood-building – idealized location, emotional connection, and even narration about a local legend about eternal passion and "limitless devotion." However, there are also aspects of profane sex in the scene as well, including a lot of performative erotic moaning from Triss and an emphasis on the lovers engaging in multiple positions, enthusiastic thrusting, almost clumsy eagerness, etc. This is a vision of sex that emphasizes both the spiritual connection and the heated physical lust between the characters.

Just as you can use the Venn diagram model to analyze and break down the components of an existing sex scene, you can also use it to plot out where your own sex scenes fall on this "spectrum". Using a model similar to this can help greatly in judging the mood, aesthetic, thematic drive, and final outcome of your sex scenes. By positioning your sex scenes as points on this Venn diagram, you can provide a good guide to you and your team of what the overall impact and tone of a scene needs to be, and from that, inspires you and others with how to reach that impact.

Most importantly, this model can also help you work out that tone and mood in the larger scope of your game.

NOT JUST FOR GETTING NAKED ANYMORE!

As some of you might suspect, this Venn diagram can be adapted for a wide variety of *nonsexual* themes, themes that can be core to the message or world of the game itself. As an example, if the theme is humanity, then sacred might equate to, "humans are good and enlightened", profane might be "humans are savage monsters", while mundane might be "humans are a mixed bag, both good and bad". The diagram can also be used to model things like the state of the game world (e.g., beautiful and enlightened, a total hellhole, or boringly ordinary?) or where a character is on their arc (e.g., heroic and optimistic, brutal and pessimistic, or something else entirely?).

This means that on top of using the Venn diagram to plot out the general mood of a sex scene, you can also use it to plot out how that sex scene fits in the general mood and theme of your game, as well as the emotional states of the characters involved. You can avoid tonal dissonance by either matching the type of sex to the type of world and narrative, or carefully and deliberately choosing ways to contrast the two to reveal a twist or new aspect of the story you're telling.

Matching – In this model, whatever the dominant tone of the world, game, or characters is, that's what the type of sex scene is. A dramatic, hopeful fantasy game where true love wins over evil? Probably easiest if consummating that "true love" is treated with the dramatic, sweeping, hopeful tones of sacred sex. But sacred sex would be out of place in *Grand Theft Auto*! A gritty, cynical tale about selfish people who are only out for themselves lends itself far more strongly to mundane or profane sex (Figure 7.9).

However, that's not to say that the tone of the sex and the tone of the larger world ALWAYS have to match…

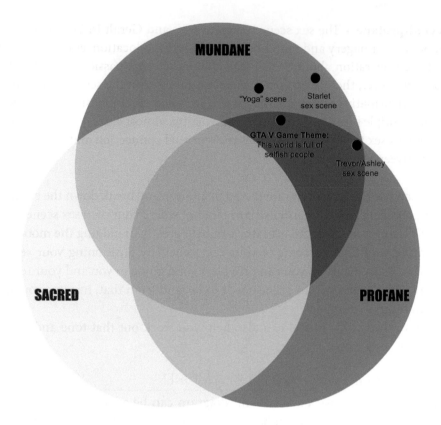

FIGURE 7.9 Plotting out *GTA V*'s theme vs. some of its sex scenes and how they match. Note the thematic clustering in profane/mundane.

Contrasting – Depending on the world or tone you're building and the nuances of your characters, you may wish to create sex scenes that deliberately contrast the dominant tone of the game. This can reveal more about your characters and world, or provide a counterpoint or underlying message beyond the surface-level mood. For example, the general, nonsexual "feel" of *Wolfenstein* is probably nudging into the profane end of the model: War is hellish, Nazis are loose, and life as a resistance fighter is grimy and harsh. BJ and Anya both suffer traumas, and while they keep their sense of goodness, they both are also in dark mental places at various points of the narrative. In such a brutal, dark world, sacred sex would seem to be discordant.

And yet, both sex scenes feature heavy sacred elements to great effect. It showcases the sexual and romantic connection between BJ and Anya as a respite from the darkness, as the one pure and bright spot in a world of horrors. It also reveals new depths to BJ and Anya as characters and sets this side of their personality against the grimy harshness of their surroundings. While using contrast in this way may not work with every game, thoughtful application in the right settings can only make both the scene and the larger world and characters feel more compelling (Figure 7.10).

Again, this model is a suggestion; feel free to adapt and adjust it based on your needs and aesthetic approaches. But consider the usefulness of adopting this "trifecta" model or a

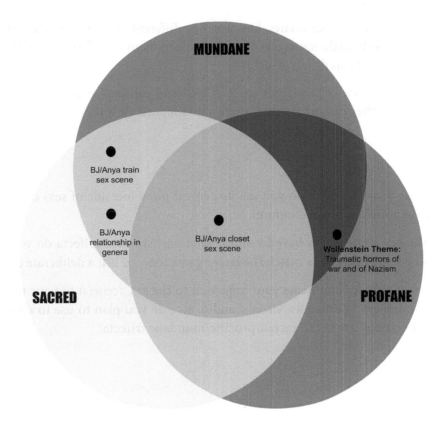

FIGURE 7.10 Plotting out *Wolfenstein: The New Order's* theme vs. some of its sex scenes and how they deliberately contrast. Note the contrast between the harsh profane/mundane core themes and the sweet sacred/mundane sexual relationship between BJ and Anya.

similar model for mapping out your sex scenes in the larger scheme of your game. It helps name and maintain a consistent tone, grounds the details of a presentation, and most of all, inspires you to consider the sex scene's role in the large themes of the game.

CONCLUSION

Creating sexual content in games is a nuanced process, and you may find it easier to go in with no preconceptions or structures to work off of. But if not, consider using the sacred/profane/mundane model as a lens and a tool for conceptualizing the larger tone, aesthetics, and themes of your sexual content, and for nailing down that structure in the early stages of development so that you and your team know what to aim for from here on!

WORKSHOP QUESTIONS

Analysis

- Examine the overall tone of the sex scene(s) in the game you're analyzing. Would you describe it as more sacred, profane, or mundane? Or a mix of the three? Can you point to specific aspects, moments, visuals, etc., that reflect its place in the trifecta?

- If there are multiple sex scenes, how are they different in relation to the trifecta? Are they all roughly in the same place, or are some of them in different areas? What's the general effect of this difference, if so?

- Consider the tone of the larger work as well and compare it to the tone of the sex scene(s). Do they match? If not, is there a dissonance, or is there more of a deliberate contrast?

Creative:

- For your project, where do you see its general place (outside of sex) on the sacred/profane/mundane Venn diagram?

- For the sex scene(s) you have in mind, what part(s) of the trifecta do you see them most evoking? Does this match the larger game tone, or is it a deliberate contrast?

- How will you communicate your approach to the sex scene(s) to your team and to your audience? What tools, visuals, audio, etc., do you plan to use to convey where the sex scene(s) are in the sacred/profane/mundane trifecta?

CHAPTER 8

Teamwork Makes the Dream Work!

Main Author: Souha Al-Samkari
Sidebar Author: Michelle Clough

This chapter is brought to you by the amazing Souha Al-Samkari, VP of Truant Pixel and veteran of multiple sexy visual novel teams such as Akash and When the Night Comes! She has a lot of experience to share about leading teams in creating sexy content, experience she's been kind enough to share for this book. As for me, I have a few thoughts on the subject as well, which I've added in the sidebars. For now, take it away, Souha!

MICHELLE

If you're referencing this chapter, then you're thinking about or embarking on a project that's going to require you to work in a team. Working with others can be deeply fulfilling, especially if you're used to working solo, but it brings a new set of challenges in an arena that can already be a bit fraught and stressful. The good news, however, is that you can navigate these challenges the same way as any other in development – good communication, mindfulness, and consistently modeling the sort of behavior you want to see on your team. This chapter is only an overview, but we'll cover some of the most important things to keep in mind when you're leading a team working on sexual content.

SIDEBAR 8.1 – THE AWKWARD, NAKED ELEPHANT IN THE ROOM (BY MICHELLE CLOUGH)

While one of the goals of this book is to normalize the use of sexual content in creating games, the truth is, of course, that there are some pretty unique challenges… and handling sex-related awkwardness in your team is one of them. Many of us live in sex-negative cultures where discussing sex frankly is Not Done. Talking about sex is awkward enough when it's with friends or partners; in creative and professional

DOI: 10.1201/9780429356650-10

settings, it can be almost crippling. Not even teams and studios famous for their sex scenes are immune. Jakub Szamalek, lead writer for *The Witcher 3*, had this to say about how the sex scenes got "handled" at CD Projekt Red:

> At one point, a producer came in to the writing room and said, 'we need 12 cut scenes with sex – who wants to write them?' Nobody wanted to do it. If I remember correctly, I wrote them all. It was a pretty awkward process for everyone involved. First I had to come up with the scenario, and describe it – and writing it down for other people to comment on was awkward, and then the animation staff had to figure out how to show it and then they have to direct the mo-cap actors, which is awkward, and then the actors have to perform it and deliver the lines, which is also awkward. But sex is awkward anyway so it all works out fine in the end.[1]

If that's what happens at a studio that is already known for sex and "comfortable" putting that content in a game, imagine a new studio trying it for the first time! But awkwardness can mean more than just blushing a bit during scrum; if not handled carefully, it can cause breakdowns in communication and workflow, where different team members can't get on the same page of what they're making or can't collaborate properly because it's too embarrassing to discuss the details of a sex scene. Part of leading a team (or just being part of one) that's working on sexual content is to not only be aware of awkwardness, but to know how best to handle it in a way that respects your team and supports them through minor embarrassment to create effective, meaningful, and sexy game content.

Note, though, that there's a BIG difference between "working through cultural awkwardness to collaborate" and "making your team uncomfortable," as Souha will discuss.

SETTING EXPECTATIONS

If your project requires you to seek out and interview contractors, or if you're in charge of onboarding for your team members, be sure to let them know what to expect. If your game will be rated M and contains full frontal nudity, let your potential team members know the content they'll potentially be working with or have their names on when it comes time to ship. The games industry is notoriously tight-lipped, so if this is a concern for you, be sure to slip your potential hires an NDA before you get into the interview process.

If you're working with a team you've already assembled, then it's important before the project starts that you have a good understanding of everyone's comfort level with the project. It may not always be possible with your setup/financial situation to create something that everyone agrees on, in which case you'll need to deploy team members as effectively and strategically as you can. Some folks might be fine working on a game that contains sexual content but not working directly on a sex scene, some folks might be fine working on the game but request that their name not appear in the credits, and so on and so forth.

As a team leader, it's your job to ensure that everyone has a clear understanding of both the project content and vision and their options for assuring their comfort going forward.

Beyond that, however, all of your noble efforts to be transparent and accommodating will fall apart if your team members aren't comfortable coming to you to express their reservations and concerns, which leads us to our next point.

SIDEBAR 8.2 – TOOLS FOR SHARING THE VISION (BY MICHELLE CLOUGH)

So you're on board with making sure the team has full understanding of the content and vision of the project…but how exactly do you do that? What are the nuts and bolts involved? Here are some tips and techniques that may help.

- **Communicate clearly and in detail** – This may seem obvious, but once that awkwardness we mentioned enters the picture, it can be easy to slip into hazy, vague descriptors like, "and then things get sexy." Call out specific images, moments, or details that are important to the scene or project in general. Use storyboards if appropriate, and ensure different disciplines have all the information they need to do their job. There's no need to go into porn-level detail (unless you're making porn, of course!) but the clearer the picture you can paint for your team, the better.
- **Use visualizations (e.g., the sacred/profane/mundane Venn diagram)** – Want to ensure your composer doesn't deliver jazzy porn music for a gentle, tender sex scene? On top of clear verbal and written communication, be ready to provide visual guidance, not only as visual references but also in diagrams, models, etc. This is a place where the sacred/profane/mundane Venn diagram, or similar materials, can be useful for providing your team quick tonal and thematic guidelines at a glance.
- **Keep a resource bank of references** – Sometimes, the easiest way to get the team on the same page for a sex scene is to be able to point to an existing scene or image and say, "yes, like that." It's worth taking the time to collect and curate examples and references from games, movies, TV, books, and even art or stock photography. These can either be general mood pieces to get the "feel" of your scene, or more specific shots, positions, or dynamics. An added bonus: If discussions about sexual content still feel a little awkward, it's often much easier if the team has a shared point of reference that they can consult at their comfort and convenience.

MODEL WHAT YOU EXPECT FROM YOUR TEAM

You can tell people anything you like, but until and unless they see you putting all those lovely ideas about transparency, communication, and professionalism into practice yourself, they're not going to believe it fully. As a team leader, you set the tone for what goes on in your project, from everything to work ethic to communication. If you care for the well-being of your team, it is your job to model the standards of behavior you wish to see.

Discussion of romantic and sexual content must be handled with care, especially in an industry that is rife with issues of sexual harassment thanks to bad actors who take advantage of the power imbalances and instability present in many game studios. One way to combat this within your own project is to ensure that you keep a professional distance from the material itself. Be cognizant of how you talk about the material itself – take for example, discussion of an explicit sex scene. Comments like "wow, this is so hot! If anyone needs me, I'll be in my bunk," dated reference and all, might seem really obviously like a bad idea, but you have to watch out for subtler things as well. No one on your team should be able to divine that you're into tickling or that you moonlight as a domme when you're discussing your in-game content unless it's directly relevant in some way to the discussion at hand.

SIDEBAR 8.3 – "BUT WHAT IF WE WANT TO GET THIRSTY ON MAIN?" (BY MICHELLE CLOUGH)

Souha makes an excellent point about the importance of professionalism when it comes to sexual material, and not being, as they say, "thirsty on main." But I can hear at least a few of you at the back asking, "but what if I want to have a company where we can talk openly about our desires and what turns us on? What if I want to foster an environment where everyone feels empowered to make their thirstiest tweets about the characters and scenes we're making? What if I want us all to be free to say, yes, that's hot and I *will* be in my bunk?"

Here's the thing; companies with that level of sexual openness can and do exist, BUT only with an extremely high level of both professional and personal trust, and that is a step you CANNOT skip or rush. If you are forming a very small company or team from existing close friendships – friendships originally based around, say, sharing smutty fanfic or gushing explicitly over sexy characters – then talking frankly about your desires, turn-ons, and sex lives might be fine! The problem comes, however, when people start unloading in similar detail to new hires, contractors, or people whose level of comfort and trust hasn't been established. Suddenly, thrusting them into the middle of explicit thirst and sexual enthusiasm can be off-putting at best, and outright hostile and harmful at worst. That goes double for team members who are marginalized and at heightened risk of gross behavior in the industry (e.g., harassment, sexual jokes, etc.); blasting them with "I'LL BE IN MY BUNK!" without knowing or caring if they're comfortable with that is only going to compound their bad experiences.

In general, **you will never, EVER go wrong by keeping things professional.** And if you are hoping for more "enthusiastic" and personal engagement with the content you're making (e.g., getting excited about your sex scenes), then remember: **trust first, thirst second**. Take the time to establish mutual trust and understanding between you and your team *before* getting overly enthusiastic about the sexual content; don't force it by oversharing at the start! As Souha notes, make it clear from the beginning what the content is, and always put the comfort and safety of your teammates first. If people are going to become more relaxed and less reserved about the sexual content, let it happen organically, and let them set their pace and comfort level. By creating an atmosphere of trust, where ALL teammates feel safe, both your content and your company culture will be the better for it…and if discussion of your game eventually gets thirsty, it will have gotten there the healthy way!

CHECK IN WITH YOUR TEAM AS YOU GO

Projects evolve naturally as you progress, adding and removing content on the fly, and sometimes people's tolerances for the romantic and sexual content you're producing may change quite suddenly for a variety of reasons – for this reason, it's imperative to continue to check in on your team as you continue along. Some folks may not feel comfortable discussing their feelings on such matters or the reasons that drive them, so it's important to allow people to opt out, no questions asked, if working on certain content wherever possible. There are certain financial realities that must be considered when working on a small team, but in that case it's even more important to be as honest and communicative as possible with your team at every step to ensure that you don't paint yourself into a financial corner by forcing a team member to work on something potentially triggering or massively uncomfortable for them – this can be hugely damaging and exploitative.

Outside of comfort with the material, it's imperative that you keep communication open with your team members when it comes to the content itself. Your team may have notes for you that will help you make your scene more realistic or sensitive, or they may save you from disaster in the event that something is simply not working. If you are creating content that pertains to or features people of marginalized races, genders, or sexualities outside of your own experience, it's even more important that your team be able to speak to you on these issues. In such a case, strongly consider hiring a sensitivity reader or consultant.

SIDEBAR 8.4 – TIPS FOR COMMUNICATION AND CHECKING IN (BY MICHELLE CLOUGH)

Communicating with your team to keep tabs on their comfort level is important, but part of their comfort also comes from how you communicate, and whether you have made it safe for them to do so. Again, this goes double for marginalized team members, who may be under cultural pressure to downplay their own discomfort and laugh along with uncomfortable subject matter rather than complaining. Beyond being consistently respectful and supportive to these team members, here are some other ideas on how to keep the lines of communication open:

- **Provide avenues both for public AND for private discussion** – Some team members may only feel comfortable talking about sexual content, or their level of comfort, in a personal one-on-one setting, or over text and email. Others may be resistant to private one-on-ones and instead prefer to share feedback only with the rest of the team as witnesses. A lead should ensure both approaches are supported within your structure, that any and all team members have a way to give feedback that is most comfortable to them.

- **Check what's going well** – While it's important to touch base with your team to check if they're still okay and comfortable with the sexual content, it's equally important to check what they definitely DO like, what they are comfortable and happy with, and what is going well. Obviously, this should not be applied in a toxic positivity way (Say something nice about the sex scene, or else!) but in a way that allows for enthusiastic, celebratory feedback just as much as more cautious or uncomfortable responses.
- **Encourage use of references** – As mentioned above, it can be hard to say, "I want to see X in this sex scene," but easier to say, "I want this scene to be like X moment in Y movie/game/show." Having a large library of media references for your sex scene isn't just helpful in terms of visual and creative references, but for giving your shyer team members a useful toolbox for communicating their preferences with a minimum of awkwardness or embarrassment. Keep the references at roughly the same level of explicitness and rating as your game; in other words, no pornographic references unless you are actually making a pornographic game!
- **Consider anonymous methods of feedback** – A comment box or jar might sound like a ridiculous notion, but setting one up for brainstorming or feedback on sexual game content can be a freeing, low-stakes way to allow devs to have their say without any fear of having to justify themselves or having it thrown back at them later. Digital methods such as Google Forms or SurveyMonkey can allow for easy compilation of feedback in one place with no identifying markers (e.g., handwriting, etc.), meaning your team can speak completely freely and without shame.

Of course, none of these can "replace" being honest and respectful to your regular team communication, and fostering those values in the team as a whole. They can, however, provide ways to reinforce those values, to protect vulnerable teammates, and take a bit of the pressure off when talking about sexy stuff.

WORKING WITH ARTISTS

When working with artists on romantic and sexual content, you may find yourself necessarily working with references that feature nudity or sexual content – in such instances, it's vital to ensure that you are as professional as possible at all times. Before you've brought your artist onboard or assigned them this particular content, you should have already ascertained whether or not they're up for this particular task. Once you've gotten the groundwork done, be sensitive to the way this material is handled and discussed. When sharing references, keep it clinical – don't offer commentary on how sexy or not you find something, and don't send your artist explicit references in a private message or mix in regular everyday conversation. If such references are shared in common workspaces, make sure you have something like a click through link or other barrier to ensure no one blunders into this kind of content without a warning.

WORKING WITH ACTORS

Working with actors is an amazing way to bring your scenes to life, but when you're dealing with sensitive content, it's even more vital to ensure that you're doing everything you can to create a safe environment. To that end, communication is your greatest tool at every stage in the process.

Before you bring an actor on board, make sure you're providing them with all the information they need to make an informed decision about this audition – Does the game have sexual content? Does this character have a sex scene? Will there be nudity? If you are working with actors with agents or union actors, they may have more detailed questions for you about the game's content, so be prepared to answer.

Once you've selected your actors and are ready to record, be just as aware of their comfort levels as you go through as you would to your own team members. When recording an intimate scene, ensure you don't have any extraneous staff hanging around the session, and keep your comments and reactions professional, always. If you're doing mo-cap, consider hiring an intimacy coordinator if you have the budget – an intimacy coordinator's entire job is to ensure that your actors are feeling safe and secure throughout this vulnerable process.

If your actors bring up a concern with some dialogue mid-session, listen with an open mind – particularly when it comes to content that involves people of marginalized races, genders, and sexualities. If someone says they're uncomfortable with a line or a piece of direction, respect their boundary and stop there. Just as with other processes, apologize if it's warranted, take a break if needed, and continue on when you can. Acting can put a person in a very vulnerable space, so it's especially important that your actors know they can trust you.

SIDEBAR 8.5 – WARNING SIGNS OF SEX NEGATIVITY (BY MICHELLE CLOUGH)

Respecting your team's comfort levels (or lack thereof) about sexual content is one thing and an incredibly important thing at that. But, there's a difference between discomfort with discussing sex and outright sex negativity; while the former can and should be accommodated, the latter can be poisonous to creating sexual content in a mature, meaningful, and/or fun way. Here are some warning signs of a sex-negative team culture taking root:

- **Dismissiveness** – Ignoring feedback for sex scenes, minimizing importance, questioning the need for in-depth discussion.
- **Authoritarian view of morality** – for example, "think of the children" for a game that is not in any way intended for children.
- **Aggression** – harassment, disdain, open anger at teammates working in good faith
- **Mockery** – teasing, targeted jokes, backhanded compliments/insults.

- **Sleaziness** – oversexualizing, painting all sexual content as automatically "lewd," conflating creative sexual content with personal sexual tastes/availability.
- Any kind of "punishment," intrinsic or extrinsic, for speaking in good faith about sexual game content or creative ideas for said content.
- **Sex-based shaming** – for example, homophobia, ace-shaming, kink-shaming, slut-shaming, virgin-shaming, vanilla-shaming, etc. – any kind of shame placed on team members for their sexualities or contributions to the sexual content.

As a team lead, it is vital you shut any and all of these behaviors down early, particularly those that could lead to abuse of your team members or those tied up with sexism, homophobia, etc. While no team member should be *forced* to be "comfortable" with sexual content, or to work on material they find triggering or painful, your team should at least be a place where sexual content is seen as *valid* and not either dismissed out of hand or used as a cudgel to shame others. Thus, as Souha says, early and clear communication is vital. Addressing harmful sex-negative behavior is important, but if you've hired the right team and shared the right vision with them… chances are, you'll find you won't need to.

IN SUMMARY

- Set expectations!
- Communicate!
- Check in!
- Respect boundaries!
- Model the behavior you want to see from your team!

Follow these steps and you'll be on your way to creating the romantic and sexual content of your dreams with as smooth a ride as possible. Remember: If your team feels safe, respected, and valued, the end product will be vastly superior to anything produced under conditions to the contrary. It's also just the right thing to do, but in an industry often driven by the bottom line, it's important to remind folks that creating games ethically also results in a better product made by happier, healthier people who will then stick around to continue making games.

SIDEBAR 8.6 – WHAT IF YOU'RE NOT THE LEAD? (BY MICHELLE CLOUGH)

While Souha has provided a fantastic outline of how to lead a team working on steamy sexual content…sometimes, you're not the lead! Some of you reading right now might be part of the larger team, or contractors, or even remote freelancers, all working in your own discipline with no lead power at all.

But, this chapter is still useful in that anyone on a team, regardless of their rank or authority, can do their part in promoting trust, honesty, and sex positivity in their team. You do not have to be a lead to be a comforting, supportive ear to your colleagues as they discuss their thoughts on the sexual content you're making. You do not have to be a lead to curate and provide useful reference material for your teammates and your team lead to use as guidelines for your intimate scenes. You do not have to be a lead to model good communication about the goals of your game's content, or to model respectful professionalism when talking about sex with your peers. And of course, you certainly don't have to be a lead to turn in sexy, effective, high-quality sexual content in your discipline.

As we all know, making games is a team effort – well, unless you're a solo dev, and even then! As vital as the lead is in setting the tone, don't discount your own contributions, no matter how small. You can be a big part of ensuring your team is happy, comfortable, and making some damn fine sex scenes.

WORKSHOP QUESTIONS

Analysis: Research the team behind the game you're analyzing, and if possible, seek out any interviews, reports, or details on how they approached the sex scenes (e.g., the CD Projekt Red example above). How did their team tackle sexual content? How did they handle discomfort (if any) about the subject matter?

Creative:

- Imagine an interview with a prospective new hire for your project. Consider how you would communicate your plans re: sexual content in game, how to ensure the interviewee's comfort, and how to evaluate their interest and suitability for both the scenes in question and the game as a whole. With these in mind, compose some interview questions on the topic. If at all possible, ask some friends and colleagues outside of the team to take a look at the questions and offer feedback on them, particularly in regards to their potential to discomfort new hires, etc.

- Draft a vision document for your (hypothetical) existing team to refer to for your game's sexual content. Create a list of similar sex scenes from games and other media (or, alternatively, a few examples of what NOT to go for). If needed, use visual aids and diagrams such as the sacred/profane/mundane Venn diagram. The goal is to have useful documentation to ensure your team remains on the same page going forward.

NOTE

1 K. Stuart, Eurogamer, "The Writing of The Witcher 3," October 15, 2019, https://www.eurogamer.net/articles/2019-10-15-the-writing-of-witcher-3.

PART 3

Sex in the Larger Game Structure

CHAPTER 9

Characters and Sex

Unless you are doing an extremely abstract, experimental game about sex – in which case, Godspeed! – chances are that your sex scenes are going to involve people…more specifically, characters. To create compelling sex scenes – and, on a larger level, compelling sexual and romantic relationships – your creative team should always know the following:

- **Who** are these characters?

- **How** do they express themselves sexually?

- **What** is the nature of their relationship?

- **Why** are they having/going to have sex?

And yet, surprisingly, a lot of sex scenes fall at the very first hurdle (Figure 9.1).

FIGURE 9.1   Whoa there! (horsemen/Shutterstock.com.)

DOI: 10.1201/9780429356650-12

When games with sex in their narrative fall flat, players will often complain about sex scenes feeling "forced" or "pasted on." Very often, there are also complaints that the characters involved had no chemistry or felt "forced" as sexual partners. In cases like these, the core of the problem is often due to the characters being underdeveloped – specifically, in terms of what their sexual side actually is. And without fleshing that out, it becomes that much harder – arguably impossible – to write interesting, sexy ways that their sexual side both matches and clashes with their partner's ways that generate heat and tension and that finally burst forth into sexual action. Those dynamics are the core of good sexual chemistry, but without a sense of your characters' desires and sexuality, there's no strong foundation to build that chemistry on, meaning it will almost certainly fizzle (Figure 9.2).

This isn't necessarily a sign of "laziness," mind you! Many writers and designers will pour huge amounts of effort into detailed character bios and worksheets in the aim of fleshing out their characters and making them fully believable. Those bios will often cover everything from their likes/dislikes, goals, and dressing style, all the way down to things like, "what was this character's first job?" or "what's their relationship with authority?" or "describe their extended family." Game writers often use these templates or bios to help create compelling and "real" characters in the game world (Figure 9.3).

But…these bios and worksheets and templates tend to miss one major aspect of the characters, because there's one thing that most of them do *not* include…"what, if anything, makes this character horny?"

Part of truly knowing your characters – both as the writer writing them AND as the rest of the team bringing them to life – is knowing about their sexual life. But too often,

FIGURE 9.2 It's like building a castle in the swamp. It sinks into the swamp, so you build a second castle, then THAT sinks into the swamp… (Benny Marty/Shutterstock.com.)

FIGURE 9.3 It's like tabletop RPG character sheets, but with "Greatest Regret" and "Educational Background" instead of DEX and INT. (Collective Arcana/Shutterstock.com.)

the buck stops at, "this character is straight/gay/bisexual/asexual/etc." without any further, deeper exploration of their sexual side. In a shocking twist that surprises no one, there's a lot of cultural resistance to digging any deeper than that, an artifact of the idea that sex should be something "private." Laying out someone's kinks, turn-ons, sexual fantasies, and so on – even if that "someone" is fictional – is seen as "unnecessary" at best, "indecent" or "salacious" at worst.

But sexuality isn't only who someone's currently having sex with, or what gender they prefer, or even whether they're kinky or not. It's also how and why they experience and express arousal, how their sexual desires and attitudes inform their behavior and thoughts, and what being a sexual being means to them. If you've worked out your characters' favorite breakfast cereals but *not* what makes them fan themselves off or invite someone to bed, then you're actively shortchanging your characters and denying a potentially huge part of their inner lives.

The good news is, if you DO consider these questions – not just consider them, but codify them in the character documentation – you're in a much better position to explore sex and sexual content in a way that is helpful to your team AND resonates with your players. To that end, consider adding these (non-exhaustive) questions and sections to your character bios and documentation.

- **What is their cultural background in regards to sex?**

- **Personal attitudes toward sex?**

- **Goals/reasons for having sex?**

- **What are their turn-ons?**

- **How do they act when sexually attracted?**

- **How do they initiate sex or respond to sexual invitations?**

- **What are their sexual preferences?**

- **Why do they want to have sex with X character?**

The earlier you ask these questions and know the answers, the better. They will be the foundations of the romantic and/or sexual stories your writers tell, and they will greatly inform the work of your artists, directors, designers, and audio engineers. After all, there's no good deciding that a character likes to stare at someone they dig with a smoldering, intense gaze if no one in the cinematics department or gameplay design got that memo! By making sure everyone at every level of the project understands the characters in the context of their erotic feelings and desires, you can ensure that that context gets communicated well, through visuals, audio, gameplay, and dialogue.

One vital thing to note: characterS, not just character. It is not enough to do this only for your main character(s); if you do, you're going to end up with a potentially worse scenario where your NPCs end up as shallow props only to be used for the PC's gratification. You can come up with all the detail in the world as to why Dudeface McKnightALot might find Lady Elfears Silknightie the hottest thing since sliced bread (She's so gentle! I love pointy ears! She has such huge…responsibility on her shoulders!). But if you're not going to define and explore what SHE finds hot, then the fantasy is lopsided, and any sexual relationship they begin will feel more like one-sided wish-fulfillment for him rather than mutually heated desire and erotic interest. To create compelling, sexy relationships and sexual encounters in games, you need to have the same level of detail and thought for all the characters involved. Truly successful chemistry and mutual desire comes from ALL participants finding their kinks, turn-ons, and sexual interest piqued, not just the player and their avatar, and taking the time to work out those things for *everyone* means more opportunity for sexy tension, and more fully realized characters in your work.[1]

Let's break down those sexual character bio questions in more detail.

CULTURAL BACKGROUND AROUND SEX

As mentioned several chapters ago, different cultures have different attitudes toward sex, and many of those attitudes are deeply woven into larger life. Some cultures might take a rigid, moralistic viewpoint against sex, while others might treat it as a status symbol and still others might be relaxed and open. Some cultures have strong ideas of when sex is "good" and when it's "bad"; others might have different expectations about emotional entanglements (or lack thereof). And of course, cultures are not wholly uniform; even if the dominant culture in an area may espouse one view on sex, that doesn't preclude different schools of thought, countercultural ideals, or even just privately held viewpoints passed through family connections.

The point, in the end, is…which of these cultural viewpoints on sex has your character been marinating in? (Figure 9.4).

That is not to say that your character has exactly the same cultural values that they have been brought up in or that they are part of. We can see countless examples in real life of young adults rejecting the sexual rules of their upbringing and embracing new models and

FIGURE 9.4   And how have they…uh…"interpreted" those values? (Lana K/Shutterstock.com.)

perspectives on sexuality. However, it is still important to know what a character's relevant cultural background is, as it can often have a massive impact on their character and where they are now. Even if they no longer adopt those views, certain aspects may still make their way into their subconscious assumptions or knee-jerk reactions (Well, of course, X is good/bad…wait…). Alternatively, their current views might be a deliberate rebellion against the culture(s) they were once part of. And of course, some characters will still hold the same viewpoints as their culture when the player meets them. Whether they keep true to them or change their mind in the course of the game is, naturally, part of crafting their character arc.

It's worth noting that while knowing cultural attitudes toward sex is, of course, relevant and important in realistic moral settings, it is also vital to consider in games set in speculative settings, like fantasy and sci-fi. Indeed, this goes beyond developing your characters and into developing your world as a whole. How DO the dominant cultures (if they exist) of elves, dwarves, and orcs view sex? What about aliens like the asari or salarians in *Mass Effect*? What sexual attitudes might robots get programmed with? There's tons of world-building to be done around sexual attitudes and politics in fantasy and sci-fi, and your designers and writers should be considering it both in terms of fleshing out the world and in terms of what it means for your characters.

In any case, establish early what sorts of sexual attitudes your character has grown up with and been exposed to, both in their youth and later in life. At worst, it will simply help with subtle characterization around sex; at best, it can provide some interesting plot hooks and possibilities for character development.

GENERAL ATTITUDE TOWARD SEX

As mentioned above, your character may not hold the same attitudes and perspectives toward sex that their culture does…so what attitudes and perspectives DO they hold? Do they see sex as an amusing diversion? A physical need? Something deeply meaningful?

FIGURE 9.5 Of course, don't forget the classic, "all of the above!" (Mix and Match Studio/ Shutterstock.com.)

Something they just gotta have? A status symbol? A dangerous temptation? Something only for holy matrimony? Something only for hot people? An act of deep intimacy? A blot on morality? Or just something that fills them with a profound sense of "meh?" (Figure 9.5).

Not everyone has strong opinions about sex, but chances are they at least have AN opinion (arguably, not having a strong opinion IS an opinion in itself). Your character will start the game with certain preconceptions and feelings about the role of sex in people's lives. Those thoughts may hold steady throughout the game, or they may change, particularly if player control and input is taken into consideration (e.g., choosing the player character's responses, or convincing NPCs). Like the cultural attitudes above, their personal viewpoints on sex can have both subtle and dramatic effects on their characterization, how that gets expressed to the player, and what the player's impressions of the character are. For example, a character who considers sex "sinful" can be handled in many different ways, to many different effects:

- Loudly slut-shaming and moralizing may mark them as an obvious jerk right out the gate.

- Quiet and subtle insinuations and offhand comments, on the other hand, may tip off their true feelings to alert players, while flying under the radar of others; this could be a simple character Easter egg, or it could lead to a much larger surprise reveal later (Wait, he was with the Evil Church the whole time? I was wondering why he was slightly standoffish to our professional domme friend…)

- Of course, you can also go the route of having a sympathetic character struggling with newfound sexual feelings and trying to reconcile them with their old views. Watching someone who once saw sex as sinful now having their own desires and longing spill over their reserves can, depending on the intent, be dramatic, tragic, or very, very, VERY hot.

Note that this is more about exploring the character's general thoughts about sex as opposed to their specific sexual desires or goals for themselves. These might align completely, or they might be different due to nuance, situation, hypocrisy, etc. For example, the slut-shaming jerk mentioned above might be insisting on general celibacy and abstinence…all while secretly carrying on multiple affairs (Oh, it's different for ME!). Alternatively, a character might be completely respectful of casual sex, promiscuity, etc., but still want a long-term sexual relationship for themselves. In any event, it can be very handy to have an idea of how the character views sex in *general*, not just how they view their own personal experiences and desires.

But now that we've brought it up…

GOALS FOR SEX IN GENERAL

Regardless of their larger thoughts about sex, the character may have very specific expectations, goals, and hopes for their own sexual experiences. This can look like them not wanting at all (e.g., asexuals) to wanting it all the time, to wanting it only in the context of an emotional relationship, and all the variants in between.

How much time and effort do they spend pursuing sexual relationships? What are they looking for when they have sex, and what do they get out of it? Pleasure? Connection? Numbness? Or something else? In general, why do they tend to have sex, how do they feel about the sex they have, and who ARE they in regards to their sexual life? Are they a grumpy, antisocial type who prefer to avoid any sexual entanglements? Are they a Casanova always eager to bed as many people as possible? Are they a consummate professional who's totally comfortable with having sex as part of "the mission?" Are they someone who just needs an hour or two of pleasure from time to time to ease the pain of their lives? Or are they someone with romantic dreams of giving themselves completely to someone they love, and won't tumble into bed for anything less? What kind of sexual life does the character seek, in the end?

The sexual needs and wants (or lack thereof) of a character can inform many aspects of their behavior, or how the player interprets their emotions or goals. Writers and designers should consider the context of the character's sex life and how they pursue or prioritize it in their life, as again it will subtly (and not-so-subtly!) inform how and why the character acts and behaves certain ways. Sex may (or may not!) influence or reflect the character's larger long-term goals, even the ones that may not be obviously to do with sex. A character whose only goal is "survival" will likely have a different place in their life for sex – or, at least, different priorities re: sex – compared to a character whose goal is "find a place to belong," or "live a life of power and pleasure," etc. When considering what your character wants from life, what role, if any, does sex play in that larger life goal? (Figure 9.6).

While laying out the character's goals and approach to sex is important for set characters, it's worth also considering how player agency and choice can play into this. In some cases, the player will be the ones who dictate a character's approach to sex, frequency, even emotional responses. We can see this in play particularly in *The Witcher 3*, for example. There are subtle character differences between a Geralt who pursues sex with casual partners and sex workers, a Geralt who only has sex with Yennefer, a Geralt who only has sex with Triss, a Geralt who tries to have sex with both Yennefer AND Triss, a Geralt who sleeps with one

FIGURE 9.6 "At last, our dreams have come true. A lasting peace in the realm, a home of our own… and a wall strong enough for us to bang against until we're old and grey!" (Evgeny Atamanenko/Shutterstock.com.)

of them but also with casual partners or sex workers, and a Geralt who doesn't have sex with *anyone*. None of these Geralts are "better" or "more correct" than the other, but they are all subtly different, with different goals and priorities than the others, at least as far as his sex life goes. And while Geralt/the player's choice of sex partner(s) does not fundamentally change his dialogue or any big aspect of the plot, it provides the player a lens (chosen BY the player!) on how to interpret the rest of his actions and behavior in the game – whether he comes over more as a rolling stone, a man looking for a home and family, or just someone who is Done With Everyone's Crap. Keep this in mind when creating, designing, and documenting player avatar characters or characters with player control; ensure that they are offered a range of in-character approaches to their sexual life (Figure 9.7).

Lastly, it's worth noting that, just like regular character goals, sexual goals do NOT have to be static and unchanging. Plenty of emotional drama and character development can come from characters wanting one kind of sexual life but getting quite another, or evolving over time to be more interested in a different kind of lifestyle. The most common form of this is a free-spirited promiscuous character (e.g., Isabella or Zevran in the *Dragon Age* series) falling in love and deciding to "settle down," but there are plenty of other possibilities for shifts in sexual goals and approaches, all up and down the spectrum. For example, in *Star Wars: The Old Republic*, the character Jaesa Willsaam begins as a dutiful Jedi padawan; while we do not see her in sexual situations, the Jedi background would suggest a life of celibacy, or at least a nonhedonistic approach to sex. However, if she falls to the Dark Side, she soon gains a taste for hedonism and passion; she starts actively chasing sexual experiences whenever the ship comes to port, and her hunger for new sexual experiences is a major factor if she begins a romantic relationship with a male player character.[2]

FIGURE 9.7 "Is it just me, or does my heroine feel 75% more badass and confident after picking the threesome option?" (Volodymyr Tverdokhlib/Shutterstock.com.)

Remember that just because your game character begins the game with one kind of sex life or sexual goals…does not mean they will end with the same thing!

In the end, establishing and documenting what your characters get out of sex, what and why they seek it – even if it's just at the beginning or before the player makes their own decisions – goes a long way to fleshing out your characters' scenes, expressions, even animations and even in games without any sex, this sort of character nuance can really make them come alive!

But don't get too settled; you're not done yet. While exploring your characters' attitudes and needs around sex is important, going off of that alone can still result in somewhat sterile or underdeveloped sexual relationships and encounters. To bring the heat, you need to get down to the vital core…what makes your character actually *heated* in the first place.

CHARACTER TURN-ONS AND ATTRACTIONS

This is arguably one of the most important aspects of writing a character through a sexual lens. Seriously, if you add only one sex-related note to your character documentation, let it be this one. Laying out exactly what your character finds attractive and what arouses them is one of the quickest and best ways to make their sexual storylines come alive, to create other characters they are drawn to, and to ensure that their interactions and sexual encounters feel organic, in-character, and appropriately hot!

Unfortunately, the question of what a character considers sexually attractive often gets ignored at a fundamental level, or handwaved into something that just "happens" as long as two people are in proximity for long enough. Many games treat any sort of character bonding as a stand-in for attraction, or worse, and reduce it to its simplest and often crudest form (e.g., "pretty woman has boobs"). But if it were that easy, we would be falling in lust with literally anyone we came into contact with! Sexual attraction can be complex and nuanced, anything from "a type" to a specific moment or gesture that grabs the attention. And of course, attraction and desire are also unique and internal to each and every person, even occasionally unique to a moment in time! That's why it's important to fully flesh out what turns your character on; you'll be in a position to craft cool character-specific moments, details, and flashes of attraction, as opposed to going with, "just because."[3]

Turn-ons and points of attraction can, of course, be extremely varied. Some are purely physical, from an appreciation for a particularly nice ass or a set of abs, to being aroused by extra weight, or someone's feet, or the angle of someone's neck as they turn. Some might tie into certain clothing, grooming, or other ways the character physically presents themselves. Other turn-ons are more based on another character's behavior, actions, or personality – a rush of heat and desire caused by, say, a sense of humor, or the way they smile, or someone fiercely protecting a helpless kitten. And of course, the most potent sexual attractions and turn-ons may be a mix of physical and behavioral – watching someone physically strong lift something heavy while their muscles flex, or seeing the way someone smiles in a certain light, or just pulling off their gloves and tie a certain way, all can cause a sudden rush of "I NEED TO HAVE _THE SEX_ WITH THIS PERSON NOW."

Note that, in many cases, this is where the dynamics of sexual attraction may overlap heavily with romantic attraction, particularly when it comes to personality or behavior. Becoming romantically attracted or enchanted by a character may lead to an increase in sexual attraction, or vice versa. A common dynamic is as follows:

- Character A displays a particular admirable trait or act (e.g., determination, kindness, strength, saving puppies, etc.)

- Character B admires them warmly for this trait

- Character B's admiration and feelings toward Character A become romantic

- Character B's romantic feelings give rise to sexual feelings as well

- When Character A returns the romantic feelings, Characters A and B consummate those feelings by having sex

There's nothing inherently wrong with this model, and there are plenty of examples where love and romance successfully pave the way for sexual desire and interest. However, a dynamic like this can sometimes shortchange or ignore the role of sexual attraction, or moreover, conflate romantic and sexual feelings as exactly the same thing. While they certainly CAN be, it's not at all guaranteed, and the responses they evoke can be quite different. Thus, it's important to develop your character with _both_ in mind, not just one or the other. There's fertile ground to explore the difference between what inspires a dreamy sigh of, "god, they're so wonderful," and a lustful growl of, "god, they're so hot!" Just as there's fertile ground to explore what might evoke BOTH reactions... (Figure 9.8).

Also, it's definitely worth considering turnoffs as well as turn-ons, along the same lines of distinction. There are definite traits and behaviors that can lessen a character's sexual interest, prevent any from forming to begin with, or even kill budding desire entirely in

FIGURE 9.8 "Oof, that cocky smile...I think my heart AND my pants just exploded." (Image Point Fr/Shutterstock.com.)

a moment. While many of them may be larger personality-driven factors (e.g., someone being an asshole totally killing all sexual or romantic interest in them), others might be more instinctive or physical, like body odor or annoying voice. Sometimes they're not even actual negatives! What turns off one character – a body shape, a style of dress, a personality type – might be ridiculously sexy to another. So don't be afraid to mix and match turn-ons and turnoffs in your cast of characters, particularly when there might be multiple potential partners!

Whatever the turn-ons (and turnoffs) may be, it's important to give genuine creative and foundational thought to which ones your characters have and why – not from the perspective of simply checking off boxes when crafting a love interest character, but from the perspective of knowing your characters more fully and being able to dig down into the actual details of what excites them and evokes their desires. Summing up a sexual attraction just as "straight male character thinks straight female character is hot" (or way worse, "he's a [straight man], she's a [straight woman], obviously things will progress that way") is just lazy writing. But exploring it as, say, "this secret agent is turned on by ruthlessness, intelligence, and women in glasses," that can give much more nuance, subtlety, and heat to the moment when the sexy scientist ally removes her glasses and uses them to stab someone in the eye (Figure 9.9).

Lastly, tracking what your characters' turn-ons and attractions are can have major impact on gameplay considerations, particularly in branching games where sexual relationships and encounters are optional and depend on player actions. We'll get into this in the later chapter about the chemistry casino, but knowing what intensifies a character's attraction can be vital to designing game systems that leverage and model interpersonal attraction.

FIGURE 9.9 "…I have never been more aroused than I am right now, Dr. Honeypot." (Podvysotskiy Roman/Shutterstock.com.)

ATTRACTED? WHAT NOW?

So your character meets someone who's the answer to their most erotic dreams, who checks off every single turn-on they have. Fantastic!

What do they do about it, and how do they react? Do they walk up and deliver a suave, charming line? Stammer and blush and try to awkwardly stammer something? Engage in aggressive, sexually charged bantering and arguing? Or do they remain totally calm, not saying a word…but casting longing, heated, emotionally devastating looks at the person they're drawn to, hoping against hope that their crush notices their gaze? (Figure 9.10).

The way the character generally expresses sexual interest in someone – even if it's just a completely private reaction as opposed to flirtation – should reflect who they are as a person and what their relationship with sex is. Are they someone who approaches sex with a calm, laissez faire attitude? Then they may be confident, relaxed, and take rejection well. Are they not very good with words at the best of times? Then perhaps they stutter or stumble. Of course, seeing a character who is USUALLY confident tripping over themselves can be an important character moment (not such a badass when it comes to talking to burly hunky men, is he?), doubly so if it's specific to a particular romantic interest (not such a badass when it comes to talking to That One Specific Man, mm?). So consider how Character X's desire and attraction might express itself in unexpected ways as well, or how their usual mode of flirtation or interaction might fall to bits and change entirely only

FIGURE 9.10   Or, you know, screaming and running the other way when their crush talks to them. That works too. (fizkes/Shutterstock.com.)

when around Character Y. Figuring out how the character comports themselves around people they desire BEFORE you write the scene will help you create scenes that feel less like artificial constructs and more like two (or more) fully realized people reacting to sexual attraction in a way that makes sense for them.

Documenting in detail how a character approaches or flirts with people they're sexually interested in, or what signals they give off when they're interested, is not only a huge part of writing those scenes in a way that's relatable to players. It also has an enormous impact on how your art, audio, and cinematics team creates content for those interactions. Even if there's no explicitly flirtatious dialogue, there are subtler signals that are no less powerful, and in fact can grant a scene much more erotic weight and relatability, signals that art, animation, cinematics, and audio need to integrate into every scene. These signals could be things like as follows:

- Long, drawn-out eye contact

- Fluttering eyelids/eyelashes

- A longing gaze from across a room

- A slightly huskier/softer tone of voice

- "Accidental" and/or lingering physical contact – for example, fingers brushing against each other when handing something over

- Leaning toward the person subtly (or not so subtly!)

- Relatable awkwardness (e.g., jumping in place, surprised recoils, etc. Tali in *Mass Effect 2* is a good example of this.)

And of course, this is just talking about general sexual interest. You can also explore how the character reacts to a moment of intense, blinding arousal. When all the blood is rushing somewhere other than the brain, it can provoke some rather striking reactions…and depending on who your character is, those reactions can be erotic, funny, emotional, or intensely relatable.

Seeding these sorts of details in a scene can make the sexual connection between characters feel more genuine and more palpable, as well as avoiding the refrain of the badly setup sex scene, "wait, since when were these two ever interested in each other?" Even if you're not making a character's sexual interest explicit, making the effort to include these physical, subtle details gives the scene more emotional charge, as well as (as always) revealing more of the characters doing it. Plus, you know…it can be really, really hot!

INITIATING SEX OR RESPONDING

The previous point considered how the characters behave around someone they want to have sex with. But what about the moment when they actually START having sex? When things have progressed to a point where sexual intimacy is on the table, how do they make that first touch, that first kiss, and that first invitation that results in a moment of passion?

This question is a little more situational than the others. For one, sexual logistics can differ wildly based on the context of the sex in question; for example, Geralt may engage in calm, detailed communication about sex with a sex worker, describing the sort of experience he'd like to hire them for…but he still gets flustered and clumsy when Triss gives him a come-hither look in the underground baths. On top of that, there are nonsexual logistics to consider as well. It's all very well to say, "this character wouldn't beat around the bush, they'd throw everything off the table in a moment of passion!" but that if they're trying to signal sexy times to their lover in the middle of, say, a mission briefing…well, they might have to make an exception (Figure 9.11).

FIGURE 9.11 "I want you to plop your naked ass down right *here*…" (Gorodenkoff/Shutterstock.com.)

Still, it's worth exploring how your characters might transition from "I am not having sex" to "let's have sex NOW!" Are they the kind to get swept up in desire and arousal and just *act*, or are they more deliberate in planning out their tryst? Do they prefer to "talk about it" or "let things happen"? Do they make the first move, and do they do it boldly, gently, nervously? Or do they prefer to wait until their partner approaches them, and if so, how do they react in the heat of the moment?

As an example as to how this can matter in terms of narrative and characterization, imagine a scene in which two sexually attracted characters are going into a dangerous mission that they do not expect to survive. Consider the different characterizations of the following:

- A character who openly invites the other to spend the night, that is "If this is my last night on earth, I want it to be with you."…

- VS a character who shows up on the other's doorstep at midnight, mutters, "can't sleep," then rushes into them in a blazing fit of passion

- VS a character comforts the other, gives a long, warm hug of support…only for the contact to linger, then slowly transition into a more intimate embrace…

- VS a character who in no way shape or form will EVER make the first move and will only respond enthusiastically if the other approaches first.

There are a thousand different ways a character might initiate sex in the moment, and much of it has to do with their personality, their relationship to sex, and their relationship with the other character. Having an idea of how your characters initiate makes writing sexy, believable sex scenes all the easier, giving you a framework for how their interactions will play out and what the crucial details are to get the scene rolling.

SEXUAL PREFERENCES

By now, you have the turn-ons that make your characters want to have sex, as well as their thoughts about sex, but don't start skimping on the low-level, nitty-gritty details… in other words, *how* do they actually like to have sex? Do they like it slow and leisurely, or frenzied and impatient? Are they rough, or gentle? Playful, or serious? Do they tend to be deliberate and conscious in what they do, or do they surrender to their passions and act on their erotic whims? Do they like to be on top or bottom, or does that never even enter the picture? Are they kinky, and if so, what sort of kinks are they into? Do they talk dirty, or poetically, or just not talk at all? Are they vocal in other ways, or totally silent? Do they like to be active, or lie back and experience the sensations? What's their preferred aftercare? Are they up for anything, or do they prefer very specific sexual experiences? Really think about these questions and what they mean for your character; don't just shrug and answer at random, or you'll miss out on some good characterization opportunities.

There are a hundred different small but evocative details to have in mind in terms of your character's sexual side. Many of these details can be vital to document for the benefit of other members of your team – art, cinematics, etc. – so as to block out the scenes in question. But more importantly, getting to know the intimate details of your character's sexual preferences helps to know the *character* more. Why do they like the things they do? Do they "fit" with the other aspects of their personality, or is there a disconnect, and why? What sort of person do they become in moments of private intimacy or sexual release? While you don't have to hang the Entire Secret of Their Inner Character on whether they like whips and chains or if they grunt while orgasming, treating those aspects of their character like they're unnecessary or spurious locks off entire avenues of character development and character exploration.

Also, consider that sexual pleasure can also extend outside the bedroom and outside partnered intercourse. There are many ways that a character might express, indulge, or enjoy their sexual side without having sex with anyone. For example, they may seek out sensual indulgences – certain fabrics or foods, or even just the act of touch – and enjoy them in an erotic way. They may wear particularly evocative or "sexy" clothing, not just to attract others but in a way of expressing their own sexuality. Similarly, they may enjoy flirting not as a way to gain new lovers, but as a playful way to enjoy their sexual side safely. Making sexual jokes, enjoying erotic stories or art, using sex toys, speaking frankly about sexual fantasies, masturbation – all of these are examples of ways that characters can express their sexual side and sexual preferences on a day-to-day basis, as something for themselves as opposed to only something that is done with or for others. Sexuality, after all, is something that's holistic as opposed to specific, and sometimes even a small detail – wearing silk against bare skin, or a collar – can be a nod to that part of oneself.

Use character creation as a time to interrogate and consider how your characters indulge in or express their sexuality both inside and outside the bedroom, with partners or alone. Some of the ways will lead to dramatically obvious game content like animated sex scenes or erotic art on a character's bedroom wall. But others can point to unique, expressive details (say, a single article of clothing) that honor the character's sexual life in public and private.

WHY SEX WITH THIS CHARACTER? (CHEMISTRY VS. OPPORTUNITY, ETC.)

So you've figured out what turns your character's crank, how they feel about sex, what kind of sex they enjoy, and how they react when they meet someone they want to have sex with. Now comes the million dollar question, the question on which so much of your game is going to rest…why does this character want to have sex with this other specific character?

It is, in many ways, the most important question of the entire process. But here's the good news; if you have done your due diligence for the characters involved, then this part is also the easiest.

That's because the answer to this question comes out of all the answers and biographical information you have already compiled for the characters. You know who your characters are, and now you know what they're attracted to; you now have a blueprint for crafting a believable, compelling attraction between them, as well as a rough roadmap of how and why they may eventually come to act on it. You know which traits to enhance or highlight in each character so that the other will be drawn to them, and if things aren't coming together, you now have a pretty good idea of why not (e.g., Character A not matching what Character B actually digs, etc.).

FIGURE 9.12 It's like this, but with beakers full of "finds aggressive arguing sexy," "likes the look of them shirtless," and "I intend to blow off some steam and break the bed in the process." (Romolo Tavani/Shutterstock.com.)

The creative dance of who these characters are and what about them attracts the other, how they express or hide their sexual desires, whether they even intend to act on their desires, the delicious friction that all of these cause when coming together…there's another word for it when it's done well. And that word…is chemistry! (Figure 9.12).

Sexual chemistry can be one of the most important keys to making a compelling, believable, erotic sexual scene. While it's very possible to have a great and memorable sex scene that doesn't hinge on chemistry – for example, a tense thriller where a spy must coldheartedly seduce someone, or two friends coming together for comfort and warmth on the eve of battle, or someone hiring a sex worker – having that sexual tension building between characters over time is a truly fantastic way to engage your players and make them invest in the final sex scene…or heck, even head to fanfiction and fanart to create more sex scenes of their own! And when that sex scene finally arrives, if you've done your characterization correctly, then every interaction, every delicious bit of friction between the characters you've created should generate the heat and tension that leads to their eventual erotic encounter…and that encounter, in turn, should play out in a way that reflects their individual feelings, needs, and motives around the act of sex.

But as for the question of why that chemistry and tension finally translates into actually taking the plunge and having sex…well, that will be a question for another chapter!

CONCLUSION

Unless you're making an abstract game (in which case, awesome!), then characters will be the foundation on which you build everything about your sexual content – the relationship dynamics, the tension, and the final sex scene. It's not enough to stick to the nonsexy parts of your characters; you need to dig deeper into their sexual, erotic side from the beginning of development, or at least as early as possible. But with that knowledge comes better, more fully realized characters, more engaging and sexy relationships, and – of course – better and more memorable sex in your game.

WORKSHOP QUESTIONS

Before Starting:

- Research and select a template for a character bio, if you do not already use one yourself. I highly recommend the character bio template in *The Game Narrative Toolbox* by Tobias Heussner and Toiya Kristen Finley, but you can also find plenty of character bio templates for writers on the web; just Google "character bio templates" and pick one that works for you.

- Add the following questions to the template, either as-is or rephrased to match the formatting of the template (e.g., titles instead of questions)

  - **Cultural background in regards to sex?**

  - **Personal attitudes toward sex?**

  - **Goals/reasons for having sex?**

  - **What are their turn-ons?**

  - **How do they act when sexually attracted?**

  - **How do they initiate sex or respond to sexual invitations?**

  - **What are their sexual preferences?**

  - **Why do they want to have sex with X character?**

Analysis: Fill out the character bios, or at least the sex-related questions above, for at least *two* of the characters in the video game you are analyzing (ideally two who have sex with each other!). Using context from the game, do your best to "reverse engineer" the characters and give your best guess for their turn-ons, attitudes toward sex, etc. Feel free to incorporate out-of-game research as well (e.g., interviews with the developers).

Once you have answered the questions to the best of your knowledge, examine how their sexual turn-ons, attitudes, etc., affect and shape the characters' interactions. If the two characters end up having sex, how do these elements interlock and create sexual tension? How are these elements expressed not only in dialogue, but in body language, facial expressions, audio cues, and other methods?

Creative: Fill out the character bios fully for at least two characters in your video game who will participate in sexual content. These can be two characters who have sex with each other, two optional love interests for the player character, or just two sexually active characters. Fill out the sexual AND nonsexual questions, then compare the two.

Consider how these answers will guide dialogue, art, animation, and audio in depicting these characters; jot down your thoughts to share with the rest of your team.

Consider if/how the information in these bios may affect development of your other characters. For example, will you tailor a character in ways to be more sexually appealing to one of the characters you fleshed out?

Lastly, consider how this information will affect character interactions going forward, particularly with potential sexual partners. How will you use the turn-ons, attitudes, and other information in this bio to generate meaningful chemistry before any sexual encounters?

NOTES

1 Of course, not every sexual narrative is about mutual desire and sexual tension – some scenes are based around manipulation or comfort – but it's just as important to fully develop your characters and how they relate to their own sexuality to make *those* scenes hit too.

2 BioWare, *Star Wars: The Old Republic*, published by Electronic Arts, PC, December 20, 2011.

3 In reality, of course, people are attracted to people outside their usual turn-ons all the time – you hear plenty of stories about finding someone attractive despite not being "their type," or someone's personality making them sexy, etc. This can certainly be the case in games, but that doesn't mean you shouldn't work out a character's usual "type" or turn-ons; it just means you have to go a step further and figure out what unique turn-ons the "exception" character brings to the table!

CHAPTER 10

Sex and the Three-Act Structure (Part 1)

E STABLISHING YOUR CHARACTERS IS vital to crafting good game sex scenes, not to mention a good game narrative in general! But that doesn't necessarily mean you can just "wing it" as far as the larger story. If nothing else, the realities of game development – needing to know what assets to create, what levels to design, how gameplay ramps up, etc. – means you need to have a strong sense of exactly where your story is going and how it plays out. Similarly, your writers and narrative designers need to plot out the major story beats, how they relate to each other, how to pace those beats, etc. And sex, in the end, is a form of story beat, needing similar respect and consideration as any other story beat. The point is, whether your game is purely about sex or whether sex is just a brief encounter in the larger story, your sexual content is going to be part of a larger narrative structure.

(Unless you're still making that Sexy Tetris game with no story at all. In which case, carry on!)

It's that larger structure we'll be discussing in this chapter, at least as it relates to sex. And while every story brings different, important context to the table of sex scenes – different characters, chains of events, worldbuilding, etc. – it's also worth taking a large step back and looking at sex scenes from a bird's-eye view of general story structure. Do these moments occur at the beginning, middle, or end? Do they play out as part of the resolution of a story, or as the building tension and action...or maybe even the thing that kicks things off? How does a sex scene's place in the overall structure affect its impact – and how might that impact change by having more than one sex scene?

With a more structural approach to these scenes' places in the game narrative – and to the game narrative in general – it can be helpful to use tools like diagrams or templates for dramatic structure, just like we used Venn diagrams to visualize the theme and aesthetic earlier in the book. There are well-known existing diagrams used by writers and story analysts to lay out the plot and tension of a story; we can use those same diagrams to map out

DOI: 10.1201/9780429356650-13

FIGURE 10.1 That screaming sound you just heard was a thousand writers suddenly crying out in terror, and then suddenly silenced. (Stokkete/Shutterstock.com.)

sexual moments and their place in the larger story. And for this chapter, we'll be focusing on one of the most widely known and arguably useful types of these diagrams: the three-act structure and Freytag's Pyramid (Figure 10.1).

The three-act structure, for those that don't know, is a popular narrative model for story progression that many novels, movies, and other stories can be organized or classified by. The model has been put forward in some fashion by various Western writers and scholars as early as the 4th century BCE, when Aristotle claimed that tragedies must have a beginning, a middle, and an end; much later in the 20th century, screenwriters such as Syd Field helped to repackage and codify this structure as a paradigm for Hollywood screenplays.[1] While there are certainly other narrative structures and models, particularly from non-Western traditions, the three-act structure is arguably the most well known, and given how many AAA games aim for "cinematic" storytelling, it makes sense that the narrative structure follows the one most common in Hollywood screenwriting.

Roughly, it breaks down as follows:

- The first act **(or beginning)** is the establishing setup, where readers/viewers/players are introduced to the main characters (particularly the protagonist) and their relationships, the world setting, and the "normal" state of affairs (sometimes called exposition). Later in Act 1, however, there is an **inciting incident** – a major event or catalyst, usually but not always negative, that happens to the protagonist (or their loved ones, or their home, or to a larger group of people, etc.) It introduces **conflict** that drives the protagonist forward in the story – usually to solve or respond to a major problem or conflict, either inner or outer. Some writers also call this phase or related decisions from the protagonist the **First Plot Point** that sets up the protagonist's goal. Here are some (fictional) examples of what these might be in a game:

- An RPG in which, after scenes establishing the protagonist's hometown, it's destroyed by the evil empire (inciting incident/conflict). The protagonist swears vengeance and goes on a quest to defeat the empire (First Plot Point). Protagonist's goal: defeat the empire.

- A dating sim where the protagonist has a meet-cute with one of the love interests on the way to the first day at work (inciting incident) and then discovers that they'll be working with them+a host of other attractive love interests (conflict/First Plot Point) Protagonist's goal: find true love! (Figure 10.2).

- The second act is **rising action (or middle)**, where the action builds, and the protagonist attempts to resolve the problem or conflict. Obviously, this is easier said than done (otherwise the story would be over immediately!) so this is often where the protagonist must develop in terms of skills, relationships, or character arcs. It may end with an escalation of conflict or crisis that triggers the beginning of Act 3. Continuing the examples:

  - In the RPG, this would be the bulk of the game where the player quests, gains party members, gets better skills and gear, and discovers more about the world and themselves, all while they struggle against the empire and other antagonists. At the end of Act 2, the heroes discover that the evil emperor is behind everything that the empire has done and that if he is not stopped, he will summon an army of demons to conquer the entire world!

FIGURE 10.2 A hypothetical erotica game first act – the protagonist sees someone who inflames their desires (inciting incident/conflict) and decides to approach them (First Plot Point). Protagonist's goal: Tap That (or at least try and see what happens!). (stockyimages/Shutterstock.com.)

FIGURE 10.3   In the erotica game second act, this would be where sexual heat and tension builds between player and NPC through interaction, physical contact, etc. The "conflict" comes from uncertainty: is the attraction mutual? Will either act on it? How "hot" does it need to get? etc. (New Africa/Shutterstock.com.)

- In the dating sim, this would be where the player deepens their relationships with the various love interests and/or other NPCs, possibly forming a romantic connection with one of them. However, there are still major and/or minor obstacles to the relationship (everything from "he is actually a secret vampire, and we can never be together" to "we're dating and in a great relationship, but I'm too nervous to confess that I actually love her!") (Figure 10.3).

- The third act is **the resolution of the story (or end)**. Story threads are wrapped up and the story gears up for the **climax**, where all the conflict and tension are brought to their highest point, and then resolved. This also includes the **denouement**, or **falling action**, the time after the climax where the consequences and results of that climax are revealed and the story "winds down," with remaining plot threads getting resolved. The ending may be happy, unhappy, or simply "an ending," and the characters move on, their lives either better or worse for their experience in the story.

  - In the RPG, the third act would be "endgame" phase, when the player is on the final quest to defeat the evil emperor. This might be a time when the player is also wrapping up sidequests and other optional content. The climax is the fight with the final boss, the evil emperor. Defeating him triggers the ending of the game, which functions as the denouement. In an RPG with branching choices, this denouement will likely reflect player choices; a linear RPG might just feature a prescribed wrap-up of the protagonist riding off into the sunset.

FIGURE 10.4 In the erotica game, the third act would be...well, you know. (PinkCoffee Studio/ Shutterstock.com.)

- In the dating sim, the third act would focus on surmounting the final challenges and obstacles to the protagonist and love interest being together. These could be external challenges (the LI is relocating to another country!) or internal (I can't confess my feelings!) The climax would be the protagonist chasing the LI to the airport and finally confessing their love, resulting in the love interest reciprocating. The denouement focuses on their newfound happiness, either in the short term ("getting together") or long term (marriage, etc.) (Figure 10.4).

So where do plot diagrams come into play? Simply put, they visualize how action rises and falls throughout a story, and at what points. The most famous example is Freytag's Pyramid (named after the 19th-century playwright and novelist Gustav Freytag[2]), which adopts an inverted "V" structure for stories, but many modern variants use slightly different models that draw out the first and second acts slightly longer (Figure 10.5). While basic diagrams just have smooth slopes and lines to indicate rising action, longer stories might have also "jagged" rising action, with subplots, mini-climaxes, and small resolutions before returning to the rising action. For example, a side quest that involves saving a particular character might have its own mini-three-act structure that then rejoins the main story, causing little peaks and valleys through the beginning and middle of the game's rising action.

It should be stressed that three-act structures are not necessarily universal or mandatory! Many writers and narrative designers recommend against relying too hard on the three-act structure in both movies and games. My mentor Tom Abernathy has done a fantastic talk on this very topic that suggests, among other things, focusing less on structure altogether![3] Some games eschew the concept of rising action and tension altogether, embracing new ways of storytelling. And if that's what works for your game, that is awesome; please embrace it! Having said that, it can still be useful to know the three-act structure, or at the very least a similar model of rising/falling action, if only to recognize it if

PLOT DIAGRAM

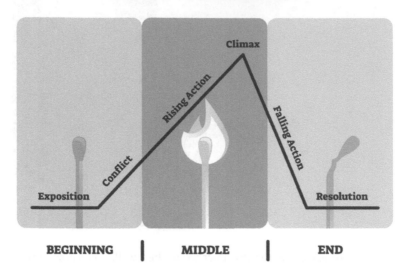

FIGURE 10.5   An example of a plot diagram. This example does NOT have the climax in the end phase, but other diagrams do; the basic premise – rising action that builds to a peak, then resolves – is still the same. (VectorMine/Shutterstock.com.)

the game narrative you're creating starts feeling like it matches the same pattern, or to recognize how and why to go against it.

But what does ANY of this have to do with sex? How on earth does larger narrative structure have any bearing on sexual content, other than the fact that both of them tend to involve a climax of some sort? (Figure 10.6).

FIGURE 10.6   "Oh god, she wrote this whole chapter just for that climax joke, didn't she?" (Mix and Match Studio/Shutterstock.com.)

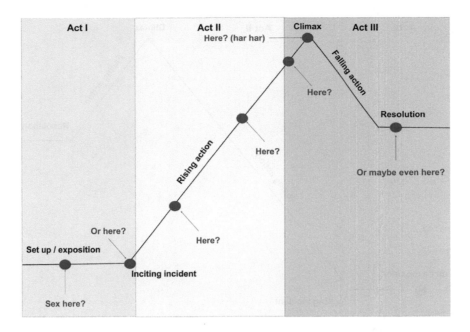

FIGURE 10.7   An outlook of where sex might happen in the larger story structure.

The reason all this story structure discussion is important is because where your narrative designers put sex scenes in the game, where they might appear on the diagram, can have major significance, both in terms of the rising/falling action of the story arcs, and the – well, you know, the *action* – action of the sex. This is doubly true if you only have one sex scene in the entire game – but we'll get into that later (Figure 10.7).

So, let's look into how the placement of a scene in the game's larger narrative structure can give it an extra context that you may – or may not! – intend.

SEX IN ACT 1: ESTABLISHMENT PHASE

Remember all that work we did in the previous chapter to explore your character's sex life and sexual attitudes at the start of the story? Well, good news: showing sexual content here is your big chance to drive it home. Sex scenes in the exposition or setup phase not only establish your character's sex life, or the relationships they have with their lovers; it underlines it as a major aspect of their character arc, who they are, and where they are now. Spending precious time during your narrative exposition to highlight this aspect of their lives tends to signal its importance to the character and the narrative, which tends to mean one of three things (Figure 10.8):

- This character's sex life, enjoyment of sex, or relationship with their sexual partner is one of their defining personality traits – e.g., "This character is a suave Casanova!"

- This character's sex life, enjoyment of sex, or relationship with their sexual partner is going to be a driving force in the story – e.g., "This character is going to do anything to rescue their lover!"

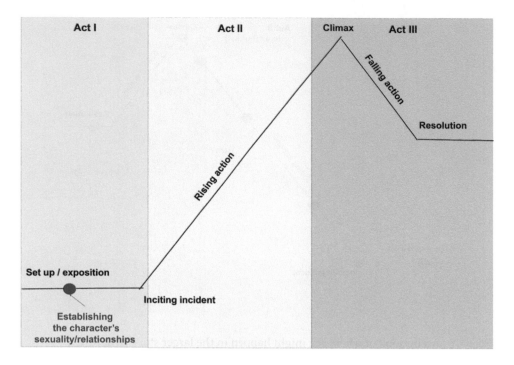

FIGURE 10.8   The implications of sex in the exposition/setup phase of Act 1.

- This character's sex life, enjoyment of sex, or relationship with their sexual partner is about to take a dramatic turn for the worse – e.g., "This character was a fun-loving libertine until their village burnt down, and now they've lost interest in sex" (Figure 10.9).

FIGURE 10.9   "Boy, we sure do enjoy sex! I'm sure we'll continue living our regular lives, enjoying sex, and nothing bad will ever happen to us sex-enjoyers…" (NDAB Creativity/Shutterstock.com.)

There are several good examples of this kind of sex-as-character-establishment, particularly in AAA games. One of my favorite examples is from *Assassin's Creed II*, which stars the particularly charismatic and charming Ezio. The beginning of the game follows him before he becomes embroiled in larger affairs, depicting him as a hot-blooded but charming and likable young man who gets along well with his brothers and family, enjoys a bit of mischief (climbing over things, getting in street brawls), and generally enjoys having fun. As night falls, he goes to visit his girlfriend Cristina, who happily invites her into her bedroom and engages in playful sexual banter with him before the two of them immediately make love; the scene is followed by a comedic sequence the next morning of her father chasing Ezio out. While the scene is lightly sketched – Cristina does not have much dialogue – it drives home the foundations of Ezio as a character: he's youthful, hot-blooded, an enthusiastic ladies' man, attractive to women, and not above a bit of trouble and fun. Things DO get markedly worse for his sex life soon after – after losing his family and becoming an assassin, we don't see him have sex again until the sequel, when we also discover how things ended with Cristina. But even so, the establishing sex scene sets the tone for the character; he never loses his flirtatiousness, sensuality, or warm admiration for women, and his sexuality shines through much of his character arc for that game and its sequels.

There are also darker examples of sex scenes as character establishment:

- As discussed previously, the sex scene between Trevor and Ashley in *Grand Theft Auto V* is joyless, messy, and mundane; moreover, it quickly establishes Trevor as a selfish character who's disrespectful and uncaring of others, based on how he physically treats Ashley during the sex and how he doesn't even talk to her afterward. And while the rest of the game does not center his sexuality as much, it certainly centers his selfishness and disregard for others that we see glimpses of here!

- The very first *God of War* game has several courtesans lying in Kratos' bed; the player can interact with them to trigger a sex scene at the very start of the game. Thus, one of the first snapshots we get of Kratos is his open and casual attitude toward sex, his frequent use of sex workers, and his willingness to have sex at a moment's notice. But we also establish his disconnection and apparent lack of enthusiasm about sex and the women he sleeps with (e.g., he doesn't speak to the courtesans, he shows no vocal or visual sign of pleasure) The sex scene establishes Kratos as going through the motions of sex, of using it more as a numbing agent than a source of joy or pleasure. As the series progresses, this lack of interest and enthusiasm about sex becomes more pronounced, but again, the foundations are laid at the very start.

SEX IN ACT 1: INCITING INCIDENT

Using sex as an inciting incident is a lot rarer in video games – at least in terms of a larger plot – but depending on the setting and the theme of the game, there are a lot of potentially interesting stories that could be told that get kicked off by a sexual encounter. Romance games and dating sims are a fertile ground for this, as having sex with someone – either a major love interest or even just a casual fling – can be the inspiration for all sorts of romantic or sexy driving goals for the protagonist. For example, the protagonist could have a hot one-night stand with an attractive stranger, and this one-night stand inspires them to go out and seek a more satisfying, sexy relationship with one of the dating sim's love interests (including, of course, the attractive stranger!). Outside of dating sims, sex as inciting incident could have a lot of potentials in relation to noir games (where having sex with a character might then kick off a murder plot!) or in games with heavy political intrigue (e.g., a war kicking off because of two cheating rulers being caught in the act) (Figure 10.10).

Also, note that while it can be rare and difficult to make a sex scene the inciting incident of an entire game narrative, it can quite easily be the inciting incident of a smaller, more character-heavy sub-plot. Again, romantic subplots are an obvious example of where they could be done – for example, a one-night stand with a friend that then sets them on a romantic course – but sex can also be used as the kickoff for sidequests. This could be particularly interesting in nonlinear or open-world games where players can pursue sex with NPCs. Imagine the player meeting an NPC offering sex and taking them up on it only to then trigger a quest chain in which the NPC's annoyed spouse chases the player through the town!

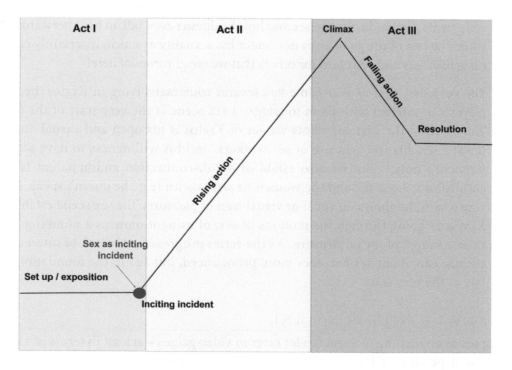

FIGURE 10.10 The implications of sex at the inciting incident/start of rising action in Act 1.

SEX IN ACT 2: RISING ACTION OR TURNING POINT

The vast majority of RPGs that touch on sex and scenes of intimacy place their sex scenes in this phase, during the rising action when the protagonist is still working toward their final goal (usually to defeat the final boss). *Dragon Age* and *The Witcher* are very well-known examples of this, with their sex scenes taking place long after Act 1 but well before the final act. This is the phase of the story in which things are intensifying at a slow and steady rate, where the stakes get bigger and the characters move more and more quickly down the road they're taking, but where there is still room for the story to "breathe" and have lulls or quiet moments. Thus, it's quite common for sex scenes to happen in this phase of the story, either as part of the general exploration and progression of the game, or particularly as part of longer-term romantic side plots (Figure 10.11).

These romantic side plots deserve special attention as, quite often, sex scenes and sexual activities are used as a major turning point in the romantic relationship, either in terms of "building" or "defusing" the romantic tension and arc. If a turning point is defined as "and then nothing was the same again!" sex can certainly have that effect on some people and relationships, whether the relationship gets more romantic or ends up putting distance between the characters. How these encounters play out, and where they fall in their side plots, is variable and depends a lot on the relationships and the characters involved.

- For example, one love interest might invite the player to have casual sex early in their story arc; in many games, this then opens up a player-driven turning point in the relationship, either in whether the player says yes or no, or how they react in the

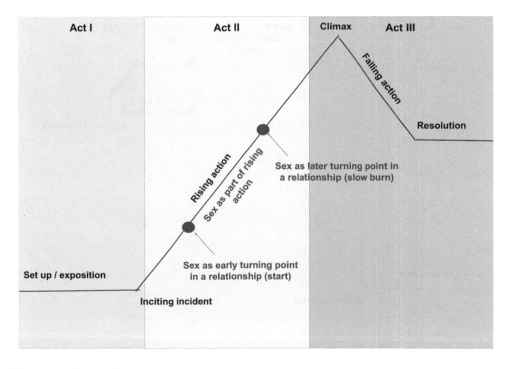

FIGURE 10.11   The implications of sex as part of rising action in Act 2.

aftermath. The early "casual" encounter with Jack in *Mass Effect 2* is an example of this, where choosing to have sex early actually ends the romantic arc entirely, while refusing allows it to continue.

- Other romance side plots might feature a romance at a midpoint in the arc of the relationship, after certain feelings have come to a head or certain desires communicated. This can be a sudden, unexpected development (e.g., characters arguing, then falling into each other's arms – e.g., Fenris in *Dragon Age II*), or it can be a carefully chosen act (e.g., part of a romantic confession of love – e.g., Jaal in *Mass Effect: Andromeda*). The sex may be the first explicit "admission" of romantic or sexual interest, or it may be something where romantic interest is established and where this sexual scene deepens or lessens that relationship.

- In relationships that are already established – for example, married couples or long-term relationships – the use of sex scenes as part of rising action can serve to bring them closer together while providing an emotional release amid the building tension. Couples in established relationships may find comfort, pleasure, and connection in sex scenes amid the struggles that the characters have to go through.

SEX IN ACT 3: MOMENT BEFORE STORY CLIMAX + CLIMAX ITSELF

It's almost time. We're about to go and fight the final boss. We might not come back alive from this…and no matter what, nothing will ever be the same.

Time to screw like bunnies! (Figure 10.12).

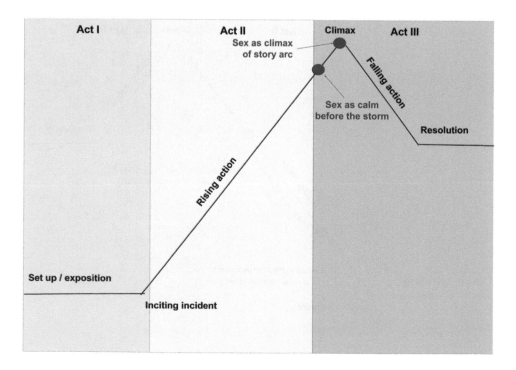

FIGURE 10.12   The implications of sex as part of the climax and/or transition into Act 3.

Sex scenes before the end climax of the game often bring a sort of intense, dramatic emotion to them, a sort of end-of-the-world sentiment that imbues even the sweetest, most wholesome sexual encounter with added emotional and dramatic weight. The most famous examples of these sorts of scenes can be seen in the original *Mass Effect* trilogy. The majority of the sex scenes are triggered only as the player journeys to the final conflict, when the love interest approaches Shepard privately and an intimate encounter plays out; some of them are steamy and fun, some of them awkward and cute, and some of them emotional and bittersweet. Regardless of the tone, they play out as a moment of pleasure, peace, and intimacy before things go haywire.

In this dynamic, usually a romantic relationship has been established throughout the rest of the game, or at the very least a platonic relationship that has the potential to become sexual or romantic. These sex scenes often serve as a sort of "deep breath before the plunge," a chance to put a short pause and a quieter story beat before the more dire stakes and intensity of the big climax. It's also a chance to step back and reveal the characters' mindsets at this phase of the story as well as their relationships with each other. Sex before a major event – particularly a life-threatening one that may involve combat – can be a very intense experience where characters are trying to reaffirm their humanity, get their minds off the stress, or even ensure that they can die with no regrets, either in regard to their partner or themselves.

Also, depending on the setting, don't discount the possibility of having a sex scene near the final climax be actually *related* to the main story or be a major turning point. Remember our earlier discussion about how sex scenes can serve a plot function? The example we used – of Morrigan sleeping with one of the male Grey Wardens – also takes place at this point in the story structure, just before the climax. And while the sex scene doesn't fundamentally change the gameplay climax – you do still fight the Archdemon as the final battle – it does radically recontextualize the narrative and completely changes its outcome. Thus, this sex scene is not only "the calm before the storm," but a scene that changes the nature of the storm. This sort of scene is dependent on specific worldbuilding – in this case, aspects of the lore, theology, and magic of Thedas – but may be applicable in your game.

Of course, there is also the possibility that sex might be the final climax itself. This is actually rarer than you might think, and usually only in the context of romantic or erotic subplots – and even then, the actual sex scene may take place just before the climax and build toward it. But if the rising action you've been building throughout the arc is filled with sexual tension or romantic longing, if literally everything in their relationship arc has been building to this encounter…then sex can be one hell of a climax, pun or no pun.

SEX IN ACT 3: DENOUEMENT

Having a full-on sex scene during the denouement or falling action of a story is quite rare, mostly because a sex scene often involves some building of tension and activity during a phase of the story when things are being wrapped up and the tension is defusing. However, some games use the iconography of sexual intimacy – things like nudity, cuddling in bed, and foreplay – to signal that sex has happened or is about to happen. This is used to create a subtle atmosphere – usually a happy one – to signal that the crisis or conflict is finally over, that our characters have either returned to normal or to a new normal (e.g., new relationship and new situation in life), and that they are now in a place to enjoy or seek physical intimacy after the intensity of the climax. Seeing our favorite characters snuggling in bed together after the final battle and sharing pillow talk (e.g., "I want to wake up next to you like this forever!") can serve to tie up emotional narrative threads in satisfying ways, letting the players know that they are entering a new, happier phase of their lives and their relationships – the dawn of a new day, possibly even literally! (Figure 10.13).

One example of a game with sex in the resolution phase is the original *Catherine*, by Atlus. The game has multiple endings, several of which show the protagonist Vincent in sexual contexts:

- In the Good Katherine ending, he lies in bed with his human fiancée, Katherine, while she looks through catalogs and plans out their wedding. Although their conversation is nonsexual and they don't engage in sex, both are depicted as naked, and Katherine straddles Vincent's hips in a suggestive way; the implication is an easy sexual intimacy and an implication that they may have been having sex not long before.

- In the Good Catherine ending, he wakes up in bed with his new lover, the succubus Catherine; again, both are naked, and the dialogue heavily implies they've been having a lot of sex (Catherine mentions that Vincent doesn't let her get any sleep). Vincent grabs her and is about to have sex with her again when they're interrupted by Boss (another character), resulting in a comedic panic from Vincent. But Catherine comments that "it's better when someone's watching," and pushes Vincent beneath her, murmuring that she loves him as they begin making love.

- In the True Catherine ending, after the events of the previous ending, it shows Vincent several weeks later, now a naked and powerful demon lord, surrounded by aroused

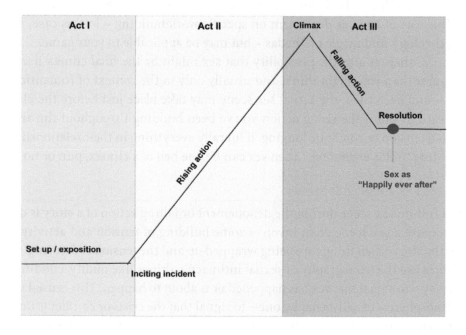

FIGURE 10.13   Implications of sex as part of resolution phase in Act 3.

succubi (including Catherine); the succubi comment on how attractive he is and how he makes them feel heated, and Catherine comments that she has less interest in the work of tempting men because none of them compare to Vincent. While no one has sex during the scene, the eroticism and sexual subtext is clear from the dialogue, voice direction, and the way nudity is used.[4]

In all of these scenes, the theme of resolution – for Vincent and for his romantic partners – is carried through by the sexual intimacy. The player gets a look at the new (sexual) normal, and a sense of happily ever after, as unusual as it might be.

SEX OUTSIDE THE THREE-ACT STRUCTURE

Lastly, it's worth noting that, even in games that have rising/falling actions or three-act structure, there are plenty of cases where sex does NOT occur as part of that larger narrative arc, where players may encounter sexual content in places, moments, and contexts that aren't part of a traditional narrative structure. This is particularly true of games with more emergent gameplay and storytelling, where the "story" comes about more from player experimentation and engagement with the world and systems. It's also true of games that allow more freeform exploration in and around their central storylines. Note that these scenes, due to their disconnection from traditional narrative, may not have the same meaning or narrative impact of their more structured counterparts, though it is still possible! Rather, instead of reflecting a key turning point or story beat in the main story, these outside moments serve either to illustrate the larger world and/or allow the player room to experiment and play in the margins (Figure 10.14).

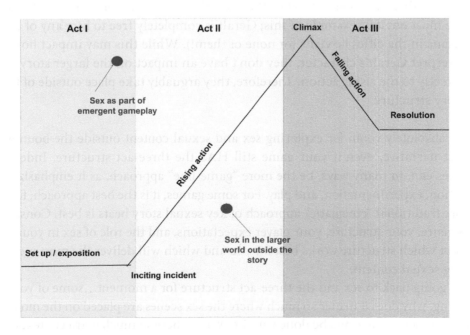

FIGURE 10.14   Sex outside rising/falling action and three-act structure.

The three biggest examples of sex outside the three-act structure that follows these models:

- Life simulation games that eschew a central storyline in favor of allowing the player to create and manipulate characters in life situations, where the player can also direct the avatars to have sex or allowing the AI to pursue it. *The Sims* franchise is the obvious example here; after two characters gain romantic interest in each other, the player can command them to have sex, or "WooHoo," in certain locations like beds and hot tubs; this triggers a suggestive comedic animation in the bed, hot tub, etc. If the couple is heterosexual, they can even "Try for Baby" with the same effects. None of this is tied to a larger story, only to the player's experimentation and interaction with the game's systems.

- Open-world exploration and adventure games in which the player can explore and encounter denizens of the world (i.e., minor random NPCs) engaging in their regular daily life, including having sex. An example of this is in *Assassin's Creed Origins*, where Bayek can visit historically accurate brothels in Ptolemaic Egypt; there are period-appropriate pornographic paintings on the walls, and Bayek can spy on or listen in to clients and courtesans having sex in various chambers. These encounters have nothing to do with the central storyline or the rising action of the plot; they are simply there for the player to encounter them.

- Games where the player can hire and interact with sex workers at any point in the story without prior narrative buildup. Sex workers can absolutely be part of the central narrative, but here we are speaking specifically to hiring them separately from the main story. Since these encounters can take place at any time, they usually are not directly connected with the central narrative action. The *Witcher* series is the most obvious example of this; Geralt is completely free to hire any of the courtesans in the cities he visits (or none of them!). While this may impact how players interpret Geralt's character, they don't have an impact on the larger story or relate directly to the rising action. Therefore, they arguably take place outside of the main story structure.

There is absolutely room for exploring sex and sexual content outside the bounds of the three-act narrative, even if your game still HAS the three-act structure. Indeed, these sex scenes can, in many ways, be the more "game-like" approach, as it emphasizes player exploration, experimentation, and play. For some games, it is the best approach; for others, the more traditional "cinematic" approach of key sexual story beats is best. Consider your game's genre, your structure, your player expectations, and the role of sex in your game to figure out which structure works best for you and which will deliver the most memorable, engaging sexual content.

Now, going back to sex and the three-act structure for a moment…some of you may be wondering, why does it matter so much where the sex scenes are placed on the model? Why not just have a sex scene and be done with it? Why is there so much extra context based on where this sex scene occurs in the story?

The answer lies partially in how narrative structure works in the first place – something that happens during the establishing phase is going to be "establishing," after all! But the real answer ties in with a common habit in many video games: only having one sex scene. In truth, that can end up putting *far* more narrative weight on a sex scene than might normally happen, or that the game designers might intend.

SCENE PLACEMENT FOR ONLY ONE SEX SCENE

In real life, barring one-night stands, sexual relationships (usually) involve having sex more than one time. However, for various reasons – pacing, resources, development struggles – a large number of games only have a single-sex scene, or maybe one sex scene per romance route. This means that, rather than the scene being simply one point of many on a graph, it becomes the ONLY sexual scene. As such, it becomes the main weight on which all the sexual relationship pivots on. This, combined with the narrative structure, can grant a sex scene more significance than its narrative context might usually entail.

To show what I mean, let's go through examples of the different stages that we discussed above, but through the lens of being the ONLY sex scene (Figure 10.15).

- **Sex in the character/world establishing part of Act 1** – This scene establishes the character as having an active sexuality and a personality in which their interest (or lack thereof) of sex is notable. That was important, because we're not actually going to see them having sex again and this aspect of their character will probably be dropped.

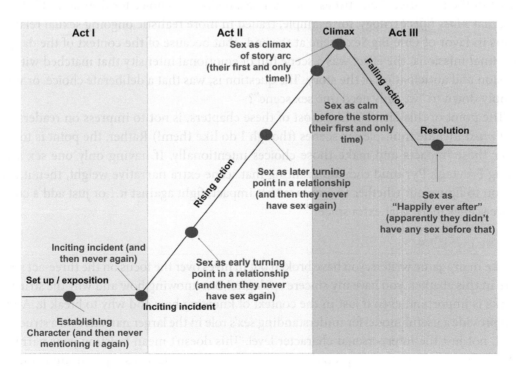

FIGURE 10.15 A refresher on the points in which sex might happen...and what the implications are if each point is the ONLY sex scene in a game.

- **Sex as inciting incident in Act 1** – Wow, having sex has triggered a story arc or relationship! This is/was a really major event…and we know that because it's the only time any of these characters ever have sex!

- **Sex as a turning point in Act 2** – Wow, the characters have finally fallen into bed together, and, in the aftermath of their first lovemaking, have confessed their love! How romantic! I guess now they've had sex, now *that's* out of the way and their feelings are clear, *they never have to have sex ever again…*

- **Sex as a prelude to Act 3 climax** – Wow, the characters who have been together through so much have finally consummated their relationship! Well, that's the ending right there! This relationship is over in a story sense, much like the game. What, you thought things were going to stick around and see how things developed between them? Pff.

- **Sex as a denouement** – Well, wrap it up, everyone! We have our happily ever after! And we all know that sex is always a part of the happily ever after, and only that. Not like it's part of a living, growing relationship like the one we've just been following through the game! Nope, they had sex, and now everything is finished and wrapped up neatly. Happily ever after!

Sex scenes should always have an impact – the same as any scene – but the reluctance to have more than one sex scene means that that sex scene ends up having extra impact due to just being The One Sex Scene; this means it can take on relevance that's even larger than its place in the narrative. Sometimes, that can be a deliberate choice for dramatic effect! The original *Mass Effect* trilogy, for example, traded in more realistic ongoing sexual relationships in favor of One Big Sex Scene at the end…but because of the context of the dangerous final missions, the effect was a scene full of emotional intensity that matched with the tension and anticipation of the story. The question is, was that a deliberate choice, or was it simply down to "we only need one sex scene"?

The point of this chapter, like most of these chapters, is not to impress on readers that you *must* include multiple sex scenes (though I do like them!) Rather, the point is to *consider* these impacts and make those choices intentionally. If having only one sex scene along Freytag's Pyramid ends up granting that scene extra narrative weight, then it is up to you to figure out whether to embrace that impact, fight against it…or just add a couple more scenes in for that extra spice!

CONCLUSION

If, like many game writers, you have broken out in hives over the focus on the three-act structure in this chapter, you have my sincere apologies! But knowing how and why the structure works is important, even if just in the context of knowing how and why to break it. And, it can provide a useful model for understanding sex's role in the larger narrative on a structural level, not just the interpersonal character level. This doesn't mean twisting your narrative, characters, or sex scenes into pretzels to make them fit the model; it simply means being able to look at your structure, your sexual content, and the characters that are part of both, and understanding how they all interrelate. Easier said than done…but well worth the effort!

WORKSHOP QUESTIONS

Analysis: If the game you're analyzing has a traditional narrative with rising/falling action, try to construct a three-act plot diagram for the game's core story similar to the diagrams we've shown in this chapter. Figure out the establishing setup, the inciting incident, what phases are rising action, what the climax is, and how much resolution the ending has.

Then plot out the game's sex scenes on that diagram. Are there more than one, and where do they go? Are they part of the core storyline, or optional side content; if the latter, does that side content have its own rising/falling action? What is the general impact and impression of those scenes (e.g., turning point or calm before the storm?)

Creative: Do the same thing, but this time for your own project. Lay out your story (if applicable) along a story diagram that showcases the rising/falling action, climax, etc. Then consider:

- Where in the storyline you see the scenes in question happening

- What impact you want those scenes to have as they appear in the story arc

Do the two match? For example, if you have a sex scene in the rising action but want it to feel like the calm before the storm, does the context work for this? If there seems to be a disconnect, would it help to change the timing, or does the scene's theme and role need rethinking?

NOTES

1 J. Lanouette, Screentakes, "A History of Three-Act Structure," December 24, 2012 (originally published December 1999), https://www.screentakes.com/an-evolutionary-study-of-the-three-act-structure-model-in-drama/.

2 J. Bunting, The Write Practice, "Freytag's Pyramid: Definition, Examples, and How to Use this Dramatic Structure in Your Writing," accessed August 23, 2021, https://thewritepractice.com/freytags-pyramid/.

3 T. Abernathy, R. Rouse III, GDC Vault, "Death to the Three Act Structure! Toward a Unique Structure for Game Narratives," accessed August 23, 2021, https://www.gdcvault.com/play/1020050/Death-to-the-Three-Act.

4 Atlus, *Catherine*, published by Atlus, PC/PS3/Xbox 360, February 17, 2011.

CHAPTER 11

Kindness Coins and the Chemistry Casino

IF YOU KEEP UP with online game developer discourse about romance and sex in video games, chances are you may have heard of something called "kindness coins" – usually in a critical, negative context. Kindness coins are used as an emblem of a particular romantic or sexual game design approach that is often regarded as, at best, shallow and lazy, and at worst actively harmful. But what is it, and how does it work in a sexual context? Is it actually bad, and if so, in what particular ways? Are there better ways to design and write these encounters and dynamics? And most importantly of all, is there a way to make these elements feel more organic, natural, and compelling while still keeping some of the benefits of the kindness coin model? (Figure 11.1)

FIGURE 11.1 Well, hold onto your butts, because we might be onto something...(fizkes/ Shutterstock.com.)

DOI: 10.1201/9780429356650-14

WHAT ARE KINDNESS COINS?

- The term "kindness coins" refers to a particular design dynamic, found mostly in nonlinear games which allow players to choose and pursue romantic or sexual relationships with NPCs. In this model, the player can do optional "nice" or "kind" things for an NPC, like favors, compliments, or otherwise positive interactions; these are the "kindness coins." Every time they do one of these things, it increases a certain value with the NPC – we'll call it an Affection meter, but some games have Approval, Relationship, etc. When this value reaches a particular level, the player will get the option to make the relationship sexual (or romantic), or at the very least nudge it in that direction (Figure 11.2). This may be expressed by:

  - Unlocking certain "flirt" choices, or allowing the player to flirt successfully (e.g., you can flirt at any time, but only once Affection meter is high enough will the NPC respond well).

  - Triggering certain scenes in which the PC and/or NPC expressly negotiate the nature of their relationship, ask for sex, actually HAVE sex, etc.

  - Other events that shift the relationship from platonic to firmly sexual and/or romantic.

Some games will hide the NPC Affection value from the player's view, dealing with it purely in hidden coding and scripting; the player may never know exactly how much Affection the NPC has. Other games, however, will show this value as a meter, number, or bar and will allow players to see how they are progressing the relationship and how close they are

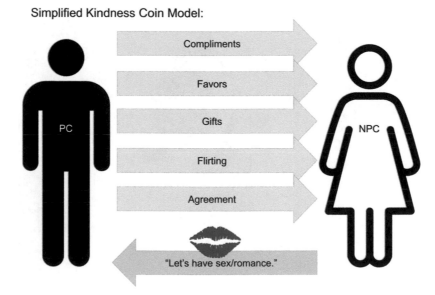

FIGURE 11.2 The Kindness Coin model of sex and romance design. This diagram depicts a heterosexual couple with a male PC and female NPC, but this dynamic can still play out with other permutations (e.g., same-sex relationships and female PC/male NPC)

to certain milestones (e.g., sex, love confession, or offer of marriage). It's worth noting that many games also have a platonic version of this model (i.e., where you do "nice" things and increase friendship with an NPC), and very often, the two overlap. In other words, doing a "nice" thing might advance both their friendship AND their romantic interest in you.

Kindness coins cover a wide range of in-game actions and player choices. They can be based on dialogue, gestures, or even physical objects! Examples can include:

- Complimenting the NPC.

- Always agreeing with them (even on nonsexual or non-romantic topics)

- Doing favors for them (e.g., loyalty missions and quests)

- Constantly choosing the flirt dialogue options.

- Giving them gifts, particularly gifts that are tailored to the NPCs' interests (e.g., giving books to a booklover).

- Continually choosing positive interactions with the NPC, particularly flirtatious ones.

Note that "flirting" comes up on this list a lot! A common variant of the kindness coin model is "flirting coins," where the player only has to choose the "flirty" options in dialogue in order to increase Affection; choose enough of them, and the player unlocks the "romance" or "sex" path. Flirting and kindness aren't exactly the same thing, but this *particular* dynamic is close enough that this model of "do flirty thing, Affection goes up" is counted under kindness coins. To put it another way, this flirting is basically another "nice" thing, just with a more obvious sexual or romantic tone to it.

(Note that some games will often have systems that allow players to go an "anti-kindness coin" route – being cruel and insulting, for example, or disagreeing with the NPC's values, will drive down the NPC's meter and make them less likely to desire you.)

The original *Dragon Age: Origins* provides examples of all of the above types of kindness coins, with various levels of nuance. While initiating a romance requires choosing particular dialogue options at key moments in the story, the actual "level" of that romance – Interested/Care/Adore/Love – is tied to kindness coin mechanics and character approval. Character approval increases if the player is friendly and kind to the NPC in question, if they agree with their worldview (e.g., agreeing with Morrigan that the Chantry is bad), if they complete a personal quest for the NPC, or if the player gives them a gift that the NPC particularly likes. As the player goes up in NPC approval, they reach higher "levels" of the romance and trigger new optional conversations with the NPC. And sure enough, sex scenes unlock at specific "levels," albeit different levels for each NPC – for example, Alistair is a romantic and only has sex at the Love level, while the casually promiscuous Zevran will have sex at much lower levels. In all romances, however, the core loop is the same: do things the NPC will like -> increase the NPC's level of Approval/Affection -> Unlock sex and romance scenes when this level is high enough for that character. Regardless of the character, the progression of romantic and sexual relations is at least partially gated by

FIGURE 11.3 "Whew, just five more gifts and this NPC will like me enough to take my pants off!" (VGstockstudio/Shutterstock.com.)

kindness coin options such as gift-giving, agreeing with them, flirting, and compliments. This is a model used by many other games, both in AAA and indie space (Figure 11.3).

But why kindness *coins*, as opposed to kindness tokens or kindness models? Well, it's because, on a systemic level, they are the "currency" which the player can "spend" to increase the meter and unlock romantic or sexual content. Naming this dynamic "kindness coins" emphasizes the underlying transactional nature of the design – that if you "pay" enough "kindness" to the NPC in question, you will inevitably be "repaid" by a sex scene (or a romantic relationship, or some other sexual or romantic connection). There are several issues with this dynamic – by this point, you've probably already thought of a few – but first, let's discuss why this model is so prevalent, what it gets right, and why it's appealing.

THE PERKS OF KINDNESS COIN DESIGN

There are plenty of reasons that developers and designers go with a kindness coin model, and not all of those reasons have to do with nefarious or ignorantly unhealthy attitudes toward sex and relationships. Many of them have to do with trying to find simple, clean models to deal with, and in a nonlinear system, kindness coins are one of the easiest in terms of design and programming.

On a coding level, the equations required to keep this design loop are very simple to manage and only involve basic math and conditionals (Figure 11.4).

- Establish a counter for affection, attraction, etc. as X.

- For every "kindness coin" action, increase X by 1.

- At appropriate points in the game (e.g., at particular story beats, or when speaking to the character), check the value of X against a certain target number (let's say 10).

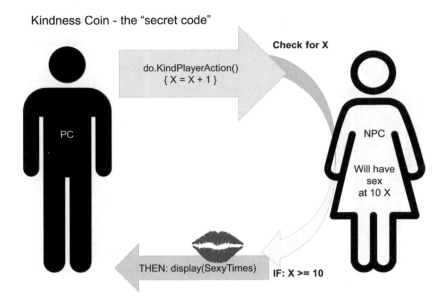

FIGURE 11.4 The very, very basic gist of how the programming, coding, and design work for kindness coins. Apologies to any programmers who are reading my terrible attempt at code!

- If X is greater than or equal to the target number (if $X \geq 10$), then unlock or trigger a sex scene (or other intimate moments).

- If needed, this loop can be repeated for other target numbers (e.g., further sex scenes if $X \geq 20$ and $X \geq 30$)

This core loop is very easy to design and equally easy to program and is surprisingly flexible for games where multiple optional sexual partners are available; it's easy to track different Xs for multiple characters! It's understandable that, with all the other pressures of designing, writing, and coding games, many developers would embrace a simplified system like this.

There is also something to be said for *players* enjoying a system that is transparent and predictable. Players engage with sex and romance in games for different reasons, and while sometimes they may be seeking a deeper, more realistic, and nuanced representation of how romantic and sexual dynamics work…at other times, they may just want something simple and "dependable" to enjoy as an escape or fantasy. And there's absolutely *nothing* wrong with that. In the context of fiction, sometimes it IS nice to know that exploring a romantic or sexual relationship with your favorite character can be simple and straightforward that you're not going to "fail" as long as you talk to them and treat them well and pick the right conversation choices. If you believe your player base will be that way inclined – that players will be engaging in the romance or sex in your game looking for something simple and easy to experience with a little affectionate effort – then there's nothing inherently wrong with embracing a system that's straightforward, simplified, and easy to "game."

But although kindness coins offer all of those elements, it's worth reconsidering it as the go-to model.

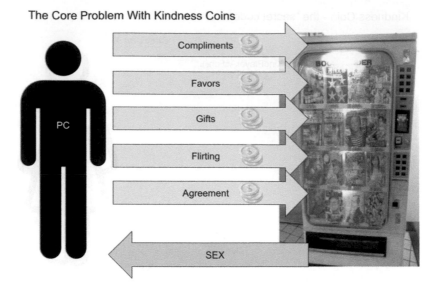

FIGURE 11.5   Hmm, I wonder what happened to that interesting NPC that was just here…

SEXUAL VENDING MACHINES: ISSUES WITH KINDNESS COINS

Despite the appealing simplicity of the kindness coin model, there are several major issues with it, many of which can be summed up in a simple visual (Figure 11.5).

This is the issue at the heart of the criticism of the kindness coin model. By turning certain actions and good deeds into something the player does in order to unlock sex, the designers inadvertently turn the NPC in question into a glorified sexual vending machine that will deliver sex if the player puts in enough kindness coins (favors, compliments, gifts, etc.)

There are, naturally, several major issues with this, a big one of which is the reduction of the NPC to "sex dispenser" status and ignoring their sexual agency. Even if the character is generally well written and fully realized outside of romance and sex, boiling their sexuality down to, "will bone player if player jumps through hoops and does nice things for me" is incredibly reductive and flattens their character and personality. Rather than the sex feeling like two fully independent adults deciding they want to have sex, it ends up feeling like a "reward" that the player unlocks independent of the NPC's interest or wishes. Good writing can mitigate this effect somewhat – for example, emphasizing the NPC's romantic or sexual response to the kindness, friendliness, or flirtiness of the player – but if you scratch the surface, the transactional and reactive nature of the underlying design ends up shining through, and the result feels less like an interested NPC who's made an enthusiastic choice and more… well, the vending machine who just spits out sex when the player has "paid enough kindness."

Worse, if the designers and writers are not careful, the transactional nature of the design can, in some instances, get reinforced in the writing and end up derailing the character entirely. For example, if the game allows players to gain affection by giving gifts, you run the risk of portraying the character to be actively mercenary in their affections, only showing interest if you bribe them with trinkets or other items – literally buying their love or sex via trade. Unless the NPC is explicitly the sort of character who is interested in that kind of transaction, it's either going to feel out of character, suggest mercenary qualities, or result in the relationship dynamics feeling flat and shallow. Do they like the player only because they buy gifts? Gifts *can* be used in meaningful ways, of course. *Dragon Age: Inquisition* goes out of its way to emphasize both the romantic nature and the Inquisitor's thoughtfulness and care in giving Cassandra a romantic gift; *Hades*, on the other hand, emphasizes how the culture of the game world gives special meaning to the exchange of nectar. But meaningful gift-giving, or other "kindness coin" gestures, requires effort and planning in terms of the narrative, worldbuilding, and characterization. Otherwise, it's far too easy for the character's personality to slip into a reductive, flattened state of, "get good stuff, repay with sex." Even in games where gifts don't enter into the picture, would your NPC really fall in love or want to have sex just "because the player was nice to me?" Is that really the kind of character they are, and if not, why are they being designed and written that way?

Another related but equally major issue with this approach is how it directly ties kindness and sexuality together. Don't get me wrong, a lot of characters (and people) prefer kind sexual partners, and there are ways in which showing kindness may spark romantic or sexual interest. But there's a lot of difference between that and, "showing someone kindness automatically makes them fall in love/lust with you." If the latter were true, I'd be lusting after pretty much every human being I've ever met! Clearly, there's more to it than that, but there are games that still fall into the trap. In some games, even being *friendly* toward a character can put you on their "romance and sex" track and cause them to become attracted, or at the very least open to your advances. Tightly connecting "be nice to character" with "character wants to sleep with you" can send wildly irregular messages, both in terms of gameplay and in real life, about the nature of kindness and good treatment in sexual relationships, making it the sole end-all-and-be-all of whether or not someone will sleep with you.

And this, in turn, can feed into some extremely unhealthy stereotypes about relationships in real life, which brings us to another major issue with kindness coins – reinforcing negative real-life behavior. Game depictions of sex and relationships don't always need to be perfectly healthy or unproblematic – there's definite room for messy, problematic themes and fantasies! – but in this case, the overlap with real-world issues is difficult to ignore. While this kindness coin structure might be harmless enough in the context of a game, it is *not* so harmless when the players expect these dynamics in real-world relationships. This attitude causes problems in all sorts of sexual relationships, though it can hit particularly badly across certain gender lines and along patriarchal models of heterosexuality. Go to any relationship forum on the Internet, and you can find countless examples of straight men who feel entitled to have sex with a particular woman because the man was "nice" or "kind" or "did them favors" – which sure enough sounds exactly like the kindness coin model. Clearly, this is not a problem specific to games, but more of a larger cultural issue…but reinforcing these expectations in a fictional game setting isn't doing a great job of challenging this perspective, or conveying attraction and sexual relationships in a more holistic light. Worse, in some cases, it may inadvertently reinforce the behavior by showing a gameplay loop where it does, in fact, work (Figure 11.6).

FIGURE 11.6 "But I gave you 10 rides to work and complimented your outfit 15 times! Why haven't I unlocked getting in your pants yet? Is there a loyalty mission I missed?" (fizkes/Shutterstock.com.)

OUT WITH THE KINDNESS COINS, AND IN WITH…CHEMISTRY CASINO?

So, we have a design model with some major pluses – simplicity of design, programming, and approach, as well as predictable and easy experience – with some even more major minuses – reducing sexual relationships to a tryst with a sexual vending machine. Surely there's no way to mitigate the latter so as to enjoy the former? Surely we can't use such a simple base to build something more nuanced and interesting?

Well, I would argue that we can. It just involves a significant reframing in how we think about the core loop and how to use it for building sexual attraction. It means linking the simple core gameplay to something more profound and potentially romantic/erotic than "niceness" or "flirting," and defining it more broadly than before. It means making it less about admiration or gratefulness – though those can still play a part! – and more about *attraction*.

As such, I suggest we replace the kindness coin model with an alternative I like to call… the chemistry casino (Figure 11.7).

At their core, kindness coins and chemistry casino may have the same loop – do X thing, increase attraction meter, trigger sex – but the fundamental difference is in what "X thing" actually is. While the model for kindness coins is "do nice things for an NPC until they want to have sex with you," the model for the chemistry casino is, **"do things that the NPC finds sexually attractive until they decide to act on their sexual attraction."**

At first glance, this might seem like hair-splitting, but it's an absolutely critical difference. The former flattens characters and makes their sexual interest only hinge on general kindness or flirting. The latter is focused on arousing the NPC's sexual interest in an organic way that reflects their personalities and turn-ons. It results in a more holistic vision of how sex and sexual attraction work, one that is better rooted in the NPC's identity and

FIGURE 11.7 "I'm betting it all on the sexy voice and the quirky sense of humor!" (Studio Romantic/Shutterstock.com.)

agency and that offers new and interesting opportunities for players to "role-play" and inhabit their player character in the game.

And where does the casino element come into play? Well, we'll get to that in a bit, but first, the most important thing…

REDESIGNING THE LOOP FOR CHEMISTRY

The chemistry casino is, at its simplest programming level, functionally similar to the kindness coin model:

- Establish a counter for attraction/chemistry as X.

- For every action that *increases attraction and chemistry*, increase X by 1.

- At appropriate points in the game, check value of X.

- If X is greater than or equal to the target number, trigger sex scene or other intimate moments (e.g., flirtatious sequence and love confession)

- Repeat loop as needed

In this case, however, the actions that increase X are fundamentally different in that they are tailored to the NPC's turn-ons and what they find attractive. In other words, chemistry casino bases its loop on actively displaying traits that the NPC finds sexy and doing things that spark chemistry between you. Remember two chapters ago, when we were discussing the importance of knowing and developing your characters' turn-ons and turn-offs? This is where they become crucial in a narrative AND gameplay sense, because they will be providing the baseline for what actions the player can take and what erotic chemical reactions they inspire.

By redesigning the "kindness coin" loop around what NPCs find attractive vs. just "being nice" to them, the transactional nature of the model is replaced with – or at least modified by – a more organic model focused on arousing their genuine desires, matching their sexual interests, and just acting in a way that gets them hot under the collar. The sex results from the NPC actively pursuing sexual fulfillment; while they are still "reacting" to the player's actions, it's a reaction to how *hot* the player character is to them. It's less about "dispensing" sex, and more about actively WANTING to have sex (Figure 11.8).

The best part of this approach is just how many potential "attractive actions" there can be in a game. If you've fully fleshed out your NPC's desires, then you have the foundation for an almost limitless variety of gameplay actions and player choices that can excite that NPC and their desires. This can go far beyond simple dialogue choices; these can be baked into every element of gameplay, down to character creation, cosmetics, and combat! Let's look at how some particular types of turn-ons might translate into gameplay features:

- **Appearance** – NPCs may have a thing for certain physical features, such as long hair, muscles, extra plumpness, or the simple pleasures of a nice butt! While this should not be the key deciding factor for sexual chemistry – people fall madly in lust outside of their physical "type" all the time! – it can provide a fascinating additional aspect to character creation. Imagine if choosing certain appearances granted small bonuses to attraction to different characters; one might like the big muscular look,

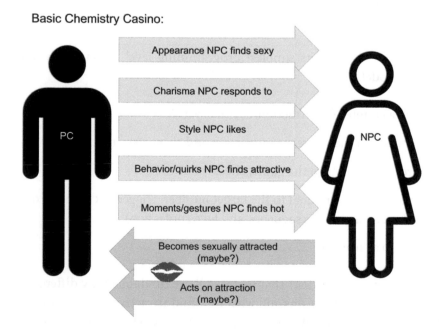

FIGURE 11.8 A layout of the basic chemistry casino model: instead of generic favors and compliments, the player must display traits that the NPC finds sexy. Note the "maybe" and potential uncertainty, i.e., the "casino" element, which we'll discuss later.

while another likes the soft and cuddly aesthetic.[1] Changing non-body cosmetic appearances in-game is also a great potential source of attraction mechanics and chemistry casino. Dying or cutting your hair, for example, or getting tattoos could evoke some very *interesting* responses from an NPC who's Into That Sort of Thing. Lastly, never discount the potential of clothes and accessories and how they can be used to build attractiveness. This could tie in with in-game cosmetics, transmogrification, armor sets, or even just the character's "default" clothing. Of course, you can always dress in something skimpy that shows off your favorite *ass*ets (pun intended), but…it may be that what *really* gets an NPC going is a person in a finely tailored suit…(Figure 11.9)

- **Physical activities and displays** – many of us have had moments where we've seen a person or character do something physical – something that shows physical strength, dexterity, or grace of a certain kind – and gone, "That's really hot." NPCs are no different! By matching what your player can physically do in the game with what arouses the NPCs, you can build their attraction to you by performing actions that stir their desires. These actions can be tied directly into gameplay such as combat, platforming, running, or other physical gameplay feats. And you can tie attraction to the WAY these things are done as well. For example, someone who is turned on by strength might be interested in a combat style that favors brute force. They also might be attracted by the player applying their strength to in-game challenges (e.g., using a high strength stat to hold up a collapsing beam could make the NPC ogle them all the more). In contrast, another NPC might like someone who's a good dancer, and their attraction would improve the more/the better you dance, or if you fight in a particularly graceful dancer-like way (Figure 11.10).

FIGURE 11.9 "The Suit and Tie armor set grants +500 sex appeal with the high fashion party member…as well as half the player base." (Viorel Sima/Shutterstock.com.)

FIGURE 11.10   Some characters would consider this sort of thing to be foreplay. (Pixel-Shot/ Shutterstock.com.)

- **Personality/behavior traits** – this can be anything from a general personality type that your NPC has a "thing" for – for example, broody angsty goth boys, or sweet and gentlewomen, or quirky idiots with a hilarious murderous streak – to the character doing particular actions or choosing particular types of responses. For example, if an NPC really likes funny partners, consistently choosing humorous and witty dialogue options may turn them on. Alternatively, another partner may be more and more intrigued the more you pick poetic, eloquent turns of phrase. Beyond branching dialogue choices, there can be other actions to take in game that might stir someone's romantic or sexual interest. Consider in real life how many people respond to a picture of a muscled strongman celebrity cuddling a puppy with some variant of, "I want to have his children" or "I want him in my bed immediately." Depending on your game, having the player (and by extension, their character) stop their combat or exploration and take time to pet a dog might have the same effect on NPCs! This is an area that heavily overlaps between sex and romance, with the latter more focused on personality compatibility than sheer lust factor…but don't discount the lust factor an appealing personality can have! (Figure 11.11)

- **Values and viewpoints** – lastly, beyond behavior and physicality, there's the component of personal admiration tying into physical attraction. We're familiar with scenes in movies and books where a character will be making a passionate speech about something important and noble, only for another character to suddenly fall on them kissing them wildly. While this can be clumsy if done poorly, it can be an interesting kickoff to a sexual or romantic relationship, either in a dramatic moment like the one above or a more subtle, long-term approach. Of course, this is also something that can be done in reverse, with characters becoming LESS attracted

FIGURE 11.11 For some people, this is pure sexual catnip. Get it? Catnip? (Alena Ozerova/ Shutterstock.com.)

to you the more and more they realize you have opposing viewpoints. Developing sexual chemistry around values and viewpoints alone is usually not enough – you can agree with someone in pretty much everything and still not want to have sex with them! – but it can add an interesting dimension when paired with the other elements. It can also be a major aspect of romantic relationships, which in turn can then affect sexual desire (e.g., respect and admiration mixing with romantic feelings to deepen desire) (Figure 11.12).

And of course, all of these can overlap in interesting ways. An NPC who is attracted to sophistication, for example, might respond both to suave dialogue choices *and* to wearing suits or evening dresses. Another who likes strength and forcefulness might be equally weak in the knees whether the player is punching down doors, shouting down a particularly loathsome enemy, or taking their shirt off to show off their muscles.

Again, many of these are less about single-dialogue options or one-off choices and more about what your character actually *does* on a regular basis. It can be an inherent part of the core gameplay, trickling into combat, movement, exploration, strategy, and anything tied to the player's control of their avatar and how they engage with the game world. This is another strength of the chemistry casino: it allows the player to role-play their character much more and to craft a persona for them. **It's not about saying "the right thing," it's about being the "right person" for the NPC,** sexually and/or romantically. It's about role-playing the player character as an individual who sparks chemistry with this particular person, who inspires desire and interest based on who they are and how they're seen rather than just always picking the "nice" option. Players may still be able to "game" their way to a romance or sex scene by picking particular actions, but in the process, they end up developing who their character actually is and how they interact with the world in general.

FIGURE 11.12 "Ironic, all your talk about freeing the mages from oppression has got me in the mood to tie you to my bed. Weird, that." (Star Stock/Shutterstock.com.)

Sticking with a simple chemistry casino – where actions that match an NPC's turn-ons increase their attraction – can already offer a lot of possibilities, particularly when the potential pool of actions is so large. But there are even more variants and refinements game designers can make on this.

- Any meters or variables tracking "attraction" and (and should?) be completely separate from ones that track relationships, friendships, or respect. This is about what turns the NPC on, not what makes them like you! Disconnecting them can result in some fascinating combinations and potential sexual relationships. What if they have high attraction but very low respect or affection scores? Could you be in for some hot, angry hatesex? Or possibly something extremely casual? What if you have high romantic compatibility but not a lot of sexual chemistry? Could that be a companionate relationship?

- Beyond tracking the meters and values, there's also the question of how and when they increase, and under what conditions. If you have an NPC that's turned on by aggression, for example, the simplest way to handle the core chemistry equation is to simply have attraction go up every time your character is aggressive. Simple enough… but that would include times that the NPC isn't there as well as when they are. What if you also had the game check for the NPC's presence and only increase their attraction if they're actually in your presence, experiencing the arousal firsthand?

- And if you wanted to push this even further…what if they became aware that you were only acting aggressively when they were present, and not the rest of the time? Could they become aware and react appropriately if they realize you're deliberately altering your actions or appearance just to attract them? (Figure 11.13)

FIGURE 11.13 "Mind explaining why you only bother saving orphans whenever *I* am in the party?" (NDAB Creativity/Shutterstock.com.)

All of these questions can be remarkably complex and involve a lot of resources and content development, so they may not always be possible to do, but the results can offer a lot of nuanced narratives and gameplay possibilities, so it can be worth the effort.

So to a certain extent, this is the kindness coin model reworked to better reflect NPC attraction and agency and to incorporate gameplay beyond dialogue choices…so why is this chapter not pushing "the chemistry coin model?" Where does the casino element come into play?

HOW ABOUT THAT CASINO?

As discussed earlier, there's nothing necessarily wrong with creating a system that is dependable and straightforward. Sometimes, that's exactly what the player wants, and a chemistry coin model is perfect for that. However, in reality, romantic and sexual relationships, and the mechanics of attraction, are not so predictable. How many among us have met someone who technically ticks off ALL our attraction boxes…and yet not really felt that spark? Conversely, how many of us have met someone who, on paper, wouldn't attract us at all or hit any of our turn-ons, but somehow manage to become devastatingly sexy after a single conversation? How do you know that being sexy, even your partner's perfect version of sexy, will hit home? Even when all the ingredients for blazing hot attraction are in place, who is to say when – or if – it all finally ignites? (Figure 11.14)

That's why I advocate for "chemistry casino" as opposed to "chemistry coins" – to stress the erotic appeal of uncertainty and to incorporate it into design, narrative, or both. After all, romantic and sexual relationships, particularly in the early days of heady attraction, carry a lot of uncertainty. Do they like me? Do I like them? What are these feelings? How far do I want to go with them? How far do THEY want to go? Exactly how much do I want them to throw me on the nearest flat surface and have their wicked way with me? And

FIGURE 11.14 Attraction is less a series of steps and more a sexy dice roll…you can increase your chances of success, but in the end, you need the right number to set things aflame. (galaxy67/Shutterstock.com.)

if it looks like things are going that way, how much will I nudge it along? Uncertainty, employed correctly in this way, can be engaging, suspenseful, and very, VERY hot.

The element of randomness can also play a part in erotic connections and can add further spice to the gameplay and narrative, if done correctly. Consider, for example, how classic "meet-cutes" in romance have a heavy element of randomness in them – bumping into each other accidentally, or both missing the last train together, or just happening to be at the right place at the right moment. Sexual connections can use similar structures, often with an extra erotic charge – two people's eyes meeting across a crowded bar at *just* the right time, for example, and the resulting sizzle between them. This sense of random chance, of sexy serendipity, can add a sense of organic tension and anticipation to players' experience of sexual game content, supported by the turn-ons and chemistry we've already discussed. Even if an encounter is entirely scripted, approaching the design and/or narrative presentation with an erotic element of randomness and uncertainty – winning at a casino as opposed to trading in coins – can make sexual storylines more vivid and more exciting for your players, and get them even more invested in the outcome.

In other words,

- If kindness coins can be summed as, "be nice to someone until they fall into bed with you…"

- And chemistry coins can be summed up as, "do attractive things until someone is so overwhelmed with attraction that they fall into bed with you…"

- Then, the chemistry casino might be summed up as, "do attractive things to roll the dice, see if a spark catches fire, and see if that spark inspires them to fall into bed with you." (Figure 11.15)

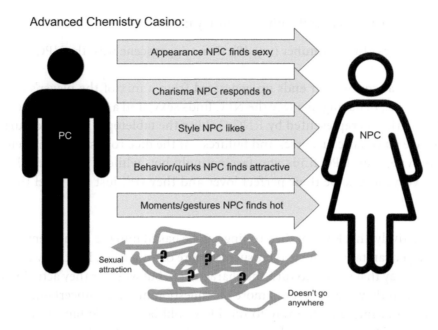

Advanced Chemistry Casino:

- Appearance NPC finds sexy
- Charisma NPC responds to
- Style NPC likes
- Behavior/quirks NPC finds attractive
- Moments/gestures NPC finds hot

PC

NPC

Sexual attraction

Doesn't go anywhere

FIGURE 11.15 An advanced chemistry casino, where the NPC's response to your attractive behavior is uncertain, or at least APPEARS uncertain.

Of course, the question then arises: should it be a LITERAL roll of the dice – something that incorporates genuine random elements in the game's systems? Unsurprisingly, the answer is…it depends.

In some cases, a more randomized system – one that incorporates genuine random elements that the player cannot predict – may be the right call for the sex in your game! Games like roguelikes and grand strategy games already incorporate randomized elements, events, and even characters in their structure – it's not impossible to imagine how a "roguelike" romance or erotica might similarly randomize certain aspects so as to make the journey and the outcomes of your romantic or sexual pursuits different every time, even to the point of being impossible in some playthroughs! Having this random element can encourage multiple playthroughs as well as stimulate community discussion, as no two players will end up with the same experiences in terms of their romantic and sexual explorations of the game.

Some ideas of how to introduce randomness to the design of romance and sex include:

- Instead of triggering sexual or romantic scenes at specific levels of user-generated chemistry with an NPC, the scene triggers can instead be designed around random number generators (RNGs), with the user-generated chemistry modifying or improving those results with the NPC. The system could be something like *Dungeons and Dragons*, which uses dice rolls and skill modifiers to hit a target number:

  - X=chemistry with the NPC (increased by the player's deliberate actions)

  - Y=random dice roll or equivalent (say, between 1 and 10)

- **Z** = X + Y (i.e., dice roll with a chemistry modifier)

- If **Z** > SexyTargetNumber (say, 10), then trigger scene with the NPC, etc.

Thus, the sexual connection ends up generated from a mix of the player's actions and role-playing (i.e., behaving in a way the NPC finds sexy) and a random, unknowable element (the spark?) as represented by RNG. Taking the tabletop RPG model further, one can also have automatic successes and failures – if the dice roll is 10, then even if you're not "their type," the NPC finds you fascinatingly hot, while if the dice roll is 1, you could do everything to be their perfect lover and they still just don't feel that *spark*… (Figure 11.16)

- Alternatively, this RNG or dice-rolling can be baked into the high-chemistry actions the player can take, to make their success more of a question. In other words, you can act in a way that's likely to turn the character on, but whether they actually ARE – or how much they are – becomes more of a question mark, an uncertainty that sparks tension and interest. One way to do this would be a simple binary success/failure check every time the player does something "attractive," but this could be frustrating and dissuade players from making the effort, and may not properly reflect the smaller nuances of attractions and turn-ons. A better approach might be to guarantee that doing "attractive" things will attract the NPC, but randomize how MUCH it attracts them. Sometimes, they may react to a gesture, behavior, or appearance with a mild interest, while other times it hits them in the gut. Which reaction the NPC has can be set to vary based on their moods, their situation, and even pure random chance.

FIGURE 11.16 Botching your roll has literally never been so unsexy! (paulzhuk/Shutterstock.com.)

- Depending on your game and narrative structure, you may want to consider having the *chance* of a scene triggering at certain chemistry levels as opposed to a *guarantee*. In this model, rather than cueing up the intimate scene as soon as the player hits their SexyTargetNumber, the game makes a hidden coin flip, where heads will trigger the intimate scene. If it comes up tails, the player continues the game as normally, but the game will make another hidden coin flip at a later point (and will keep doing so until the scene is finally triggered). This works particularly well in games where the players or characters have day cycles, sleep cycles, or other cycles of downtime (e.g., returning to a spaceship, setting up camp); every time the player "rests," the game can check to see if their chemistry with an NPC is still high enough, then flip the coin to see if something comes of it. It encourages players to engage in the downtime loop and builds anticipation. Imagine, after so many days of flirting and so many nights going to bed as normal gameplay, the player and player character's reaction, when a cutscene begins, there's an unexpected knock on the door and the NPC they desire is standing there, eager and hopeful and horny. This is basically the model that *Hades* uses for its sex scenes; attraction is built in a structured way, but the actual encounters themselves are randomized, and you never know when Meg or Thanatos will finally visit your room…

- Another source of randomization can be the attractions themselves. While some attractions are certainly reflections of the specific character personality that you've already constructed, not all attractions work that way. Some can seem entirely random, even to the character in question! One could, in theory, generate new and different turn-ons for a character in every playthrough. Having ALL of the turn-ons randomized is not the best idea, as it negates the characterization work discussed in the earlier chapter…but you could go with a hybrid model! For example, an NPC who focuses on money and luxury might "canonically" be turned on by sophistication and high-end suits, but also have a random attraction that's different in every playthrough: big butts, radical honesty, good dancing skills, etc. This would mean players would not be as able to "game" their romance or sexual route by simply choosing the "right" options every time and would have to pay close attention in order to pick up on what excites them in each playthrough. Of course, if you wanted to take this to a natural extreme, you could also randomize whether they're even open to romance, sex, or other intimate relations in the first place. It could be intriguing and amusing to have a game with a set cast of characters but with a different selection of them being romanceable on every playthrough…

- And of course, depending on the game, randomizing the characters themselves may be an option. Obviously, this is not a solution that works for all games, particularly those that depend heavily on established characters. There, the only option might be to randomize which characters end up appearing, or whether they are or aren't open to sexual relationships. But in games that incorporate randomization or procedural generation, particularly as part of the narrative, randomizing a potential sexual partner (complete with turn-ons, turn-offs, preferences, etc.) has potential to be explored…an even sexier *Crusader Kings III*, if you will!

In the right game, introducing a genuine random design element – the "casino" to the chemistry – can make the experience hotter and more interesting for players, as well as encouraging replayability and community discussion and sharing. But for other games, including randomness on the *design* level may not be the right call. Sometimes, it's simply a matter of scope, on either a technical level or a budget level (or both). Coding and designing around randomization can result in a huge level of complexity, and if your game is already complex (e.g., RPGs), it can be beyond the technical or design limitations of the game. Also, in terms of content, it might be too much time, effort, and expense to create scenarios or interactions that may end up never actually appearing! And of course, your players might not appreciate getting those scenes or content by luck of the draw either. While some will be seeking a challenging or randomized experience, others will be seeking a dependable, easily followed route to being with the NPC of their choice – and again, there's nothing wrong with that! But those players are likely to be frustrated if that route to their dream NPC ends up being totally different and randomized every time. If they end up being sidelined or even blocked from pursuing the sexual relationship they want to play because of the roll of a dice, they're going to be deeply unhappy, and possibly give up playing (Figure 11.17).

So there are always going to be games where the design of the sexual relationship progression isn't a random casino of chance, but rather a more linear or dependable model with no random gameplay elements. That's fine! But that doesn't mean you have to abandon the idea of sexy uncertainty and random chance entirely. In these sorts of games, the chemistry casino becomes less about the design and more about the narrative and UI wrapping *around* the design. The development of the sexual connection should still FEEL like a lucky win, even if the mechanics behind the curtain basically guarantee success if done right. Players may still be going through a chain of predictable action-reactions – doing

FIGURE 11.17 "I'm sorry, did the woman of my dreams suddenly disappear permanently from the game after losing a random coin flip...FOR THE FIFTH TIME?!" (Krakenimages.com/Shutterstock.com.)

specific high-chemistry actions to evoke a dependable sexual reaction from the NPC – but in terms of their moment-to-moment experience, they should still feel the same sort of tension, anticipation, and uncertainty that enhances the sexy mood of a scene or dynamic between characters.

And yes, making a system nonrandom DOES mean that players will find ways to min-max or "game" the system, working out THE way to romance or seduce an NPC. But that, in and of itself, is not necessarily negative; arguably, it encourages player engagement as they try to puzzle things out. By cloaking the straightforward system in a more mysterious or "lucky" wrapping, you invite your early players to experiment and explore to find out how that system actually works, and to engage with the NPCs in ways that reflect their understanding of those characters, before sharing what they learn with the rest of the player community.

Applying a chemistry casino narrative or experience to a non-casino design can be done in several ways:

- Remove or hide immediate feedback of player "success." Many games with romance or sex in them clearly signal to the player when their actions are impressing or winning over a potential sexual partner. There may be pop-up messages like "[NPC] liked that" or "[NPC] Affection + 10!," or a visual meter that shows increases, or even just the NPC having very bluntly positive verbal responses. If you hide this feedback, however, it makes the process of sexual connection much more mysterious and random-feeling, drawing a veil over the systemic workings of the sexual relationship system and leaving the players deliciously in the dark. *Did* they just like me flexing my biceps? What does that smile mean? Were they watching while I took my shirt off, or did they look away?

- If you *do* want to provide feedback to players, use subtle character-appropriate narrative clues as opposed to explicit UI text or other signifiers. This may be easier to do for games with large budgets or particular art styles, but consider giving positive feedback to players via subtle cues like facial expressions, small smiles, body language, and other signifiers. Dancing with an NPC and having a simple pop-up saying "NPC liked that" isn't desperately mysterious or erotic. Dancing with them and then noticing them smiling at you and leaning subtly closer…way hotter. To run with the casino metaphor, think of it like poker: your players might be playing the game right, but the only way they can guess that is to interpret the "tells" of your characters (Figure 11.18).

- Consider making the major beats of the sexual relationship trigger in unpredictable ways, or at least ways that APPEAR unpredictable. If EVERY character's sex scene triggers at 75 attraction or just before going into the final mission, for example, players know exactly what to expect, particularly on subsequent run-throughs. But if the player character is going to bed, night after night, thinking of the sexual tension between them and an NPC, hopeful for them to knock one night, yet never quite sure when the knock will come…that lends itself to powerful sexual tension and curiosity. We discussed the possibilities for genuine randomization of this above, but even if the major beats are set in stone, they can be set in interesting, organic, and

FIGURE 11.18 "She only raises her eyebrow that way when I recite my poetry. Hmmm..." (LightField Studios/Shutterstock.com.)

random-feeling ways. Don't bind all the characters to the same relationship, sexual, or narrative milestones; mix them up, and trigger them at unusual times. Think beyond the big, dramatic, "obvious" moments to have sex – or at least, beyond having The Obligatory Sex Scene for every character at the same dramatic point – and consider smaller, character-appropriate moments for sexual intimacy. Embrace the idea of the sexual relationship unfolding in front of the player and revealing itself, rather than setting out a set of goalposts or story beats for players to chug along for until they hit!

- And above all, write the sexual and romantic relationships in question with a sense of chance, randomness, and unpredictability! Even if the underlying system is set in stone and always guaranteed to work, *the characters don't know that.* Have characters wonder about their connection, have them encounter misunderstandings, have them carry on nonsexual conversations that are clearly about Something Else, have them be genuinely scared or confused or excited or hopeful about what they're feeling and seeing between the two of them. Above all, when the two characters finally tumble into bed together, it shouldn't feel like it got that way just by one character (the player) doing a thing or being sexy often enough, even if that IS what is happening on a systemic level. To continue hounding the casino metaphor to death: write it with at least a *little* of the breathless excitement and mix of fate vs chance that winning a contest of dice might have...even if you've been carefully weighing those dice specifically for this moment to happen!

CONCLUSION

Kindness coins were a useful starting point for designing sexual and romantic relationships in games, and there are certain approaches and benefits we can take from the model.

If your goal is to provide your player safe and idealized sexual fantasies and a fun escape from "real life" complications, you can still do that by trading out bland "acts of kindness" for acts and gestures that increase chemistry and attraction. But if desired, we can also push this model into more realistic, more random-feeling reflections of real-life sexual dynamics. By focusing on the nuances of physical and emotional chemistry and mixing it with a little bit of random chance and unpredictability, writers and designers can create more compelling, passionate, and exciting sexual relationships and encounters, and tell new and interesting stories in the process. It's time players and developers alike tried their hand at playing a game at the chemistry casino!

WORKSHOP QUESTIONS

Analysis: If the game you're analyzing has branching or optional sexual encounters or relationships in it, analyze what actions, dialogues, and choices the player makes in order to trigger the sex. Is it a kindness coin model? If so, can you point to the sorts of actions the player is encouraged to take in order to romance/sleep with the character they desire? Is the final result organic, and does the NPC still maintain their sexual agency, or do they end up as a temporary sex dispenser as opposed to an active sexual partner?

As a mental exercise, try reimagining this structure as a chemistry casino instead. How would the actions differ? What things would you imagine the player would need to do to "turn on" the NPC? Are there ways you could expand the scope of player action (e.g., combat and cosmetics) to arouse the NPC?

Creative: If appropriate to your game, design and document the core romantic/sexual gameplay loop with the principles of chemistry casinos in mind. Create a minigame design document or other reference documents to lay out:

- What the turn-ons of your NPCs are.

- What in-game actions and choices trigger these turn-ons. Where appropriate, expand this to include:

  - Dialogues

  - Branching choices

  - Combat (style, success, etc.)

  - Character creation

  - In-game cosmetics (e.g., clothing choice)

  - In-game movements (e.g., body language)

  - Other gameplay elements

  - Randomness (expanded below)

- How the NPCs react to players displaying attractive traits.

  - Do they notice only when they're in the room? Do they detect inconsistency?

  - What are in-character, diegetic ways of responding positively?

  - What is the designed progression of the NPC's sexual interest? When do they express initial interest? When do they escalate to sex?

- Will sexual relationships in this game include randomized elements?

  - If so, which ones? How is the randomization achieved? Can randomized elements act as blockers against the characters?

  - If not, what UI and narrative tricks can be used to keep the players engaged and maintain positive tension in the story?

Use this chapter as a reference and inspiration, and get as detailed as you need to; this will be one of the most important mechanisms for players engaging with your sexual content, so your design documents should offer a robust overview of your approach.

NOTE

1 Note, of course, that designers should take special care not to use attraction to appearance in a way that reinforces harmful real-life prejudices or beliefs (e.g., being more attracted to certain skin colors than others, or only being attracted to fully able-bodied characters or skinny body types).

CHAPTER 12

Sex in Quest Design

Y ES, YOU READ THAT title right – sex in quest design. A surprising number of games incorporate sex or sexual moments in a quest or mission, either as part of the main story campaign or as optional sidequests for the player to complete. In some cases, the sex is part of the quest itself, but in most cases, the sex is part of the outcome or reward of a quest or quest chain. When well-done, this incorporation of sexual content can feel like an organic part of the narrative arc; when poorly done, the results can be sleazy, transactional, and clumsy wish-fulfillment. In this chapter, we'll explore some of the different approaches and what the best practices are for each.

For the purposes of this chapter, a quest refers to a distinct task (or series of tasks) with clearly stated and tracked objectives and a clear "end" to the mission or mission chain (Figure 12.1). These may be strung along a central story arc to further the plot (i.e., critical path missions),

FIGURE 12.1   New quest unlocked: "Have Sex, Will Travail!" (solarseven/Shutterstock.com.)

DOI: 10.1201/9780429356650-15

or they may be sidequests, optional stories, and other content that players engage with separately from the central narrative. Sex can figure into three phases of the quest:

- The inciting incident or reason for the quest assignment

- The quest itself

- The quest outcome or reward.

SEX AS INCITING INCIDENT FOR QUESTS

A few chapters ago, we discussed the possibility of sex as an inciting incident in a larger three-act narrative, but it can also function that way within the more limited scope of a quest's storyline. Quest and questlines usually get kicked off by something, and while rare, one possible kickoff is either the use of a sex scene/erotic moment or the fallout of a prior sexual encounter or sexual relationship.

Sex Scene as Inciting Incident

In this model, a character, likely the player character, has a sexual encounter at the start of a quest; almost immediately afterward, however, they are suddenly thrown into the action or directive of the quest, usually as a direct or indirect result of the sexual encounter. The most obvious example, and arguably the most common, is one where the character has sex with someone, then awakens after sex to discover that their partner is now missing or has left for certain reasons. This then transitions into a gameplay mission to follow them, investigate their disappearance, or deal with the immediate impact of their departure. The stakes are immediately made clear (whether high/dramatic or low/comedic), and the motives and goals of the player character are immediately made clear. It is also followed up with a clear course of action with driving, active game design verbs: to investigate, to chase, to follow, etc.

A good example of this is the 2003 release of *Prince of Persia: The Sands of Time*. In the third act, the Prince and Farah have a mysterious, magical sexual encounter in a bathhouse; it's unclear whether it's only a dream, or if it's reality. Either way, when the Prince awakens, he discovers that Farah used the distraction and his (post-coital?) slumber to steal his weapons and go on alone. The penultimate quest of the game centers around attempting to follow her and recover the stolen weapons, all while navigating a dangerous tower without the time rewind ability granted by one of the weapons. In the context of the game's larger three-act structure, this sex scene would come at the transition into Act 3, but within the context of the actual mission – ascend the tower – this is actually the inciting incident, or at least leads directly to it.

Another example of sex as inciting a quest or mission is one where, during or after sex, the hero is interrupted by an unrelated group (anything from town guards to an angry parent to a villain's armed forces) and needs to effect a daring escape. In terms of quest design, this can be used to lead into tense, action-packed sequences in which the player character may or may not have access to their usual equipment (due to being undressed for sex). Two good examples of this can be seen in the *Assassin's Creed* franchise:

- In *Assassin's Creed II*, after spending the night with Cristina, Ezio is discovered the next morning by her angry father, who calls for the city guards to apprehend him. This immediately triggers a mission to "escape the guards," where Ezio must run away or hide from the aggressive guard enemies until they lose track of him. The sex with Cristina is clearly the inciting incident for this short quest, leading directly to the chain of events where Ezio must escape.

- In *Assassin's Creed Brotherhood*, there's a slightly less direct example where the sex scene does not directly incite the quest, but adds complications to it. At the start of the game, Ezio and Caterina Sforza have sex, and afterward, they cuddle in bed in a state of undress. However, unexpectedly, the Borgia forces attack their stronghold, destroying part of the room and much of Ezio's armor in the process. Ezio has barely enough time to get dressed before rushing out and being swept up in the next mission: defend the walls from the attackers. While the sex does not "trigger" this mission, it does affect how it plays out; since Ezio is in a naked and vulnerable state when the attack begins, he's caught off-guard and is unable to use any of the powerful weapons or armor he gathered in the previous game. Not only does the sex function as a character moment, but also as a useful "power reset" before engaging in the next mission.

Quest as Fallout from Past Sexual Encounter

Another approach to having sex as a catalyst for a mission is to explore the fallout or consequences of past sexual encounters or sexual relationships. In this model, a character – most often an NPC – has engaged in sexual intimacy some time before the player encounters the quest. By now, however, some sort of consequences (usually negative) have transpired, and the NPC requires assistance from the player in order to restore order. The most common examples are cases of scorned lovers making trouble for the other, but other examples could include social repercussions and blackmail, overly enthusiastic lovers making trouble, or even issues with sexually transmitted diseases!

- In the Fevered Note questline (now defunct) in *World of Warcraft* during the *Legion* expansion, the player discovers a note from an unnamed NPC who requests medical assistance due to a poisoning…caused by an amorous encounter with a harpy (a feminine-presenting monster) with a poisonous kiss. While it's left vague how far the encounter got, the implications of sexual or near-sexual dalliance are clear, and the player is left to find a cure to help the NPC recover.[1]

- In another *World of Warcraft* example, the Arelion's Journal quest chain in *Burning Crusade* begins with a blood elf woman requesting help to find her missing husband and his journal. The player finds his body and returns his journal to the wife…only for her to read it and discover her husband was having a sexual affair! This then leads directly to a quest chain where the player must help the wife uncover the identity of Arelion's mistress, then assist her in getting revenge.[2]

- In *Mass Effect*, the player receives a questline related to the former client of a respected courtesan and sex worker, the Asari Consort Sha'ira. It is revealed that the client developed feelings for Sha'ira in the course of their professional relationship and spread vicious rumors after being rejected; the player must approach the client and convince them to restore Sha'ira's reputation.

As a general rule, quests dealing with the fallout of sexual liaisons and relationships should be treated with a very light touch. Fallout should be either touched on only briefly, played purely for laughs, or presented with sincere goodwill regarding those involved. The characters involved *can* be spiteful or mean-spirited, but the outcome can be presented on a cartoonish or comedic level as opposed to a deeper, darker exploration of sexual malice. More serious explorations of fallout from sex can be done, particularly in games with darker stories, but only with a very high level of respect and caution. Care must be taken not to slip into shock value or misanthropy, and writers and other developers must be cautious not to trigger actively painful or unpleasant memories in players, particularly those relating to toxic or abusive sexual partners. In other words, a quest about turning a cheating lover into a lizard is an emotionally safer, less harmful narrative avenue to explore than a quest about slashing a cheating lover's tires and killing them (Figure 12.2).

Sexual Desire as Quest Motive

Lastly, there are also examples of quests where the quest or task does not center around fallout from sex that already happened and instead centers around sex that a character *wants* to have. In this model, a character – almost always an NPC – wishes to have sex with another character, but, before doing so, must ask the player to complete a task that will assist them in either wooing the object of their desire or in arranging circumstances for an

FIGURE 12.2 "That'll show the cheating jerk! Thanks for your help, hero…here's your gold!" (Alfa Photostudio/Shutterstock.com.)

intimate rendezvous. Many games use the less sexual version of this model, which focuses on romance as the end goal; the player may be assigned to find a particular item or kill a special monster so that the quest-giver NPC can impress someone they're attracted to and ask them on a date, or create the perfect date experience. More explicitly sexual versions can focus on:

- Second-hand wooing of the partner in question (successful or not)
- Passing messages, either of a sexual nature or to arrange a sexual encounter
- Ingredients for aphrodisiacs or other sexual aides
- Access to a private location for a tryst
- A particularly lustful or insatiable character seeking ways to be "satisfied."

An example of this can be found in *Assassin's Creed* again: this time in *Odyssey* as part of the optional questline Age is Just a Number. The player character, Alexious/Kassandra, encounters an insatiable older woman called Auxesia who asks Alexios/Kassandra for assistance. Her elderly husband is no longer able to satisfy her lust, and though she has other lovers, she loves her husband deeply and wants him above all others, describing (in detail) their sexual exploits. She commissions Alexios/Kassandra to find ingredients for an aphrodisiac elixir that will strengthen and invigorate him. Alexios/Kassandra must then hunt several animals to find the parts for the potion in order to complete the mission.

Given how many strange and interesting things real-life humans do in pursuit of sex, the use of sexuality as a quest motive has a lot of narrative potentials. With the right world-building, characterization, and narrative design, this motive can be applied to a broad variety of quests, including fetch quests, resource gathering, kill quests, persuasive or dialogue-heavy quests, and environment investigation/manipulation. The quest can be played for light-hearted laughs, but can also be a sincere exploration of human desire, passion, and how far a character will go to satisfy their sexual needs or lust.

Note, however, that unless the tone of the game is extremely dark and the subject matter is handled delicately, consent of all parties should be emphasized in the work. For example, using an aphrodisiac on a non-consenting, unwilling, or unaware target amounts to sexual assault and should not be something players engage in, unless it is to actively prevent the attempt (i.e., quest is to warn the target or stop the perpetrator). Keeping things consensual maintains a fun and enjoyable experience for the player, whether they are comically assisting a horny old woman to seduce her husband or sincerely helping a pair of lovers slip away to enjoy each other's company.

SEX AS QUEST ITSELF

Actually solving or completing quests by having sex is a pretty rare edge case outside of pornographic or erotic games, but not unheard of. While usually played for laughs or for light-hearted fun, occasionally it can be a more dramatic event. The sex can be transactional, a supernatural plot device (such as a magic ritual), or just a way to please one or more parties in the questline. Completing the quest via sex is usually accomplished by a player choice such as a dialogue option and is usually one of several ways to complete the mission. Some examples:

- While the *Dragon Age: Origins* sex ritual with Morrigan has been discussed in previous chapters, it's also worth noting here as an example of completing a quest via sex. In this case, the questline, Morrigan's Ritual, literally revolves around sex and the player's choice to go ahead with it or refuse. At the start of the questline, Morrigan lays out her proposal – perform the ritual and conceive a child with one of the male Grey Wardens, allowing them to survive the final battle against the Archdemon. The player can complete the quest by convincing the male Grey Warden companion (either Alistair or Loghain) to have sex with Morrigan and impregnate her, or by having sex with Morrigan themselves (if playing a male Grey Warden). The quest ends with a short intimate scene. Alternatively, the player can also choose NOT to do the ritual and to refuse Morrigan; this also completes the quest.

- In *Dragon Age: Inquisition*, during a loyalty mission for Josephine Montilyet, the player must seek an audience with an elderly aristocrat, Minister Bellise, in order to convince her to elevate a particular family to nobility. During the conversation, Bellise makes it clear that she requires a tangible trade for her favor. The player has the option to offer troops, information, or influence…but they also can offer "an unforgettable night" and sexually proposition the minister. She asks if the player is serious, in which case the player can either claim they were making a joke or confirm that the offer was a serious one (with the caption "Carpe diem!" for the option). If the player doubles down on the offer, the minister reacts in surprise, but the screen fades to black, and some short pre-sex banter occurs followed by sound effects of rustling clothes and kissing.

- In the aforementioned "Age is Just a Number" quest in *Assassin's Creed Odyssey*, upon finding all the required items, the player returns to Auxesia and her husband, who expresses exhaustion at the prospect of bedding her. The player can choose to give them the ingredients for the aphrodisiac elixir OR offer to sexually satisfy Auxesia themselves. She immediately agrees, and a short scene shows the husband waiting outside as day turns to sunset, then to night, and then to morning. When the player emerges, the husband thanks them for their help and pays them for their service.

It is important to note that in all of these examples, the option to have sex to complete a quest is just that: an option. Unless your game is purely linear with set narratives and quests (e.g., *Wolfenstein*), players should never be "forced" to engage in sex in order to complete a quest or questline; there should always be either an alternative option (e.g., giving the aphrodisiac ingredients to Auxesia and leaving) or turning down the quest entirely (e.g., refusing Morrigan's ritual in *Dragon Age: Origins*). Otherwise, forcing players to actively engage in sex as the only way to complete a quest is questionable design at best, harmful, and upsetting for the players at worst. So always design quests with alternative non-sexual solutions in mind!

One last note for optional sexual quest completion: while the player may choose the sexual option for a variety of reasons, the motives of the player *character* are often non-explicit and open to interpretation, even with dialogue. For example, the player character in *Dragon Age: Inquisition* comments that they seek the "pleasure of [Minister Bellise's] company," but in context, it's unclear if this is genuine or simply an act to charm her. Leaving the player character's motives lightly sketched or with alternate interpretations allows the player to experiment and to put their own spin on their character's choice, particularly in cases where the player character is a blank slate vs. an established character.

SEX AS QUEST ENDING

These are quests where a sex scene or implied sexual activity is triggered upon completing a quest. This usually falls into two categories:

- **Sex as situational outcome** – This is when the circumstances, context, or emotional state of characters at the end of a quest leads naturally to the player character and NPC having sex.

- **Sex as quest reward** – This is when the player/player character is explicitly rewarded for completion of the quest by a character offering sex as a reward.

While the line between these two types of outcomes can blur, it is very important to be aware of the distinction and the underlying tropes and stereotypes beneath each, as they are not interchangeable. While sex-as-outcome can offer an organic, narrative way to transition into sex while still "rewarding" the player, sex-as-explicit-reward can result in clumsy, sex-negative, and often sexist presentation unless handled carefully and in specific contexts.

Sex as Situational Quest Outcome

Sex as a non-reward quest outcome can take many different forms but is usually directly informed by the narrative and the context of the quest in question. The common structure is that the player will complete the quest by handing in an item, reaching a destination, or speaking with a relevant NPC. In the immediate aftermath of the quest or event being over, either the player character or the NPC (or both) initiates a sexual encounter. The reason for this depends, of course, on the game, the characters, the dynamics between the characters, the context of the quest, and the larger narrative and game design in play. The possibilities are vast, but here are some starter examples:

- After a tense and dangerous mission is complete, the characters escape by the skin of their teeth, look at each other…and fall into each other's arms for the first time.

- Two characters are established as sexually active lovers; the end of the quest offers circumstances in which they can meet and engage in intimacy (e.g., a private room and a quiet moment)

- In the course of the quest, one character *becomes* physically and/or romantically attracted to the other(s) – for example, being impressed by their physical strength, looks, dedication, and personality – and at the end of the quest, acts on their attraction and initiate sex.

- In combination with the earlier discussed "sex as motive," the NPC may wish to have sex with the player character, but circumstances prevent it (e.g., they're too busy with other work, or they need a private space). If the player is willing to have sex, they may complete quests to improve these circumstances (e.g., taking work off the NPC's plate, arranging a private room). Once the quest is complete, the NPC and player take advantage of the more intimate situation.

In games with linear narratives broken down into quests and tasks, these sexual quest outcomes are often an organic part of the larger game narrative. For example, in *Wolfenstein: The New Order*, BJ and Anya first have sex after a short quest where BJ goes to the dining car for coffee and is waylaid by Nazis. The quest ends with a task to return to BJ's sleeping car. He does so, triggering a cutscene where BJ offers Anya the coffee, after which they have sex. In *Assassin's Creed Origins*, the rooftop sex scene between Bayek and Aya only happens after completing two assassination quests: one to kill a soldier tracking Aya and another to kill the last conspirator responsible for their child's death. Once both men are dead, and the quests are complete, Bayek reports back to Aya; the sex happens as both characters are overwhelmed with emotion and relief. In both cases, these sequences are triggered by the completion of a task or mission, but still within the context of the critical narrative path. The sex is also an organic part of both the quests and the larger story; it's not that sex is "rewarded" by the quest, but that the characters are in a more intimate mind state in the aftermath.

In games with branching narratives or sidequests, these encounters that end in intimacy can be part of larger relationship arcs or can be completely self-contained. As the name would suggest, sidequests are optional, and sexual sidequests are no exception; players should have the option to engage or refuse, either within the quest ending (e.g., refusing sex at the end) or by clearly signposting a sidequest's sexual nature BEFORE the player engages in it. Sometimes, these quests center around a minor NPC who is interested in the player character but has a minor role in the story; this might result in a quest spurring the NPC to suggest a one-night stand at the end. Other times, they relate to squadmates and love interest NPCs, doubling as personal quests to deepen a romantic relationship as well as having sex. This allows for greater development of the character relationships, as well as exploring their sexual side and tastes.

An excellent example of this latter kind can be found in Cassandra's relationship quest in *Dragon Age: Inquisition*. The quest centers around learning of Cassandra's long list of demands for what she considers romantic: candles, flowery poetry, and so on. The player/Inquisitor collects a series of these items, then sets up a romantic rendezvous in the nearby woods for her, and invites her to meet them. When she arrives, she discovers a romantic candlelit grove, and the Inquisitor reading aloud from a book of romantic, intimate poetry.

Touched and enticed by the gesture, the atmosphere, and the erotic poetry, Cassandra embraces the Inquisitor, and they have sex. It's a great example of how quest design can tie into sexuality and eroticism, tying the building of sexual tension to the progression and completion of tasks while not reducing those tasks to generic kindness coins or just "giving gifts" until she has sex. It highlights how quest tasks can connect more deeply with the characters' sexualities and fantasies, as at its heart, the quest is about Cassandra's erotic desires and romantic fantasies and seeking ways to fulfill them. The resulting sex is not a "reward" as much as a natural outflow of the feeling that the player has inspired.

But what is wrong with sex as "reward" anyway?

Sex as Quest Reward

Any sex scene after a quest is arguably a "reward" for the player, in the sense that any/all narrative scenes "reward" players who progress through the quest or game. Sex as quest reward, however, refers to a specific dynamic where an NPC, usually a quest-giver, explicitly indicates either at the beginning or end of the quest that the player will be rewarded sexually for their assistance or for completing the quest. A common variant of this is the "gratitude" approach, where the NPC will have coy dialogue asking, "how can I repay you?" or "allow me to show you how grateful I am" or "I'll make it worth your while," then initiating sex on quest completion. Depending on the game, sometimes they don't even bother with the dialogue! The key difference between "sex as quest reward" and "sex as quest outcome" is the explicit connection of sex as payment, reward, or in-world "gratitude" or trade for the player's in-game services (Figure 12.3).

There are several key issues with this model. The first and most important is that it moves away from a model of reciprocal enjoyment and engagement in sex, and downplays the NPC's sexuality and erotic interest. In the previous "sex as situational outcome" model, NPCs in might joke about being "grateful" for something the player did, but it's clearly not

FIGURE 12.3 "Thank goodness you came, hero! My car battery is dead. If you could help me jumpstart it, I'd be ever so…'grateful.'" (Daria Lukoiko/Shutterstock.com.)

the reason the NPC has sex. Rather, it is the NPC's own sexual interest in the player that spurs the intimacy. Their sexual interest is acknowledged openly, given weight, and made part of the larger text.

For "sex as reward," however, the sex isn't happening because of the NPC's sexual interest. Rather, sex is used as a bargaining chip or method of payment, stripped of pleasure or excitement for the NPC in question. While they still consent, they aren't having sex because they're eager to, or because they're attracted to the player, or because of their own desires. They are only having sex as a method of payment or reciprocation for the player's assistance. In other words, the *player*'s sexual pleasure and satisfaction (both in the game world and out of it) is the only thing considered and the only important element of the transaction, with little to no consideration of the pleasure or desire of the partner (Figure 12.4).

Of course, some NPCs use coy dialogue and offers of sex as a reward as a cover for genuine sexual interest – they DO actively desire the player character but offer a sexual reward as an "excuse" to act on that desire. But this raises the question of why they need an "excuse" to initiate sex in the first place? Use of this dynamic, even as a joke, can support some unhealthy sex-negative attitudes toward intimacy and sex, subsuming genuine desire as something that can't or mustn't be communicated openly, and covering it over with a one-sided transactional model that, again, prioritizes the player's interest, satisfaction, and pleasure over the NPCs.

It also leans heavily into a transactional model of sex. In short, sexual favors are being traded for an "equal value" of non-sexual favors – in this case, the tasks in the quest, such as killing monsters or collecting items (Figure 12.5). Sexual transactions do happen in real life and can work in certain contexts (which we'll discuss later). But in terms of modeling human interactions or relationships, there are some major problems. At best, it can miss out on opportunities for deeper exploration of character and sexuality, and at worst,

FIGURE 12.4 "…I mean, it's not like I'm actually interested in you or anything. I just left my wallet in my other car, and I gotta pay you back SOMEhow, I guess." (Daria Lukoiko/Shutterstock.com.)

Sex as Quest Reward:

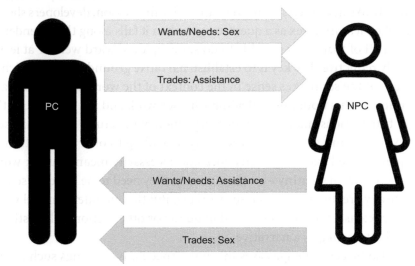

FIGURE 12.5 A breakdown of the transactional dynamics of sex as quest reward. In this case, "assistance" can mean anything to do with the non-sexual part of the quest (e.g., "Help, my farm's being harassed by bandits!") Also, note the gender dynamic…

it can be cold, impersonal, and reducing sex to a supply and demand trade. Rather than both characters wanting sex, one character (the player) wants sex but only has a specific non-sexual skill (e.g., combat skills) to offer, whereas the other wants a non-sexual problem solved with that skill, but…apparently only has sex to offer? The resulting trade is sterile, economic, and frankly, not particularly hot.

Also, we would also be remiss if we didn't note the huge role that gender and sexuality play in this dynamic. In quests that "reward" sex, overwhelmingly the player character is straight and male, while the character *doing* the rewarding (the NPC) is a convention-ally attractive cis female. Other gender combinations – e.g., a conventionally attractive male NPC offering sex as a reward to straight female player characters or queer male characters – are much, much rarer. Obviously, this has concerning implications in regard to which players are being catered to and which aren't. The persistence of "male player avatar rewarded with sex by attractive women" sounds like a sexual fantasy catered only to straight male players, meaning players of other genders and sexualities are ignored at best and made uncomfortable at worst.

But more importantly, this dynamic plays into a negative stereotype about women as "gatekeepers" and distributors of sex in return for favors, as opposed to enthusiastic part-ners and participants. In this model, sex is not portrayed as something the female NPCs want to have for its own sake; instead, sex is a bargaining chip or a form of payment, only to be given in return for the male PC doing something for them. It's a highly transac-tional, highly one-sided model of heterosexual sex, in which men are the only group who are interested in sex and are given sexual pleasure. Female desire is denied, and erotic agency and pleasure are diminished only to "giving the men what they want in trade for X."

It can also fuel highly sexist attitudes and stereotypes about women manipulating with sex or being useful only to satisfy men's sexual demands. For this reason, developers should be very, very careful when featuring sex as a quest reward when it falls along these gendered lines.

Having said all of that…it *is* possible to do sex as quest reward well, or at least in a way that isn't totally reductive. The key is to establish narrative ground rules in which the transactional nature of the sex makes sense in the context of the world and the characters. One obvious example of this would be in dealing with sex work and sex workers. In the context of sex work, transactions make sense: one pays money in return for certain sexual acts. In the context of a game, sex worker NPCs may be willing to offer similar transactions in return for quest-related assistance. This does not necessarily mean that sex worker NPCs and quests are free from scrutiny – on the contrary, they need to be handled sensitively and ideally with heavy creative input from sex workers. But they do offer a model where a character may offer sex as a transaction related to quests or other actions while still remaining consistent and interesting as a narrative.

There can also be certain edge cases involving speculative settings such as fantasy and science fiction. Depending on the worldbuilding of your game, certain cultural situations could call for offering sex as a reward or as a trade for something. This is particularly worth considering in terms of non-human characters such as aliens, demons, or other magical creatures and for situations where the player can choose a particular boon from these characters. If the player is dealing with a non-human entity who, in the context of the world, grants sexual wishes or favors in some capacity, it may be appropriate for the setting and the story to allow players to request sex as a reward for a quest or as a payment for some service or decision.

Some examples of sex as quest rewards:

- **Sex worker example** – In the first *Mass Effect* game, after completing Consort Sha'ira's quest regarding her previous client, the player returns to her and is given a non-sexual reward as well as some unique advice for the future. If the player expresses dissatisfaction with their reward ("That's it?"), Sha'ira then invites the player to close their eyes and then initiates a sexual encounter with them. The implication is that the sex is a further reward for the player's help (albeit a reward that must be asked for). It's implied that Sha'ira also enjoys the encounter; one shot shows a close-up of her hand slamming against a window or headboard as if in pleasure. While the scene is slightly awkward in its execution, it makes sense that Sha'ira is willing to offer sex as a further reward, given how she approaches sex as part of her work. Moreover, it establishes Sha'ira as being empathetic and insightful; she recognizes Shepard's dissatisfaction, sees exactly what WILL satisfy them, and offers that as a voluntary gesture of gratitude.

- **Speculative example** – In *Dragon Age: Origins*, to save a young boy called Connor, the player may confront the creature possessing him, a desire demon. Desire demons appear as beautiful, half-naked women with some monstrous features, and their modus operandi is to offer mortals their heart's desire in exchange for services or other boons. Upon meeting the player, in an effort to avoid combat, she offers a deal.

She asks that the player allows her to leave the boy peacefully and to return to repossess him at a later date. In return, she will give something "of value" to the player. She claims she offers "power, knowledge…pleasure…" The player can refuse and fight her, or accept her offer and request one of several boons in trade, including magic specialization, information, or a rune that offers in-game combat bonuses. The player can also demand "pleasure" as their boon. If they make this request, the desire demon will comment that the experience of sex with a desire demon will be unforgettable; she then approaches the player and kisses them as the screen fades to black. While the sex in this scene is transactional (sex in return for sparing the desire demon's life), it makes sense for the specific nature of the desire demon and how her magic, deals, and worldview operate. It also makes sense as a possible reward for the quest, in that the demons are explicitly connected to desire (sexual and otherwise), and it makes sense why a character might be intrigued enough by a desire demon to take her up on her offer and have sex with her.

CONCLUSION

Sex can serve many roles in quest design, whether serving as the initial motive, the final outcome, or even the actual quest itself. Ensuring that it remains narratively and ludically compelling without sliding into harmful stereotypes or dynamics requires careful thought, but the results can be well worth it and can add a note of romance, sensuality, excitement, and sexiness amid the many quests of your game.

WORKSHOP QUESTIONS

Analysis: Consider the game you're analyzing and its sex scenes. Would you say that the sex scenes function as part of a quest (i.e., a player mission or task, or chain of missions/tasks?). If so, do the sex scenes serve as the start of a quest, the quest itself, an outcome of the quest, or a quest reward? Is the sex integrated well into the quests, or does it end up feeling disconnected from either gameplay or storyline?

Creative: If appropriate to your project, design a quest or quest chain for your game that incorporates sexual content. Write out:

- Quest or quest chain title

- Summary of quest

- Opening of quest (e.g., first contact with quest-giver)

- Solution(s) for quest (include all possible solutions)

- Quest outcome(s) (include all possible branches and details)

- Quest rewards (if applicable)

Which of these phases is your sexual content in? How is it incorporated, connected, or related to the quest? Have you ensured that players can choose other solutions or paths in the quest? Is your aim to create organic sexual relationships, or explore sex as transaction? If so, how? What are the sexual themes and goals of your quest?

Document the important design details of your quest, along with your notes on the sexual content, and organize them in a format that is easily shareable with other team members and disciplines.

NOTES

1 Blizzard Entertainment, *World of Warcraft: Legion,* published by Blizzard Entertainment, PC/Mac, August 30, 2016.
2 Blizzard Entertainment, *World of Warcraft: The Burning Crusade,* published by Blizzard Entertainment, PC/Mac, January 16, 2007.

PART 4

The Craft of Sex Scenes

CHAPTER 13

Queer Sex in Games

Contributors: Kris Wise, Monica Fan,
Aubrey Jane Scott, and Antonin Fusco

THIS BOOK IS INTENDED to be used (and useful!) for all kinds of sexual content in games, regardless of the orientation of the content or the creators. My hope is that many of the tips, tricks, and considerations herein are universally applicable enough to be used for any and all sex scenes. After all, considerations like pacing, building tension, visual, audio, and quest design are always things you're going to need to consider for your sex scenes, whether they're queer or straight!

However, there are still unique considerations to keep in mind when creating and presenting queer sexual material in games, considerations that are subtly or not-so-subtly different from creating heterosexual scenes. These deserve their own chapter because, quite frankly, they rarely get their chance to be explored in mainstream gaming, and as a result, many developers may be unfamiliar or uncomfortable dealing with them. We all know how heterosexual scenes tend to play out in games – the vast majority of AAA or mainstream scenes are heterosexual – so we're all at least somewhat familiar with the mechanics and the details (even if some of them should be challenged from a gender POV) But it's worth focusing on tips and considerations unique to queer sex because, depending on what games they're playing, it can be easy for non-queer developers to remain blissfully ignorant of what they might need to approach differently, whether they're larger thematic differences or specific sex-related details that reflect the realities of queer sex.

For example, in the erotic queer visual novel, *Ladykiller in a Bind*, some lines of dialogue refer to the main character (The Beast) noticing that a female NPC (The Beauty) has short nails on her middle and index finger; from this, she realizes that the Beauty has sex with cis women (or, at least, people with vaginas) because…well, let's just say that having those nails be short is a VERY useful thing comfort-wise when sticking

DOI: 10.1201/9780429356650-17

those fingers inside certain places! That line, and the sexual connotations attendant to it, are a meaningful detail, not to mention an authentic one. The creator, Christine Love, knew to add details like these thanks to her own experience as a queer woman. But how many AAA games include these sorts of details, or even know to consider them in the first place? How many AAA queer women do we see with that particular manicure? In contrast, we have issues with scenes like the Peebee sex scene in *Mass Effect: Andromeda*, which reuses male Ryder sex animations and positions in the female Ryder version of the scene. This results in a somewhat awkward setup where Peebee is riding and grinding on…uh…nothing, it seems? It's the sort of accidental error that, while likely not meant in malice or disrespect, could have been avoided if the people involved had considered the logistics better and not assumed the same act in heterosexual sex would work the same way in sapphic sex.

So yes, a book about sex needs at least one chapter focusing on queer sex specifically. Moreover, though, it needs to be written from the perspective of queer creators – a variety of them, more importantly – and emphasizing their voice. And I'm not the right person to be writing this chapter, as my sexuality is…uh…let's just say it involves a lot of drooling over beautiful men and leave it at that.

But luckily, I was able to reach out to some great queer developers who were willing to answer some questions and give their perspective on queer sex in games – what games are doing it well, what they want to see more of, and what advice they'd give to developers who want to make compelling LGBTQ+ sexual content (both in general and for specific orientations of L, G, etc.). So, please meet my wonderful contributors:

- **Kris Wise (they/them)** – director and narrative designer of *Lunaris Games*, creator of steamy queer visual novels *When the Night Comes, Errant Kingdom, Call Me Under*, and upcoming *In The Blood*.

- **Antonin Fusco (he/him)** – game designer, and creator of the in-development queer male dating sim *Catboy Café*. His day job is patient information app development, but his free time is focused on queer-friendly and queer-focused games with cute catboys.

- **Monica Fan (she/they)** – game designer, graduate of Depaul University, treasurer of the IGDA Romance and Sexuality Special Interest Group, and (as of writing) a game design fellow at Schell Games.

- **Aubrey Jane Scott (she/her)** – trans woman of color working as a gameplay engineer at Monster Games, with experience making trans-inclusive character creators in the *NASCAR Heat* series; she also created the game *Goddess Grotto* which marries gardening with sexual identity.

Take it away, gang!

What are some games with sex/sex scenes that showcased hot/effective/good queer sex?

Kris – My first real experience with queer sex in video games was playing *Dragon Age Origins*. Despite those sex scenes being awkward thanks to the limited technology and also the choir as the backing track to our pants-on lovemaking, I still felt seen. To be able to flirt with the object of your affection without having to worry about the gender of your character is something that might be seen as insignificant to some, but as a queer gamer, it just adds that extra layer of immersion and inclusion that we crave, and that is often overlooked by a lot of the larger studios as a whole.

BioWare has always provided this in some shape or form in all *Dragon Age* and *Mass Effect* games, but I'd say that the most notable for me was Dorian Pavus in *Inquisition*. The fact that he was a gay man and that, not only did his whole story arc and romance route reflect that and stay true to him and his unique experiences as a queer person, but he had a sex scene in which the developers quite clearly went out of their way to make special, from the wonderful, thoughtful dialogue, to the stunning graphics and composition of the scene as a whole.

Another of my recent favorites has been *Hades* by Supergiant Games. Supergiant so perfectly encapsulated how important being thirsty for your own characters is when writing. You have little to no input in the narrative of the game, and the sex scenes included are simple fade-to-blacks with a few suggestive noises from the voice actors, and yet I thought it was incredibly well-executed and very, very hot. As well as the simplicity of their sex scenes being inspiring, I loved the very healthy polyamorous representation and the inclusion of a threesome; something we very rarely see in games, and if we do, they're usually pretty tasteless.

Antonin – Strange as it is to say, the pickings are extremely thin for queer masc people (I'll say MLM, queer men, or men from now on for brevity, but consider the terms to be inclusive of any masc-identifying person who experiences attraction to other masc-identifying people). Despite having no interest in them myself, I can more readily name acclaimed games that represent WLW relationships than any that do a good job portraying MLM experiences. The closest I feel that I can come is *Dragon Age II*, which accomplishes the task by creating MLM-romanceable characters that feel believable as queer men, even though they don't do anything within those romance tracks to situate the romance as specifically MLM. I still have strongly fond memories of Fenris, whose eyebrows I credit with getting me into game development (more on that later), and while I think that the carefully non-MLM-specific approach taken to romance there has limits, it is nonetheless a good primer.

That said, I'm thinking specifically of English-language and -localized games. If you can read the original Japanese or get direct translations, I'm told that some games there do portray MLM relationships with more specificity than even their own English localizations do.

Monica – This is a hard one as I don't think I have played a lot of games with queer sex (if there are many?). But one I recently played I really like is actually *Coming Out On Top* (2014). I like it because it shows a lot of porn tropes but then flip it on its head and constantly remind you this is not porn. I feel a lot of games/media like to use sex either for a shocking topic or reason or as a reward of some sort. As a sexual person who has survived more than one sexual assault, neither approach sits well with me. I like how *Coming Out On Top* (2014) treats sex as just sex. It is something on our minds a lot and something we do as humans. There isn't any shame or pink bubbles surrounding the topic of queer sex (Figure 13.1).

Don't stare at it. Don't stare at it. Don't. stare. at. it.

FIGURE 13.1 *Coming Out On Top* treats sex between gay men as a regular fact of life, rather than a shocking or shameful act. (Obscurasoft, *Coming Out On Top*, published by Obscurasoft, PC/Mac/Linux, December 10, 2014. Screenshot taken from C Ellison, Rock Paper Shotgun, "S.EXE: Coming Out On Top (NSFW)," December 19, 2014, https://www.rockpapershotgun. com/s-exe-coming-out-on-top-nsfw.)

> Personally as someone who studied sexuality in college and worked in safe sex activism, I appreciate the fact that the game does not shy away from showing sex scenes (instead of… fade to back with background noises). In addition, it is an R-rated game that shows a wide range of sex, including masturbation and fantasy towards forbidden partners.

> **Aubrey** – TBH, I haven't played many mainstream games that have queer sex scenes in them. I adored the sex scenes in *Ladykiller in a Bind*. I tend to think of games as an opportunity to explore different facets of my many overlapping identities It was great to get a chance to explore some of my submissive identity through the nightly sex scenes available. The way that it slowly and sensually takes you in deeper through conversation and the commanding presence of a lady domme gets me all in the mood. It was beautiful having agency in these scenes. I felt like I could stop where I wanted and every scene left me satisfied and wanting to come back each night to see where it would develop. I really appreciated seeing the vulnerability and care that went into the nightly sessions of the character practicing their knotwork and preparing for the scenes. It shows the level of commitment that is necessary for healthy dom/sub relationships to progress in a way that is so often glossed over in movies, books, and games.
> I think more than anything the intimacy that is created through these scenes is ideal for queer sex scenes. This of course is present in cis heterosexual sex scenes when done well, but the vulnerability of that intimacy is something that is really palpably present in queer sex for me. Something about having shared trauma and feeling seen in that moment by each other feels wholly more connecting than just screwing each other hard and having a good finish. I mean we do that too, many times over, but like the space and safety of checking in with

each other, helping each other feel seen, and staying connected is an incredibly vital part to a good sex scene for me.

Blood Pact from Ana Valens was also lovely hot erotic and kinky. Sure, this scene is between a trans girl and a demonic being who can control disembodied tentacles, but there is a slow sink towards the depths of eroticism this visual novel reaches. The inner thoughts of the character, the insecurities brushed away, and the absolute burning lust that cannot be contained within her. It is a show of letting yourself want something deeply and then realizing the having it and reveling in the enjoyment of it. There are all kinds of space in kink for queer sex because it inherently does not shame and is open to the possibilities of what feels good and welcomes consent. The combination is incredibly intoxicating and hot.

What are some recommendations you'd make for showcasing authentic, compelling, and hot scenes that are specific to queer sex?

Kris – One of the most important things I try to remember when I'm writing a sex scene is that everyone's experience as a queer person is different. We aren't a monolith, we're a community of incredibly diverse people who experience sexuality and relate to gender in a multitude of different ways. Whether you're writing a sex scene purely for eroticism, or if you're using that scene to try and convey a deeper meaning and further your narrative, then you need to keep that in mind and act accordingly. Also, as I said previously, being thirsty for your own characters is vital, especially if you're writing from the point of view of the player.

When writing my own games, I have to respect that our main character can have any pronouns and that anyone of any sexual orientation or gender could be playing. This means I tend to lean towards using prose and metaphorical language instead of being overly anatomical with my descriptions when referring to the player. Of course, you can still talk about anatomy, but I suggest approaching it as if you were choreographing a dance, but your dancers are…naked. Think about the rhythm and the flow, even the breathing. All of these things can be described in incredibly thirsty ways without straight-up mentioning genitals. Use the location of the act and focus on things within and around the scene other than the characters to evocatively imply what's happening. Suggestive things like crumpled sheets and bare skin bathed in neon light.

I write Visual Novels, which are obviously a little more reliant on just the narrative itself than games that might have more elaborate ways of showing sex scenes, so I think it's really important to make sure that I'm writing something that will both leave the player hot under the collar, but also wanting more. Unless you're writing in first person, and maybe even then, sex scenes in media are inherently voyeuristic, so treating them as such when writing can actually assist you in discovering what people will enjoy observing.

Of course, if you are creating a game where you can show and not just tell, if we take look at a certain cyberpunk RPG that came out recently I think it's safe to say that if you half-arse your representation when it comes to things like genital customization in an effort to be "inclusive," then you're going to simply end up doing more harm than good for your queer players. If you're going to give them the option in character creation to have different genitals, pronouns, and to pick their voice, then go to the effort to actually make those selections meaningful and not just a cheap trick. If you're not going to be able to find meaning in those things outside of character creation, then I would advise you to ask yourself what the purpose of it is and if it's really necessary. Sometimes less is more, especially when you're trying to represent a wide and varied range of human beings who are really just looking to feel included and like there's a place for them within these games that they so often get left out of or misrepresented in.

Antonin – Facial expressions are your golden ticket. Queer men emote differently than straight men, and your romances won't be exciting to your audience unless you capture how we relate to each other. For a quick example, look up images of Claude, Felix, and Dimitri from *Fire Emblem: Three Houses*: the first one's expression is warm, soft, and welcoming. He's a frequent subject of complaints that he's not romanceable by us. The other two are comparatively less popular, even among the considerable number of us who like partners to be a little mean in the bedroom. While I won't speak for anyone else, to me they look distant and cagey in a way that sends massive "don't touch" vibes and are therefore unappealing.

There's also a tendency to assume that "tops" (i.e., people who prefer to be the penetrative partner) are normatively masculine or straight-reading and -acting, and "bottoms" (receptive partners) are not. MLM do advertise their preferences to each other in their behavior and appearance, but it is at best orthogonal to the gender norms that straight people are used to. What really defines such preferences are what kinds of physical sensations you enjoy and, more tenuously, what your ideal relationship to power and desire is. Furthermore, most MLM I know have at least a weak preference for one or the other, but they rarely have a no-exceptions policy and will play around with other positions given comfort with their partner. Take this as an invitation to play around yourself! Give your bottoms facial hair and make your tops 5'2" and paint their nails on occasion. You'll probably find that they are easier to characterize as human beings if you let them live outside their role, and your audience will understand what you are going for.

Monica – I think the biggest thing is to not trying to fit queer sex into a heterosexual lens. For this, I blame lesbian porn that is made for straight guys, ha-ha! I feel as a queer person, it can be very upsetting to see queerbaiting these days (while decades ago, any queer representation would make me happy). I am a game designer, so I tend to focus on whether the system design and interaction design work with the story they are trying to tell and whether it is designed with care.

My biggest recommendation is to do a lot of research on the topic, as well as talk to people from that demographic. A lot of queer persons would be happy to help be your sensitivity reader when you show you care. Whenever I go to indie dev events that showcase queer games made by cisgender straight (usually male) people, I would like to ask them what games they play that have inspired their design process. I have been told by more than one designer that they never bothered to play many romance games and just decided to make dating sims because it's easy. It was even more concerning when someone proudly told me they didn't think the gender or racial identity matters in the story they tell. Maybe because I came out many years ago when it was a lot less safe to do so, my queer identity has been very important to me as a person especially when it comes to dating.

Another thing I care about is to make sure the players are protected. Being a female-presenting game dev and gamer, I encountered a lot of violence in both physical and digital places (unsurprisingly), and I have got into panic attacks/depression spirals while playing games either due to the content or due to the interaction with other players. I am an advocate of enough content warnings+options to block out content that includes sexual violence or stalking; I don't want to harm my players the way I have been, and I want my players to be able to go back to their normal lives after playing the game. Sometimes those topics can be empowering or educational, but only when the players are ready to face it. But sometimes, those issues can be solved with design, like allowing your player to block the stalker or fight back anytime, as opposed to forcing the player to receive the hate until a certain story point.

Aubrey – When talking about hot, erotic, and kinky, preferences tend to be so vast. I personally love the feeling of agency within a sex scene allowing me to be able to speed up or slow down the action at any point and still feel connected to my virtual partner. I want to be able to embody the character, but also be able to guide and choose in these most intimate moments. Sex is full of physical and connecting acts that have a way of bringing up strong emotions that surprise or overwhelm us. To be able to be held in the moment by the characters who we are connecting with and then be able to continue or just cuddle can be an extremely validating and hot experience all at once. Frequently these sorts of choices don't have to mean an end to the action and will often lead to hotter scenes shortly after or in a future encounter.

Queer sex also tends to allow us to encounter a variety of sexual and gender identities and figuring out the right way to support each other in the moment is quite common. We don't always match up, but often we can get all our needs met without anyone getting hurt through communication in the moment. Feeling heard tends to deepen my connection and allow me to push past barriers that may have stopped me even moments before. This is not always the case and choice of the player and their preferences should definitely be respected.

I'd love to see more sex scenes with characters who are figuring themselves out and growing in the moment. Scenes where both characters experience emotional growth through the experience. Sex that isn't the culmination and reward of the relationship but is just another part of the relationship that grows and changes as your characters get closer. For some, sex and sexuality is what makes them different. For others, sex is just the piece of their identity or may be relatively unimportant or they actively avoid it. The thing about queer sex is we hold space for all these people and experiences, but that need to connect is present, whether it is through physical touch or just existing in the same space as someone else while you each do your own thing.

What details would you like to see more of in queer sex/sex scenes (within your interest/ orientation, etc.) that ground it in reality, make it more sexy, make it more authentic, etc.?

Kris – One of the things that we've always done in our games is to give the player the option to express themselves sexually in a way that feels authentic to them. Most of the time in sex scenes in gaming, you find yourself being told which way you're going to do it and to just sit back and watch, but in reality, there's a wealth of different preferences when it comes to *how* you have sex. From positions to speed, to dirty talk, and more, sexual experience customization is something that can be achieved if you're using a branching narrative or options system. For example, giving the player the option to either take the lead or to be the one being led by their partner during sex, and beyond that, you can give them further options to pick between getting really hot and heavy or keeping it relatively sweet and sensual (Figure 13.2).

Working with sexuality and gender as a more fluid concept when writing queer characters is essential, and be realistic when portraying these scenes. Whether it's your lesbian character cutting her fingernails to ensure she doesn't hurt her partner, or your queer characters having a drawer full of lube in their bedside table, every little detail is appreciated when it comes to this kind of much-needed authentic representation. There are so many great guides to having queer sex available for free online, and also researching queer erotic literature to see how others write it can be incredibly helpful.

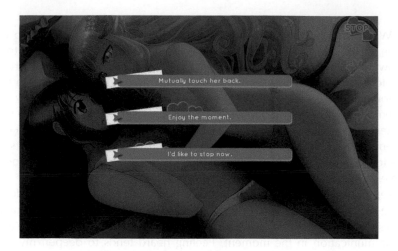

FIGURE 13.2 *Cute Demon Crashers!* depicts queer sex (and straight sex, for that matter!) in the context of the player choosing what they want and how they express themselves sexually. (SugarScript, *Cute Demon Crashers!*, PC/Mac/Linux, partial version published April 7, 2015, full version published August 15, 2015. Screenshot from English Otome Games, "Cute Demon Crashers!" April 8, 2015, https://www.englishotomegames.net/post/115877512766/cutedemoncrashers.)

Antonin – Anal sex requires some combination of lube, practice, and considerable patience at first. Lack of the former especially involves a lot of friction and is not fun unless you are specifically into it. Eliding this isn't really the end of the world, especially if your setting makes lube difficult to find (middle of the woods, anyone?), but reference to going slower during initial penetration makes it more realistic and is a good way to subtly show that a top who is playing rough still is caring for his partner.

In my experience, there seems to be a difference in preferred terminology. Among the men I've talked with, tops seem to prefer the word "cock" and bottoms the word "dick" in reference to their own genitalia.

Monica – What I would like to see more is normalization of the fact that everyone has different sexual histories and attitudes towards sex. I have played many games where sex is the final reward, which doesn't always make sense to everyone. There are people who prefer to never have sex, and there are people who like to have sex early on before settling into relationships. I get annoyed whenever I see discourse in the lane of, "She's not into you now, but if you send her enough gifts and compliments, she will open up to you," because I blame a lot of dating violence in my generation on this discourse. I wish I could see more acknowledgment that everyone has different preferences and limits when it comes to sex and that we should respect that instead of trying to push the limit.

Another thing I want to see more is masturbation, because I think it is an amazing way to experience sex, and it is empowering. One thing some non-profit organizations do to help women suffering domestic violence is to teach them how to masturbate as a way to help establish their independence and autonomy. I want to see it to be more normalized, especially with non-cis-male characters. Also when designed/written the right way, masturbation scenes can be useful to help players understand the character better.

Aubrey – I would love to see a separation of agency between the player and the character. There have been times where I want a fade to black button to get me out of the scene now, but I want the characters to continue their experience because it is what is right for them. I would also love the opportunity to turn off the visuals or sound in the moment to continue to read the text and maybe bring them back when I feel I am ready to re-engage or choose to fade to black completely and pick up in the next scene. Sex with queer folks tends to bump up against a lot of trauma and sensitive subjects. It is hard to predict what will come up, but it is important that I be able to continue to progress through the game even if the particular scene is not for me. Controls like this also allow me to engage in such a way that is similar to having a partner who checks in with me throughout our experience. It would feel connecting and important to have this level of flexibility and control over the content.

I tend to react completely differently to full-on animation than I do to illustrations or simply text descriptions. As a gameplay engineer, I understand that creating a dynamic system like this is not simple, but being able to close my eyes and listen through a scene or quietly read through it without whatever bits were triggering to me is incredibly important to being able to continue to engage with the game and content in which I am otherwise interested.

I would also love to see more aftercare as that closeness is such an important part of the sex and connecting process. You see this in some movies where the scene fades out and then comes back in during a close moment. In queer sex, this aftercare can happen just after before more sex happens, when you wake up in the morning or even days later. The important thing, checking in with your partner and connecting is just so frequently brushed over that we don't get to complete the feeling. Movies often have a scene after the climax to show the reactions of characters so the viewers know how to feel. Seeing aftercare accomplishes this but also models healthy behaviors that are important for anyone engaging in intimate sexual experiences. Being intentional about what we model and show in our sex scenes is incredibly important and should be carried through with thoughtfulness and care.

If you were speaking to developers who do not share your orientation (particularly cis/straight developers, but also queer developers who may be of different orientations than you)

1. **What are good resources you would recommend for them to learn more about writing queer sex geared for your orientation/attraction/interest?**

Antonin – Your gay friends. Seriously. We're all extremely opinionated as a product of living in a world without many guide rails on how to behave as ourselves. Failing that, look up queer masc artists on Twitter and see what you see. (Though do be prepared for a lot of penises. Perhaps unsurprisingly, we're pretty fond of them.)

Though you might be tempted to look at them, almost all of the romance games that depict MLM scenes that I have encountered are produced by female creatives for a female audience, and so they aren't representative of what MLM themselves would like to see.

Aubrey – *Sense8* is a beautiful love letter on the LGBTQ+ experience of found family and has many beautifully done queer sex scenes. Most of the orgy scenes from the show result from the queer characters' deep connecting sexual acts rippling through the rest of the cluster. Small details that they add to let you know Nomi is trans, like her estrogen injection before their passionate sex, which closes the scene on the lubed, discarded, rainbow strap-on. Their inclusion of these scenes at points to affirm their love for their partners and in response to really feeling seen by them is essential to the scenes feeling so well crafted. They have story purpose as well as titillating properties.

Boy Meets Girl is a lovely film about the trans experience, and the sex scene between the main character and her love interest is particularly good to me because of the exploration, intimacy, and accepting nature of it.

Girl Sex 101 by Allison Moon is a lovely trans-inclusive primer on everything surrounding girl sex. It is far and away one of the best sex education books on a variety of sex education topics through a lens of femme sexuality with inclusive pieces for all sorts of anatomy.

Come as You Are by Emily Nagoski was pivotal in changing how I approach women's sexual functioning and how I write and shape my sex scenes.

Crazy for You by Harper Bliss – Lovely hot lesbian sex scenes full of intimacy and deep connection.

Queens of Geek by Jen Wilde – The chase and the soft romance here is so utterly wholesome and hot mixed into one. I regularly return to this book for the gooey amazing queer take on classic rom com story with a bit of nerdy ambiance thrown in.

Everything Leads to You by Nina LaCour – A slow burn soft romance novel developing as the main character solves a mystery involving her love interest.

Bad Dyke by Allison Moon – A memoir of a kinky queer sex educator with amazing touchstones for queer sex.

Nevada by Imogen Bennie – A hot kinky sex scene opening up an incredibly authentic take on the trans existence. I've heard this is the novel where the term egg originally comes from as there is a clear example of a very eggy trans girl who denies her trans experience for the longest time. Has many different windows into the trans experience through a fictional narrative.

The Ethical Slut by Dossie Easton and Janet W Hardy – kinky queer sex and how to approach it with ethics and morals.

The New Bottoming Book and *The New Topping Book* by Dossie Easton and Janet W Hardy – Sub and Dom counterparts on how to safely and healthily engage in these dynamics. These can be essential primers if you are exploring dom/sub dynamics in your sex scenes.

Sexy Microtalks GDC 2019 - Christine Love's section especially, but all of them are amazing examples. This whole microtalk series each year is amazing and lovely.

2. **Beyond differences in physical detail different kinds of queer sex and/or non-queer sex (e.g., "X position works for a partner with a penis, not a partner with a vagina,"), are there any larger, more fundamental differences developers should be aware of?**

Antonin – Probably the single best piece of advice that I can give is this: treat your straight female audience as completely separate from your queer male audience, *even and especially when designing MLM content*. In my experience, women generally consume MLM content looking for totally different things than men, and what turns one audience on often alienates the other. Some examples:

- Most women I have talked to have expressed distaste for unminimized bulges on clothed characters, especially outside of actively sexual scenes; every MLM I've spoken to enjoys them. (Though they want the ability to pick their own size if their avatar is represented! Small penises are a thing for some folks.)

- Characters who present a cold or distant demeanor are dramatically more popular with women I have spoken to than men. More emotive characters, and especially more sexually forward or flirty characters, are very popular with men but often cause women to express alarm, disgust, or discomfort.
- Characters expressing self-loathing or disgust with homosexuality before/during a romance scene is a specific fetish for some men and should be handled carefully, though most women consumers of MLM seem to take it as a standard trope.
- Queer men are significantly more interested in strongly queer-coded and non-normative gender performances than most women consumers of MLM that I've interacted with, whose tolerance for such behaviors is generally dramatically smaller. On the flip side, though they are wildly popular with women, very straight-coding male characters are begrudgingly accepted in MLM communities as the best we're likely to get. (There is an active fetish community for straight-acting men, but that's not broadly indicative of the audience.)

Aubrey – Sex for me as a lesbian tends to happen regardless of how clothed or unclothed I am. We can have a really lovely moment quickly and passionately without having to shed all our clothes and get down to business. The preamble is part of the main event and in many cases is a whole act or 3 in a marathon of lovemaking. Building up the headspace of sexiness, grinding on your partner's leg while she pins you to the wall kissing you hard, and fondling your breasts beneath your shirt can be what you're here for, and that's totally normal. These scenes can also be asymmetrical, one partner getting some then the other reciprocating in a later scene. Queer sex is about equity and not as much about equality of every scene. It is a long game of meeting each other's needs at each new opportunity.

There is also quite a variety of folks and preferences in this space. One partner may be poly-orgasmic and climax multiple times in short spans, heightening the feeling each time to the point that they may orgasm just from giving pleasure to their partner or being told when to orgasm depending on the power dynamic of the relationship. The other partner may need time and rest after their orgasm and may spend most of their time pleasing their poly-orgasmic counterpart to have a really connecting powerful orgasm together when it is their turn and their partner worships them and their body.

The thing about queer sex is that it breaks a lot of rules and norms. There are much more open boundaries giving you a more, "mix and match," or, "figure it out as you go," sort of feel. This is a shift from heterosexual sex because there is more of a common script with, "p in v," sex. You have to think about queer sex in a more creative way because the shortcuts don't get you there as easily or worse are active turn-offs that can be ramps out of the action for many queer folks.

[...] Spend some time reading trans stories written by trans folks. Read queer sex education books written by queer kinky people. Understand how women have a mostly different and more widely varied experience than men. Read some primers on LGBTQIA+ communities and the multitude of people who make them up. These are all the basis for which queer people understand themselves and others. Usually we have to figure it out, but this shared connection allows us to shed prescribed identities to uncover authentic experiences full of our deepest desires. We have to completely reinvent ourselves and it is hard to understand how it changes everything about you including sex and romance without experiencing it first hand or immersing yourself in the culture.

I do not recommend reading and watching stuff mostly created by cis and non-queer folks. People outside the community have been telling our stories for a long time, so it is important to make sure you have a strong basis in how queer, trans, and gender non-conforming folks understand their own experiences. You have plenty of time to read the take of cis straight folks on trans and queer relationships after you have a good base. Understand that there is a growing amount of queer content, but it is so much smaller in comparison to cis het experiences. So you will need to do some legwork to find good content and sources.

WORKSHOP QUESTIONS

Analysis: Did the game you have chosen to analyze include queer sex as part of its content? Was it part of the main storyline, or relegated to "background" (e.g., minor dialogue implying off-screen sex between NPCs?) Was it optional, or part of the core critical path?

- Queer readers: How did this content make you feel? Do you feel it did a good job presenting queer sex and queer characters in the context of sex? If it was geared towards you as a target audience (e.g., a gay male sex scene geared towards gay male players), did it appeal to you on that level? How would you make it differently?

- Non-queer readers: Research online responses from queer fans, players, and critics towards this content. Read their feedback and focus on their reasoning (do not pester them online, though!) In your own words, try to describe your understanding of why they like or DON'T like certain aspects of the scene(s) in question. Prioritize listening to what queer players and game critics have to say!

Creative: Consider the role of queer content in your game, particularly in regards to sex. Do you intend to have queer sex scenes, straight sex scenes, or a mix? If you are doing a mix, how will you ensure that the queer sex scenes are given the same amount of time, detail, eroticism, etc., as any straight scenes?

- Queer creators: Are you creating content aimed at a broad spectrum of queer players, or at a specific queer subculture (e.g., gay men using hookup apps, or queer trans women)? There's no right answer here, but it will help you tailor the sex scenes you're creating. What realistic (or idealized?) details might you include in sexual content? What, in a perfect world, do YOU want to see in your game that reflects your sexual experience or desire?

- Non-queer creators: If at *all* possible, bring on team members or contractors who are queer and have personal experience with the sort of content you are trying to make, and ensure their input is not ignored. Their perspective will be invaluable in creating better content. If expanding your team is not possible (or if you are working on this game solo), research and budget queer sensitivity readers for your content. Lastly, as Aubrey recommends, research media and games created by queer writers and designers and take notes on how they present this content.

CHAPTER 14

Initiating Sex with Branching Choices

I N LINEAR GAMES, THE transition from the main narrative to a sex scene is usually triggered if the player reaches a particular story beat; they occur regardless of the player's input. In contrast, nonlinear games put the "if" and sometimes the "when" more in the control of the player. We've discussed how nonlinear games can track certain values (affection, attraction) to trigger sexual encounters with characters. However, in many visual novels, indie games, and AAA RPGs, regardless of how the attraction has developed or the relationship has been built, there is often still a key conversation or choice that the whole thing pivots on, a single question that you as the player and character must answer…

So, are you *actually* going to have sex, or what?

A lot of modern game and narrative design around sex and romance revolves around designing singular key decisions that trigger a sex scene. There may need to be prerequisites to getting these key decisions – e.g., having to build up enough attraction or develop a deep relationship – and of course, we'll be talking in other chapters about how to build the sexual tension in the scene leading up to the final decision. But there is still usually at least a single choice that serves as a turning point, that takes a "detour" from the main story to focus on a moment of sexual intimacy. Games like *Mass Effect* allow players to build relationships with characters, culminating in an intimate visit or moment, but when that moment comes, whether the sex happens or not depends on a single yes/no choice.

Having a clear "opt-in/opt-out" decision is important for allowing players to tailor their experience around their comfort and their vision for the relationship, but there is so much more that can be done with these choice points. Later, we'll also discuss how choice-based design (and other kinds of player agency) can be employed IN the sex scene itself, how players can choose what to say to their sexual partner or even what sorts of sexual acts to perform. But here, we'll focus on the initial choice to suggest or accept a sexual encounter and how it can be approached in a broader perspective than just "yes" and "no."

DOI: 10.1201/9780429356650-18

THE BIG Y/N QUESTION

That's not to downplay the importance of offering players a choice to refuse a sexual encounter. As discussed in an earlier chapter, it's one of the most important choices that should be offered. Linear games can get away with prescribed, mandatory sex scenes, partly because the player characters (PCs) are separate enough from the players that they make their own sexual decisions. In a branching, choice-guided narrative, however, **the player should always have an in-character opt-out of any and all sexual and/or romantic content.** This gives the players options both in and out of game narrative; they may want to develop or role-play their character in a way where that character would refuse sex or they may be opting out purely for personal comfort reasons, and doing so in a way that doesn't disrupt the flow of the narrative. As such, there should always be a clearly signposted, in-character option that ends the encounter or at least the sexual aspect of the encounter.

Similarly, any choices that *do* lead to sex should be equally clearly signposted; an innocent or accidental choice should not lead to unexpected sex. This is an issue that several games have, including some sex scenes we've already discussed (e.g., the Sha'ira scene in *Mass Effect*); quite often, the relevant option to start the sexual encounter doesn't actually signal anything inherently sexual about it. Care should be taken to ensure that every choice for agreeing to sex is clear to the player and that they won't be completely surprised by what happens. This does not necessarily mean needing to explicitly spell it out in dialogue ("Let's have sex!") or action choice ("Make Love"). But it does mean clearly signposting that there is an erotic undertone to it, an invitation charged with a meaning that is clear to the player AND the character…"Stay the night," "Be with me," and so on. The point is, you do not want your players choosing an innocuous-sounding dialogue option or even a romantic but nonsexual gesture like a kiss, with no hint of what it is going to escalate to (Figure 14.1).

FIGURE 14.1   "All I did was pick the option for, 'Brag about how white my sheets are!' I didn't think I'd be inviting him to come up and see for himself!" (WAYHOME studio/Shutterstock.com.)

Eagle-eyed readers will likely, at this point, be putting two and two together and asking, "Hang on, giving players and characters the choice to knowingly accept or refuse sex? This is about consent, isn't it?" And indeed, it is. Consent for both player and PC is absolutely vital...SO vital that, well, the entire next chapter is going to focus on it! So, I won't dwell on it here for too long, but suffice to say, yes, the *bare minimum* of respecting player and character consent is to give them the key choice, clearly marked, to say yes or no to sex.

But designers and writers should not stop there.

BEYOND THE YES/NO BINARY

If writers and designers only go so far as giving players the ability to say yes or no to a sex scene and do not take the time to explore the nuances of the choice, this can result in larger narrative problems (Figure 14.2). Many of these problems are compounded if there is only one sex scene with a character, as discussed in the chapter on sex and three-act structure. If there is only one choice to have sex with, say, a romanced love interest, and the choice boils down to a yes or no:

- There may be no further opportunities to pursue or engage in sex in the game, placing unnecessary weight on this one option; it becomes less a question of, "do you want to have sex now" and more "do you want to have sex *ever* in this game?"

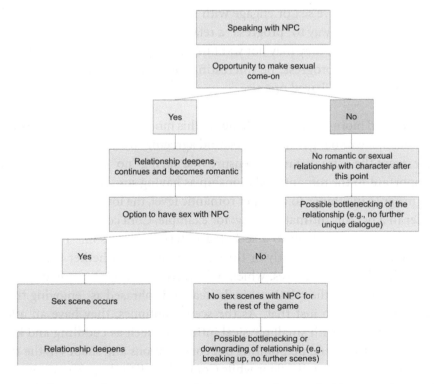

FIGURE 14.2 A diagram of common game design centered around a binary yes/no model for sex scenes. Note the relationship bottlenecking for both romantic AND sexual content and how they can also bottleneck platonic interactions and dialogue.

- A binary choice does not allow for nuance in the acceptance or refusal, either in terms of the player's own wishes or the way they are role-playing their characters. In many cases, a person may have a nuanced refusal of sex, for example, they may not be ready yet but would be interested in later opportunities, even if those later opportunities may not occur within the scope of the game. By reducing it to a binary yes/no, it becomes a permanent, simplified state for the entire relationship; do you want sex now or never have sex with this character again?

- A particularly egregious problem with some of the yes/no choices is to connect the "no" directly with the relationship itself, phrasing the "no" as "Let's just be friends," or "This isn't going to work out." In other words, if you refuse sex, it's equivalent to breaking up. This obviously has hugely problematic implications, suggesting that players have to agree to sex in order to "keep" a lover, suggesting that sexual desire is binary (i.e., if you don't want to have sex NOW, you're not interested ever) and conflating sexual desire with romantic feelings (i.e., if you don't want sex, then clearly, you're totally disinterested in a romantic relationship!).

- Even in games where the "no" isn't tied to a breakup, there can still be problems where refusing sex may result in being "stuck in a rut." If the only way to develop or deepen a relationship is to have sex with a character, then refusing results in the relationship being frozen in place at best or, at worst, being ended entirely. This results in players who prefer not to have sex or engage with sexual content in an uncomfortable position, where the only way to "progress" a relationship route (or even get new dialogue) is to agree to sex that they may not want to have. Again, the theme seems to be "relationships can only progress, be interesting, or deepen if the characters have sex," which is obviously a flawed premise.

To be fair, more and more games are challenging this model and finding ways to keep developing relationships without gating them behind agreeing to sex. *Mass Effect: Andromeda*, for example, went the extra distance to ensure that saying "no" felt as meaningful, engaging, and important to the romantic relationship as having sex. For several of the relationships, after progressing things to a deeper romantic level, the love interest would approach the PC Ryder in a private, intimate setting; for example, Cora comes to visit Ryder in their bedroom, while Jaal takes them to a secluded waterfall. After some romantic conversations, the love interest asks (directly or through implication) whether the player is interested in sex. The player can say yes, which will trigger an erotic sex scene, but saying no does not end the scene or the relationship. Instead, it is phrased as "enjoying the moment as it is," and the lovers do just that. As the scene continues, they have an affectionate, emotional conversation, with small physical intimacies such as cuddling and kissing: For example, Cora and Ryder end up pointing out constellations and shapes in the stars, eventually sitting and cuddling on the floor while Cora drifts off to sleep. These scenes are given similar narrative attention and weight as the sex scenes; in fact, in some cases, the conversations you have with your love interest can ONLY be had by choosing to refrain from sex. The design for these choices allows players who are not interested in sexual encounters to continue deepening the connection between their characters and to experience meaning-ful, unique content. Here, we can see another best practice for branching choices and sex: **do not gate or bottleneck relationship development behind choosing to have sex with a character,** and wherever possible, offer those who choose the nonsexual route an equally meaningful narrative and gameplay experience.

This is a clear improvement over a model that bottlenecks relationships, but there is still a small, niggling issue; the fact that, as the only possible sex scene with the love interest, it still serves as a yes/no binary, just along a different axis. Instead of "do these characters have a relationship (with sex) or break up/not get together," now the question is, "do these characters have a sexual relationship or never bring up sex ever again?" There is still room for greater nuance and better reflection of how human beings (or their nearest equivalents in sci-fi and fantasy settings) can negotiate and initiate sex, and how the game systems can allow for more experimentation and looseness in the initial conversation.

MOVING FROM QUESTION TO CONVERSATION

In terms of designing choices around initiating, rejecting, or accepting sex, there should be room for actual play and back-and-forth. This should not be approached in a coercive way (neither PC nor nonplayer character (NPC) should be able to keep pestering a character who has already said no!) but in a way that allows greater scope for different kinds of hesi-tation vs. eagerness and allows for the player to experiment within those boundaries. And sometimes, even just adding an extra option can be enough to expand the decision past the simple binary and give the scene greater nuance or role-playing potential.

Let's walk through a potential example. Let's say you have an NPC love interest who is written to be very forward, sex-positive, and open about their interest in others. Not long after they join the party, after a series of reasonably positive interactions, the NPC approaches you and propositions you for sex. A binary answer would boil down to "yes" or "no" but consider adding a single extra option and expanding it to, "Yes," "Not inter-ested,"…and "Not right now."

While this might seem like hairsplitting between negative responses, there is a lot of poten-tials as far as narrative design and game design can expand from here. Not interested would shut down any sexual relationship for good. Depending on the characters (or, potentially, another conversation subtree where the player can clarify further), it may also result in shut-ting down any possibility of romance. In contrast, "not right now" leaves the future open, both to the characters themselves and to player interpretation. Even if there is no more sex in the game, "fanon" (i.e., fandom's shared interpretations or expansions on the canon) can often spring up about how things develop "off-camera," and leaving the door open to it can encour-age players to use their imaginations. On top of this, "not right now" can offer some intriguing opportunities for further storytelling, role-playing, and character exploration (Figure 14.3):

- It could immediately lead to another conversation tree in which the love interest and the player talk out where the player is at. The player could then choose dialogue options to reflect their character's reason for hesitating. It could be due to unresolved feelings for another NPC, or uncertainty about their feelings for the NPC they're with, or a

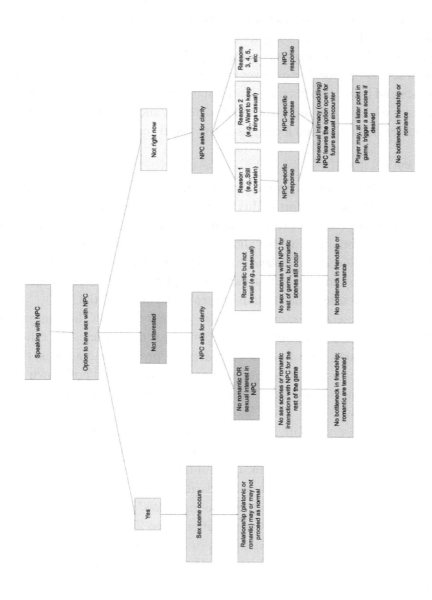

FIGURE 14.3 An expanded flowchart showing how an extra choice+subtrees can make for a more nuanced, fluid conversation about accepting/refusing sex.

need for a deeper, more committed relationship before taking that step, or even something like, "I want to make love on a comfortable bed, not in a camp in the middle of nowhere!" Options like these allow the player to better develop the PC's personality, both in terms of how they communicate and in terms of what their inner feelings are. In turn, the love interest's responses reveal more about them as a character – are they warm and understanding, hurt and wary, or even annoying and persistent?[1]

- In terms of long-term narrative, the love interest can back off and tell the player to "come find them if they change their mind," or other indications that are progressing to sex will be left up to the player. Other romance or relationship conversations will still take place in the future, with no bottleneck due to the sex choice. Moreover, the player can approach the love interest at a future time to talk about the subject again and will have an option to pursue sex again ("About your proposition..."). This can trigger a short contextual dialogue ("Oh, so you've been thinking about it, hmm?") and another choice between yes, no, or not right now. And if the player picks yes...then yes, they still get the sex scene.[2]

This branching choice tree can be expanded and refined even further. For example, what if saying "yes" had as many variants and shades of nuance as the refusals? For example, perhaps the player can answer, "Yes, but only if it's casual," or "Yes, but only if it means something." This can prompt different responses from their sexual partners, possibly even entire new conversational trees. What if the love interest replies, "I can't promise it will be casual/meaningful, is that okay?" What new responses can this prompt from the player? Acceptances/refusals can also be explored through the lens of different personalities ("I guess" vs "Hell yeah!" vs "I've been dreaming of this" etc. etc.) If designers and writers are willing to broaden and deepen these trees, the results can produce a lot of interesting character interaction and dynamic narrative around sex and the invitations to have it.

Of course, once we get into the sex itself, both player and NPC might want to say yes or no to specific acts or things...but we'll get into that when we talk about consent and/or branching choices in a sex scene.

PLAYER AS INITIATOR

So far, we've been mostly discussing scenarios where the player is responding to an invitation from an NPC, either positively or negatively. But what if the player is the one inviting the NPC to have sex? If they have already been building attraction and sexual tension with a character (via chemistry casino or other means), how to handle moments where the player is the one who decides to act on that attraction and tension first?

Firstly, the issue of yes/no may be a little different here depending on the narrative design of your sexual and romantic relationships. There may be less need for an explicit opt-out choice, because...well, players can already "opt out" by not pursuing an NPC in the first place! However, care must be taken to ensure that the player will never be "stuck" with no option other than to pursue a sexual encounter. Alternate choices and dialogue options should be provided on top of the sexual approach, as well as a potential "eject" button to end the conversation or scene if it gets too intense or does not feel right. This may be less of a "not-interested" or "not-right-now" choice, and more of a, "I think that's enough for now," or "hang on, second thoughts!" option. You can assume that the player is at least interested as they deliberately pursued these options, but that they may have misjudged their level of comfort. Having a soft "eject" becomes particularly useful and important once the sex scene gets underway…but again, we'll discuss that in a future chapter.

Another thing to consider when designing choices to initiate sex is to allow players to not only choose whether or not to approach but HOW to approach. In reality and fiction, the paths to two people having sex are endless. It could be a brash and blunt "Hey, wanna screw?" or a poetic, flowery declaration of passion, or something awkward and stuttered out, or even just a physical action like a glance, a kiss, or a piece of clothing dropped on the floor. The scope may stop you from giving the player an *infinite* amount of choice on how they engage their partner, but this is still a great place to give them the tools to role-play what sort of a character they are and how they express their sexual side. Will they be suave, gentle, or awkward? How will they phrase their questions and invitations to their lover? Will they communicate through words or will they show their intentions through physical actions like passionate kissing – and if so, do they wait for the verbal confirmation to do it, or is it the fantasy of sweeping someone off their feet mid-sentence?

And how will the NPC react? In some games, once the baseline attraction/romance is set, the NPCs may respond positively to *all* approaches, just in different ways (e.g., responding tenderly to a romantic proposition vs. getting hot and bothered with a more lustful approach). In other games, the player's approach might actually tie into a failstate if you don't approach the NPC in the right way. The NPC may react positively or negatively to certain approaches, possibly refusing sex altogether if they don't feel aroused or engaged by the player's approach (Figure 14.4).

FIGURE 14.4 "Ugh, I was all for it until he picked the 'Nice tits, wanna do it?' dialogue option." (Antonio Guillem/Shutterstock.com.)

CONCLUSION

Branching choices are only one way to grant a player agency and to apply a nonlinear design to the story, but they're still a powerful way of navigating sex, consent, and character connection. Again, sex is not where one wants to start skimping on thoughtful game/narrative design, and rethinking how branching choices can work to initiate or reciprocate invitations to sex can be the foundation for new stories, character moments, and gameplay experiences.

It is also one of the cornerstones of designing around consent…which leads us to the next chapter…

WORKSHOP QUESTIONS

Analysis: Examine the lead-in to the game's sex scene and pinpoint the key decision point that triggers it. Is it a choice to approach a character, or is it a yes/no/other response to a character's sexual proposition? What are the different outcomes for each choice? (e.g., agreeing vs. refusing)? Do these outcomes seem sufficient, or is there room for other variations and nuances in terms of the player choice?

Creative: If appropriate to your game design (e.g., if you are using branching choices like in visual novels or RPGs), plot out the key initiation decision that triggers (or doesn't trigger) a sex scene in your game.

- Consider **at least three** possible choices that the player can take and model out how each choice plays out.

- Where appropriate, outline other dialogue or choice subtrees that these choices lead to (e.g., letting the player choose their reason for hesitating, clarify their lack of interest, respond to NPC questions, etc.)

- If there is a potential for a romantic relationship, ensure that there is a route to continue the romance without needing to agree to sex.

Outline the decision tree in a flow chart similar to Figure 14.3 or in another format that works for you and your team.

NOTES

1 Be very careful about making characters whiny or persistent around sex. This is another area where one can easily hit real-world triggers and bad memories, particularly for marginalized people, of previous sexual partners who would not take no for an answer. When in doubt, always default to your NPCs respecting your PC's refusals.

2 Whether it's the same sex scene that was offered earlier in the game (i.e., reusing the same sexual content) or whether it's a brand-new sex scene depends heavily on your game's scope, budget, locations, and narrative – perhaps the characters are now in an entirely new place that requires new positions, etc.

CHAPTER 15

Consent in Video Game Sex

N o discussion of sex would be complete without touching on the all-important theme of consent. As discussed at the start of the book, this book is focused purely on mutually consensual sex scenes. Themes like rape, sexual violence, and coercion are not in the scope of this book, and the tools we've detailed so far are not intended for that kind of content. So if you've read this far, we'll assume that the sexual content you're intending for your game is the kind where everyone involved is actively eager to have sex or at least willing to do it for their own reasons.

Consent is vital to the success of almost all sex scenes, but many games, particularly in the mainstream, are somewhat hazy and vague on the subject and never really tackle it head-on. That is NOT to say that the scenes in question are nonconsensual – it's clear from the context and the eagerness of the characters involved that all parties are consenting. It's more that, unless you have one of those "key decisions" we mentioned in the previous chapter, the actual consent just kind of...happens. Two or more characters come into a room, they talk for a bit, and then, at the "perfect moment" (which is magically the same for both of them), they fall into each other's arms without any discussion, proceeding to have sex in which everyone gets exactly the sorts of intimate contact they want and nothing else. There are even more forceful depictions where someone grabs another character, slams them against the wall, and kisses them without so much as a heads up or a check-in...but it's all okay because hey, they're into it!

To be clear, this doesn't mean these scenes are awful or should never be done. They can be a useful shorthand to communicate mutual passion and in some cases fulfill certain player fantasies (e.g., some people find "forcefulness" sexy!). The point is, very few games really address the logistics and the meaning of consent directly. Even the games that present the key choice that we discussed in the previous chapter tend to approach consent as a simple binary on/off switch, and once you've picked the "on" switch...that's it, it's *on*. But consent is an active, ongoing process, one that can shift and flow, one that involves communication – though that communication does not always have to be verbal! – and one that engages all parties, ideally with enthusiasm!

So, let's discuss the logistics of consent in game sex scenes and how it can be approached.

DOI: 10.1201/9780429356650-19

CONSENT OF PLAYER VS. CONSENT OF CHARACTERS

Firstly, consider that there are actually two threads of consent that should be followed up on – the consent of the characters involved, but also the consent of the player involved, which we touched on heavily in prior chapters. Some people have used player agency as a metaphor for real-life consent, and though imperfect, there's a grain of useful truth here – that agency and consent both involve respecting the player/partner's choices and actions and NOT forcing them into taking actions (gameplay, story, or sexual) against their will. The same can be argued for the player's consent to witness or partake in sexual activity – that it should be through their choice and action and that it should not ever be against their will.

This is, of course, more difficult to do with linear games like, say, *The Last of Us II* or *Assassin's Creed: Origins*, where sex scenes are unavoidable beats in the storyline. One could argue that in these games, players may not "consent" to see these sex scenes (i.e., may not want to see these characters have sex or any sex in general), but must watch them anyway to play the game and further the plot. However, this isn't quite the same sort of infraction on the player agency as in other games, as the player is often not directly influencing the characters or story, and there is far more division between the player and the character they play. In other words, they are playing *Abby or Bayek's* story and seeing those characters' experiences (including sexual ones) almost like a movie, as opposed to the player actually participating in those moments personally. Thus, player consent is not violated in the same way that it would be in a branching game with more direct control, as they are not forced to actively partake in a sex scene against their will. It's more that they play the game, then watch (or are "forced to watch"?) while the CHARACTER has sex of their own free will (Figure 15.1).

FIGURE 15.1 In linear games with established protagonists and noninteractive cutscenes, the player is cast more in this perspective, a camera or observer to the characters as *they* have consensual sex. (Kaspars Grinvalds/Shutterstock.com.)

Having said that, being "forced to watch" is still not ideal, to put it mildly, and there are still ways to ensure that player consent is still respected in the context of these scenes:

- For nonoptional sex scenes, keep the sex purely to cutscenes, NOT gameplay. Unless you are making a deliberately experimental game that explores the idea of consent, this is not the time to pull a *BioShock* and "force" the player to take certain actions to progress the story or the scene. There's a big difference between passively watching an unwanted sex scene (where, in theory, the player can simply get up and walk away until it's done) and being forced to participate by touching, thrusting, or other physical/gameplay actions. The former may be annoying to some players, but they can at least leave the room or check their phone until it's done; the latter has more potential to feel violating and gross, as well as require participation to progress the game.

- As much as appropriate, signal to the player what may happen (in terms of sex) and what they can expect. Much of this is actually part of making a good sex scene in the first place – building a mood, setting up a connection, and so on – and we'll be discussing it more in the chapter on sexual tension. This obviously works to engage and excite your players who want to see the characters have sex, but it also warns the players who don't that they may want to prepare themselves or wander off to get a coffee, or so on.

- Also, consider how the pacing and presentation of the cutscene can allow players to opt in and out as they need. A slam-cut from polite talking straight to nudity and sex might be a cool and engaging cinematic trick (and the right one for some scenes!), but the abrupt shift offers no chance for disinterested players to step away. In contrast, showing the characters passionately kiss for a lengthy period before throwing each other on the table gives plenty of "warning" for those players to step away while still internalizing the narrative note of, "okay, those two had/are about to have sex."

- Lastly, consider giving the player the option to opt out, either as a menu setting (e.g., "Hide scenes with sexual content") or as the ability to skip cutscenes in general so that, if they prefer not to watch the scene, they don't have to. Unskippable cutscenes can be a fraught topic among game writers and narrative designers (believe me, as a writer, I Have Thoughts™) but if your game has sexual content that will make some of your players uncomfortable, then giving them an option to opt out while still being able to continue the game is a thoughtful and respectful way to accommodate them.

In games that heavily emphasize player choice, however, the consent of the player becomes vital, as well as inexorably connected with the consent of the player character. If a player takes the option to pursue or refuse sex, then that choice becomes that of the player characters as well. In games with branching choice, particularly with the "key decision" we examined the last chapter, there is usually no design structure in place for a player to opt out of sex but have the character opt in...or vice versa, for that matter. This makes sense:

FIGURE 15.2 "What the hell, dude? I avoided the "grab his ass" option for a reason!" (Roman Kosolapov/Shutterstock.com.)

in these games, there is a much closer connection between character and player, where the player is encouraged to either identify personally with the character (e.g., the Warden in *Dragon Age: Origins*) or to shape the character's desires and actions (e.g., Geralt in *The Witcher*). Thus, it wouldn't make sense for the player to choose one thing for that character ("Have sex!") and for the character to suddenly develop their own free will, "rebel", ignore the player's choice, and do their own thing ("No, I don't think I will.") (Figure 15.2)[1]

I know I already emphasized the importance of allowing players the option to refuse sex or sexual scenes several times, but frankly, in the context of consent, it's important enough that I'm going to repeat it here again: if your game has the option for sexual relationships or sexual connections, **it also MUST have the option to refuse them**. Furthermore, that refusal MUST be respected by the game and the other characters; that means no scenarios where the player refuses sex, but the game pushes through anyway. Refusing to grant the player agency over sex is bad enough, but it's almost equally bad (if not worse) to grant them agency to refuse, only to rip it away. At best, it frustrates the player as their agency and control is removed; at worst, that removal can be profoundly violating in terms of the intimate context. If the player chooses to refuse sex, ensure that choice is enforced and respected both in and out of the game world, ensure that the refusal is diegetic and in-character (as opposed to suddenly breaking immersion and character or having the player character suddenly ignore player input), and ensure that the nonplayer characters (NPCs) involved back off and accept the refusal (Figure 15.3).

So, we've driven home the importance of respecting a blanket no from the player that shuts down sexual activity. But as the previous chapter drove home, consent is more than a binary. We'll talk a bit later about more specific, qualified no's (i.e., refusing certain things but consenting to others), but right now, let's talk about an equally, if not, more important aspect of consent…the importance, nuance, and power of YES, and what it means for your game characters.

FIGURE 15.3 When the player does this, the characters involved should follow suit. (Lijphoto/Shutterstock.com.)

NO MORE "MOTHER MAY I!" ENTHUSIASTIC CONSENT

In discussions about consent, either depicting it or actually getting it in real life, there's a common thread of criticism that often pops up: the idea that it's somehow "unsexy" to be asking permission for EVERYTHING, that having to gain/portray consent means an endless stream of, "Is this okay? Is this okay?" or "may I do this?" that takes people out of the mood (Figure 15.4).

FIGURE 15.4 How do most people seem to think asking for sexual consent works? (Prostock-studio/Shutterstock.com.)

Assuming this criticism is in good faith – because let's face it, it very often isn't! – it misses several important aspects – first, that there is more than one way to communicate and gain consent, and second, that even those requests can be done in a sexy, erotic way as opposed to plaintive and demanding. But most importantly, this criticism makes some reductionist assumptions about consent and sex – that consent is about getting "permission" or someone "allowing" you to do something.

Screw that…what about someone full-throatedly saying YES, PLEASE, I WANT YOU TO DO THE THING!

This is the concept of enthusiastic consent. While simple consent is often boiled down to saying "yes" (or, worse, "not saying no"), enthusiastic consent is more like saying "hell yes!" or "yes please!" It's a model of consent in which all parties are participating in sexual acts because they are excited and/or aroused about the acts in question, rather than because of pressure or because the other party "demands" it.

Recasting consent in this enthusiastic, affirmative, and eager way has a profound effect on how to write and design the ways the characters communicate with each other in terms of sex. The context and design of the dialogue and gameplay interaction become less about "Mother May I," demanding permission for what one person wants to do, and more about pleasurable collaboration and negotiation about what all parties want and what they're all eager and willing to do. This affects not only how a character might "ask" for consent but also how someone might answer. How your characters seek and express enthusiastic consent depends on how you've conceived, developed, and written them – and hopefully the earlier chapter on characterization helps! – but here are some ideas:

- For example, "may I do x?" can be less of a rote request and more of a question of invitation and seduction, looking into the partner's eyes and asking, husky and eager, if the partner will enjoy it as much as the speaker will. And in turn, the partner's response can be much more eager and active than a "yes" or "okay" – everything from "HELL YES!" to "God, I've been dreaming of you doing X all night!" to "Yes, do X, then Y, then Z, *please*…" It can even be a clear physical demonstration or action (e.g., nodding before kissing them, grabbing their hand and placing it somewhere, etc.)

- Since enthusiastic consent is a model which seeks for and finds sexual activities that both parties are eager for, there's a lot of room for sexy, erotic ways to share one's own desires and ask (emphasis *ask*) a partner to relieve them. Imagine a character, aroused and yearning, saying something like, "Please touch my X," or "God, I want to do X to you," and the partner replying with heated, passionate agreement…or encouragement to keep talking more *explicitly*.

- And yes, because someone is probably going to bring it up, consent does not ALWAYS have to be explicitly verbal. While verbal consent has the benefit of being clear and easily understood, there are times when certain body language – making significant eye contact, biting a lip, nodding, or loosening/tightening of posture – can speak volumes as to the characters' excitement and eagerness for sex and their enthusiastic consent. And don't discount what hands can communicate either – they might guide someone's touch to a particularly aroused spot or simply pull the partner closer in pleasure and desire for more.

On top of characterization, enthusiastic consent also has ramifications and potential for actual gameplay. For example, imagine a 3D or VR game in which the player has full control over the player character (PC)'s hands during an intimate scene and can touch their NPC partner or guide the NPC's hands in turn. Enthusiastic consent can serve as the in-game positive feedback and vice versa! The core gameplay loop can center around the players placing their hands somewhere and waiting for eager reactions as a sign to continue. Those eager reactions could be dialogue-based, ("Yes, right there." "A little lower… mm…"), nonverbal responses (moaning, blushing, tensing, etc.), or even interactions with the players' controls (guiding their hands somewhere sensitive, etc.). And, of course, the player can similarly give nonverbal enthusiastic consent to the NPC's activities by guiding their hands, nodding, pulling them in, or touching them in encouragement. Designing sexual gameplay around enthusiastic consent is not only erotic as hell, but reinforces the act of sex as mutual consensual interaction, experimentation, and play…which sounds like a good goal for games to aim for in general! (Figure 15.5)

Establishing mutual enthusiasm and interest in sex is an important part of most sex scenes – it represents healthy models of consent, it allows for more exploration of character development, and it's just plain hot. But it's fair to note that there are some sex scenes where one or more partners may be consenting, but not with enthusiasm…at least, not based on lust, attraction, or desire for sex. Going back to Morrigan's blood ritual in *Dragon Age: Origins*, for example, her encounters with the male warden NPCs (Alistair or Loghain) are not exactly enthusiastic for anyone. Neither of the men is exactly eager; they consent willingly, but only to circumvent the fatal effects of killing the Archdemon, and are not the least

FIGURE 15.5 "Ooh, she really liked that. C'mere…" (Insta_photos/Shutterstock.com.)

bit interested in the sex itself. As for Morrigan, she is only enthusiastic about the child she will conceive for the ritual. Both parties see the sex as purely functional, not something to be excited about. Other examples of nonenthusiastic consent and context could include:

- a spy seducing a mark for information or other mission reasons

- a sex worker having sex willingly for financial reasons as opposed to desire

- characters who are bored and figuring, "meh, why not?"

In writing and designing these sorts of scenes, presenting these characters with the same level of excitement and enthusiasm as described earlier may not work thematically with where their characters are or what their relationships with their partners are. Unless they are deliberately putting on an enthusiastic face for some reason, it may make more sense for them to be less eager, more passive, and generally a little bit more staid and more neutral in their responses and consent (Figure 15.6).

However, it is still important to portray their participation in sex as active and willing, rather than passive or against their will. In the examples given – manipulative spies, sex workers, bored characters – while they may not be ECSTATIC to be having sex, it is still a choice they are actively willingly making, and their agency should be expressed through their consent. In other words, while they may have nonsexual reasons for pursuing sex or accepting sexual offers…in the end, they still *want* to have sex, even if sexual desire and attraction don't enter the equation. If you want to ensure that the sex scene keeps your audience engaged and interested (as opposed to revolted or deeply uncomfortable), then it's important to show all parties as actively agreeing and consenting to the sex of their own free will, as opposed to doing it due to pressure, duress, or desperation.

FIGURE 15.6 "I mean, yeah, sure, I *guess*…" (tommaso79/Shutterstock.com.)

This brings us to the topic of reluctant consent, where a character may actively NOT want to have sex – as in, would rather do almost anything else, actively dreading it, etc., – but agrees to it due to pressure (from the other character, from society, etc.) or some other pressing external need or situation. While such topics can be handled delicately and carefully, my recommendation is: unless your game's intention is to focus specifically and deliberately on that experience, **avoid situations and scenes with reluctant consent**. This is a topic that too many of your audience will have had bad or traumatic experiences with, and unless the entire point of the game is a thoughtful and sensitive exploration of these situations (and *clearly signaled* as such to prospective players), you run far too much risk of blindsiding them, triggering them, or just plain annoying them. Even your players that have not had negative experiences are unlikely to enjoy these sorts of experiences, and if these players went into your game expecting Happy Fun Consensual Sexy Time Adventure only to have this dropped on them, it will jar them even more. And if your design includes the *player* forced into giving reluctant consent, then that's even worse. Unless this is an exploration of a specific kink or a personal experience – i.e., a member of your team actively wants to create a game to explore, process, or represent a similar encounter that they had – I would think twice about exploring reluctant consent as a game narrative.

NO BUTTS, OR NO, BUT?

Part of enthusiastic consent is, naturally, respecting a "no" and backing off from anyone who is not enthusiastically into the sexual act(s) in question. In the last chapter, we explored what a no might mean, what the difference is between "no, never" and "not right now," and the importance of respecting whatever "no" the player (or character!) might say. But what about situations where characters may say "no" to certain things, but "yes" to others? What about situations where characters may enthusiastically consent to begin with, then withdraw consent later? How can we portray consent with this additional nuance?

Of course, the approach depends heavily on the nature of your game and the narrative context of the sex. For example, if you are looking to explore how a character might explicitly refuse some forms of intimacy but enthusiastically jump for others, you can employ a "no but" model.

"No, but…" works along somewhat similar principles as "Yes, and…", a well-known rule of thumb in improv theater that involves accepting what the other participant has stated ("yes") and then expanding on it ("and"). In the "no, but" model of writing and designing consent, things are a little different: the person or character may not consent to the other participant's suggestion ("no"), but they are still willing to suggest alternatives or other ways to be together that they ARE enthusiastic about ("but…"). Rather than simply ending the scene after a player or character's refusal, there is still room to have them interested in other activities, even sexual activities. This goes beyond the "key decision" from the last chapter in that this option is not a way to end the scene or even to end the sexual encounter, but to continue it under other parameters they enjoy and consent to. It respects and underlines the character's agency and consent (or refusal of consent, in this case) while keeping the interaction (or the relationship!) going in a way that is comfortable to them. There are countless examples of this phrasing or dynamic, not limited to:

- No, I'm not comfortable with [X sexual act], but I would love it if we did [Y sexual act].

- No, I'm not up for that…but let me show you what I AM up for.

- No, I'm not ready to "go all the way," but I'd be up for touching/making out/kissing/etc.

- No, not there…but…yesssss, *there*.

- No, not tonight…but later, we will revisit this conversation, nudge nudge, wink wink.

- No, I'm not ready for sex, but…I don't want to be alone tonight, so will you just stay and hold me?

Obviously, there are other ways you can express this dynamic or similar nuanced expressions of consent. The variety is endless – is it a playful suggestion or a vulnerable confession? Is it something that is touched on briefly, understood, then moved on from, or something the characters might have a conversation about? Does the "mood" of the evening continue or does it shift into something different (e.g., playful to serious)? Are there other models besides "no, but…?" Perhaps "yes, if you'd be willing to try X as well" or "yes, at least until Y happens"? As we stressed in the previous chapter, consent has so much potential beyond the two extremes of, "yes, anything goes" and "no, stop and leave now."

There is, however, one important thing to note with this nuance and the "no, but" approach – that in all cases, **the nuance, negotiation, and agency should rest in the person who said "no, but" in the first place**. The alternatives should be coming from the one who initially "refused," not from the one who initially asked. That's because if Character A says, "no to X" and Character B replies with, "Fine, but what about Y? Or Z?" then this can be interpreted as B trying to "get around" A's refusal or that they don't respect Character A's refusal. In this case, it's better to have Character B allow Character A to set the subsequent tone and pace, either by explicitly saying, "cool, let's do what you're comfortable with" or by listening to their suggestions and consenting (or not!) to that. When in doubt of how to write and structure a scene, Character A's refusal should ALWAYS be upheld and respected ludically and narratively, both in the world and out, and whatever "negotiations" take place between the lovers should never infringe on that refusal (Figure 15.7).

There is also the possible dynamic where a character (or player, for that matter!) consents to sex, begins to have sex, and then midway through, wants to stop. Perhaps the experience is too overwhelming, or they are no longer enjoying themselves, or maybe they're just no longer in the mood. Whatever the reason, they want to slam on the brakes and end the scene. And as a general best practice, **players and characters should always be allowed to do so**, both within the story and by the game UI. Consent is not permanent and can be revoked, and a nuanced portrayal or presentation of sex should recognize that and, where appropriate, allow it to be a part of the experience. On a narrative level, this may mean having characters, both PC and NPCs, pause in the middle of sex and ask to stop, and having both their partner and the larger story respect this: no shaming, no weirdness, simply stopping immediately and checking in with them. On a gameplay, player-focused level,

FIGURE 15.7 "No handcuffs tonight, sweetheart. But I'd be up for a round of blindfolds and ice cubes if you are…" (sakkmesterke/Shutterstock.com.)

this may mean giving the player multiple choices throughout a sex scene where, on top of other dialogue or action choices, they can also choose to stop or ask their partner to stop.

One excellent character-focused way to handle revoking consent in the middle of a scene is the concept of a safeword. Used heavily but not exclusively in the kink community, safewords came about from a need to unambiguously demand a halt or a pause to the sex, particularly in situations where yelling "no, stop!" might be part of role-playing a particular fantasy, or even just them complaining that the ropes are too tight! The safeword is something that would not be accidentally yelled out in a fit of passion…things like rutabaga or credenza. Some people use multiple safewords to communicate different levels of comfort (e.g., the old traffic lights: green means go, red means stop, yellow means slow down). People may also use particular gestures like tapping someone's hand if they are unable to speak. Whatever the safeword or safe gesture, when someone uses it, that means that the sex ends (or slows down, if that's what's used), absolutely no questions asked. Games can incorporate this structure as part of player choice: always giving players the option, even in the middle of a sex scene, to pull the plug (or ask for things to slow down) and end the encounter. And as a bonus, coming up with safewords for your characters can be a great exercise in characterization. One of the few mainstream games that explore this is Dragon

Age: Inquisition. If Iron Bull and the Inquisitor are in a relationship, they will jokingly discuss what the other characters' safewords (or "watchwords") would be and how they relate to their personalities (e.g., Iron Bull commenting on Blackwall choosing a safeword from "the good life," or that Vivienne is a "periwinkle" sort of woman).

One of the best examples of nuanced consent, both of "no, but X" and of safeword/revoking consent mid-sex, is an indie dating sim called *Cute Demon Crashers!* While they do use refusal of consent to "end" the scene, they do so in an interesting way that integrates it with the PC's preferences AND the UI (Figure 15.8). The premise of *Cute Demon Crashers!* is that the player character, a virginal female college student, accidentally summons four friendly and kind sex demons to her house; stuck there until the next morning, they make an open offer to be her first sexual experience in a safe, controlled space that she can be comfortable in. During the game, players get to know the different demons, then in the evening can choose which demon, if any, to have sex with. This is where consent comes into play:

- Firstly, the player can decide not to have sex with any of them, but still spend friendly platonic time with them. This triggers an ending in which all the characters spend the evening playing video games. Care is taken to make the scene still feel meaningful and engaging as opposed to being "punished" for refusing consent to sex or not pursuing sex.

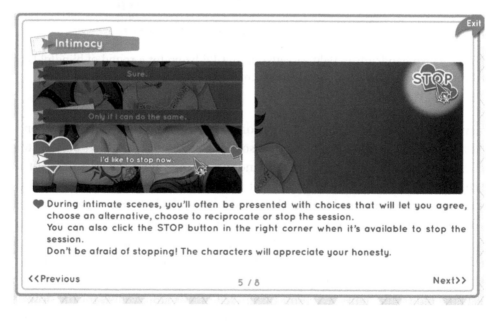

FIGURE 15.8 A screenshot of *Cute Demon Crashers!'s* tutorial about consent in its sex scenes. Note the two options for enthusiastic consent, the option to stop now, and the extra UI "stop" button in the upper right corner (which can be used at any time, even outside choice points). (SugarScript, Cute Demon Crashers!, PC/Mac/Linux, partial version published April 7, 2015, full version published August 15, 2015. Screenshot from A Henderson, AZE Journal, "Asexual Positivity in a Game About Sexy Demons," July 1, 2018, https://azejournal.com/article/2018/6/29/asexual-positivity-in-a-game-about-sexy-demons.)

- If the player chooses one of the demons, the demon consents enthusiastically. A lengthy sex scene begins with multiple choices, going through first the preparation (e.g., do you want the demon naked or not), then certain preferences throughout the scene (e.g., positions, types of sensation play, use of a blindfold, etc.). Almost all these scenes are couched in terms of the demon asking what YOU want to do, rather than them asking permission to do something. As a result, the "no, but" structure becomes more of a "yes, if" as you are constantly offering active engagement on your preferences, comfort level, etc., to proceed.

- Importantly, EVERY choice point during the sex scene presents the option to withdraw consent and say, "I want to stop" (or, in the case of the BDSM-practicing demon, to say the safeword, "red"). Choosing this immediately ends the sexual activity, but the demon checks in on you, offers aftercare, etc. Having this choice available at multiple points throughout the sex scene, it allows players to go exactly as far as they wish before saying no. Players may find themselves comfortable with most of the scenes until a particularly intense moment or choice, at which point they are completely free to stop. This would be a "yes, until…" model (i.e., being enthusiastic to do something but stopping when it's no longer wanted). It's worth noting that the demons are always extremely respectful and kind at these moments, ensuring that the player feels reaffirmed in their choice rather than punished.

- As an added excellent touch, on top of the choices to withdraw consent and ask to stop in the key choices, the game also offers an extra gameplay way to stop by including an extra button in the upper right corner of the UI with "stop" or the safeword written on it. At any time during the scene, even during the middle of linear non-branching text, the player can hit the button and demand to stop. It's a small but very well-thought-out detail, as players are never forced to "endure" the current activity until the next choice point. There could be ways to improve on this model – for example, rather than immediately ending and winding down the sexual activity, also offer options to pause, then continue (in case the player just needed a moment to collect themselves), revert to an earlier choice point, etc., – but it's a great start to giving the player more tools to consent or withdraw consent in ways that allow experimentation with the story.

Hopefully, as sex becomes less of a pearl-clutching concept for games and more of a natural, integrated work, we'll see more games exploring models like *Cute Demon Crashers!* and other indie games for how consent can be something fun whether you accept OR refuse and how that consent might be baked into gameplay in interesting ways.

BITS AND PIECES

A few random thoughts about consent that don't fit into the previous sections:

- Consent should always, ALWAYS be given freely. We touched on this before, but if consent is given under duress (e.g., "sleep with me or I will kill this puppy!") or other pressures, it's not consent. Always ask yourself, "if this character says no, what will happen to them?" And if the answer is anything actively harmful to their safety, others' safety, their livelihood, etc..., then your scene is NOT consensual.

- There are players of all genders and sexualities that can and DO find stories that have problematic consent issues hot and interesting. For some people, they like the power differential of "my hot boss," while for others, the idea of a dark sexy villain demanding their sexual submission "or the puppy dies" is their idea of a good time! We touched on this earlier in the book in the discussion on porn games, but what I will say on this account is that, if this is an aspect of sexual fantasy you wish to explore in your game, it should be the main, heavily signposted focus of the entire game, not something that you introduce into your broader work. If I am into games with dark sexy villains who trap me in their castle and have their way with me, then I will be picking up a game ABOUT that. Including that content in a game that's actually about saving the world, or even springing it on players as a surprise, is just going to annoy and upset the people who did not come for this content and are repelled by it.

- Avoid sexual activity centered around heavy alcohol use, particularly to the point of blackout. A glass of wine to get in the mood is one thing, but if your characters are inebriated to the point where, the next day, they can't remember what they did, then they were incapable of proper consent! Unfortunately, many games, even otherwise well-intentioned ones, fail to recognize this and treat these encounters as completely consensual. The game *Catherine* was a particularly bad example of this; in the early game, Vincent drinks with the eponymous Catherine at a bar, gets ridiculously drunk, and wakes up the next morning to find her in his bed, with the heavy implication that sexual things happened. Vincent is arguably a sexual assault victim in this scenario, given that he seems to have been inebriated enough to black out, and yet the story, characters, and even articles about the game all focus on him "cheating" on his girlfriend as if he fully consented to the sex. Content like these support harmful real-world assumptions about sex and sexual assault and should be fully avoided.

CONCLUSION

If there's one thing that's important to get right for a sex scene, it's the concept of consent. It's one thing to mess up something that hurts your game's appeal or sales, but quite another to mess up something that hurts your *players*. But consent doesn't have to be a giant dangerous thing or something laden with shame and begging permission. Consent can be something joyous, fun, and enthusiastic, where "yes" is a "hell, yes!" and everyone involved can communicate and collaborate in finding something that everyone enjoys. Bring that energy to your game design, your design around agency and consent, and you can move so much further than "Mother May I" or "yes or no"?

(Oh, and if you're curious about how choice and agency might work within a sex scene? Stay tuned for a future chapter...)

WORKSHOP QUESTIONS

Analysis: Look at the choice you examined in the previous chapter workshop – the "key decision point" for the sex scene in the game you're analyzing – and reexamine it through the lens of consent. Does it function as enthusiastic consent? Are there ways that it could depict consent for the following sex scene as more nuanced or granular?

Creative: Consider ways in which your game can model enthusiastic consent. What in your narrative and/or game mechanics can reinforce mutual pleasure, play, and agreement in the context of sex? How do you reinforce the eagerness and enthusiasm of the characters involved? How do you present and explore the nuances of their sexual boundaries in terms of consent: do they have certain things they prefer not to do or only do in certain circumstances? What things DO they like to do instead? How do they negotiate their limits and desires with their partners? If relevant, add these details to the character bios and/or the flowchart you created in the previous chapter.

Also, consider ways that the UI can provide "opt-outs" for the player if they do not wish to partake in sexual content. Is it worth creating menu options that block certain content for players who don't wish to see it? UI elements like *Cute Demon Crashers!* that allow players to stop the sex scenes in an in-character way? Or simply provide the option to skip a sex cutscene? Work this out with your UI team to find a way to ensure your players can have a comfortable experience, even if they're not fully comfortable with sex.

NOTE

1 That's not to say that there can't be out-of-game options like skippable cutscenes or menu settings to allow the player to choose that their character has sex but still opt out of SEEING the sex themselves.

CHAPTER 16

Building Anticipation!

Sex Scenes and the Four Types of Tension

I N GENERAL, THE TIGHTER you can wind someone up, the more satisfying the release will be (Figure 16.1).

Am I talking about game design and gameplay? Real-life sex? Or how sex is presented in video games? The answer to all of these is 'yes,' but since you're reading a book about the last one, let's focus on that.

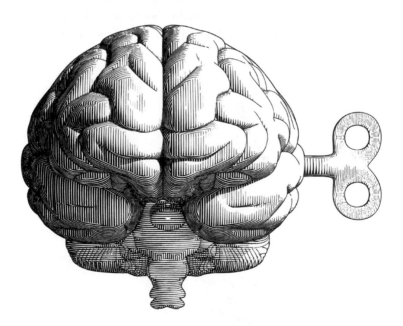

FIGURE 16.1   Your target audience might have sex on the brain, but your game still needs to wind them up a little…(Jolygon/Shutterstock.com.)

DOI: 10.1201/9780429356650-20

In the previous chapter, we spoke about how nonlinear games need to allow players a choice about consenting to sex, how linear games establish a distance between the character's consent and the player's…, and how, in both cases, the scenes need to be telegraphed well in advance so that the players understand what they're getting into. But the telegraphing doesn't have to be blaring red flags or giant neon signs saying, "SEX SCENE AHEAD." In fact, arguably, the "telegraphing" is the real meat of a sex scene…because what we're actually talking about is the tension of the sexual kind.

While there are many reasons that a sex scene might fall flat, one common issue – hard to diagnose but vital to get right – is a lack of the right kind of tension, be it sexual tension between the characters, general tension of the scene, and the tension generated by the overlap of those two elements. A well-executed sex scene should have your players bouncing in their seats with the anticipation of what's about to happen long enough so that when it does happen, they have a burst of satisfaction and emotion.[1] That satisfaction can come whether it's "Yay, they got together after a whole game's worth of romantic tension!" or "Yay, that flirtation and banter at the start of the scene was superhot, and I finally got to see it pay off!" In contrast, a badly executed sex scene may drag things out too long, or more commonly, not take long enough to set up the sexual chemistry and tension. Instead, the sex scene feels rushed, forced, or just generally "dropped on" the player, and whatever emotions or sexiness it was meant to convey can fizzle out (Figure 16.2).

Building tension, sexual and otherwise, is a holistic task that requires patience and taking time to not only construct the scene and the characters involved, but to allow the emotions space and time to simmer, build, and eventually coalesce in sex. How this coalescing actually happens depends massively on the scene. Some sex scenes are like warm baths that you ease into, where each step is comforting and "right" as the lovers slowly but surely

FIGURE 16.2 "I am overwhelmed with a deep and passionate feeling of 'meh.'" (Billion Photos/ Shutterstock.com.)

come together. Others are like rubber bands or striking a match, all drawn out tension and smoldering gazes until something snaps, desire bursts into flame, and the lovers suddenly jump on each other. Some scenes require a long period of time to build up the tension; others can be very short thanks to a small amount of perfectly placed detail…or a lot of tension building up over the entire game, not just the one scene! Knowing what sort of effect your scene is going for, and what will work the best for your players and your game, helps your designers, writers, and cinematic directors focus on how to pace the scene and how to build the tension using all of their tools (including the ones in this book). Giving tension room to breathe and infuse every detail of the scene – the dialogue, the body language, the environment, and the lighting – helps that tension to build organically and allows players even more ways to sense that tension, internalize it, and get excited about it.

Tension is also something that can be generated by the players themselves, either in terms of explicit choice or in terms of how they play the game. Even choosing to hold off on a particular quest or story beat that is telegraphed to be a sex scene ("I'm gonna do all the sidequests before I finally push on with the main story and see these two get together!") has the effect of building the tension by choice. But once players are in the scene, if it is interactive, it's important to design the choices in a way that doesn't defuse or dull the tension and ruin the impact. If the scene only works with a slow, smoldering buildup, then allowing the player to have the choice to rush through and get "straight to the sex" can end up in a much less effective scene. However, that doesn't mean that players should not have the agency in how the tension is built or even how and when it eventually culminates!

- If designers are able to establish a satisfying baseline tension via set elements like cutscenes, dialogue, or camera tricks, then they can offer players meaningful choices on whether to build the tension higher or make it explode. For example, a game with a branching narrative might have a "set" sequence of sexy banter between two characters, full of secret meaning, which then results in the nonplayer character (NPC) confessing their desire ("I want you…") at the height of the tension. The player can then either enthusiastically reciprocate immediately (triggering the sex right away) or teasingly play innocent ("You want me? You want me to…what?" with a big wink), drawing out the sexual tension between the NPC and the player character (PC), as well as the tension of the scene. If they choose that option, they can then continue teasing and edging the NPC until both of them are ready to jump on each other even more.

- Alternately, the designers could go a different direction – only allow a sex scene to play out if the player sufficiently ramps up the sexual tension in the scene or ramps it up in a certain way. Perhaps they have to stand just a little closer to their potential partner or show certain expressions, or have to choose dialogue options that build the sexual tension between the partners. This is basically a "chemistry casino speed round," where your moment-by-moment actions are all focused on building the NPC's arousal and attraction to a final, irresistible peak. "Failing" to do so would not necessarily mean a "failure state" for the sex or the relationship, only that you didn't build the mood high enough to "boil over." The end of the scene could still

FIGURE 16.3 Has this player built enough tension for a good time...or a "Maybe next time?" (Real_World_Stu/Shutterstock.com.)

be brimming with the potential for future connection – an almost kiss, a pregnant pause, hesitating at the last moment, and unspoken attraction still bubbling between them, still simmering for a future encounter...(Figure 16.3).

Tension in sex scenes – arguably in any scenes – tends to boil down to one of the four types or four reactions from the player:

- **I don't know what's going to happen!**
- **I think I know what's going to happen, but I'm not sure how.**
- **I know exactly what's going to happen!**
- **Wait, what the hell just happened?**

Needless to say, some of these types of tension are better than others! Let's explore how each of them plays out in terms of a sex scene, which ones are the "sweet spot" to aim for and which should be avoided

MYSTERY: I DON'T KNOW WHAT'S GOING TO HAPPEN

You might think that if a player enters a sex scene not knowing what's about to happen, then the designers have not done their job in properly setting up the sexual dynamic between the characters or setting the scene itself, but this isn't necessarily true! A scene can have generalized tension as opposed to specifically sexualized tension – in other words, it can signal to the player that *something* is about to happen between these two characters, but it's unclear as to what it will be. A good example of this is scenes that are initially framed as an argument between the characters – depending on how the dynamics have been set up between the characters, building tension in the scene *could* lead to either a full-on blowout fight (punches thrown, etc.) or an explosion of kissing and sexual passion, and the player

FIGURE 16.4 We're at T-minus 30 seconds from either a giant punch-up or the most epic bed-breaking sex ever...and I don't know which!. (Red Fox studio/Shutterstock.com.)

isn't sure which is actually going to happen. When it *does* turn sexual, it's not necessarily a "surprise" (though it can be!) but more of a reveal or a resolution of the tension, something that makes the player say, "Oh, that's what that scene was building to!" (Figure 16.4)

This lends itself very well to character dynamics in which the emotions and connection are a little ambiguous as opposed to clearly sexual. The player may see their connection in a sexual OR nonsexual light, leaving things open to interpretation and less bound to specific expectations. In the "argue, argue, kiss" example above, the relationship dynamic between characters might be quite antagonistic, with a lot of snarky banter, personality clash, and so on. If handled well, this antagonistic dynamic can pair well with a certain kind of sexual tension, where the friction between the characters translates into heated attraction or at least a sort of excitement and agitation that might lead to romantic or sexual interest. Another example might be a deep friendship or comradeship with a fellow character in a similar situation. If the connection between them is ambiguous and open to interpretation, it may be that a scene where they finally kiss and make love comes as something of a pleasant surprise, where the player didn't expect it or know it would happen but enjoys how it plays out.

However, it should be stressed that in order for this sort of "surprise" tension to work out for a sex scene, there does need to be at least *something* set up between the characters that can translate to their sexual connection. Being pleasantly surprised by a sexual connection involves being able to look back at the characters' interactions and see how they came to this headspace and this new sexual relationship, even picking up on foreshadowing they might have missed before. However, if the player looks back at their interactions and sees absolutely nothing that would foreshadow or explain their sexual attraction – or just nothing that suggests they have any sexual interest in each other at all! – the scene is going to feel out of left field and fundamentally dissatisfying, possibly even falling into "Wait, what the hell just happened?" territory. In other words, the chemistry just isn't there, casino or otherwise.

Examples of this model are somewhat rare, as many games telegraph their sex scenes from a mile away or they allow the player to actively choose what will happen. However, there are some that are close enough that suggest possible models for these scenes.

For example, in *InFAMOUS: Second Son*, the player character, Delsin, is a Conduit, a sub-species of humans with supernatural powers who are hated and feared by normal humans. During one mission, Delsin can encourage a fellow Conduit NPC called Fetch to pursue a dark path of killing an anti-Conduit activist. Their vibe together during the mission is exuberant and defiant rebels against a system that hates them. After Fetch kills the activist, she mentions feeling extremely keyed up and needing to burn off all the energy she has. Delsin begins mentioning that there are other activists to kill, but Fetch suddenly interrupts him with, "You wanna hook up?" Delsin replies, "activists can wait," and kisses her. The scene capitalizes on the general tension of the previous murder scene and its aftermath – will Fetch murder the activist? What is she planning? What will these two do next? How will she burn off her steam? And while the sex is a surprise (deliberately and played for some comedic value), the two characters have good chemistry that lends itself well to their sexual connection, even if it is just on a casual level.

To create a successful scene where players have no idea how it will play out, writers and designers need to seed tension – both in the character interactions before the scene and in the scene itself – that does "double duty." In other words, it needs to serve as both sexual tension and a second, narrative-appropriate tension between the characters and their interpersonal dynamic. This could be anything from bitter rivalry to warm camaraderie to desperately seeking comfort in a moment of crisis. It could also be an external tension over a particular action (e.g., is Fetch about to kill that guy? Is she about to kill MORE activists?). The scene is then structured to primarily build that tension and then at the appropriate moment use sex to resolve the tension in a semi-surprising way.

In terms of more interactive scenes where the scene tension is guided by player choices, this is harder to do as the player usually has much clearer control of whether the tension of the scene is actually sexual. However, it can be accomplished by using the same structure – build nonsexual tension, reveal a sexual element (for example, an NPC suddenly kissing them), and THEN allow the player the opportunity to respond. Alternately, their choices could be building a nonspecific tension that the player then decides how to resolve (e.g., whether to respond at a critical moment with a derisive laugh or a kiss). Just remember to keep the consent of the player, PC, and NPC in mind while designing this…if one character "surprises" the other with a kiss or other sexual gesture without even giving them a chance to agree or respond, that can nudge up against some problematic consent issues. Whenever possible, show both parties reaching the same page (i.e., "let's bone") at the same time or at least in quick succession ("Oh, well, in that case…").

ANTICIPATION: I THINK I KNOW WHAT'S ABOUT TO HAPPEN, BUT HOW?

This is arguably the sweet spot for most sex scenes, at least those that are intended to be erotic and sexy. This is a scene where the sexual attraction is obvious and heavy, and the player knows (or at least suspects) that the characters are going to have sex…but what they don't know is *how* it will happen. This, in a sense, is sexual tension distilled to its purest form – the conflict of the characters' awareness (or lack thereof) of their own desires and that of their partner versus the uncertainty of how or if they will act on it. The result is a very heady kind of anticipation that, if the player is invested in the couple, will result in both edge-of-the-seat nail-biting but also in deep satisfaction of seeing a long-awaited intimate moment take place. Unlike "I don't know what's about to happen," this is something that has likely been marinating a long time or, at least, for the length of the scene! The building sexual attraction and erotic connection have also been clearly signaled to the player. As a result, they anticipate the resolution of that sexual tension in the scene, but are still ready to be surprised and delighted with how that resolution plays out, particularly if they had some agency in bringing it to be!

Obviously, this sort of tension is easiest to bring to the surface for the characters first time together, when many aspects of the relationship may still be unclear. This may even be the first time either character expresses sexual or romantic interest in the other, and thus, there isn't a clear map of how they will get together or how the sex will play out. However, there's no reason you can't make an equally sexy building of tension between longtime lovers (e.g., Bayek/Aya in *Assassin's Creed Origins*) or casual sexual partners (e.g., Geralt/Keira in *The Witcher 3*). Don't restrict sexual tension only to "will they get together" or "how will they get together" – expand the erotic and sensual tension to include, "what will they say to each other?" "What will they *do* to each other?" and most of all, **"what will be the moment that pushes them over the edge and into each other's arms?"**

A good metaphor for this kind of tension is that of a rubber band being stretched. You know, at some point, the band will snap (and the characters will jump each other), but you're not quite sure how long before the band snaps or how much tension it will take. As the scene progresses, the rubber band continues to stretch, stretch, and stretch, and you're waiting for the moment it snaps back – and when it does, it's incredibly satisfying (Figure 16.5).

Creating a scene that capitalizes on this sort of anticipation – suspecting what's coming, but not being sure how it will play out – is something that depends heavily on the characters involved and the style of writing, game design, cutscenes, and so on. There is no one perfect

FIGURE 16.5 When this rubber band snaps, the heroine and her bodyguard are going to have SOOOOO much sex…(edwardolive/Shutterstock.com.)

formula, but one best practice is to write and design as if the sex and sexual attraction is an elephant in the room (Figure 16.6). The characters aren't necessarily talking about it and might be trying to ignore it for various reasons, but it's a looming presence that they're both aware of and that they can only ignore for so long before either tackling it head-on (actually talking about their desire to have sex) or getting stomped on (falling into each other's arms without discussion). Their mutual desire should always be palpable and in the background of every interaction, unable to be escaped, and every action, line of dialogue, expression, and piece of body language should serve to deepen that desire, bring the characters a little closer, and ramp up the tension and heat just a little more, until it finally spills over. And don't be afraid to take your time in pacing and drawing out the scene – giving these details time to breathe, particularly the more subtle ones like facial expressions or body language, also means that you can draw out the tension and hone it to a knife's edge.

Unsurprisingly, this model of anticipatory sexual tension in a scene is very easy to build in a game with plenty of player choice in regard to sex and romance, where the player has been flirting with the character over the course of the game and building sexual tension from the start. In dating sims or games like BioWare's, as discussed earlier, the sex scenes are usually triggered at a particular moment of the plot or at a certain level of connection between the two characters, so the player often knows or suspects when an intimate moment is coming. But they can still be surprised, teased, or intrigued by how the scene plays out, particularly if they still have plenty of dialogue or action choices during the scene that affect how the scene plays out. This is another reason why going beyond the key

FIGURE 16.6 "Oops, don't mind me, just your seething, overwhelming desire to rip off their clothes and taste every inch of their skin. Don't worry, you won't even notice I'm here." (Zastolskiy Victor/Shutterstock.com.)

decision of "do you want to have sex, yes/no" is so important. Letting players play with the tension in the context of the scene by flirting, glances, or talking in heated subtext allows them to steer their course toward the long-awaited destination while still keeping an element of pleasant, erotic mystery and uncertainty.

SATISFACTION(?): I KNOW EXACTLY WHAT'S GOING TO HAPPEN

If "I suspect what will happen, but not how" is the perfect sweet spot for erotic, passionate sex scenes, then "I know exactly what will happen" is just a little to the left of that sweet spot, almost right on top of it...IF it's executed correctly. When done well, the scene will play out exactly as your players always dream with the same sense of "rightness" as dropping in the perfect Tetris piece. When done poorly, a highly telegraphed sex scene can be a little...well...boring. The difference? How and when to apply the dramatic tension... because yes, even when you know what's about to happen, tension is still important!

A good scene where the player knows what is going to happen should, above all, be satisfying. I'm sure we can all think of a favorite scene from a game (or show or movie or book) where, as the scene began, you knew *exactly* how it was going to play out, whether it was a sex scene or something else like horror, drama, or comedy. And unlike the previous type of tension, this isn't something where you suspected how a scene might end but was blanking on the rest. In this sort of scene, you know exactly when the jump scare is going to be, or when the gag is going to hit, or when and how the characters are going to kiss. But rather than being derivative, the predictability here is comforting; the dominant feeling is of "rightness" and satisfaction. The player or viewer has expectations, but rather than being bored by their predictions coming true, they feel a sense of satisfaction and pleasure in seeing their expectations play out as they'd hoped. That's the sort of feeling this sort of tension should aim for; a sense of fulfilling player expectations in the most satisfying way possible.

When done well, this results in a sex scene where the sexual connection and the way sex plays out, feels so *right* that it's like the universe falling into place. Of COURSE, they're going to kiss gently and tentatively just as they're saying good night. Of COURSE, they're then going to deepen the kiss and show hunger for each other. Of COURSE, they're going to tumble onto the bed at just that moment. In a sense, this is similar to the "sweet spot" tension of "I think I know what will happen but not how," but while that version emphasizes the sexy tension between uncertainty and erotic hope, this emphasizes the sweet inevitability of how things work out perfectly. The player knows to expect every single moment and feel satisfaction in seeing it all play out. To set this up, designers can be much more blatant in signaling their intentions with the scene – the environment and music, for example, may be extremely suggestive, and every gesture and action that the characters do are both teased in advance and left with no doubt that their lover will reciprocate. The designers still build tension, but in a way where each action that builds the tension is expected and points to the final satisfying conclusion.

Most of all, however, designers have to make sure that they build tension BEFORE the scene occurs. In a sense, a sex scene with this satisfying "I know what will happen" energy is actually the *resolution* of a tension that's lasted throughout a lot of the game up to this point. Perhaps there's been a lot of tension over whether the characters will get together.

Alternately, perhaps they're together, but the tension has been when they will ever get a break from the current crisis to take a moment in each other's arms. When the player has become invested in the rising tension of the characters' sexual connection, a "predictable" but satisfying sex scene hits home because it feels earned. You expect every little touch or kiss, but in the context of the characters "earning" a perfect (or not-so-perfect) moment together. If the previous tension of "I know they will, but how?" is a rubber band, this is a warm, relaxing bath that the player and characters sink into comfortably – one that is all the more satisfying if it's after a proverbial hard day! (Figure 16.7)

So that's how one kind of "I know what will happen" scene plays out, but there are other models in which a player will know what to expect. For the most part, these other kinds can be summed up in two steps:

- One character says, "let's have sex,"

- The other says, "Sure."

And next to nothing else: no romantic or sexual connection, no flirting, no nothing, just cutting straight to the chase. The beats of the actual sex scene might be a bit more up in the air, but the actual having of sex is bluntly laid out on the line. This is less sinking into a warm bath and more taking a glass of water; it's straightforward, gets the job done, no surprises, but isn't exactly a drawn-out indulgent experience unless you're really, REALLY thirsty (pun intended).

A commonplace where this sort of dynamic occurs is in scenes involving sex work, e.g., where the player can hire a sex worker for a sex scene by paying some in-game

FIGURE 16.7 Pictured: your players and characters soaking up the pleasure of watching the sexual tension come to fruition exactly how they always imagined. (Poznyakov/Shutterstock.com.)

currency. These scenes tend to be predictable as they usually have a clear and dependable structure for communicating and negotiating sex (offer pay, and sex will happen). Also, in most contexts, there isn't really any buildup of tension from previous scenes; the client may not have met the sex worker before and may be choosing them purely in the spur of the moment (or with input from the player). And of course, there isn't a lot of uncertainty around the sex actually happening! The *Witcher* series has many of these scenes in various brothels – for example, in *The Witcher 3*, choosing to hire a sex worker is clearly marked and triggers only a short two-line conversation in which Geralt expresses interest and the courtesan invites him somewhere private or begins negotiating. There's never any doubt that sex is going to happen, though. Of course, this dynamic can happen in non-sex work situations as well.

To be fair, there's nothing necessarily wrong with this structure, and there are arguments to be made in favor of clear communication ("wanna sex?" "sure"), particularly in relation to player choice and/or sex work. If a player chooses to have sex, then yes, probably sex should happen! And of course, as discussed before, there is absolutely a value in depicting clear communication in sex work and sex in general. However, if there is no attempt at building up of tension in the scene – if the sex just *happens* – the results can often be a bit flat and unsexy without taking the time to prime the engine, as it were. It may be instant gratification, but without a chance to build the appetite for that gratification, the results are often not as satisfying. Taken to an extreme, it can even be a little silly: *Saints Row 4* lampooned this by having amusing sex scenes triggered just by walking up to characters and hitting a button to "romance" them.

If you're designing a scene with a clear "on-demand" setup where the player knows what happens – hiring a sex worker, for example, or simply inviting someone to go and have sex – letting the player guess exactly what will happen can sometimes work. But consider that it may be better to go for more of a "I think I know what, but not how" dynamic or introduce some tension, no matter how minor, to leave the player either guessing or eagerly awaiting the expected outcome.

SURPRISE: WAIT, WHAT THE HELL JUST HAPPENED?

This structure – where the player is taken by total surprise and confusion by a sex scene – is actually less about a certain kind of tension and more about the *lack* of tension, or at least the lack of any sort of buildup, warning, or telegraphing. This is what differentiates it from "I don't know what's about to happen." In that, the player may not have any clue that the impending climax of the scene will involve sex, but they can always tell that *something* is about to happen, or that something has been building to a head. In this "what the hell just happened?" model, even if there is "buildup" (e.g., the romantic tension between characters), the presentation of the actual scene is so surprising and so jarring that the player is left flat-footed and taken aback.

A "what the hell just happened" sex scene is usually defined by a surprise reveal of two or more characters having sex with next to no buildup, warning, or even context. Often, this sex is juxtaposed against a totally non-sexual scene that has little to nothing to do with the sex, unless in a humorous context (e.g., people talking about a suggestive statue, then smash cut to two other characters having sex). These sexual reveals tend to fall into one of two categories:

- **In-world reveal** – the OTHER characters are going about their business when they suddenly stumble upon two other characters having sex. For example, they may be headed to the briefing room to discuss strategy, open the door, and find two lovers having sex on the desk. Another example might be opening a closet to get something and finding the lovers banging away in there. The running theme is that of game characters getting surprised and shocked by discovering their friends, colleagues, or even enemies right in the middle of sex.

- **Player-only reveal** – this structure is rarer but refers to meta-reveals such as camera smash cuts or sudden loud moaning, etc. If the player is going along with a nonsexual plot point or gameplay aspect and then, out of nowhere, the camera smash cuts to two characters suddenly having sex out of nowhere, without any tension or buildup to it, it probably evokes the "wait, what the hell just happened?" reaction.

It's important to note that, as a rule, sex scenes that come out of nowhere like this are usually not particularly erotic or intended to be. Because there isn't a lot of time to build sexual tension and heat in a scene and the sex just sort of happens, the player hasn't really "warmed up" to the idea or the visuals and is left more confused or surprised than aroused. This confusion and surprise are best used in one of two ways:

- The best and most narratively engaging way is to use this to reveal surprises and hidden information about a character or their relationships, either to set up or reverse expectations about them. This can particularly go well if the nonsexual scene you're cutting from is set up to contrast the surprise sex in some ways. As an example, imagine you're hearing about how two NPCs are rivals and enemies, always hating each other…then cut suddenly to those same NPCs having wild sex in a backroom! It's a striking, often amusing way to reverse assumptions and reveal new context to the situation.

- On a slightly less elevated level, these scenes can also be used as cheap but reliable sources of shock value and comedy. The sheer surprise of suddenly changing to a sex scene out of nowhere can often provoke laughter from players, and if that is the point of the scene, a well-executed "WTF" sexual moment can be great for a giggle or a gasp.

A good example of this sort of sex scene can be seen in *Wolfenstein II: The New Colossus*, between Sigrun and Bombate. While the game does establish some sexual interest from Sigrun, it's left ambiguous as to whether it's reciprocated, and things are kept lowkey until a particular scene. As part of an unrelated storyline, the other characters make their way to the dock where one of their submarines is parked to take it on a mission. However, as soon as they get into the dock, they hear extremely loud and enthusiastic moans; when they open the hatch, they find Sigrun and Bombate having exuberant sex. When they realize everyone is staring at them in shock, Bombate's only response is, "…I'm sorry, do you need this boat?" The sudden surprise of the scene works for comedy purposes and helps cut the tension of the more serious storyline, while also having a surprise reveal about Sigrun and Bombate's relationship.

Obviously, this is the sort of sex scene that should be written with care and with an eye for timing and pacing. Designers must identify the best moment in the scene to spring the "surprise" but also identify what the nature of the surprise is. What expectation is it subverting? Is the intended reaction shock, laughter, confusion, or something else? What are the benefits of dropping the sequence on the player with no warning? What did they "know" before and what will they "know" after? Approaching the scene as a carefully crafted comedy or dramatic reveal can help guide the execution and develop a memorable moment that people will be amused by, moved by, or shocked by.

Also, this is another place where extra care should definitely be taken if the player has some agency and control in the scene. For one thing, the interface will often give the game away; if a player sees a choice to have sex, then it's not exactly a surprise anymore, is it? The closest equivalent would be something like the Minister Bellise sequence in *Dragon Age: Inquisition*, where the actual presence of the choice is the surprise ("Wait, I can...I can DO that?") But more importantly, sex is not something you want to have as a "hidden" consequence of a nonsexual choice. I know I've said variants on this thirty times so far, but it's so important that I'm going to say it again: **you should never spring surprise sex on a player character based on their choice!** Having players blissfully making nonsexual choices only to be suddenly blindsided by their character having sex is going to result in frustration, confusion, and in some cases, even deep discomfort over the lack of informed consent. Restrict your WTF surprise sex sequences to NPCs or to PCs in linear games and find a different approach in games where the player agency is the key.

CONCLUSION

Building sexual tension is one of the best ways to make a game's sex scene hotter, and there are so many ways to do it and experiment with it, from dialogue with a double meaning to lingering glances to pregnant pauses before the storm breaks. If your game's sex scenes are not hitting the mark or come through as sterile, take a step back and analyze the way that tension works in the scene, and which of these four models are currently in play. You may find that shifting to a different approach for tension results in a scene that's far more effective...and far hotter to boot.

WORKSHOP QUESTIONS

Analysis: Looking at the sex scenes in the game you're analyzing, which of the four types of tension do the scenes try to build? How do they do it? Is it the right kind of tension for the story context?

Creative: Consider at least one of the sex scenes you plan to include in your game and how you intend to build sexual tension in the scene. Which of the four types of tension work best for your scene in terms of theme, goal, and impact on the player and characters? Brainstorm some ways you can build that tension, both inside the scene (i.e., when the characters are in the same space just before the sex) and outside (in the rest of the story). If appropriate, consider doing some live playtesting or script reads of the sequence to ensure that the gameplay and story are building the tension in the way you intend.

NOTE

1 Assuming the sex scene is meant to be sexy or positive! For sex scenes that are intended to be more "negative" (e.g., partners who are bored and joyless or who are engaging in unhealthy sexual behavior), tension might need to be handled differently (i.e., with more negative anticipation) or dispensed with completely.

CHAPTER 17

Bringing to a Climax

Sex and the Three-Act Structure (Part 2)

R EMEMBER THIS LITTLE DIAGRAM from earlier in the book? (Figure 17.1)
What would you say if I told you this structure could be applied to individual sex scenes as well? (Figure 17.2)

Okay, that might be a bit reductive. As we discussed in the chapter about larger narrative structure, not everything is a three-act story and that includes sex. However, in many cases, the structure does actually map scarily well onto how many sex scenes play out. Sex scenes are, in many ways, a microcosm of the larger narrative arcs of the sexual relationship and the game narrative as a whole. And like many larger arcs, many sex scenes follow a common structure: build tension, rise to a peak, release the tension through the climax,

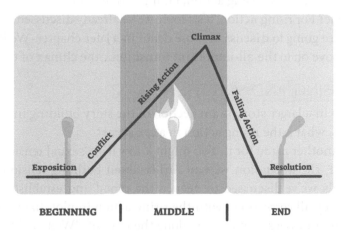

FIGURE 17.1   Yeah, that one, the three-act structure one? (VectorMine/Shutterstock.com.)

DOI: 10.1201/9780429356650-21

FIGURE 17.2 There's that anguished screaming again…. (Stokkete/Shutterstock.com.)

and then (optionally) tie up loose ends. In fact, the diagram above even provides a usefusl metaphor of the match as it relates to sex: the unlit match ready for the slightest spark, the all-consuming flame, and the cooling, spent match afterward. Given that fire imagery is often entwined with sex, it's likely not too difficult to connect that with aspects of sex: the potential, the passion, and the aftermath. While, again, this structure is not necessarily universal and should not be used as a limiting, constrictive rule set, it can be a useful foundation to approach a scene, to analyze how its sexual and narrative tension plays out, and to ensure that the emotional beats of the scene are hitting in the right way.

Also, it means thinking about climaxes…and not always the obvious one.

So, how do the concepts of rising action, falling action, and climax work in the context of a single sex scene? For rising action, it's a topic we've already discussed; for falling action, it's something we're going to discuss in more detail in a later chapter. We'll touch on them both here, then move on to the all-important transition…the climax of the scene.

THE HEAT IS RISING, AND SO'S THE ACTION?

So, if rising action in a larger story is a reflection of the story building intensity and stakes as things progress, what is the rising action in a sex scene?

Well, we have another name for it. You might know it as "sexual tension."

Yes, that's right, the discussion we had earlier about building tension in a scene and all the little details we've discussed to deepen the mood and establish the emotions of the characters…they all correspond with the rising action in plot diagrams like Freytag's pyramid. After all, unless it's a smash cut along the lines of, "Wait, WTF just happened?" tension, most sex scenes don't just jump straight to the sex. There are usually at least some establishing moments where the scene is set, the characters meet, and the tension begins to rise, particularly around what is going to happen and when they are going to fall into each other's arms.

It's also worth noting, however, that on top of the "will they, won't they" sort of sexual tension, there's another stage of sexual tension that, depending on the nature of the sex and the characters taking part, might be long and deliberately drawn out to its height, a short burst before getting down to business, or not even happening at all. I'm referring to *foreplay* and other physical intimacies that may take place before the sex begins: anything from light kissing and cuddling to extremely sexual make-outs, groping, or even fondling. The role of foreplay as a tension-builder depends heavily on the structure of the scene; in some cases, some of the foreplay itself might actually end up being the *climax*, as we'll see later in this chapter. But in other kinds of scenes where the climax is a later part of the sex (say, for example, an actual physical climax,) the foreplay might be as much a part of the tension as the verbal or body language dance the characters do before they act on their desires or get swept away by them! Imagine a scene where the characters might start out with a very tentative romantic gesture, a peck on the lips… then a deeper kiss…then even deeper as their hands begin to wander…growing bolder and bolder with foreplay, no one sure how far it will go, until they're overwhelmed with desire and have sex. In this sort of a dynamic, the characters' arousal becomes inextricable from the mounting tension of the scene, which makes for an extremely erotic, pleasurable rising action.

In general, just as rising action in a story should feel like it's building to a resolution, so should the tension of the scene – sexual tension, anticipation of the player, or whatever other tension you're building – feel like it's getting higher and higher until it reaches a peak. In most games, this rising action can map to dialogue or to gameplay actions, and depending on your scene and the "peak" it's building to, can be anything from understated gazes, touches, and speeches, all the way up to extremely explicit sex (Figure 17.3).

FIGURE 17.3   Rising action in a sex scene is the equivalent of striking the match until it sparks to life, the tip growing hotter and hotter, until…. (KConstantine/Shutterstock.com.)

DOES FALLING ASLEEP COUNT AS A FALLING ACTION?

Falling action or resolution in a sex scene, after the climax, usually corresponds to any scene or aspect of the scene that deals with the moments immediately after sex, such as pillow talk, afterglow, getting dressed, or silent moments of physical affection. There are some cases where the scene actually doesn't have a resolution – where right after the climax, the scene ends, and the narrative transitions back to the main game story. But in other cases, there is at least a short sequence that serves as a coda to the sex scene, knitting up the emotional threads and letting the heat and tension of the scene fade and process naturally (Figure 17.4).

These scenes – "aftermath" scenes, as I call them – are the topic of a future chapter, so like the rising action/tension, we'll just do a quick overview here. But it's still worth noting quickly how these scenes function and why, and how to recognize when they're needed to tie up loose threads. Those loose threads often relate to the characters: What are they going to say to each other? How are they going to treat each other now that this has happened? What does this mean for their relationship? Or it might just mean transitioning them to the right mind-space for the next phase of the non-sexual story; otherwise, it can be rough to go from postcoital afterglow straight into "have to go shoot/stab/fight lots of things!" It is certainly possible to keep some loose threads "dangling" for a future resolution later in

FIGURE 17.4 Falling action in a sex scene is the equivalent of when the match is on its last embers, its warmth and glow still there but gently fading. (FotomanufakturZ/Shutterstock.com.)

the story (e.g., a character might need time to figure out how they actually feel). But even when the plot and relationship threads aren't resolved, the scene should at least leave off on a satisfying "breakpoint." The player should also be clear that the thread will be picked up again, rather than feeling like it's simply "dropped" in a jarring way. In general, a good rule of thumb is to have the falling action last as long as it needs to wrap up those threads or get them to a satisfying break and then consider moving on.

So, having tackled the question of rising action/tension in the last chapter and planning to tackle falling action/aftermath later on in another chapter, let's focus on the key transition point between them, get our giggles out of the way…, and talk about climaxes in sex scenes (Figure 17.5).

THE CLIMAX OF THE SCENE

The climax of a sex scene, like the climax of an arc or story, is meant to be the high point of the scene, the point where all the tension and action has been built to, where it all reaches a fever pitch of intensity, sometimes even a narrative explosion of sorts, leaving catharsis and resolution in its wake as the tension, at last, is resolved.

And believe it or not, that fevered, explosive climax is not always the thing you're thinking of. (Though yes, it absolutely CAN be…)

The moment of orgasm – the "climax" of sex – can indeed sometimes be the perfect high point for the narrative and emotional climax, but it is not the only option; otherwise, scenes that fade to black or have a less explicit depiction would never be able to have a climax of their own. And what the team chooses to make the climactic moment or shot of the scene – or what plays out as the climactic moment as the scene is developed and iterated on – has a fundamental impact on the mood and emotional takeaway of the scene. This can be a useful lens (one of many) to look at the scene, identify key moments, and experiment with moving them around, emphasizing them, and seeing what the resulting outcome may be.

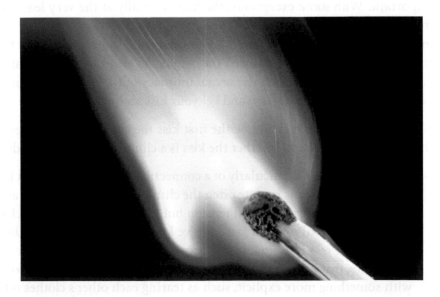

FIGURE 17.5 A climax of a sex scene is…well, you get the idea. (sergo iv/Shutterstock.com.)

In general, it's worth noting that once you hit the climax of the scene, that is usually when the actual *sex* (as in, the physical activity) should end – cutting away to another scene or to falling action (e.g., the aftermath) is usually the way to go. Showing further details of what happens after the climax (e.g., continued touching, thrusting, etc.) may offer realism, but also serves as *more* rising action to the structure of the scene. You may end up needing ANOTHER climax to resolve it. In general, less can be more with these sequences.

So, let's take a look at the different kinds of climactic moments that a sex scene can focus on. Note that, depending on the structure of the scene, these can also all be used as part of rising action and building sexual tension as well; here, we are considering them in the context of a final climactic moment.

- **The kiss** – specifically, the "first" kiss of the scene, the one that initiates the sex. The kiss will usually be the climax for "I don't know what's about to happen" or "I know what's about to happen, but not how" tension. In these cases, the sexual tension is building but not "certain" to be acted upon. The kiss-as-climax then becomes the answer to the question of "will they or won't they" – they will! – and that makes it the high point of the scene, usually before finishing on a quick fade to black or pan away. Focusing on the kiss as the climax grounds the scene in the evolution of the character's relationship. This expression of affection, love, or attraction is the high point AND the turning point for both characters, the moment they and the players have been waiting for. It emphasizes intimacy, affection, and connection as a theme, as opposed to more earthy, fleshy elements of sex.

  - It's important to note that, even in scenes where a kiss isn't the climax, **it is almost always still an extremely important beat in the scene**, if not one of the most important. With some exceptions, the kiss is usually at the very least an "inciting incident" of sorts which shifts the mood and direction of the scene toward intimacy, as well as building upon that intimacy and those emotions of the scene. In other words, even if the kiss isn't the climax, it's almost always a turning point and the foundation on which the sexual intimacy of the rest of the scene is built. So, whatever you do, always try and get your kiss scenes hitting right!

  - Note that this may or may not be the first kiss the characters have ever had and that can have an effect on whether the kiss is a climax or just the prelude to it

    - If it is the first kiss, particularly of a connection that has built over a large part of the game, then this is quite often the climax as it serves not only as the culmination of the scene's sexual tension but the culmination of the characters' attraction up until now. At last, they've kissed! Of course, depending on the nature of the relationship and the sexual desire that's been built between the characters, that may not be the full "climax" – full resolution may only come with something more explicit, such as tearing each other's clothes off or even a full orgasm. But the kiss will still be a standout moment in the scene.

– If the characters have kissed before, however, then it is a little less likely to be the climax of the scene, as kissing alone is already a bridge that has been crossed; however, it can still be positioned as such, particularly if dialogue or other context clues make it clear that sex is about to happen. Kissing in this context can be a little bit less of a "dramatic" moment depending on how it's positioned; it can be played off as an easy intimacy between the characters rather than a big action. However, this works best if you show the same easy intimate kissing throughout the earlier parts of the relationship.

- **The fade/cut to black** – In scenes that are less explicit about sex, the fade to black often features as the high moment of the scene, the climactic beat. In some cases, this fade to black can be immediately after the kiss or after some similar nonexplicit but intimate gesture – the characters moving together toward the bed, for example. In these cases, this kind of a climax works more as a gentle confirmation – yes, they're going to have sex! In slightly more explicit works – where, for example, the characters are shown passionately kissing or embracing sexually before the fade to black – it hits more as a substitute for, well, the climax of a sexual encounter, but without the explicitness. We already know they were going to have sex and have partaken of their rising sexual tension, and the fade to black provides catharsis and climax in the form of allowing us to imagine a satisfying consummation of what we've witnessed. A good example of this is the Garrus love scene in *Mass Effect 2*, where we see Shepard and Garrus gently bow their heads close together and tentatively touch each other as things fade to black poignantly. This model, to a certain extent, is the most flexible as it allows players to substitute their own imagined climax, guided by the context leading up to it, whether it's heated and passionate, sweet and romantic, casual and playful, or any other kind of emotional state. We'll be talking more at length about fades to black in a subsequent chapter.

- **The disrobe** – Having the moment that the clothes come off as the climax of the scene can be a really meaningful, erotic resolution to the rising action of the scene and of the character's relationship, and it can be done in a variety of ways: ripping off clothing in a desperate frenzy, gently disrobing each other, or pausing a moment before deliberately letting clothes fall to the floor. Having this as the high point of a scene serves as an even clearer, more delineated transition point of the characters' narrative arc, one that grounds it in both eroticism and vulnerability. To a certain extent, there is a sense of "no turning back" once the clothes are off and the characters are naked; even if they suddenly decide not to have sex, it's not like their lover can now "unsee" their nudity. As such, this sort of climax tends to feel dramatic and "final," unless the disrobing is being played in a very light-hearted fun kind of way. How that drama plays out and what sort of climax and catharsis it serves as depends heavily on the kind of disrobing that happens:

  - A frenzied disrobing usually serves as the climax and catharsis of intense lust and passion. This is a climax where these emotions involved become overwhelming and impossible to control, where the emphasis is on these tensions becoming so

FIGURE 17.6 Sometimes, just ending on an image like this – or even just the clothing on the floor – is enough to communicate the scene's emotional and erotic climax. (Kaspars Grinvalds/ Shutterstock.com.)

powerful that they just "snap" and bust open as violently as the clothing involved. In this, the characters may seem like they're being swept up in things as opposed to making an active, thought-out choice; indeed, it's arguably a climax in which reason is completely lost and overwhelmed by desire.

- In contrast, a more deliberate disrobing – for example, carefully and deliberately letting each piece of clothing fall to the floor, while making eye contact – ends up with a climax that is less about getting "swept up" in the rising action and more about the characters making a conscious choice of what to do about it…in other words, to act on the sexual tension. That doesn't necessarily make it less erotic – it can be just as sexy and just as informed by desire – but if ripping each other's clothes off is an explosion, this is the pause before a plunge off the diving board. It emphasizes the high point of the scene as the character stepping through a doorway and setting their course ahead, rather than being rushed through that door by lust (Figure 17.6).

- **The transitional movement** – In some sex scenes, the climax comes, usually just before a fade to black, from a significant transition or movement between the characters as they move from a neutral position (e.g., standing) to a more intimate position (e.g., lying down, sitting on laps, slammed onto a table, etc.). One common example is one character leading another to a bed or other flat surface as a prelude to the sex; another is what I jokingly call "the sexy collapse," where the characters passionately kiss and embrace and end up sinking or falling out of frame. This kind of climax, similar to the fade to black, is a gentler transitional moment, a resolution of tension in the form of moving to a literal physical space of intimacy (e.g., a bed, the floor, etc.). Like disrobing, it's also something that can feel either like a deliberate choice from the characters (e.g., guiding their lover to a particular space) or the climax of repressed emotions that are now bursting forth uncontrollably (e.g., tossing things off a table before both slamming onto it). This is also a climax that, thanks to the way it relocates the characters, can resolve a tension between the "public" and the "private." These characters may have been interacting in "polite society" (e.g., standing, clothes on, etc.), but now they have moved their relationship into more private, personal spaces like bedrooms or places that represent more physical vulnerability (e.g., beds where one sleeps). Examples of this are particularly common in *Dragon Age II*, where the majority of sex scenes reach their peak as someone either falls into bed with someone or slams someone up against a wall.

- **The dramatic physical connection** – Sometimes, the climax of the scene is on a particular physical gesture, act, or touch. This can be something as simple as a meaningful touch or caress as part of foreplay or as explicit as the moment of a sexual act (e.g., penetration, manual contact with genitals, etc.). It can also focus on the character's response to this touch (e.g., rapt pleasure, teasing smile, etc.). This sort of climax is moving further down the physical act of the spectrum, grounding the catharsis in the physical, sometimes even more than actual orgasm (which we deal with next). It provides a useful shorthand for the physicality of sex, of the fact that yes, sex is not just tasteful fades to black but also involves touching, stroking, arousal, and other physical contacts. When paired with a fade to black, it can be a useful way to resolve the sexual tension with a dramatic, sexy touch, gesture, or act while still allowing the player to imagine their own further resolution in the following moments. A good example can be seen in the Lair of the Shadow Broker DLC for *Mass Effect 2*; the optional Liara love scene reaches a climax as Shepard places a hand in the small of Liara's back (an erogenous zone for asari) and she gasps in pleasure.

- **The moment of orgasm** – yes, sometimes a sexual climax is, in fact, a climax. Focusing on a character's final moment of bliss (or both characters') is, out of all the climaxes, the one most grounded in the physical and primal. It puts the lens squarely on the physical realities of sex and of bodies coming together and on the pleasure of the characters. This pleasure may be simply physical or may take on emotional or spiritual qualities based on the context of the characters involved, their relationship, and their personal experience of what sex is like. This context affects how the climax and how the scene itself is read by the audience; is it simply a titillating, erotic moment that serves as the satisfaction of the player's arousal or is it a profound and moving climax to the emotions that have been building in the entire scene, with every kiss, with every touch? Either way, having this as your climax ensures that your scene is "about" sex, that there is no way of avoiding or minimizing the sexual nature of the moment. It's neither "polite" nor "modest," but it offers a primal note that may be exactly what your scene and your characters need to drive the emotions home. *The Witcher 3* offers several examples of "climax as climax" with the Keira Metz scene as well as several courtesan scenes; there is a particular visual and narrative emphasis on the women's orgasm as the encounter builds to a climax.

- Note that focusing on orgasm as the narrative climax does not mean having to actually SHOW it with explicit visuals (e.g., facial expressions). It can also be alluded to by other visuals (e.g., a hand slamming against a glass window, similar to the Consort sex scene in *Mass Effect*) or with audio cues such as vocalized moans, etc.

There are other potential climaxes to a sex scene (for example, confession of feelings or someone bursting in), but for now, these are a good baseline to work from; you may be able to think of more.

A few other tidbits to consider when considering climaxes and scene structure for sex scenes:

- One of the most powerful companions to scene structure, in this case, is, funnily enough, music. Consider having music that guides the player through the rising action, climax, and falling action. Many sex scenes feature music that builds to a very clear and identifiable "peak," and as such, this often matches almost perfectly with the actual climax of the scene. Alternatively, if you're finding that a scene is not quite hitting right in later production, ensure that the narrative structure and the musical structure are not at odds with each other.

- Don't be afraid to storyboard out a sex scene ahead of time and use that phase to work out the order and the structure of your scene. It may be useful to place key moments (e.g., the first kiss, getting undressed, certain moments of foreplay, etc.) on cards that can then be shuffled, reordered, removed, etc., and then prototype out the scene with your team or playtesters. That way, you can get an early sense of what the real high point of a scene might be, how best to raise the tension and action to get there, and what sort of resolution is needed for falling action afterward.

- Ensure all contributors to the scene – cinematics, writers, animators, audio, etc., – are in sync with each other and are all aware of the technical limitations, budget, scope, etc. It's all very well for your writer to detail out a deeply meaningful, photorealistic expression of physical ecstasy as the pinnacle of your scene, but it's not going to help if you don't have high fidelity models or mocap suits! If tech limitations are an issue, let your developers know early and often so that they can compensate and work around the problem. Much better if that writer can collaborate with audio to do one sexy, breathy fade to black…

CONCLUSION

The building of tension, the resolution of it, the unwinding in the aftermath – just as these can be useful storytelling tools for larger story arcs, so too can they be for sex scenes. And just like a big heroic story, the climax should be the high point of the scene's energy, the moment when all that sexual (or regular) tension you've built finally explodes and releases in a satisfying way. So, when you're building your rising action, make sure it's rising toward a meaningful, cathartic destination…and when you get there, make sure it's a hell of a high point to end on!

(And as for what comes after that climax? Well, you'll find out a little later…)

WORKSHOP QUESTIONS

Analysis: Looking at the sex scene(s) from the game you're analyzing, can you identify what the climax of the scene is? Look for the moment where the tension resolves or the moment of highest energy. Is the climax one of the types we've discussed so far or is it something else? Describe the energy and impact of that moment/visual/etc., as the climax of the scene. How would the energy and structure of the scene be different if the scene climaxed earlier or at a different moment?

Creative: If appropriate for your game, consider what you imagine as the climactic moment of your game's sex scenes, the highest point of the action, and the moment that resolves the tension. What kind of climax do you want it to be, a physical climax or some other narrative moment? Consider the suggestions above, but don't be afraid to explore other kinds of narrative climaxes as well.

Ask yourself the following questions:

- What do I feel the mood and thematic impact of the climax should be on my players? How should they feel after this climax?

- Is it something that keeps the sex vague or explicit?

- Are there any unique technical challenges to take into consideration (e.g., facial rigging, clothing, etc.)?

- Will you be able to execute the climax as planned? If not, what are some other alternatives?

CHAPTER 18

Sex Cutscene Direction and Design

An Interview with Ashley Ruhl

Author/Interviewee: Ashley Ruhl

Interview questions by: Michelle Clough

For 3D games, creating convincing cutscenes can be difficult at the best of times, and that can be doubly true for creating sex cutscenes! Yet, a well-done cutscene can be the erotic capstone to an amazing romance, or a passionate lust, or even just a one-night stand. And while this book discusses considerations for narrative, visuals, game design, etc…what about the cinematics design itself? I had a chat with Ashley Ruhl, one of the lead cinematic designers at BioWare and a good friend of mine to get her insight on the subject, and this is what she had to say!

- MICHELLE

Firstly, thank you for agreeing to be part of this book!

Let's start off with a very quick introduction of who you are, your background in cinematics, and your experience in doing sex/romance cutscenes.

Hello, my name is Ashley Ruhl! I'm a Lead Cinematic Designer at BioWare, meaning my focus is on visual narrative and cutscenes. I'm really passionate about sex/romance cutscenes in games because, like most interactive media, they have an opportunity to connect very personally with the player and allow them to express and discover more about themselves. Thoughtful representation, variety of player expression, and relatable experiences are all really important to me in making scenes that matter to the player.

DOI: 10.1201/9780429356650-22

As a cinematic designer, what are the biggest challenges (technical or otherwise) of creating good sex scenes?

I think that one of the biggest cinematic challenges (for choice-based romances especially) is making sure that the PC (player character) animations in the sex scene do not betray the player's concept of who that character is. Similar to writing, a cine designer wants the scene pacing to visually flow well, which means taking some authority out of the player's hands to keep the action moving. I can't make a player choice for every single kiss/caress/thrust, but I don't want to give the PC any actions that feel out of character. This requires a lot of the "flow" animations to be "personality agnostic," for example, "this kiss animation works fairly well for all PC personality types." Longer scenes can branch the PC's behavior thematically, like taking a dominant or submissive role and creating different performances for each. For cine designers, it's always finding that balance between good scene flow with more generalized animations and preserving the player's agency and roleplay in the scene.

I remember you once told me that a lot of cinematic design was like "smashing Barbie dolls together convincingly." (Great image, btw!) What goes into "smashing dolls" together in a way that looks like intimate contact (whether it be embracing, caressing, thrusting, etc.) and avoids the dreaded uncanny valley?

I love that imagery because I often feel like my job is making dolls move around a scene. Specifically for sex scenes though, it's how I highlight the difference between game characters and living people. As humans, we are very squishy. We change shape, we're full of liquids and expanding/contracting muscles, and we have skin that stretches all over that shape-shifting form. In contrast, digital characters are essentially working backward from a robot skeleton to make something that resembles a squishy human. But even without completely realistic human characters, we can still create intimacy with clever cinematography that hides the limitations of the tech.

One of the things I see in great sex scenes is cropping in the frame, meaning that the shot doesn't show the entire character. Instead, the cine designer creates a series of "inserts" and cuts between them. For example: Picture a moment when one character is thrusting into another character from behind. Instead of shooting from a wide profile angle that shows both characters entirely, the cine designer creates a series of insert shots:

- A hand on the hips as they move rhythmically to establish the main action
- A close-up on the characters' faces, expressions of ecstasy
- Fingers gripping the edge of a table

Not only do these shots hide the technical shortcomings of the digital characters, but they do a better job of expressing the emotional intent of the scene, placing the viewer inside the experience instead of a neutral wide shot on the outside.

What are some of the technical hurdles to convincingly conveying "touch" in cinematics?

The vast majority of sex cutscenes in modern games are motion-captured from live actors on a set wearing mocap suits that transpose their movement onto digital characters. Unfortunately, these animations can't go straight from mocap to game; the animation data requires a lot of cleanup by animators to get it to look right on game skeletons. Then, the game characters have different body types/clothes/hair from the live actors, so animators need to adjust contact points to make sure that there isn't a lot of clipping or "air-kissing" (this becomes EXTRA complicated if the player can customize their character, making it difficult for developers to line up with every possible player creation). On top of that, "real-time" scenes mean that the animation data is streamed live to the game characters, and any slight hiccup that could cause one animation to start a little early/late, or optimization in animation data, can result in contact points between two characters not lining up perfectly. Details like this aren't as noticeable when characters are by themselves, but in the intimacy of a sex scene, it becomes much more obvious.

Tell us a little bit about the role of the camera in a sexual cutscene. What should a cinematic director/designer be thinking of in terms of the use of the camera?

One of my guiding principles in cinematic design is "the camera is an actor." But unlike the other characters in the scene, the camera guides the emotional tone of the whole scene. Additionally, in games, the camera is a proxy for the experience of the player, giving specific weight and intentionality that must be carefully considered in an intimate scene.

The first thing a cinematic designer needs to consider is how to plan a series of shots that build upon the predicted state of mind of the player. As an artist, my personal feelings will always be intertwined in my creation, but the scene can't be solely built on my gaze/desires.

An exaggerated example, consider a scenario where the player controls a female protagonist with a male love interest. If the camera lingered on the body of the female protagonist longer/more intimately than the male love interest (i.e., showing intimate shots of her body more than his), that's the camera taking authority in who the player should be ogling in the scene. But if the player chose to romance this male love interest, their focus is on the love interest, so the camera work should reflect that.

As a follow-up to that, can you talk a bit about the language of camera angles/cuts and what they "say" in a sex scene?

I could probably write/cite a lot of resources for cinematic language here, but I'll try to stay on the pieces that I think are most important to consider in intimate game scenes.

* Every shot has a purpose
Like I mentioned above, I always prefer cropped insert closeups over wide shots in intimate scenes, both to bring the player closer to the action and to hide any seams in the digital performance. But these shots shouldn't just be a random assortment of body parts and physical action. Each shot means something in how it's framed, what order the shots play out, and which character perspective the shots seem to take. The camera should be expressing what the characters are feeling, as well as how the player should feel about the scene.

* Sequence of shots and meaning
Let's take an example of a simple series of shots, where the nonplayer character (NPC) is preparing to pleasure the player.

The sequence of shots goes:

1. NPC's face

2. NPC's hands travel down the player's body

3. Player's face

4. Player's hands tensing in sheets

The sequence above implies the player is reacting to the NPC's actions. If we change the order:

1. Player's hands tensing in sheets

2. Player's face

3. NPC's face

4. NPC's hands travel down the player's body

This sequence now implies that the player is *anticipating* the NPC's actions, rather than reacting. The order of the shots changes the context of how we view the scene, including the rise and fall of action, level of tension, perspective, and power dynamics.

* Power dynamics in framing
The easiest rule of thumb to establish power in a scene is where to place the camera vertically. A camera shooting a character from below (i.e., "looking up" at them) gives the character more power while shooting from above ("looking down") makes them feel weaker and smaller. In sex scenes, power often shifts between characters during the scene. The cine designer may consider shooting from below on a character when they take control, or if a character is submitting, they may fall lower in the frame. The cine designer can also give two characters of different heights the same power by tilting/"dutching" the camera so both of their heads are at the same height in the frame (the 2011 Thor movie does this for Thor and Jane's kiss).

* Speed of cuts
Rapid cuts between shots can imply a lot of passion and not a lot of thinking, as the camera is "jumping between thoughts" very quickly. In contrast, long, slow shots can imply focused intent and also build anticipation for further action. In this way, the speed of cutting changes the tone of the scene and the emotional state of the characters.

* Perspective and agency
"Eyes are the windows to the soul," but they're also where our eyes are naturally drawn because of the way our brains are wired. When we see a face on a screen, we are more inclined to empathize with that character's experience. If a camera only focuses on the

body below the face, the body becomes an object rather than a person (which is how a lot of female bodies have been objectified in modern media, see *Headless Women in Hollywood*). This is why it's important to regularly show the faces of all characters involved in a sex scene and to reconnect the physical titillation with how that titillation makes the characters feel. In the shot sequence example above, the shot of the NPC's hands on the player's body, followed by a shot of the player's face, connects the viewer with the player's experience of the physical action.

Additionally, if we want to empathize more with one character over another (like a player character over an NPC), the majority of the shots should be designed around the player character's gaze. This usually includes more shots of the PC's face as they react/show intent, over-the-shoulder shots where the camera looks where the PC is looking, and inserts on details where the PC is focusing their attention. This isn't to say we shouldn't show the NPC's face, but rather balance the time spent on the NPC's perspective to favor the PC perspective more.

Elsewhere in the book, I will talk a bit about environmental design for sex (i.e., how the location can affect mood, etc.). I'd be interested to hear the cinematic perspective on this, even if just on a technical level. What do you need to consider as part of the "set dressing" and environment where The Sexy Stuff is taking place?

Environment design definitely shapes the expectations of the scene. I think the clearest indicator is BED. Any time a conversation happens in a room where there's a bed, even if it's just sitting in the background, the player is inevitably going to consider that scene could lead to sexy times in the bed. But focusing on specific props throughout the room can also shape scene tone, especially if they take up a large chunk of screen real estate. Two out-of-focus wine glasses in the foreground versus a pile of documents change the viewer's expectations of the conversation happening in the background. A cine designer can also build intimacy by creating a frame within a frame, like placing draped curtains on either side of the shot to focus the player's eye toward the characters. I do think that framing set dressing in the shot needs to be done carefully though because it can feel very ham-fisted if it's too obviously leading the player's expectations.

Along the same line, what are your thoughts on the effects of different lighting in a scene? How do you decide what sort of lighting a sex scene should have?

We often associate sexy times with being in the dark. Darkness creates a natural vignette that brings the characters closer together. Darkness also builds drama, as the only thing that's lit (and therefore important) is the act of sex. At the other end, a cine designer can build drama by over-lighting a scene and creating a bright vignette that silhouettes the characters and draws the viewer into the only action that they can see. An evenly lit scene can make the sex scene feel unremarkable, just as common an action as a regular conversation. And that can totally be the intent! Not every sex scene needs to be world-shatteringly dramatic, but lighting plays a big role in expressing the emotional state of the characters involved.

Let's talk a bit about characters' body language. How can body language add to a sex scene? What sorts of body language can be used? What are the technical considerations/limitations/challenges that cinematic designers have to take into account for body language (and how to work within/around them)?

I consider every scene to have two scripts: the words that are being spoken and the story that the bodies are telling. There are millions of microbehaviors that humans unconsciously use to express their emotional states, and people tend to recognize them even if they can't put a name to them (unless they have a form of social–emotional agnosia that prevents processing sensory information). Knowing this, I can build character performances that imply emotional states and personalities without being too overt in their expression. Someone who is confident will step forward into the personal space bubble and with a calm direct motion place their hand on another character's cheek. Someone who is nervous will shift and fidget or during an intimate act, they will be more tentative with their touch.

In terms of technical limitations, scenes will always get more complicated the moment that characters physically touch, but clever cameras can get around that. As an example, I want the NPC to put their hand on the player's cheek, but I don't have an animation that perfectly lines the characters up without clipping. To solve this, I'll place the camera on the opposite side of the "hand–cheek" interaction, so that the player's body obscures the NPC's hand from the camera. The intent and emotional impact are still there even if I don't have the perfect animation for the moment.

Another thing that can often make a sex scene hotter is eye contact. Any tips and tricks on how cinematic designers can reproduce this and make it convincing?

I liberally use eye darts (eyes shifting focus) because humans are rarely laser-focused on one subject for more than a few seconds. This is where a lot of the "uncanny valley" feel occurs in digital characters when the eye focus doesn't shift regularly. But by making sure that the eyes and attention move more naturally for most of the scene, the contrast of long, direct eye contact will feel more intense.

The sex act of many sex scenes starts from a literal or conceptual moment of "their eyes meeting," indicating consensual intent. I try to give this moment emotional weight, telling the player, "Hey this is important, pay attention." To do this, I shoot as close to the "eyeline" as possible (the invisible line connecting two characters' faces), with a close-up shot on both characters and a cropped portion of the other character in the foreground. This builds tension by placing characters in the frame as close as they can be without actually touching, making the payoff even more exciting. This "shot, reverse shot" moment also kicks off the scene with a clear understanding of the emotional state of both characters, giving more weight to the physical act.

Besides the things we've already discussed, what are some of the more subtle aspects of sex scenes that you would recommend cinematic designers take into consideration? What are things that may often get missed, but make a scene better when done (or make a scene worse if ignored?)

Honestly, less is more. I focus on pinpointing the feeling I want the scene to have and consider which physical actions I can abstract in ways that guide the player emotionally, but also allow them to fill in the blanks. This gives the player more freedom to imagine the scene and the characters as they see them. A simple example is the fade-to-black, where anything can be implied. But in a more explicit scene, an NPC can slide down a player's body, and before the NPC reaches the player's hips, the shot cuts to the player's face in ecstasy. It still creates the emotion that the NPC is pleasing the player, but intentionally leaves the explicit action vague for the player to fill in the blanks.

And a short soapbox moment: While I do enjoy detailed sex scenes, I think that as game developers we need to be careful about how much agency we take from the player to tell a specific story. Hyperrealistic performance continues to be an overarching goal of the game industry, but I think it's easy for us to lose the magic that previous limited graphic systems required from both developers and players. What couldn't be shown on screen was implied, but it created an invitation for the player to imagine their own story in a medium that was asking them to be a part of the narrative. I think there's a balance to be struck in games, where we can create strong narrative guiding lines that still let the player fill in the rest of the canvas.

What, in your opinion, is a great example of a sex cinematic in AAA games? Can you point out on a technical and craft level what it does well?

One scene that I think is incredibly executed is the final romance scene with Kaidan in *Mass Effect 3*. The majority of the scene is clothes on, but there's a palpable connection between Kaidan and Shepard. Many sex scenes in games are "relationship initiators," whereas this is an established relationship that's confirmed earlier in the game, so the scene is of less tension and more intimacy. The camera keeps them close together in the frame, and the attention to eye and facial animation is incredible. During the sex portion, they are still clothed in classic "modesty underwear," but the little action we see implies that they're comfortable and playful with one another while still being deeply connected. I would've liked to see more during the sex portion of the scene, but I'd rather have a shorter implied scene than a longer scene that reaches beyond its technical capabilities.

What does cinematics need most from other disciplines (writing, art, sound, etc.) to succeed at better sex scenes? What would you like to ask from those disciplines if they're listening?

I think having a strong line of communication between writing, animation, and cine design produces the best scenes. A writer can outline the intent of the scene. An animator will say what is technically possible from the rigs and the animation budget. A cine designer can best strategize how to bring those two elements together. Some things written can be expressed nonverbally through animations, and sometimes writers describe actions that are difficult to accomplish well with the tools provided. I think when these three expertises build the scene collaboratively, rather than assembly line construction, they can better lean on the strengths of the others.

Obviously, cinematic cutscenes are more of a thing in 3D games as opposed to 2D. But are there any principles of creating good 3D sex cinematics that can also apply to those

other games? Can you give some good takeaways to readers who may be making, say, 2D JRPGs or visual novels with sex scenes?

If it's a series of illustrations, I think the design of purposeful insert shots still applies. It becomes more like storyboards than moving action but can produce similar experiences for the player. I also think that 2D scenes can lean heavier on sound design as well. One illustration with a short audio play of actions behind it can be incredibly impactful.

Any parting words of wisdom to your fellow cinematic designers about doing sex scenes?

Even if the animations/character rigs/environment don't quite do what you want them to do, experiment and see if you can create a strong performance from limitations, abstraction, and cheating the camera. The ultimate goal of a cinematic sex scene is to elicit powerful emotions. This gives you the flexibility to try a lot of different strategies to get there.

WORKSHOP QUESTIONS

Analysis: If the game you're analyzing presents sex in a cutscene format, examine its cutscene direction, particularly in relation to:

- Its edits (speed, order of shots, etc.)

- Camera framing

- Use of character animation for body language, etc.

- Location, environment, lighting, etc.

As a collective, what do you feel these elements combine to communicate to the player? Can you identify which (if any) of them are put into place in order to hide technical issues or solutions such as "air-kissing," etc.?

Creative: If your game is going to have sexual cutscenes, work with your cinematic team (if you have one – or maybe YOU are the cinematic team!) to plot out one of the cutscenes in a rough storyboard. Consider the following:

- Assets, animations, and resources available (e.g., are you dealing with stock animations, or do you have mocap?)

- The environment the sex scene is going to take place in (this can be a rough idea; we'll go more into environment detail later)

- The series and nature of shots in the sexual sequence (e.g., slow pan vs. frenetic cuts? Long shot vs. close-ups? Character faces vs. character body parts vs. other scene elements? Which perspective do the shots represent?)

- Technical considerations of physical contact, body language, eye contact, etc.

If you're not doing a 3D game, you can still storyboard this out for the format that your game is in (e.g., unique art or computer graphics/CGs in a visual novel).

CHAPTER 19

Fade to Black vs. Showing the Sex

V ERY OFTEN, WHEN WE talk about sex scenes in games, we're not talking about actual sex scenes in the sense of visual, on-screen sex. Many games employ what is known as a "fade to black" in lieu of an explicit sex scene. We touched on this briefly in an earlier chapter when talking about climaxes – how the fade itself can be a climax, and how otherwise the climax is usually "the last image" before the scene cuts away to black. Here, we're going to focus more on the use of fade to black and when it is (and isn't!) the right approach to use for a sex scene (Figure 19.1).

FIGURE 19.1   No joke, but this is sometimes genuinely the hottest and most engaging thing you can show your players.

DOI: 10.1201/9780429356650-23

The most common structure for fade to black sex scenes progresses as such:

1. A cutscene with initial dialogue leading to kissing, embracing, light foreplay, etc. – establishing action to indicate that the two characters are going to have sex.

2. (Optional) A transitional shot of some kind – the camera panning away from the action, or a door closing, or other refocusing away from the physical activity

3. The visuals "fade to black" as a conclusion to the scene.

4. After a few moments of black screen, the scene fades back in to show the aftermath of the sexual encounter, whether it's cuddling naked in bed or a much later scene in another location.

    a. Occasionally, some games will intersperse this with another scene entirely (e.g., in *Assassin's Creed Origins*, the sex scene fades to black, cuts to a scene with Layla Hassan in modern day, and then cuts back to Bayek and Aya cuddling after sex.)

The list of games (both AAA and indie) that utilize fade to black is so long, it's almost easier to ask which games with sex DON'T use fade to black! Even games and game franchises famous for their sex scenes are heavy in their use of fade to black; as an example, the *Dragon Age* sex scenes are legendary, but in all three of the main titles, the majority fades out before things get TOO spicy (Figure 19.2).

The use of fade to black makes a lot of sense in some cases, but it's easy to slip into the sentiment that they're the best or the "default" way to tackle sex scenes. Fades to black are seen as the "tasteful" or "mature" way to handle sex, and games that are chasing critical acclaim and praise for being "artistic" and "adult" will often only include sex in this

FIGURE 19.2   Pictured: 90% of all AAA sex scenes and probably at least another 70% of indie sex scenes too.

format. Developers when asked why they opted for fade to black or other less explicit sex scenes will often reply with a variant of, "The scene stood on its own" or "Given the lead-in/emotional context/etc., I didn't need to SHOW the sex."[1]

To be fair, in some cases, this is perfectly true. As we discussed near the start of the book, sex scenes need to fulfill a narrative or gameplay function, the same as any other scene. In cases where those functions have already been handled in other contexts, it makes at least some sense to say, "okay, yes, I don't need a sex scene to convey that they're in love/character A is a badass/etc." However, there is a difference between:

- a designer deciding, "No, I don't need a sex scene at all here..."

- a designer deciding, "Yes, I need a sex scene, but for various reasons, a fade to black will work the best for this scene..."

- and a designer deciding, "Yes, I do need a sex scene...but of *course* I don't NEED to show the details."

And there's DEFINITELY a difference when that last one is said with some sort of air of moral superiority or with the assumption that NOT showing the details is somehow inherently the ideal solution.

So...does that mean a scene that DOES get graphic is somehow signaling inadequacy? "I didn't need to SHOW the sex" might be perfectly true, but why treat it like some sort of default or design victory? Why is showing sex treated less like a creative or personal choice and more like an unwanted obligation that can be avoided if you show enough "nonsexy" work? Does that mean that games that DO show the sex have somehow "failed" to convey enough by nonsexual means? Why aren't developers saying more things like, "I decided an explicit sex scene slowed down the pace," or "I wanted to allow the player to use their imagination," rather than "I didn't NEED to (thank God) so I didn't?"

In many ways, this is the same sex-negativity we discussed in the earlier chapter about myths of sex, just slightly altered from "sex is inappropriate" to "SHOWING sex is inappropriate." While it concedes that, occasionally, sex is an acceptable and "necessary" story or game beat to explore, it posits that the "ideal" sex scene is the one that is pure implication and hinting...that somehow, using explicit sex as a storytelling tool is "unnecessary" or "overindulgent" as long as there are other nonsexual or nonexplicit tools to use. The fade to black isn't just a good way to allude to sexual activity, but it becomes THE only good way to tackle it, and only worthless "edgy" or "titillating" games would refuse to do things that way (Figure 19.3).

This approach holds back game developers from experimenting and pushing the boundaries of what they can accomplish technically or creatively. It means that anything they might explore through the medium of explicit sex – modeling realistic fleshy touching, for example, or experimenting with tactile gameplay, or showing a character's emotional journey on their way to a blissful climax – is less likely to happen because...well, what's the point if the default is always to fade to black long before the action ever gets to that point? When we establish "fade to black" as the default "best" approach, it sets up a system in

FIGURE 19.3   I mean, what kind of PERVERT would want a sex scene any more explicit than this and two seconds of kissing?

which developers have to jump through hoops to justify getting more explicit than that. At best, it's a lot of extra hassle and stress on those who want to try it; at worst, it results in stagnation as developers either give up or are blocked from trying new things.

If it sounds like I'm against fades to black, I'm not. Some of my favorite scenes in games are technically fades to black, and there are plenty of meaningful, well-executed, and even erotic examples of them (Figure 19.4). The point is not that they're "bad" any more than explicit sex is "bad." The point is that both of them are *good in different ways.* Or, to drive it home:

The fade to black *is* a good technique for dealing with sex…but it is not "the best," just one of many.

FIGURE 19.4   Showing this is a choice – and sometimes, it will be the right one.

The choice to show OR not show sex is a matter of stylistic and thematic choice, NOT of quality or morality.

But this raises the question: if fade to black is good in some ways and explicit sex is good in others, how do you know which to use? What are their pros and cons in terms of how they're implemented and what their final impact on the player is? When *should* you fade to black, anyway?

Well, with the usual caveats of, "every game is different," "these are suggestions, not rules," and of course, "you should do whatever you feel works the best with your vision," here are some guidelines on how to choose a fade to black or a more explicit scene.

In general, developers should lean toward fading to black if:

- They need to advance the core plot in a fast-paced manner

- They have meta-narrative concerns such as technical issues or censorship fears

- They prefer to tell a story through implications and hints or a story that allows the player's imagination to take precedence.

FADE TO BLACK ADVANTAGE #1: PACING

Game writers and designers often have to be highly economical when it comes to narrative and gameplay. There are certainly occasions when a story-focused game should take its time on a particular story beat or scene (like, say, a romantic scene of intimacy), but for many games, those moments must be moved through quickly and smoothly so as to return to the more exciting high-stakes moments, either in terms of cutscenes or gameplay.

This is where fading to black shines as an approach to sex scenes. It can convey the important narrative beat – "these characters are having sex" – in a much shorter amount of time than showing the act itself. While there may be a scene of conversation or foreplay beforehand, the sex scene itself "lasts" for only seconds. As such, the narrative can keep progressing at a brisk pace, often picking up immediately after things fade back in by leading into the next mission or story beat. For games that need to be economical in their storytelling or for games that need to keep a very fast pace of story and gameplay, fading to black is the safest and quickest approach to sexual storytelling. For example, in Morrigan's dark ritual in *Dragon Age: Origins*, the scene cuts to black as soon as she approaches the bed and blows at the candle, then shifts immediately to the final march on the Darkspawn; it gets the player back in the thick of the main plot almost right away.

WATCH OUT FOR: Transitions in emotions, mood, and desire. Just because you CAN get back to the "main" story as fast as possible does not *always* mean it's the right move. Transitioning from emotional and physical intimacy to a black screen and then *immediately* slam-cutting back to the combat, gameplay, or mission explanations can be jarring to players if not done well. Respect the emotional space that the sexual intimacy creates and do the work to transition the player out of that space, whether it's light pillow talk, a saucy comment, or a suitable time skip.

FADE TO BLACK ADVANTAGE #2: AVOIDING CENSORSHIP

One obvious advantage of fading to black and not showing the sex is not having to worry about issues of censorship and ratings. We discussed the issues with censorship earlier in the book – the considerations about age ratings affecting sales, for example, or the issues with government and law. The more explicit the game is the more all of those issues come to the forefront and the more chance that you or your team may end up having to remove that content to satisfy sales platforms, legal bodies, or stakeholders (Figure 19.5).

While fading to black does not completely do away with censorship issues and content ratings – the *Dragon Age* franchise has historically received M-ratings despite using mostly fade to black sex scenes – it does make these issues easier to deal with. For example, the Entertainment Software Rating Board lists "suggestive themes" and "sexual content" under the lower T-rating, suggesting that a particularly tame "fade to black" could earn a lower, more inclusive rating. This is the route *Star Wars: The Old Republic* takes; the game is rated T, and sex is restricted to veiled invitations between characters ("Let's go somewhere more…private…") before walking off and fading to black. Localization changes or cuts can be easier to apply to a fade-to-black scene as well, not only by cutting parts of the scene but by changing parts of the dialogue or interaction to make the context less erotic.

If a game developer is concerned about encountering heavy resistance to sexual content from gatekeepers, shareholders, or other organizations with clout, fading to black can be the safer option. No need to justify that bare nipple to anyone!

FADE TO BLACK ADVANTAGE #3: AVOIDING TECHNICAL ISSUES

Similarly, if there are concerns about, say, *rendering* that bare nipple or getting it to smush appropriately against another bare nipple, fade to black may be the way to go. While Ashley covered some fantastic techniques for "fooling" the camera during cinematics and

FIGURE 19.5 "I don't care how much you worked on this! You're going to have to go through and remove. Every. Single. Nipple. No excuses or your game's off our store!" (fizkes/Shutterstock.com.)

compensating for technical issues (e.g., difficulties in conveying physical contact), it can still be tricky, and getting it wrong can result in the opposite of whatever emotion you want to convey. Whether due to the uncanny valley effect of 3D models, the challenges in conveying physical touch without clipping or simply not having the hours and staff to devote to the scene, the technical challenges can be tough, and not every team may be able to do it justice. As Ashley said, sometimes less is more! Fading to black allows your team to convey the basic message – intimacy between characters – for the least amount of blood, sweat, and tears and the least number of technical challenges.

WATCH OUT FOR: Avoiding physical intimacy entirely. While skipping the sex itself can save a lot of trouble in terms of navigating character models, touch physics, etc., some game sex scenes go further by not having ANY physical contact or foreplay in the lead-up to the fade to black. Like *Star Wars: The Old Republic, Dragon Age: Origins* also has sexual encounters where there is only dialogue and no physical contact (e.g., the brothel scenes, the optional encounter with Isabela). As a result, these scenes lack the same heat and connection as other scenes in the same game which DID feature touching and kissing before the fade to black. And they didn't even have that T-rating to worry about! Thus, you have scenes like the one with Isabela, where she's enthusiastically planning out a potential foursome with you, her, Alistair, and Leiliana…and yet, *no one* has any physical contact with each other or even physical closeness! While this is likely due at least partially to technical limitations, it's something to be wary of, even as a "shortcut."

If you intend to fade to black, ensure that your lead-in (and, ideally, the aftermath) matches the emotional mood of the scene and encounter(s) with appropriate physicality, including (but not limited to) kissing, cuddling, touching, etc. If technical limitations are still an issue, refer to Ashley's chapter for some tips and tricks on how to fudge them and still present visuals that convey believable human contact. It's not about keeping the camera focused on skin-to-skin contact; it's about ensuring the player comes away believing in the characters' interaction. In contrast to the *Origins* Isabela scene, the scene with Merrill in *Dragon Age II* has plenty of physical contact both before and after the fade, ensuring that the scene still feels grounded in sweet physical intimacy.

FADE TO BLACK ADVANTAGE #4: INSPIRING PLAYER IMAGINATION

Lastly, consider that fading to black places the ultimate power and sexual agency in the player's hands; now *they* can imagine what happens next between the characters. This can be very freeing to developers as it allows them to create the groundwork and then step away to allow players to play within it, even if only in their own minds.

It also goes a long way to solving the issue of subjective tastes in sex scenes. The narrative designer Olivia Wood[2] goes into this in detail in a fantastic talk about sex in games; one of the things she discusses how one person's erotic turn-on is another person's repellant turn-off, and everything in between. For example, consider the wide variety of reactions to flowery, romantic dialogue during sex: some will find it erotic and emotional, while others will find it "cringy" or hilarious, while still others will find it boring. Similarly, for every person turned on by rough sex or dirty talk, there's another one who is repelled or just not interested. And that's not even going into the larger aspects of sexualities and sexual preferences such as enjoying straight sex scenes vs. queer sex scenes, kink scenes vs. vanilla scenes, etc. The takeaway is that there is no way to make a sex scene that appeals to EVERYONE. However, arguably, by fading to black, the developers allow every player to mentally construct a sex scene that works for them, down to the physical acts and even their personal interpretations of character dynamics. One *Dragon Age II* player can assume that Fenris and Hawke have sweet, gentle, "vanilla" sex as their first encounter, while another player might imagine an encounter full of roughness, anger, and dominant/submissive dynamics; both are right and both are supported by the same fade to black.

WATCH OUT FOR: Lack of emotional or narrative payoff. While players are more than willing to imagine entire erotic scenarios about your characters and write elaborate steamy fan fiction about them, that is separate from focusing tangible romantic and erotic fulfillment within the original story. Seeing two characters kiss on screen has a different and arguably more potent impact than just imagining that they kiss offscreen. So, it is with sex scenes; if the narrative has built up the emotional climax of two characters finally making love to each other, then that climax will fall at least a *little* flat if literally *everything* happens offscreen for players to "imagine." Keep track of the emotional beats and high points that your narrative is building to and consider what the best and *most satisfying* way to resolve them is. And again, don't skimp on the lead-in or lead-out scenes; a passionate look, a kiss, or an intense and huskily whispered confession can provide all the payout needed if placed in the right context and delivered with the right level of sincerity.

WHEN TO SHOW, NOT HINT?

Fading to black offers a host of benefits that are mostly targeted toward a particular kind of sex scene and experience, one that's rooted in implication and "hint, don't show." But showing sex explicitly offers an equal but different range of benefits, rooted instead in building drama and physical storytelling. **In general, developers should lean toward showing sex if:**

- They prefer to tell their own story through showing, i.e., visuals, physical details, movements

- They aim not only to build but *sustain* an emotional high point in the scene

- They want to emphasize the physical aspect of the intimacy

- They wish to explore the characters and/or relationship more fully

Note that, for the purposes of this discussion, "showing sex" is not restricted to hyper-detailed and explicit depictions; this can also include more stylized, "artistic" depictions that focus more on close-ups, shadows, etc., than showing nudity, bodies, or animated sex. The point is that the game is depicting sex in some way as opposed to simply "turning the camera off" at the crucial moment. Within that is a large spectrum of explicitness – from tame or tasteful shots of a bare shoulder or back to full on pornographic humping – so developers have a lot of leeways to explore.

SHOWING SEX ADVANTAGE #1: EXPRESSING TEAM IMAGINATION

Fading to black can temporarily place the narrative control of the game – art, audio, dialogue, everything – in the imagination of the player, allowing their creative vision to run free during the black screen and beyond. But sometimes, that's NOT what you want. In many cases, you and your team have your own strong creative ideas about what may happen between two characters – from how they approach each other to how they look at each other to how they touch in the throes of passion – and you may want (or need!) to keep that narrative and creative authority on the side of the developers. In other words, sometimes a team will want to say, "*here* is our idea of how it happened," and that is as legitimate a reason as any other to show those details and communicate your vision.

It's important to be aware and respectful of your players and their imaginations, but that does not mean you're not allowed to tell *your* story or present *your* game in a way that is meaningful to you. And yes, that extends to sex scenes and sexual content as much as any other gameplay, level design, narrative design, or other game elements. If your team wants to contextualize a moment of intimacy in a particular way or has a particular erotic or emotional beat they want to call the player's attention to – even just a particular shot that fired up their imagination – don't be afraid to explore that explicitly in a scene.

WATCH OUT FOR: Overindulgence and lack of awareness. There is no shame at all in wanting to depict sexual activity or sexual relationships, but again, like *any* aspect of narrative or gameplay, the team must be able to answer the question "why?" and have an answer beyond "because butts are hot." If the team has strong ideas about depicting certain aspects of the sexual encounter – for example, a particular shot, or a particular act – they should be able to back up those ideas with an understanding of what their goal is. It's also important to keep those goals in mind when doing the work of bringing a sex scene to life and not getting bogged down in unrelated (sexy?) minutiae; you may not want to spend a lot of time working out realistic jiggle physics if the main emotional thrust of a scene is going to be a slow-motion close-up of a character's expression! This is where communication between your teams – cinematic, narrative, art, audio, etc., – is important, as Ashley noted.

SHOWING SEX ADVANTAGE #2: BUILDING AND SUSTAINING EMOTION

We've discussed the role of a narrative climax in a sex scene and how a particular moment can be "the high point" of the scene. But that doesn't mean that the rest of the scene can't feel almost as high on energy and tension; in fact, that can contribute to how strong the climax feels when that tension is finally resolved. An extended, more explicit sex scene can build the erotic tension and energy of the scene in a way that's more sustained and more intense than simply cutting away and leaving everything vague. As an example, consider the narrative, thematic, and tonal differences between a character saying, "I love you," then kissing and fading to black…versus the same character whispering "I love you" over and over in the throes of passion. The Peebee encounter in *Mass Effect: Andromeda* is a good example of this done well; the confessions of love and trust and the ethereal, orgasmic experience of Peebee's meld would not hit strongly without the emotional buildup of the explicit sex leading up to it.

If the goal for a sex scene is to reach an emotional high (or low), sustain it or deepen it for the character and players, and *then* push it even higher to the climax, then developers should lean toward showing the sex more explicitly or at least avoiding simply fading to black. By using the extra screentime, visuals, and audio that go into a longer, more involved sex scene, designers can draw out the feelings and mood of a scene and let them linger with players and characters alike, whether the feelings are sweet, angry, sad, tender, or lustful. Designers can use the lead-in before the sex to establish a baseline mood and then ramp it up to 11 with subsequent sex – for example, starting with passionate kissing to establish hunger and desire, then using explicit sex to show the characters getting even hungrier for each other, and becoming even more desperate in their desire until at last, they (and the audience) are satisfied. If the game design goal is to give an erotic, romantic, or other mood time to sit or grow, then tying it to an explicit scene is one of the best ways to do so.

WATCH OUT FOR: Overstaying your welcome. While sex isn't necessarily something to rush through, a little can go a long way, and sometimes, even just a few seconds of suggestive visuals or audio can be all you need to build or sustain the mood of the scene. On the other hand, if a scene goes on for too long at the same emotional register, the player can suffer emotional fatigue, or worse, can shift out of the desired mood into boredom or hilarity. Be aware of how long a scene has gone on and when it risks shifting from a sustained or building high point to a negative state of fatigue.

SHOWING SEX ADVANTAGE #3: PHYSICAL INTIMACY

While fading to black can elide the physical realities and details of sex, showing the sex can highlight this aspect of intimacy and give a scene a more physical grounding. Sex, after all, is as much a physical experience and act as anything else – an act that involves touching bodies and the place where those bodies are. And while it's true that physical intimacy is not the be-all-end-all of intimacy (or even its so-called "highest form"), it IS still a kind of intimacy that is expressed through physical action, a kind that many characters AND players value highly and find special meaning and enjoyment in. By choosing to show this intimacy rather than keeping it hidden, developers can ground sex and sexual intimacy in the physical reality and in what the characters actually do together.

What does that mean? Consider for a moment the difference between a sex scene that is gentle and tender vs. one that is frantic and energetic. Is the sex scene idealized in that the bodies move together in graceful unison or is it realistically awkward in that people get cramps, elbow each other, get scrunched up faces, etc.? Is it romantic lovemaking after a long courtship or snatching a last-minute impulse quickie before going into a suicide mission? Is this taking place in a sumptuous boudoir, in a supply closet, on a ratty mattress? Consider how showing these kinds of physical details works in terms of storytelling and in terms of making the sex (and all that goes into it) a "real" event as opposed to something only alluded to. By telling a story through physical detail – showing rather than telling OR implying – you can convey something about the mood, the world, the situation, and of course the characters and how they inhabit their bodies and interact with those of others.

WATCH OUT FOR: Technical limitations. This is the flip side of the earlier discussion on fading to black and how it avoids issues like uncanny valley, etc. It can be very technically challenging, particularly in 3D games, to show bodies interacting with each other, and poor execution can take an otherwise well-planned, thematically resonant sex scene and turn it into something deeply awkward or unintentionally hilarious. Seeing two "plasticky" faces or bodies in the throes of passion or phasing straight through each other is a good way to undo whatever physical storytelling you're trying to do! If your team has concerns about being able to depict the sex in an attractive, realistic, or non-awkward light, but you still want to have more than just a fade to black, make sure to use the tools and tips from Ashley's chapter, and don't be afraid to lean more heavily on elements that you CAN present without a technical issue (e.g., using more audio to suggest more explicit actions, focusing on sensual environment details with the sex as a backdrop, etc.)

SHOWING SEX ADVANTAGE #4: CHARACTER REVELATION

Lastly, we come to one of the most important reasons to consider depicting sex explicitly: the chance to explore new facets of your characters and their relationships. Yes, we can learn lots about how they approach sex before the camera pans away…but we can learn just as much, if not more, from what they are like in the middle of the act. Sex is a unique opportunity to see characters in a more vulnerable or honest setting. Even if it's just a meaningless one-night stand, we can see how the character interacts with others, how they express themselves, how they experience pleasure, and what they are focused on in the moment. Key physical details such as facial expressions or touching one's partner can be intensely intimate, evocative storytelling tools that capture the essence of a character or at least the essence of their emotions and experience of a sexual moment. And if that seems a bit unbelievable, consider how we would interpret a hero and their relationship if they're looking at their lover with hungry, aching yearning vs. looking off into the distance with a bored grimace as they hump!

Like with so much else in video games, EVERYTHING in a sex scene can be used as a storytelling tool to show (not tell) more of your characters and their dynamics. Choosing to depict a scene explicitly puts these tools fully in your hands and allows you to explore an intimate and personal aspect of their lives and personalities and reveal new things to your audience…or, at the very least, communicate something that resonates.

WATCH OUT FOR: Simply repeating nonsexual character notes verbatim without further exploration. A character might be established as a sullen angry asshole outside of the bedroom, but if you then have an extended, explicit sex scene that reveals that…he's a sullen angry asshole…you're not really revealing anything new. That's not to say that a character's behavior inside the bedroom needs to be massively different than outside (though it certainly can be! It would be interesting if the sullen angry asshole was a sweet submissive in the context of sex!) But even when a sex scene reinforces what we already know ("Oh look, the sullen angry asshole treats their sexual partners badly!"), it should at least feel like we are seeing another facet of their personality rather than just a carbon copy of what we already know. We should be learning a bit about how they see sex, how they treat their partners, how they feel about themselves…even just what their favorite sexual acts are! Remember, using sex scenes to establish a character or develop a relationship means that they serve a stronger narrative function, so check in to see if this is happening and whether the characters' intimate behavior is an opportunity to show new depths or other sides to them.

CONCLUSION

Fading to black is not inherently a better way to do sex scenes, or a worse way, for that matter. It has its strengths and weaknesses as an approach, just as more explicit sex does. Keep this chapter in mind when evaluating which approach is best for your project; it'll be the difference between fading to black as a "default" and fading to black as the best choice for your scene.

WORKSHOP QUESTIONS

Analysis: For the sex scene(s) you're analyzing, would you define their approach as a "fade to black" or a more explicit sex scene? Why do you think they made that choice? How did it match the larger narrative or gameplay goals of the sex scene? What issues might that choice have caused compared to the other approach? If this scene was to be redone in the other approach (e.g., a "fade to black" made more explicit), what do you think it would feature, and what would it add/detract from the scene?

Creative: Decide whether the sex scene(s) in your game work better as fade to black or as fully explicit scenes. Consider the pacing of your game, the technical abilities of you/your team, the character beats you want to hit, and the final experience you want your players to take away. Does your game fall into any of the previously discussed categories for the best use of fade to black or of explicit sex? If it does, but you're leaning toward the other approach, why is that? Document your intent for the scene and share the vision with your team.

NOTES

1 Of course, sometimes the fade to black comes after a VERY explicit scene anyway (e.g., nudity, sexual acts, etc.). For this chapter, however, we're focusing on scenes that fade to black before any explicit activity begins.
2 VideoBrains Event, "Sex: it's complicated - Olivia Wood," YouTube video, 18:01, May 17, 2016, https://www.youtube.com/watch?v=jZle4c1wFWk.

CHAPTER 20

Coming to Grips with Gaze in Sex Scenes

W AY BACK AT THE start of the book, I talked about one of the most pervasive myths about sex scenes and sexual content in video games – that they exist only for the titillation and pleasure of straight men and that queer people and straight women are just Not Interested (™) at best and repelled at worst. In that chapter, we talked about how it was a ridiculous and false belief, that plenty of women and queer people are, in fact, extremely happy to have sexy, thirsty content in their games, to the point of even generating it themselves through fanart and fanfic when the games themselves don't provide.

Still, enjoying sexual content does not necessarily mean enjoying ALL sexual content. And if you investigate some of the history of sex scenes in games, particularly in AAA titles and series like *The Witcher*, you will often find a refrain that, while not universal, is common enough to note: straight women and queer people being turned off and exasperated by the way the sex scenes are presented, even scenes that in theory should align with their sexual orientation and preferences (e.g., heterosexual sex for straight women and lesbian sex for queer women). Specifically, the critique is that these scenes cater to something called "the male gaze" (Figure 20.1).

But what is the male gaze, and why is it such a turnoff to those other audiences? To define it, we first need to take a look at what "gaze" actually entails, as it is a huge part of any and all creation of sexy content in games. We'll look at how it's expressed both in sex scenes and in games in general, and how it affects everything from character design to camera work. From that foundation, we'll take a look at male gaze (specifically, the straight male gaze), why (or if?) it's a problem, and how developers can weave other, more inclusive gazes around it.

WHAT IS GAZE?

Wikipedia sums up the concept of gaze as a concept of "an individual or group's awareness and perception of other individuals, other groups, or oneself." The concept originated in early-20th-century psychoanalysis (Lacan, Foucault, and Satre all described or developed

DOI: 10.1201/9780429356650-24

FIGURE 20.1 A visual representation of a large majority of AAA sex scenes? (Sabphoto/Shutterstock.com.)

variants of the concept in their works), but John Berger and Laura Mulvey were among the first to really examine how it applied to creative media (as well as the first to describe the male gaze).[1] Roughly summed up, that awareness/perspective of gaze inherently colors art and media made by and for that initial individual or group, as well as coloring which groups we assume are consuming and enjoying that art and media. That's because gaze affects who "we" see as our proxy or personal avatar in a story, and who "we" see as being there for our visual pleasure…specifically, our *sexual* pleasure.

Gaze is a complex and scholarly subject, and we don't have time to go into all of it, but it's very, very worth exploring the specifics of how it relates to games and sex scenes, and how it influences the way we treat our characters, our players, and our visuals in general. In the context of sex scenes, the "gaze" is often a sexual one, looking at characters for the intent of pleasure, arousal, and desire…but only *some* characters. Who those characters are – and what the identity and role of the *other* characters in the scene are – is the core of gaze as it relates to sex in games.

When we refer to gaze in these terms, we're referring to several major interconnected parts (Figure 20.2):

- Who is creating the content (and what/who they find sexy) – the creators.

- Who the creators ASSUME is playing (and what/who they find sexy) – the "players."

- Who the creators ASSUME the "players" will identify with, and how we present them – the "gazer" characters, or subjects.

- Who the creators ASSUME the "players" will desire and find sexy, and how we present them – the "gazed at" characters, or objects.

- Who the creators ASSUME the "players" won't identify with or desire, who they'll dislike or ignore, and how we present them – "everybody else."

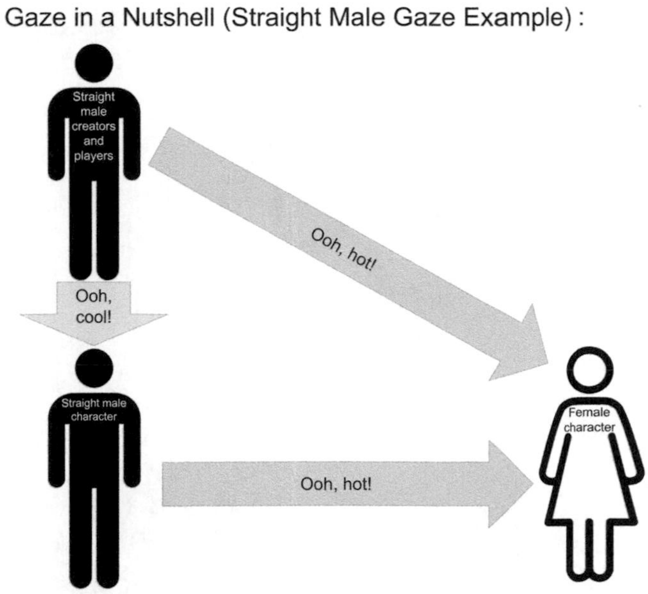

Gaze in a Nutshell (Straight Male Gaze Example) :

FIGURE 20.2 A very, VERY basic diagram of how the gaze (in this case, a straight male gaze) works in video games, media, sex scenes, etc. Notice there are no "Ooh, hot!" lines pointing from male player/creator to male character; we'll talk about that in a minute.

It's important to note, however, that all of these are not only individuals, but groups of people. It's one thing to talk about an individual creator or player identifying with a character, or finding a character hot. But gaze works on a systemic level that affects and applies this lens on a demographic level; it's less about the individual, and more the group they're part of. Also worth noting is that, in many cases, the big assumption – of who's playing, who they'll identify with, who they'll find attractive – is not a conscious act, but a mixture of unconscious bias and social expectation that we simply don't consider the larger implications of (Figure 20.3).

Let's break each of the parts of the gaze down in terms of sex in games:

The creators – Even when we are doing our best to account for our own biases and create a game that is "neutral" and can be enjoyed by everyone…let's face it, we tend to make things we like, and that extends to sex scenes. We have tinted goggles for some things and blind spots for others. Our work is influenced by what we are disinterested in, what we are enthusiastic about…and yes, what turns us on as well. And even when we are creating for audiences other than ourselves, that perspective can still slip in, giving an erotic slant to certain content or characters while completely missing the opportunity to apply that slant to others (Figure 20.4).

In some cases, like romance and sex games, embracing your own perspective and gaze and letting it guide you in sex scene creation can be fine! But for other games, what works for *you* might not work for the wider audience you're trying to reach. This is one (among many) reason that having a diverse team – spread across genders, race, sexuality, body types, disabilities, and so on – is vital, to bring those extra perspectives and gazes to the table and create a more holistic vision of desire and sexiness. Regardless, it behoves us to be

FIGURE 20.3 "This seems like a totally normal, neutral character design, right? Why would anyone think it catered to a particular perspective?" (NextMarsMedia/Shutterstock.com.)

FIGURE 20.4 "Every single sex scene in this game I'm making features sexy shirtless buff guys with abs for days. But trust me, this has *nothing* to do with the fact that I also like sexy shirtless buff guys with abs for days. It's just a weird coincidence, that's all." (Gorodenkoff/Shutterstock.com.)

aware of our gaze in terms of sex and beyond – who do we find sexy vs. who do we identify with, and how? – note how that gets expressed in our work, and if necessary, put in the work to broaden it in terms of the game we're making.

The "players" – The quotation marks here are deliberate, as it's less about who is ACTUALLY playing your game and who you subconsciously ASSUME is playing your game. This is not the same thing as a target demographic, though it can overlap. In the context of sex in games, targeting a demographic would be, say, "I want to create a steamy romance game for straight men," and actively designing for that market in mind. Gaze, however, can be much more subtle and more endemic than that, and it can wind its way into games that are NOT explicitly meant for one demographic or another. In other words, you can intend (or, at least, *claim* to intend) to make a game for everyone, like an RPG or FPS…but if the female characters dress really sexy and all the sex scenes show off the female bodies constantly, then that sends a pretty clear signal of who you expect to be playing your game and what you expect them to enjoy. And this, of course, can become a self-fulfilling prophecy: you subtly/not-so-subtly design your sexual content in a way that your assumed "players" will enjoy, and that ends up attracting that very same player base in real life, who you then make more sexual content for, etc. etc. etc.… (Figure 20.5).

This assumption of the "player's" gaze, of who the "player" is and what group they're part of, and more importantly, what that "player group" will like, affects almost everything in game design, to say nothing of sex design. And nowhere does it affect more than how the game presents its characters in the context of sex and sex appeal.

Characters the "player" identifies with (doers, gazers, *subjects*) – Characters who are usually part of the same group or groups as the "player" – e.g., same gender and/or same

FIGURE 20.5 "Hey, it's not our fault that our audience is mostly straight dudes! We just figured that everyone in our audience would appreciate and enjoy the beauty of the nude female body… and the boob jiggle physics…and the endless ass shots in every sex scene." (Koldunov Alexey/ Shutterstock.com.)

orientation – are presented as **subjects** of the sexual gaze. They are not gazed at with desire or longing or lust, but rather, *the ones doing the gazing*. And quite often, their gaze and the gaze of the "player" are treated as one and the same. Very often, these are the protagonists, heroes, and main playable characters of the game. As such, these characters will be held up as either

- identifiable – characters who the "player" can relate to and "inhabit" in the context of the game, characters who the "player" shares traits or identities with

- or aspirational – characters who the player/viewer would like to be like.

While this is not always the case – plenty of playable characters are unrelatable, unlikable, or terrible role models! – there remains a fundamental underpinning of, "this is your proxy in the game world, someone who is You/Like You in some way, someone who is active and DOING (much like you are active and PLAYING) and whose perspective shapes and/or mirrors your own." These characters may or may not be idealized, but any idealization will be focused on this axis, providing the "player" with a wish-fulfillment proxy that might be stronger, more charismatic, richer, or more of a "badass" than they are in real life.

As far as sex and sexual content go, this role of being both active doer (ha ha) and proxy viewpoint is key. The subject character represents the "player's" agency and perspective in sex, looking lustfully just like the "player" is (or rather, like the developers think the "player" is). As Ashley discussed in her chapter, a lot of camera work in sex scenes and other sexual content represents not just the gaze of the "player" but of the player character, what THEY are finding attractive and arousing in the moment.

But another key element relates to the LACK of something sexual, specifically the lack of being erotically gazed *at*. A character who's the subject of the gaze, who's *doing* the gazing, might be engaging in sexual activity, might even be desired by their partner…but that doesn't mean that they are presented as attractive or sexy, or that we see the perspective of someone gazing at *them* with lust. Whenever the camera's on them, it's not as an *erotic* gaze, but a gaze of interest or admiration or identification. Everything is in service of making these characters someone who the "player" wants to BE, not making them someone the "player" WANTS. After all, if this character isn't of the gender/type/etc., that the "player" is attracted to, why would they be attracted to them? And in that case, some might argue, what's the point of trying to make them "attractive"? And even if they are "desired" by the other character(s), it plays out less like, "of course, the subject is *hot*, let's drool over them!" and more like, "of course, the subject is *awesome*, let's enjoy the fantasy of being swooned over by the other character(s)!"

Signs that a character is being idealized as a subject and/or wish-fulfillment proxy for the player (Figure 20.6):

- Body shapes that are presented as aspirational and/or functional as opposed to sexual or sexy.

- Clothing that highlights something other than their sexual attractiveness, such as character and strength. This clothing CAN be skimpy, but unlike a character who's

FIGURE 20.6 This man is shirtless and has a muscular physique, but it is presented in the context of power and aggression, not sex appeal. This is not a character that the camera is going to be "panting over" in a sex scene, or a character "we" are intended to desire. This character is a *power fantasy*, or subject of the gaze. (FXQuadro/Shutterstock.com.)

an object of desire, the intent of this clothing is not to invite the "player" to ogle their body sexually, but to marvel at their power and strength.

- Camera angles that frame them either heroically – focus on their strength, making them tower, etc. – or neutrally – such as simple straight-on shots. The camera is not sexual in its appreciation of them – no lingering shots of body parts or slow panning over their body, and no "inviting" poses either.

Characters the "player" desires (done to, gazed at, *objects*) – Characters who are in a group that the "player" group finds sexually attractive are the "object" of the gaze and the object of desire. This does not *necessarily* mean that the character will be objectified or unimportant in the larger narrative. An "object of desire" can still be a well-written, fully realized character in their own right, with their own goals, personalities, story arcs, and roles in the story. The point is that they are seen as the desirable "other" in the narrative, not as a proxy for the player to become, but as a separate figure to be looked at and desired. More pertinently, their *bodies* are presented in order to provide the "player" erotic visual pleasure, whether in a sex scene or in other contexts.

Note that this can express itself far beyond what the subject (i.e., the "player" proxy character) is doing or how they're looking at the object of desire. This is something that, often, the entire game will emphasize, from the character design to the animation to the camera work. Whether it's the costuming of the character, the way their hips move, the way the camera frames them – it's clear that the entire game is "conspiring" to frame them in the most erotically appealing light, as someone for the assumed "player" to look at, drool over, and be aroused by (Figure 20.7).

FIGURE 20.7 This man is also shirtless and muscular, but presented in a much more sexual, sensual context. His pose and expression are more inviting and show off his body for erotic visual pleasure, not to emphasize strength or power. This DOES seem like a character "we" are invited to desire. In other words, this character is a *sexual fantasy*. (ArtOfPhotos/Shutterstock.com.)

Signs a character is being idealized as an object of desire or someone to be "gazed at":

- Body shapes that are presented purely in the context of their sexual appeal, with other considerations (e.g., strength) purely secondary. They also frequently fall along conventional lines of attraction, though some games subvert this.

- Clothing that highlights the character's sexual attractiveness and/or invites players to look at them in a sexual way. This can also extend to hairstyles, makeup, etc.

- Camera angles and poses that frame them sexually, emphasizing or calling attention to certain body parts (e.g., chest, butt, crotch, abs, and thighs) in a particularly appreciative or erotic way.

This obviously has major impact in sex scenes. While the subject is active but not erotically appealing, the object of desire is basically positioned as the dominant source of all the "sexiness" and erotic quality of the scene...the highlight of the experience, as it were. While they may be actively engaging in sex from a narrative or character framework, the framing of the scene often sidelines their desires or makes them reactive to the subject or "player." In other words, their desire isn't so much about their own sexuality and urges, or the attractiveness of the subject, or about their own sexual fantasies...it's about fulfilling the sexual desires and fantasies of the subject, or more importantly, the "player." Their pleasure may be sincere, but to an extent, it's also a performance to arouse the character and "player" looking at them. And of course, in terms of the visuals, their bodies will be held up and centered for the visual pleasure of the "player."

Characters in neither group ("everybody else") – There are, of course, characters who the player is not intended to identify with OR to desire. Either they're not part of the group that the "player" is part of/usually desires, or they are…but something about them prevents the player from either identifying with them or finding them attractive. Perhaps they're the comic relief friend more than the hero or the love interest, or maybe they're just a terrible jerk. Or maybe they simply aren't conventionally attractive enough to stir the interest of the "player."

Whatever the reason, these characters are not part of the gaze. While they may be narratively important, the "gaze" is not interested in either looking with admiration or looking with desire. In fact, in some cases, the gaze may even look at them with repulsion, doubly so when sex is involved. Consider: when was the last time you saw a video game sex scene with an overweight character where the camera either took THEIR view (i.e., posed them as the "player" proxy) or showcased their body with as much desire and appeal as a conventionally attractive character?

Sex scenes that involve "everybody else" often feel more matter-of-fact and less heated than those that might involve an object of desire. The camera may take long shots of the action rather than sensual panning shots, and the sex itself, while exciting to the characters having it, isn't presented in a way that is meant to arouse the "player." In the case of negative characters (e.g., villains, jerks, or unlikable characters) or characters who are culturally seen as "unattractive," the scenes may even end up being treated for laughs (Figure 20.8).

So, now that we've established what gaze is, time to tackle…

FIGURE 20.8 This man is ALSO shirtless, but not muscular or conventionally attractive. He isn't presented as a power fantasy or character to identify with; nor is he identified as sexy and attractive (though many would find him so!) The camera doesn't invite us to admire him or desire him. If anything, it invites us to laugh at him and assumes we find him repellant. He's not presented as a fantasy at all. (Nomad_Soul/Shutterstock.com.)

THE (STRAIGHT) MALE GAZE

Under the definition and structure of gaze as we outlined above, straight male gaze in games and game sex scenes can be boiled down as the following:

- **Who are the creators?** – Straight cisgender men.

  - This is not surprising, as the game industry remains mostly dominated by male developers. As of 2021, 61% of game developers were men (though that number was not broken down by sexual orientation).[2] As such, many games, particularly in the AAA space, are made from a male perspective and with a male gaze behind the helm.

- **Who do the creators assume are playing?** – Straight cisgender men.

  - As of 2021, male players make up approximately 55% of gamers in the United States.[3] While this isn't an overwhelming majority, it's such that plenty of the male creators in the former category assume – either consciously or unconsciously – that the audience playing their game is going to be mostly straight men, and possibly even *entirely* straight men. Thus, whatever the camera is pointed at – say, the rear end of an attractive female character – is what the creators assume the "players" want to see and what they find sexually appealing…forgetting any player who ISN'T a straight man who's Into That Sort of Thing.

- **Who are those players meant to identify with?** – A straight cisgender male hero.

  - According to a recent survey, 79.2% of video game main characters are male, with 66.5% of ALL characters also being male (again, not broken down by sexual orientation).[4] As such, we can assume that, for many video games, men and male characters are going to be the subject that they identify with.

- **Who are those players meant to desire?** – Conventionally attractive cisgender female characters.

  - The most common presentation of female characters, particularly in AAA games, tends toward hourglass body shapes, youthful faces, and tight and/or skimpy clothing that shows off their bodies. It is also usually these characters that are featured in sex scenes.

- **Who are those players not going to identify with/desire?** – Other male characters, fat or "unattractive" female characters, and trans/genderqueer characters.

  - As you can imagine, male gaze doesn't offer a lot of erotic scenes of, say, queer men having sex (though interestingly, presenting men as erotic or sexy often earns accusations of queerness and catering to gay men, as if straight and bisexual women don't also exist).

- Women who don't fall within conventional beauty standards (e.g., overweight women) also aren't shown in the context of erotic desire.

- Trans and genderqueer characters are also mostly ignored or rejected as characters to identify with or desire; they fall outside the boundaries of heterosexual desire of the straight male players that the creators assume are playing.

Some historical background: the concept of the (straight) male gaze specifically came into prominence with the work of Laura Mulvey, a feminist film theorist who applied psychoanalysis and feminist principles to the way that Hollywood movies at the time "looked at" both male and female characters, and the way it used a default heterosexual male view. According to her article, in male gaze, female characters are there to be looked at:

> [...] pleasure in looking has been split between active/male and passive/female. The determining male gaze projects its phantasy on to the female figure which is styled accordingly. In their traditional exhibitionist role women are simultaneously looked at and displayed with their appearance coded for strong visual and erotic impact so that they can be said to connote to-be-looked-at-ness. Women displayed as sexual object is the leit-motiff of erotic spectacle [...][5]

In contrast, in regard to the idea of presenting male characters as sexy, she notes, "the male figure cannot bear the burden of sexual objectification. Man is reluctant to gaze at his exhibitionist like."[6]

You can probably guess how these two contrasting strains – exhibitionist women, reluctance toward exhibitionist men – express themselves in the context of sex and sexual themes. But why guess when we can walk through a specific example? Let's take a look at the bath sex scene in *The Witcher 2* and how gaze is baked into a particular key moment in the scene: the disrobing.

- Triss – a conventionally attractive woman and off-on lover of Geralt – gets undressed first, using a magic spell to remove her clothes, and *immediately*, the camera is at her hips, only inches away from her body. It pans around slowly, seductively, over her skin, matching the curves of her body almost exactly in its movements. Her movements are sensual, erotic, and graceful, with no awkwardness from fumbling with her clothes; they simply disintegrate beneath the camera's watchful gaze until she's naked. The camera's message is clear: *Look. Savor. Enjoy.* She then jumps into the water of the bath, her naked body passing in close by the camera again as she swims under the surface. Finally, she bursts to the surface, her body glistening, her breasts exposed. Every single second of her presentation is geared toward enhancing her sexual appeal, not just to Geralt but the assumed audience of straight men who would find the display arousing.

- Then, we have Geralt start to disrobe as well, and does the camera pan over his muscled body with as much erotic pleasure and attention as Triss? Is his disrobing sexy and enticing? Is there any acknowledgment of the players who find men (and specifically, Geralt) attractive? The answer is no on all counts. The camera suddenly shifts as far as physically possible away from his body, almost to the other side of the room, as if it's afraid to get too close to his naked skin. He takes his shirt off, but there's no pause to enjoy the scene. And rather than an erotic striptease like Triss, he instead hops awkwardly on one foot, trying to remove his boot until she pulls him into the water. She even starts kissing him and initiating the sex with his pants still on, so until the sex begins properly, he remains *more* covered up than her. Despite the fact that Geralt is an attractive man, the presentation of him in this scene avoids any sort of eroticism or sexual appeal. What appeal he has in this scene is either in terms of relatability ("Oh man, I'd be tripping over myself too!") or as identification for the straight male audience ("Oh man, *I* get to bone Triss Merigold!").

- The rest of the sex scene proceeds somewhat similarly; while we do get more glimpses of Geralt's body once the sex actually begins, the main camera focus remains on Triss's body, particularly her hips, waist, and breasts, all of which are on full display to the player audience. Triss's gasps and moans of pleasure are also constant through the scene, while Geralt remains silent.

It's worth noting again that this gap between the exhibitionism of male and female characters is a little less pronounced in *The Witcher 3*, particularly when it comes to how Geralt is presented. While before he was held back and almost hidden in sex scenes, there are now several scenes that highlight his body in erotic and appreciative ways. The camera also isn't allergic to showing his body before the sex begins, allowing his body to be the center of attention in some shots, even featuring glistening musculature in a few scenes. However, in the context of the sex scenes, most of the gaze is still on the female characters. They are shown nude (while Geralt is usually clothed in modesty underwear), the action continually cuts to their bodies, and the camera remains sexually besotted with them (i.e., clinging close and focusing on their breasts or orgasmic reactions). It is still male gaze…just markedly less so than *The Witcher 2*.

Thus, male gaze in sex scenes tends to express itself through:

- **Erotic hyper-focus on the cis female body** – more female nudity, more attention of the camera on her body, more performative pleasure, more sensual animations, etc.

- **Less or no erotic focus on the male body** – less nudity, less/no camera attention, no sensual animations or actions (e.g., no sexy stripteases), less focus on their pleasure or attractiveness.

But people – including non-male players – really liked both *Witcher* 2 and 3, right? So… what is the problem with male gaze, then?

WHY IS MALE GAZE A PROBLEM IN SEXUAL CONTENT?

Male gaze as a concept – the idea of identifying with male characters and enjoying looking at/having sex with attractive female characters – is not inherently wrong at its core. It's understandable to be more sexually interested in the gender that, well, you're sexually attracted to, and to want to play a game that caters to your desires.

The problem comes when it's ***EVERY. SINGLE. GAME.***

It would be one thing if it was just the odd game once in a while that featured gruff, strong, unsexy male protagonists, large-breasted women, and sex scenes full of ogling like *The Witcher 2*. But spend any amount of time in the AAA space, or even certain indie quarters, and you will end up seeing it *everywhere*. Male gaze isn't a fun occasional treat, but the default vision of huge swathes of the game industry, the background radiation to the majority of popular mainstream games, the inescapable lens that just keeps getting used in every sex scene, with every character, with every game…

And the thing is, while there are certainly plenty of straight male players who like this gaze and find it caters to them…it can be so, so off-putting to players of other genders and sexualities. Having a sex scene which is all BOOBS BOOBS BOOBS BOOBS oh okay fine three seconds of shirtless guy BOOBS BOOBS BOOBS…it's a really, really good way to communicate to your straight female players, your gay male players, your queer female players,[7] or really anyone who isn't a straight guy that their preferences aren't being acknowledged, and their perspectives aren't being incorporated or even considered in the creation of the game. And thus, you get people fed up or feeling excluded by the game's sex scenes…and, most likely, the game itself. And when almost every single mainstream game does the exact same thing, use the exact same gaze in their sex scenes…is it any wonder that players of marginalized genders and sexualities tend to start feeling excluded by games as a whole? (Figure 20.9)

Other issues with sticking purely with male gaze:

- **Objectification and oversexualization of women** – Yes, it's perfectly possible to have a female character who's a fully realized character in her own right who's still deliberately designed to be sexy or who's presented erotically in sex scenes. There are plenty of games that have managed it! But that doesn't mean it always happens, and let's face it…if you're positioning women as "objects of desire," it doesn't take much of a leap for that concept to devolve into making her an actual *object*, to from a simple acknowledgment of attraction to making that her defining and only feature. If developers working in the male gaze start off creating every female sexual partner in a game with, "let's make her sexy," what happens when some of those developers stop there and don't go any further? And how will that make female players feel if they discover every single female character is defined primarily on how attractive she is and how good she looks during a sex scene? Even if the character IS well written and interesting, how will your female players react when the sex scene starts, and she suddenly becomes a sex doll without active desires and agency of her own?

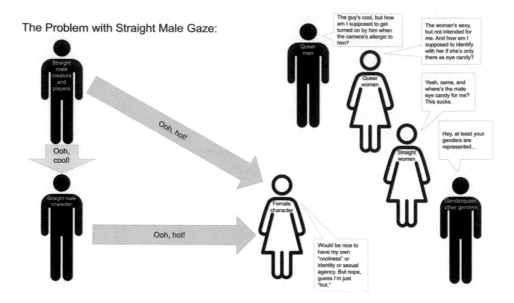

FIGURE 20.9   When you "zoom out" from the basic dynamics of Straight Male Gaze, you can see how it fails to serve, or only partially serves, people of other genders and sexualities. And when this gaze becomes the dominant model of the entire gaming industry…

- **Missed opportunities for male characters** – yes, male characters have a sexual side as well! They can be as sexy and appealing and camera-ready as the female characters around them! Completely wiping out or ignoring this sexual aspect of their character in the misguided hope of avoiding "discomfort" in a straight male audience, or triggering homophobic panic, is doing your male characters a disservice, as well as audiences who are attracted to men. Yes, sure, they might still find your male characters attractive regardless of what you do or what gaze you employ, but…let's just say it stings to get to a sex scene involving that character and have them be completely "invisible" to the camera in terms of lingering, erotic looks. And by throwing out that erotic lens for your sex scenes, you're hamstringing yourself on what you can do and show, as well as losing opportunities to explore what makes your male characters attractive, how they really express themselves sexually, etc.

- **Erasure of other genders** – Gender is not a binary, and there are plenty of players who do not identify as either male or female. But characters who reflect this reality are few, and when they do appear…well, the male gaze is so firmly set up in the binary that there isn't really space to explore what to do with them. For example, while asari in *Mass Effect* are a monogender race that don't use the same gender binary as other races like humans, the narrative and world lore still treat them invariably as cisgender female characters…and the sex scenes follow suit in how the camera frames characters like Liara or Peebee. As for genderqueer characters who don't present as female or male (e.g., androgynous characters), it's extremely hard to find mainstream games that present them as erotic and sexy in their own right…or as identifiable subjects of the gaze…or really in games at all when you get down to it…

- **Sexual erasure of "unattractive" women (or "unattractive" people)** – Heavy, heavy emphasis on the quotation marks there, but there are absolutely cultural standards of beauty, and for women (or any gender!) who deviate from those standards…the chances of them being presented as sexy and desirable by male gaze is often next to nil. Real talk? This is something I'm always painfully aware of as an overweight woman. I never get to see a body like mine shown as beautiful, sexy, or arousing in a sex scene. And while that may mean less of that objectification or sexualization, it's not like there are many sex scenes from the point of view of an overweight woman like me embracing her sexuality. The closest we get is the Sigrun/Bombate sex scene in *Wolfenstein*, and even there, though her sexual desires are treated with respect, it's not HER perspective that informs the game. WE are not invited to ogle Bombate like she does – and we are not invited to ogle her either! Her sex scene is treated as non-erotic and mostly as comedy, like *most* sex-related content involving fat people of any gender. The same is true of other characters who are not "conventionally attractive" (e.g., skinny characters, disabled characters, and characters of certain races outside Eurocentric beauty norms); male gazey sex scenes in mainstream games consistently fail to present those female characters (or male characters!) as desirable in their own right.

SUBVERTING THE MALE GAZE WITH THE POWER OF SEX SCENES

I want to stress again – the concept of "gaze" in the sense of finding some characters sexually desirable and others relatable/admirable/etc. is not inherently wrong. It's okay to approach character design or sexual content with the idea of making characters erotically appealing to your audience! The issues with male gaze sex scenes aren't, "how dare you think women are sexy!" It's more to do with the rigid gender roles, the constant application of it across the entire industry, the intersections with sexism and objectification of women, and the way all of these combine to leave non-straight male players feeling locked out.

But there is good news! Male gaze can be challenged in ways that subvert it or even broaden it to include alternative gazes and desires! And sex scenes are one of the best ways to meet that challenge, as these scenes often heavily revolve around erotic gaze and looking at characters in sexy ways. Creating scenes that allow everyone both a way to feel like they're participating (i.e., that they're the subject doing the gazing) and that they have sexy, erotic things to engage with or look at (objects of the gaze) is a great way to make your game truly inclusive. Representation is important, of course…but don't discount the power and importance of desire as well! (Figure 20.10)

The Gazes at the Table: Hiring a Diverse Team

If you aren't a straight man, then you're already bringing your much-needed perspective to your game and team; keep doing that! If you ARE a straight man, then the first, easiest, and most important step to broadening your game's gaze is to bring more gazes to the table. In other words, hire people who are not straight men and don't use that particular lens for characters and sex. Make sure not only to hire them, but to ensure they have roles in the team where their creativity, perspective, and desires will be guiding the project at its foundations. Don't settle for just hiring a few queer people in lower positions and then

The (Super-Simplified) Gaze Solution:

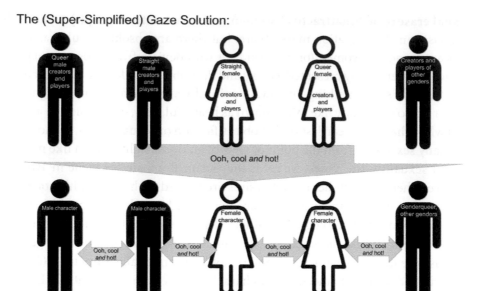

FIGURE 20.10   A very simplified way (well, *one* of them!) to subvert the effects of male gaze and make your game more inclusive. Designing *all* kinds of characters to be both the subject of the gaze (i.e., to be identified with and admired, "Ooh, cool!") and the object of erotic desire ("Ooh, hot!") allows a diverse range of players to enjoy your game on every level. But to do that properly, it helps to have an equally diverse range of creators.

handing them a ton of male gazey scripts and builds and expect them to "sign off" on them (Figure 20.11).

And before you ask, no, this is not some rule that Thou Must Never Hire Any Straight Man Ever Again, or that straight men are a hive mind. There are plenty of very cool, creative,

FIGURE 20.11   "Wait, you have the lesbians do WHAT now?!" (fizkes/Shutterstock.com.)

and open-minded straight men out there with different visions for how sex can be portrayed, and good for them! The point of prioritizing people of other genders and sexualities is that they can and will have fundamentally different perspectives and *experiences* with sex, attraction, eroticism, and people of different genders. The more of those perspectives you have, and the more those perspectives can be shared in a safe setting, the less likely you'll slip into unconsciously homogenous ideas or preferences about how to portray sex. And if you are wanting to depict sex scenes for non-straight male gazes, it really helps to have those gazes going on and telling you what they find sexy, rather than having to guess!

If, for some reason, you're not able to bring queer or straight female voices onto your team (e.g., a solo project), then be sure to budget for sensitivity reads and diversity consultation early in the project, particularly early enough that you can adjust your content or how it's presented. It will save you a lot of grief and hostility later, and will help make your sex scenes more accessible to all.

Explore beyond Heterosexuality: Embrace Queer Lenses and Couplings

To be clear, that's not to say that you should never ever, ever do heterosexual sex scenes. As you can tell from my examples, I'm quite a fan of them! And some games, like dating sims, make sense to focus their attention that way. The point here is that, in the context of male gaze, sex is always conceived of in heterosexual context, where there's a male doer/gazer and a female done-to/gazed-at. If there IS any queerness, it's usually female/female and presented predominantly in the context of "double the gazing pleasure" for the male doer/gazer behind the controller.

Yeah, screw that. There are so many other ways to explore sexuality that don't break down into heteronormative structures or reduce male and female characters to subject and object – or, for that matter, breaking down characters into male and female at all! Again, these are aspects that queer team members and/or queer sensitivity consultants will be able to explore as part of their own experience. But even with their perspective, it's worth doing your own research, re-reading the chapter in this book on queer sex, and looking at the differences in how queer games, movies, and TV depict sex for their audiences. Even if the sex scenes in your game are straight, adopting or adapting queer perspectives on what is erotic and how the camera works can be eye-opening, as well as opening up hot new sexual dynamics.

(Not to mention that you can also find some new, worthwhile perspectives in exploring how heterosexual sex is presented for a straight female audience too…)

Mind the Camera: Equal Opportunity Gaze?

One of the most obvious ways male gaze expresses itself, as mentioned above, is how the camera treats male characters vs. female characters, how it avoids the bodies of the former but hugs the bodies of the latter. Ashley touched on the camera as another character in a scene as well as how it "takes authority" about who the player is supposed to be ogling… and if the authority is male gaze, it says, "look at hot women having sex."

But that means that one of the easiest ways to subvert male gaze, or at least broaden it to include other gazes, is through the camera and what it's looking at. In other words, why not have it say, "look at hot *people* having sex?" Using the camera language of eroticism and applying it to female AND male characters (and characters of other genders, of course!) is one of the easiest ways to ameliorate the male gaze and make it more exciting and arousing for people who aren't just attracted to conventionally attractive women. It also has the added benefit of adding extra characterization and agency for the characters in the sex scene; if, in a straight sex scene, the camera drifts sensually over the male character, we can get a sense of the female character's desire and arousal. It's not exactly equal-opportunity objectification, but a little bit of equal-opportunity ogling can drastically change the impact of a sex scene and how non-straight men respond to it.

It's worth noting that "equal opportunity [whatever]" can be applied in a variety of other character aspects, both inside and outside a sex scene. For example, if your game frames all characters in skimpy, deliberately sexual clothing, that sends a very different sexual message than a game where male characters are in full armor and female characters are in chainmail bikinis! Consider things like character design, flirtation, and sensual moments to convey the idea of other characters as sexy and sexual. Even if the sex scene fades to black, you can still convey the idea that yes, it's not just conventionally hot women who are going to be exciting some desire…

Multiple Scenes for Multiple Gazes: Having Different Subjects and Objects

In games that have multiple options for sexual partners, and/or where the player can choose the gender of their avatar, this can be a great place to explore different gazes in different contexts. In this approach, rather than trying to create scenes which have something for everyone, the goal can be to create multiple scenes and options so that different members of your audience will have something, at least one scene, that's aligned to their interests, orientation, or desires. In this context, a sex scene between a male avatar and a female sex partner might be quite deliberately "male gazey," but a sex scene with a female avatar with the same female sex partner might look very different, with different camera focus and different approach to female sexualization and erotic presentation. Similarly, a scene between a female avatar/male sex partner would not play out the same way as the male/female scene, but instead might incorporate a (straight) female gaze which gives priority to the female avatar's desire and agency, and also looks at the male character with desire; this, in turn, might look very different to a male/male scene and how it presents male characters for the erotic gaze. Having this kind of variety of partnering and gazes for sex allows a lot more leeway for players to find what works for them, and for your game to experiment with a lot of different approaches to sex.

This is an approach used at least partially by a lot of queer visual novels and dating sims; there are usually a wide variety of potential romantic or sexual partners of various genders, and each gender is treated with sensual, erotic gaze as part of their sex scenes. In AAA space, BioWare also embraces this approach in a similar way, offering different sex scenes with different partners and different erotic gazes. While not always perfect – on balance, there does often seem to be a *little* more erotic female nudity than erotic male nudity, or a few more female butt shots, etc. – but in general, it does a good job of reflecting the diverse gazes of its audience and giving every player something to enjoy. Compare and contrast, for example, images of Miranda's sex scene with Jacob's sex scenes; the way they show the characters' bodies are clearly targeting very different gazes and players, with the idea of offering up different kinds of romantic and sexual content for a diverse audience.

Blurring the Gaze: Subject AND Object Combined

These five elements of gaze – creator's gaze, "player" gaze, the gazer, the gazed at, and the "not part of the gaze" – are not always set in stone. It is absolutely possible to blur the line between the subject and the object. There are games where the subject or "player" proxy is designed to be actively desirable, and where the object of desire's own sexual tastes are given just as much narrative weight, meaning, and identity as the player's. Other games might take the tack of having multiple optional sexual partners of different genders and shifting the gaze for each. Remember, gaze isn't inherently *bad* – when handled correctly, and in the context of other gazes, it can make for enjoyable and fun media, as well as characters who are both idealized power fantasies AND sexy as well. You know you've hit this for a character when you get the classic phrase, "[Group A] wants them, and [Group B] wants to BE them!"

And yes, this is a lot of words just to get across the idea, *"please make your non-female characters sexy and attractive in sex scenes as well!"*

A great example of this type of character is Ezio in the *Assassin's Creed* franchise, as he is presented both in terms of being cool AND genuinely attractive. For the former, we see his assassination skills, his active agency in driving the plot forward and fighting the Templars, and his success in bedding various women. But for the latter, we see WHY those women find him sexy; he's charming, playful, respectful, and yes, physically attractive. This comes to a head during his sex scene with Caterina Sforza in *Assassin's Creed Brotherhood*, where the "gaze" is equally on him and his body as Caterina, to the point of lingering on him while naked in the bathtub before the intimacies begin. He works as both an aspiration figure for men to admire and identify with while still managing to be an enticing, appealing figure of sexual desire for those *attracted* to men. When possible, aiming for these kinds of character types (particularly for male characters) can help make your game more widely appealing.

Acknowledge the Diverse Sexy: Treat All Bodies with Erotic Respect

Lastly, remember that providing more diverse gazes, and subverting the dominant male gaze, isn't only a matter of sexual orientation, but also of respecting and celebrating different bodies. If your sex scenes are full of sweaty camera pans and perfectly animated butt-cheeks when your characters are conventionally attractive…but not when they are UNconventionally attractive…you need to really challenge that approach. Treating some bodies as sexy and others as repulsive is not only harmful, but also neglects the diversity of what we find attractive, particularly when those attractions are outside cultural norms. Some people find overweight people sexy! Or underweight people! Or extremely short people, or extremely tall people, or people with different body constructions and functions, etc. etc. Yet you rarely see sex scenes focusing on partners with these kinds of bodies, and certainly it's rare to see scenes that treat these characters and bodies with any kind of sexiness.

So, bring the sexy to the table for ALL your characters. If your conventionally attractive characters are all having the hot and raunchy sex on every surface, then make sure your less conventionally sexy characters are getting similar attention. If your game allows for a choice of romantic or sexual partners, put these characters on the potential roster of options! I suspect you'll be amazed at how many players will genuinely love to engage with these characters, particularly if you make them charming, sexy, and appealing as people (see Varric in *Dragon Age* as an example). And as for the sex scenes, treat them with the same steamy, erotic gaze that you would treat any other character; make the sex scene a celebration of them and their bodies, rather than a moment of painful derision or insult.

CONCLUSION

Male gaze is everywhere in video games – everywhere in media, really! – and it has a particularly strong impact on how our medium tackles sex. While it's clear there's an audience interested in it, assuming that's the ONLY audience playing our games, the ONLY audience interested in sexual content and sexy eye candy, is doing our medium and our sexual content a disservice. After all, there are so many more gazes to explore, all fascinating and erotic in their own way. I hope this chapter will inspire you all to keep seeking a broader sexual gaze for your games, and creating sexy, meaningful content and characters that will be a pleasure for *all* your players to look at and play with.

WORKSHOP QUESTIONS

Analysis: Look at the sex scene(s) in the game you're analyzing. Do they exhibit male gaze? If so, in what ways – camera, character, framing, etc.? Are there other gazes in play? If so, in what capacity?

Creative: If your project is not specifically aimed at a straight male audience (e.g., a dating sim or hentai game aimed at straight men), document how you plan to avoid over-emphasizing male gaze and/or how you plan to incorporate other gazes into your scenes. Where appropriate, outline:

- Your plans regarding team composition and/or consultants to bring in other perspectives on "what is sexy," etc.

- Whether you intend to have multiple sex scenes with specific gazes in mind, or whether you want every sex scene to have something for everyone.

- How you intend to portray and present the following, if present in-game, during sex scenes. Pay particular attention to nudity, camera, animation, character design, audio, etc.

  - Conventionally attractive female characters

  - Unconventionally attractive female characters

  - Conventionally attractive male characters

  - Unconventionally attractive male characters

  - Conventionally attractive genderqueer characters

  - Unconventionally attractive genderqueer characters

- Compare and contrast the above approaches with each other. Are there certain characters that are getting more/less erotic attention than others? Different types of erotic attention? Are any of them being made the butt of jokes or awkwardness, etc.?

- With these as a baseline foundation, write appropriate notes, instructions, and checklists for your team to ensure that they are aware of the creative direction re: gaze in the sex scenes and sexual content.

  - Example: For your cinematics team, have a set of guidelines for which characters get "erotic" camera focus and in one context, for how long, how to balance it out with other characters, how to balance it out with the player's gaze, etc. etc.

NOTES

1 Wikipedia, "Gaze," accessed September 5, 2021, https://en.wikipedia.org/wiki/Gaze.
2 J Clement, Statista, "Distribution of game developers worldwide from 2014 to 2021, by gender," August 19, 2021, https://www.statista.com/statistics/453634/game-developer-gender-distribution-worldwide/.
3 J Clement, Statista, "Distribution of video gamers in the United States from 2006 to 2021, by gender," August 20, 2021, https://www.statista.com/statistics/232383/gender-split-of-us-computer-and-video-gamers/.
4 B Lin, Diamond Lobby, "Diversity in Gaming Report: An Analysis of Diversity in Video Game Characters," August 9, 2021, https://diamondlobby.com/geeky-stuff/diversity-in-gaming/.
5 L Mulvey, "Visual Pleasure and Narrative Cinema," scanned PDF, published 1975, https://www.amherst.edu/system/files/media/1021/Laura%20Mulvey,%20Visual%20Pleasure.pdf.
6 Ibid.
7 It's worth noting that some queer women can and do gain erotic pleasure from seeing women presented through the male gaze; great! But for others, there is a major gap between presenting women or sex in ways that they find erotic vs. what straight men find erotic; remember Monica's comment in the LGBTQ chapter about lesbian porn for straight men and applying heterosexual lenses to queer sex! Also, there's still the issue of whether these female characters have enough agency and identity for female players to identify with them. The point is that male gaze does not *always* translate into sex scenes having erotic enjoyment for queer women.

CHAPTER 21

Setting the Sex Scene!

Sex and Environment Design

A LOT OF FOCUS FOR sex scenes is on the human element (or alien, or fantasy race, etc.!) – of two or more characters engaging in physical intimacy. We've discussed the attraction that brings the characters together, how the camera focuses on their bodies, how to present those bodies respectfully, and so on, but in all this focus, it's easy to forget what is *around* those bodies, the place that the characters in question are having sex, and what that means for the larger narrative.

And if that doesn't seem like that would be important, then consider where *you* would prefer to have sex: a lush, candle-lit boudoir, or a rainswept neon-lit alleyway? (Figure 21.1).

FIGURE 21.1   Hey, let's hear it for Team Hot and Dirty Quickie Against the Wall in a Rainy Cyberpunk Alley! (Ian Good/Shutterstock.com.)

DOI: 10.1201/9780429356650-25

It's a trick question: there's actually no right or wrong answer. The point is that where sex takes place has a profound impact on the experience for the participants and can share a lot of thematic, character, and contextual information with the players.

Creating the environment and location for sex to take place in is an important step in creating a compelling scene, in the same way that designing a level is a vital part of narrative design and conveying a story. The chapter on cutscenes touched on props and location in a cutscene (e.g., the presence of a bed) and how it might be framed by the camera. Now let's look at some of the finer points of environment and location design as it relates to sex, as well as details that artists and environment designers should consider.

ASPECTS OF SEXUAL ENVIRONMENT DESIGN

The impact of a sex scene and its place in the narrative should be supported by the details that surround it. Therefore, it's vital for level and cinematic designers to consider how those spaces are designed, down to the supposedly insignificant details.

- **Setting of location** – in other words, what are the major considerations of era, genre, setting, etc., that shape what the location looks like? For example, bedrooms – a common location for sex – will look very different between a historical or fantasy setting vs. a sci-fi setting vs. a contemporary setting. Even contemporary settings have almost infinite variations, from the wealthy penthouse to the student dorm. Understanding the location's context within the world – and the nature of the world it's in – is an important guide to its design.

- **Nature of location** – Bedrooms are obviously a popular choice of places to have sex, but the potential locations for sex are unlimited. Is it outside or inside? Is this a place that belongs to one of the characters, or are they in some other location? Is it completely private, or is it in some sort of public or semi-public space (e.g., a closet in a space with very close quarters, like in *Wolfenstein*?) Is it an area used for sleeping, or talking, or just "any surface will do"? The choice of location can have a big impact on the intensity and feel of the sex scene. Compare the energy of a scene where the two characters deliberately withdraw to a bedroom vs. where they decide to go at it wherever they currently are.

- **Size of location** – let's face it, space matters in sex, both in terms of the logistics of the sex and in terms of how it is perceived by the audience. Large open space might suggest luxury or indulgence, while cramped tiny spaces suggest a more frantic, hurried coupling. For example, in the closet scene in *Wolfenstein: The New Order*, the cramped closet space reinforces the frantic, realistically awkward nature of the sexual encounter between BJ and Anya. The size also determines what your cinematic and narrative design teams can do with the scene leading into the sex. Are there places for the characters to pace or have a conversation? Or would any pre-sex talks have to happen somewhere else before they get in the broom closet?

- **Furniture** – the furnishing of the room reflects the world setting, but also ties into the available space and, to be blunt, the logistics of the sex. After all, the characters are going to have to be lying, sitting, or standing somewhere, and thought should be given as to exactly what it is they're up against (literally)! How much furniture is in the room, and what kind is it? Is it stuffed to the brim with cozy, comfortable pieces? Sleek, modern, and clean lines? Luxurious, glittering, dripping with decadence? Or is it just a ratty mattress on a rusty floor?

- **Smaller assets + personal effects** – many sex scenes take place in personal spaces such as bedrooms, ship quarters, or living spaces, and thus the environment designers have a chance to include small assets and props as personal effects for the room's owner – anything from photos, clothing, and books to sex paraphernalia. Even if the characters aren't having sex in a private room, however, there are still plenty of smaller assets that may be needed to make the scene look more authentic and give it more context…and after all, there's always the tried and true "throwing things off a table to have sex" move, right?

- **Lighting** – don't discount the impact of lighting in a sex scene! On top of the obvious time of day considerations – is the sex at night? During the day? – it's also worth thinking about what its source is, and whether it's a cool or warm light. As discussed before, sex scene illuminated in golden light vs. illuminated in blues can have very different moods, even if everything else is the same.

- **Materials used** – Ooh, are those *silk* sheets? The materials and textures used for the walls, floors, furniture, and other fixings can do a lot to make a scene more (or less) sexy and appealing, as well as emphasizing the context of the setting (e.g., sleek clean materials vs. scuffed and threadbare). In the case of personal settings, it can also say something about the character who owns them; are they the kind of person who demands high-quality cotton on their bedsheets, or the kind who makes do with a threadbare sheet?

- **Unique/bespoke, or reused?** – lastly, consider whether the sex is going to take place in a special cinematics-only location – a one-use-only environment – vs. a location that the player will be able to visit or navigate at other times. In some cases, entire environments are specifically crafted around a particular sex scene's blocking. However, in other games, the location may need to be designed more for general usage, with the blocking and planning of sex scenes having to work around the existing space rather than having a space made specifically for it (e.g., Shepard's quarters on the Normandy in the *Mass Effect* series).

Okay, but you may ask, WHY do you need to consider these things in such detail? And why does environmental design have such an impact; surely it doesn't matter where the boning happens as long as it happens somewhere, right? Well, let's explore some of the ways that environmental storytelling and design can be used to tell, refine, and reveal erotic narrative.

FRAMING AND CAMERA WORK

This can relate to the framing and focusing tricks discussed in the cutscene chapter (e.g., using curtains to direct the eye to the bed where the sex will happen). But it can also be important in scenes where, despite there being relatively explicit sexual content, the sex itself is not actually "shown" visually. In many cases, while the characters will clearly be having sex (as shown through silhouettes, moaning, etc.), the camera may focus on something else, whether for practical, technical, or artistic reasons. In many cases, this means that the camera will be "pointed" at parts of the room or at objects around the space.

Given that, it's important to make sure that the objects, furniture, and spaces that the camera focuses on are appropriately appealing to the eye or connected to what is happening. At the very least, it shouldn't throw the player out of the scene, or make them question what they're seeing. In other words, if the camera is going to focus on a wall for a few minutes – or possibly on the writhing shadows on the wall – while characters have sex, you don't want to have that wall be boring, or worse, thematically inappropriate (e.g., children's wallpaper!) The space where sex happens should be designed with this roving camera focus in mind, and assets should be provided to engage the frame in a way that makes the scene interesting even if the player isn't seeing any of the actual sex itself.

It should be noted that this does not have to be restricted to the immediate surroundings; some games literally go further by having the camera focus on vistas, landscapes, and other distant visuals (e.g., the end of the Bayek/Aya sex scene in *Assassin's Creed Origins* pans up to a beautiful view of Alexandria and the famous lighthouse as they tumble onto the rugs together). Thus, world design and aesthetics may need to be considered if the sex takes place in a location where vistas or other views are important.

Some games go a step further and have the camera focus on a sort of proxy image or asset for the sex. The early *God of War* games are famous for this. In the first game, the camera simply focused on a vase or jar in the room that was jostled by the passionate sex and eventually falls to the ground and shatters. Later games featured phallic or suggestive statues and imagery, such as a naked Cupid urinating a white stream or the naked candle holder discussed in an earlier chapter. In these cases, the camera is using the environment design to "suggest" the activity that they are unable or unwilling to show. The results are usually more comedic or deliberately sleazy than actively erotic. This approach should not be used for sincere or serious depictions of sex, or with the intent to arouse. In those cases, the best approach is to focus on genuine, "realistic" aspects of the scene and stick to more sensual, subtle details to convey eroticism.

REVEALING CHARACTER AND CHARACTER SEXUALITY

While sex can take place in any number of places, many scenes take place in private, personal spaces belonging to or inhabited by a character, such as bedrooms, bathrooms, and living rooms. Given this connection to the character's private life, this is an excellent opportunity to use environment design to share subtle (or not so subtle) glimpses into the personality or development of the character in question. After all, the sorts of items they keep in their intimate, private places – like beside their bed – can tell us a lot about the character, and choosing which of them to include is an important part of blocking out a scene. Do they have dirty clothes left on the floor? An orderly set of items on the bedside table that get jostled by the sex? Is their room luxurious and sensual, spartan and functional, or filled with punk aesthetic that matches their personality? Sex scenes are a great way to smoothly reveal some of the characters' inner lives through the spaces they're having sex in.

This can get a little strange if done clumsily; some personal effects might be inappropriate or unsexy and thus disrupt the mood of the scene. In *Indigo Prophecy*, for example, there's a scene in which the player takes control of a male character in their bedroom, with the character's girlfriend in bed. The player can investigate the items on the desk and find out tidbits about the character (e.g., one toy is the mascot from his favorite video game and he has several photos of his family) But if the player then initiates sex with the character's girlfriend, the subsequent scene involves the camera panning over these items. Needless to say, it's not particularly sexy, and in the case of the family photos, feels quite awkward.

Of course, part of a character's inner life is their sexuality, and environment and cinematic designers should consider what aspects of this can be shown in these private spaces. Does the character have slinky, sexy clothing? Do they have bondage gear on hand? Lube by the bedside? Do they have a drawer of sex toys, or maybe even a shelf of them? What about birth control and other forms of protection? Environmental design can convey a lot of erotic information here even without depicting the sex, revealing the sexual life of the character in the moment and beyond. It's worth noting that this sort of environment design and asset creation is worth considering even outside of sex scenes; including intimate assets and details in their living space is a great way to acknowledge their sexuality even outside of specific scenes and moments. A good example of this is in *Tacoma*; when exploring the room of a married lesbian couple called Nat and Bert, the player can find a vibrator among their personal effects, acknowledging the realities of their sexual lives – and what female sexual intimacy can look like – in a simple and effective way without showing the actual sex (Figure 21.2).

SETTING A MOOD: THE SEXUAL TRIFECTA AND OTHER CONSIDERATIONS

The location choice for a sex scene can have a massive impact on the mood of the sex scene, whether it feels raw or romantic, ecstatic or empty. In fact, design of the environment can have a major impact on how the scene is placed within the thematic trifecta – sacred, profane, or mundane – that was discussed earlier. For example, a place filled with light with a lot of space and clean lines is most likely to read as sacred. In contrast, a particularly squalid location (e.g., rundown wallpaper, old mattress on the floor) is more likely to ping as profane or the more cynical end of mundane. While there can be mismatches (e.g., *Indigo Prophecy* has a sex scene with sacred/mundane aspects take place in a dingy, ruined railway car), setting the sex scene in a location that complements the desired part of the trifecta can help keep the tone consistent (Table 21.1).

No, I think I'll just leave that there.

FIGURE 21.2 The vibrator in the drawer is a very "real" detail related to the couple who live in the room and the sex life they share together; the player doesn't need to actually see the sex to learn that about them. (Fullbright, *Tacoma*, published by Fullbright, PC/Mac/Linux/PS4/Xbox One, August 2, 2017. Screenshot from J Joho, Mashable, "There's a hidden vibrator in 'Tacoma' and here's why that's important," August 4, 2017, https://mashable.com/article/sex-toy-vibrator-tacoma-gone-home-indie.)

TABLE 21.1 A Rough Chart of Some Common Locations and Environments for Sex and the Most Common Associations and Stereotypes Players Will Likely Make Regarding the Sacred/Profane/Mundane Trifecta

Examples of Locations	Examples of Common Associations and Stereotypes Re: the Thematic Trifecta
Luxurious interiors/exteriors (silk sheets, fireplace, wine, rugs, pillows, etc.)	Sacred/mundane – romantic, heady, sensual
Lush natural environment (waterfalls, forests, caves, etc.)	Sacred – closer to nature, possible Eden-like connections
Deluxe modern locations (modern penthouses, sci-fi quarters, etc.)	Mundane – stylish, cool, self-indulgent
Standard/stock modern locations (regular bedrooms, kitchens, living rooms)	Mundane – normal, unremarkable
Dilapidated locations (abandoned buildings, alleys, old houses, etc.)	Mundane/profane – dirty, lurid, gritty
Sex-related locations (brothels, strip clubs, sex dungeons)	Profane/mundane – lustful, steamy, taboo
Personalized locations Character's bedroom, kitchen, private spaces	Mundane – personal, intimate, revealing.

Beyond the larger considerations of the trifecta, there are also more subtle connections with mood and tone that the environment design can impact. Lighting is a good example; a scene with golden light (e.g., daylight, candlelight, fires) can feel warm, heated, passionate or affectionate, while blue or silvery light (e.g., nighttime, illumination from spaceship portholes, and aquariums) can feel cooler, more relaxed and chill, and more "secretive" (in the sense of being cloaked by darkness). Environment and cinematic designers can choose which lighting to use and convey a specific erotic or emotional state, or even use multiple types of lighting to show an emotional journey. There's a good example of this in *Assassin's Creed: Origins* during Bayek and Aya's first reunion. While sex is not depicted, it is heavily suggested not only by not only their body language and interactions, but by the environmental transitions and use of light. Their first embrace is in a library lit with golden light, reflecting the warmth of their connection and their passionate embraces. Later, the scene cuts to the two of them (now undressed and engaged in grooming and intimate conversation) in a cave pool, where the light is much cooler and muted, almost nighttime; the effect is to shift them into an intimate, quiet, chill headspace, where their passions have cooled (possibly after being acted on?) to an easy, confident sexual intimacy that's reflected in their conversation and actions. Only when they return to the warmly lit library are they fully dressed and ready for action again.

Of course, lighting is not the only way to guide the mood! Indeed, everything about the environment design helps to build or tweak the mood, from subtle emotional threads to sweeping, dominant tones. For example, scenes in penthouses or futuristic quarters can feel sophisticated and "classy"; sex in an alleyway can feel exciting, urgent, and rebellious. Having candles everywhere can make a scene feel more romantic…or more deliberately erotic, like the boudoir of a courtesan or sex worker. Every asset or texture has the opportunity to reflect on the emotional core that the sex scene is trying to convey. Having a sex scene take place outdoors or in nature can create an idyllic, Eden-like atmosphere where the sex scene is seen as deeply romantic and naturalized – Cassandra's and Jaal's scenes in *Dragon Age: Inquisition* and *Mass Effect: Andromeda* come to mind. The former takes place in a beautiful, candlelit glade on a clear night; the latter takes place in a waterfall cave lined with tropical flora and fauna, a lush paradise of a backdrop. Both reinforce the romance and meaningfulness of the encounter, as well as elevate it to a perfect lovemaking fantasy.

SENSUALITY THROUGH ENVIRONMENT

Speaking of assets and textures, these are also worth paying attention to for another reason – they directly relate to the sensual nature of the scene. Sex is something closely related to all five senses – sometimes in restricting or denying them (e.g., blindfolds), but most often in pleasing them. Environment design should also be doing some heavy lifting in terms of pleasing and engaging the senses in a sensual way that matches the mood of the sex.

One example of this is fabric textures. In much of media and culture (Western culture, at least), sex and silk are interconnected – "silk sheets" are considered to be shorthand for romance and sex, sexy lingerie is silky, and a lot of romance novels describe certain sexual acts or body parts (e.g., the skin) as like silk. It offers a very particular pleasure to one of the senses – touch – and that pleasure acquires a seductive element in the context of sex. While video games may not be able to reproduce silk's exact engagement with touch – our haptics aren't quite that good yet! – the environment designer can evoke it by using silk materials and textures for certain assets in a room: the bed, the pillows, the curtains, the clothes of the lovers, and so on. Of course, using a different fabric (say, cotton) won't necessarily "ruin" the sensuality of a scene, but rather give it a different aspect (e.g., a clean, relaxing feel on the skin).

Designers can use assets and textures to evoke every sense during a sex scene or in its lead up. Adding fruits or wine, for example, evokes the concept of savoring tastes. Scents can be evoked through the presence of flowers or incense, making players imagine the scent as they inhale in the moment. Carpets and pillows can turn a cold marble floor (a sensual experience in its own right) into a lush, comfortable place for a character's naked back to rest against. Colors can guide the player's eyes to where they need to be – no one is going to miss the bed if it's covered in brilliant red sheets or pristine white! Even the sound engineering of the space can engage the senses in different ways – the crackle of a fire, or the sound of night crickets in the distance.

We can see good examples of this sort of sensual environment design in both the Bayek/Aya rooftop scene in *Assassin's Creed Origins* and in the Geralt/Keira scene in *The Witcher 3*. Both scenes are set outdoors (the former on a beautiful Grecian columned rooftop overlooking the city, the latter in an idyllic woodland glade), but both also use various game assets to enhance the luxury and pleasurable sensuality of the scene. The lovers lie on plush pillows and rugs (sensation of touch), surrounded by candles (sight) and flower petals (scent), and with various bottles and goblets of wine nearby (taste). Both scenes use their environments to provide romantic, sensual environments for the lovers, but also for the players, guiding their expectations and perceptions of pleasure in the scene.

(And of course, don't discount the power of *negative* sensuality – think of how you can deliberately make a sex scene repellant by juxtaposing it with an environment that looks like it stinks and has no pleasant surfaces to brush against! There's a reason why the scene on the dingy abandoned train car in *Indigo Prophecy* is more turn-off than turn-on!)

Regardless of the route your team takes, make sure you consider in designing the space how it will engage with your player. If you do it well, your player may already be seduced long before the characters start taking off their clothes.

BLOCKING OUT THE ACTION

We've been speaking mostly about things like moods, character revelations, and sensuality. But don't forget the most obvious consideration to environment design in a sex scene – actually corresponding with what's going on! If you have a scene in mind with a specific set of actions, camera angles, or story beats, you may find yourself needing to design the space in order to match those needs.

An amusing example of this can be seen in one of Iron Bull's scenes in *Dragon Age: Inquisition*. The scene revolves around a sex-themed gag in which Cullen, one of the advisors, walks in the door from the fortress ramparts to ask the Inquisitor a question only to find Iron Bull naked on the bed. While he reacts, Josephine and Cassandra also wander in the open door (that's open on the ramparts, mind you!) and react hilariously to Iron Bull's nakedness, culminating in a lighthearted conversation about his sexual relationship with the Inquisitor ("Nothing wrong with a bit of fun!"). It's a very funny scene that was well received by players, but what is interesting is that the team at BioWare designed an entire bedroom set purely for this scene! The Inquisitor's actual bedroom had a staircase entrance instead of a door, so the joke wouldn't work; as such, the team ended up creating a special "sex tower" for Iron Bull that was laid out specifically (e.g., bed in view of the door) so that the "everyone walks in on you" scene would actually work.[1] It was extra work to do this extra environment design, but the effectiveness of the final scene and the character dynamics speak for themselves.

There are plenty of other considerations about designing environments to match sex scenes, whether you're designing a setting purely for that one scene or repurposing an existing set or part of the level. Consider the action that is taking place and what sorts of assets it's going to affect or generate. The good old classic "shove everything off the table to have sex" isn't going to be nearly as effective if there aren't things on the table to throw off! Characters entering an apartment and going to the bedroom could scatter clothing on the floor along the way, showing their haste to get down to business. And if your intrepid heroes need an "excuse" to get into bed together, perhaps the train sleeper compartment they've been given only has one bed…

CONCLUSION

Environment and level design play a vital part in all aspects of game development and narrative, and that still holds true for sexual content and sex scenes. Don't skimp on the backgrounds just because there are characters doing sexy things in the foreground! A good environment designer or background artist will create sensual settings for the story to play out and the emotions and mood to captivate the player.

WORKSHOP QUESTIONS

Analysis: For the game you're analyzing, note where the sex scene(s) take place. Are they in private spaces, outdoors, or in more public locations? Are they luxurious, functional, or grimy? What are some of the art assets you notice in the scene – furniture, small props, etc.? Do they tell us anything about the characters (e.g., their personal effects and their standards of luxury)? What time of day is it, and what kind of lighting? And what mood do all of these elements combine to convey, either in terms of the sacred/profane/mundane trifecta or just in general?

Creative: Consider where at least one of your sex scenes will take place in your game.

- Apply the same questions as above to your proposed scene, and answer the questions as best you can, with discussion with your other teammates to get their feedback and gauge their capacity, project budget, etc. For particular consideration:

  - Can/should you reuse existing locations?

  - Will you need character models in states of undress (e.g., nude, or modesty underwear?)

  - What furniture and object assets will you need? Are these assets that you already have or that are easily made/purchased? What objects might need to be created from scratch?

- What lighting needs to be in place in the environment, and what lighting sources? (e.g., moonlight, candlelight, and fireplaces)

- If applicable, what will your camera be focusing on in the scene? Is it an interesting visual for the player?

- Document your requirements clearly for yourself and your team.

  - If applicable, create a board of visual references for the location in question (e.g., photos of similar rooms or locations and images of objects) and share this with the team.

NOTE

1 J Epler, Twitter post, October 8, 2019, 7:17 PM, https://twitter.com/eplerjc/status/11817556 24599646209.

CHAPTER 22

"Aural Sex" and Audio

Contributor: Souha Al-Samkari

WHEN WE TALK ABOUT sex scenes in games, we tend to discuss them in terms of either gameplay or visual representation. But sight is not the only sense to consider; audio also has a huge impact on sex scenes. This isn't surprising, as real-life sex often involves a wealth of sound as well, from the subtle to the outright loud and noisy. The right audio integration with your scene – appropriate music, sound effects, and vocalizations – will heighten the mood and push its emotional impact (and its hotness quotient) to the limits. The wrong audio, however, will deaden the impact or even cause it to fail entirely, possibly to comically bad levels. This is why working closely with your audio team and ensuring that they understand the emotional context and mood of the scene is so vital, and that they are in a position to use their skills and toolsets to best convey that context and match the visuals and other senses of the scene.

MUSIC SETS THE MOOD

Sexual cutscenes and sequences are usually accompanied by a musical soundtrack (except when they're not – more on that in a moment) which raises the question, what is an appropriate "soundtrack for sex," besides "whatever's on the radio at the time"? (Figure 22.1).

In popular culture, "sex soundtracks" are often jokingly connected to what is affectionately nicknamed "bow chicka wow wow" music, a reference to a stereotypical funk riff often associated with pornographic film soundtracks from the '70s. But of course, sex scenes can be scored to all kinds of music, to very different effects! The trick is to match the effect with the mood and theme that the scene is trying to convey. If there is a "mismatch," it should be done to deliberate dramatic effect. For example, juxtaposing erotic, pleasurable sex visuals to dark, tense music may make players realize that something is seriously wrong and that not all is what it seems.

More "generic" mismatches – for example, using "bom chicka wow wow" music for a gentle, tender scene – should be avoided as the disconnect ruins the mood that the scene is trying to convey. For this reason, care should be taken about "one-size-fits-all" music that's

DOI: 10.1201/9780429356650-26

FIGURE 22.1   "This evening, on NPR…" (Viktoriia Hnatiuk/Shutterstock.com.)

reused for all sex scenes. Some games have a particular musical theme that is used across multiple sex scenes, which can work well if all the scenes hit roughly the same emotional register, but if there's a variety of tones (e.g., some playful, some tender, some raunchy), using the same music for all of them will hit incorrectly. In this case, it's worth spending the extra time and money to create multiple music tracks (or remixes of a base track) to match the varying moods and emotions of the scenes. The alternative might save money and resources, but also is likely to make your players roll their eyes and disengage from the scenes you're trying to present. A good example of reused music can be heard in *Mass Effect 2* with the track "Reflections,"; while the sex scenes may be different, all of them strike at least some sort of heartfelt or bittersweet note, so the track's gentle, melancholic instrumentals work for all of them.

In terms of the types of music that can be used, the possibilities are literally endless. While it might be a little unusual to score a sex scene to, say, a triumphant high school marching band or traditional Japanese gagaku, it would certainly provide some fascinating challenges and narrative implications! Having said that, here is a quick overview of some of the more common and useful musical genres to explore for sex scenes and sexual content in games:

- **Bom-chicka-wow-wow and other "pornographic music"** – as mentioned, certain kinds of music has a heavy foundation in Western pop culture as being associated with sex and porn. As such, the emotional and thematic associations around this sort of music tend toward cheerfully, almost playfully "sleazy." If this music comes on in the context of sex, it's often as a winking nod to its history in porn. As such, it can be a good musical choice for scenes that are meant to evoke a certain playful porn-like dynamic (e.g., cheesiness, heavy flirtation, lust-based). It's also worth considering for certain period pieces. Other situations may warrant its use, but be careful; it may come off as either too pornographic for your needs, or as a parody of porn music which introduces humor/comedy that might not match what you're going for.

- **Smooth jazz / R&B** – while these genres have also gained certain connections with sex in popular culture, the associations are in many ways looser and more flexible, and less tied directly to porn. The mood is also different, often tending toward more relaxed, slow enjoyment of sensuality and sexuality. It's also quite flexible in terms of emotional dynamic between the characters; it can work equally well for long-term lovers or one-night stand. Just ensure that the general tempo of the scene matches the tempo of the music (i.e., not so much wild passion as warm, luxurious indulgence). Of course, that does not mean it works for every scene, and in certain settings (e.g., fantasy, sci-fi) it may not match the musical aesthetics of the larger world; you may need to consider period-appropriate music instead (Figure 22.2).

- **Ethereal music, choirs, etc.** – if you're going for the "sacred" part of the trifecta, can't get much more sacred than this! Music that is ethereal, elevated, or even "religious" in tone centers the scene as Something Major(™) in which the sex is highly spiritual and/ or ecstatic in nature, quite likely emotional as well. This sort of music can play well for sequences that feature dramatic or emotional intensity, particularly of a romantic sort, or scenes that are dreamy and ethereal, but for more casual or playful encounters, can often come off a little bit overwrought and over-the-top. *Dragon Age: Origins* in particular uses this style of music in its sex scenes; it worked well for certain deeply emotional encounters (e.g., Alistair), but using it for every sexual encounter resulted in things feeling a little overdone, particularly in scenes where the sex was far less emotional (e.g., Morrigan's blood ritual).

FIGURE 22.2 If this is the sort of vibe you're going for with your sex scenes, smooth jazz or R&B might be worth considering. (Civil/Shutterstock.com.)

- **Tender instrumental music (e.g., soft piano or other instruments)** – this sort of music overlaps with the previous entry slightly, but whereas ethereal music is all about ascension and transcendence, this is music that grounds itself in the current, usually vulnerable emotions of the characters – their love, their sadness, their longing or wistfulness, or even just their need for some closeness and comfort. It's great for sex scenes that incorporate vulnerability as a theme, whether in terms of love confessions or in terms of melancholy. In contrast, more playful or "performative" encounters (i.e., where the partners may be covering or hiding their vulnerabilities) might be a mismatch. You'll often hear this kind of music in big tentpole AAA games like *Mass Effect*, *The Witcher*, and later *Dragon Age* games.

- **Music with a fast tempo/percussion (e.g., heavy drums)** – you would think that "action sequence soundtrack" would not be a good match for a sex scene, right? But "action" music is designed to get the blood pumping and the heart pounding…and in the context of sex, it can be very evocative of blood pumping and heart pounding in a very different context! Using music with a fast, heavy bass or percussion – particularly one that is evocative of a heartbeat – often evokes a sense of primal heat and passion, of giving over to desire and being swept away by it. Clearly, not always the best choice for tender, gentle lovemaking – although there are some interesting examples of mixed music choice for that! – but a great call for scenes that focus on rising, irresistible passion. A good example of this is in the *Witcher 3* Kaer Morhen sex scene between Geralt and Yennefer. As their lovemaking grows more passionate, hurried, and almost desperate, the music kicks into a fast-paced, period-appropriate motif, accompanied by images of racing wolves hunting; the music, sexual imagery, and hunting imagery blend together in a metaphor of racing hearts and something untamed and primal (Figure 22.3).

FIGURE 22.3 Scoring sex scenes with fast-tempo music, or music with a heavy percussion line, can tap into something more passionate, heated, or untamed. (Prathan Nakdontree/Shutterstock.com.)

- **Harsher contemporary music (e.g., rock, metal, punk, certain kinds of techno)** – There are lots of rock, heavy metal, and punk songs about sex, and while they might not exactly be music for a petals-and-wine romantic evening, or even a night of blazing passion, they can be evocative of some extremely intense sexual experiences or emotions. After all, as many would point out, "angry sex" is a thing! Some forms of techno can also provide a heavy, harsh baseline for sex that's different than the "action" percussion discussed above. Consider this kind of music for scenes defined by their rawness or for conveying a gritty realism about the sexual encounter. The recent release (as of writing) of *Cyberpunk 2077* features some examples of this; several of the sex worker encounters feature fast-paced, somewhat "harsh" techno overlaid on top of the sex scene, making it feel raw and less idealized.

- **Music in a sinister/minor key** – sex is not always a "good" thing as far as the larger plot goes, even when it's clear both parties are enjoying it. For example, if there are two villainous antagonists that are making the heroes' lives a living hell, showing them finally giving into mutual lust and having sex might feel extremely threatening – how scary are they going to be now that they're "together"? In other cases, you may wish to signal to the audience that something is wrong, or at least ABOUT to go wrong, whether that happens to be a dire betrayal or a monster jumping in on our unsuspecting lovers. Using sinister music, or music that carries some sort of threatening undertone, can be the best way to foreshadow these events and to properly build the player's suspense. And obviously, this might work *wonderfully* for some horror games! Another excellent NON-game version of this can be found during a particular set of sex scenes during the third season of the Netflix *Castlevania* animated series; while both onscreen sexual encounters were presented erotically, the dark music in the background made them tense and unnerving, foreshadowing how both encounters would end VERY poorly for some of their participants.

- **Setting-appropriate music** – this is less of a genre, and more a lens to apply to the approaches we've discussed already. Always be sure the music in question matches the location, period, and setting that your game is established in. That means being aware of both regional differences as well as period differences; you may be calling on very different cultural and musical motifs if your game is set in, say, 1960s Philippines vs. modern day Germany vs. a futuristic Brazil! This also extends to speculative settings like fantasy and sci-fi, and the fictional cultures in them. What might the elven equivalent of smooth jazz be? How about orcs? What do aliens put on when they're "in the mood"? What do humans of the future listen to? Do the music choices feel authentic within the setting and the level of technology the world has, or do they feel anachronistic in some way? Like all music for games, these are important aspects to consider; it just has to be considered with the additional context of, you know, getting it on (Figure 22.4).

FIGURE 22.4 Don't discount the power of music to seduce outside of a modern setting. There's a reason why bards have a reputation for being love machines! (Daniel Eskridge/Shutterstock.com.)

- **No music at all!** – eschewing music entirely is absolutely a valid choice, and one with some interesting effects. In some cases, it helps to heighten the characters' hesitation and deep breath before the plunge – for example, consider the effect that a few beats of silence might have after the characters share a "platonic" hug, then part and suddenly find themselves in close proximity. The silence paired with the moment of pause, of halting movement toward each other, can really sell the scene. Another benefit of having no music at all is that the sound effects come through all the clearer, becoming in many ways the star of the scene. However, consider that if your game is otherwise heavy on music, a silent sex scene will stand out amid the larger narrative; this may be used for deliberate dramatic purpose (e.g., contrasting the loud noise and drama of the rest of the story) or just feel a little out of place.

If you're interested in further explorations of what makes a song sexy or sexual, there are also a host of music theory articles out there by academics and enthusiasts on everything from lyrical content to the sexiest Beats Per Minute for music to hit (it's apparently 119, by the way, according to an informal study of Spotify playlists.[1]) While this level of musical craft is not in the scope of this book, it can be useful inspiration and reference info for both composers and the designers working with them.

Fantastic, you've composed and chosen the right music to build the mood for a scene! But there are still a few more considerations for how to use this music.

- **Will the music block out sound effects, or will sound effects still be audible?** In many scenes (sexual or otherwise), in order to build dramatic intensity or to highlight a scene as unusual or important, the sound effects will be muted or removed entirely, with the music as the only audio connected to the scene. The result is an interesting juxtaposition between the visuals of the sex vs. not hearing the expected sounds that go with it (e.g., seeing someone moan but not hearing it); depending on the music and the scene, the effect may be a more dreamlike or more intense sequence. This technique is often used in montages, unifying the scene with the music but removing the sound effects to lessen the immediacy and reality of each individual cut.

- **Does the music come from something in the world, or is it dubbed over "out of universe"?** The former is part of something called diegetic sound (i.e., any sound that originates from within the game's world, like a speaker, radio, or singer), and can be used in interesting mood-building and character-building ways in sex scenes. For example, a character might turn on the radio or a music player to "set the mood" for the sex. Their choice of song might convey something about their character or how they envision the sexual encounter before it happens. Other examples of diegetic music in sex scenes might include background music from another source, like music playing in another room, a live singer in another cross-cut scene, or a movie soundtrack playing while characters make out in the audience, or so on. Of course, sometimes non-diegetic music is the better call, and there's nothing wrong with dubbing over a soundtrack during a sexual scene, but it's worth at least considering if your game, characters, or scene would be served by music in the universe rather than just "on the soundtrack" (Figure 22.5).

FIGURE 22.5 …not quite the diegetic music I had in mind, but hey, if you can make it work! (Wallenrock/Shutterstock.com.)

EVOCATIVE SOUND EFFECTS

This may come as a surprise, but sound effects are probably one of the most effective and versatile tools for sexual storytelling, sometimes even over visuals! Moreover, sound effects are a fantastic way to compensate for technical deficiencies in visuals and other senses while still keeping the mood erotic and sensual. Can't show a character taking their shirt off, or kissing, or entwining with their lover – or just plain don't want to? An artful cut away combined with the appropriate sound effect – rustling, kissing, skin on skin – can be intensely evocative and suggestive. Not only that, but it encourages players to engage their imaginations, each envisioning their own version of exactly what the rustling was, how the lovers kiss, and so on. Giving the player the ability to mentally compose their own sex scene with a few carefully chosen sounds is a fantastic technique for when your ability to compose a visual sex scene is limited by your tech or resources. Of course, sound effects can also hit deliciously hard for a fully visualized sex scene as well, reinforcing the visuals and expanding them to encompass all the senses.

However, if you are heavily (or even lightly) relying on sound effects for your sex scene, remember to keep accessibility in mind. You can pick the most evocative, erotic sound effects in the world, but if your players are deaf or hard of hearing and you have not accounted for that, they may be frustrated or confused, doubly so if the sounds are the only hint of what's going on. Always be sure to provide appropriate closed captioning for the sound as much as the dialogue, and ensure that those captions are written to match the mood appropriately – whether that's "spanking sounds" or "the sound of a hand smacking against flesh."

There are a wide variety of useful sound effects to consider in the midst of a sex scene:

- First and in many ways the most useful to consider are **cloth noises** – for example, the rustling of clothing as it's being removed, or the rustling of sheets as characters lie on a bed. These sounds can be deeply intimate and evocative of touch, sensation, and movement, as well as being surprisingly flexible for all kinds of scenes. Consider the removal of clothing; a soft rustle of cloth might inspire feelings of tender, gentle intimacy and sensuality, while a loud sound of cloth being *ripped* instead conveys urgency, passion, impatience and lack of restraint. Cloth noises are worth considering particularly as cloth physics are notoriously difficult for game animators to replicate in 3D games. Thus, there is a huge benefit to having a sequence that evokes removing clothes without actually having to show it. With the right sound effects and camera tricks, your team may be saving your animators a LOT of work (Figure 22.6).

- Sounds can also be used to convey the **shifting of weight and bodies** as they move in a scene, particularly as they settle (or crash!) against furniture. Shins gently hitting the edges of furniture as someone backs up, beds creaking under the weight of two people, even the noise of someone being slammed against a wall or door – these all help capture the nature of the sexual encounter. For example, soft subtle sounds or sounds that are drawn out may suggest a careful, deliberate pace; something loud and rough matches loud rough sex or desperate passion; something rhythmic and repeated evokes explicit connections with the rhythm of sex. Even loud creaking or the crash of collapsing furniture can paint a picture that's funny, gritty, or wild.

FIGURE 22.6 There's a wide range of "cloth noises" you should consider for sheets and clothing. (Tatkhagata/Shutterstock.com.)

- As discussed earlier, sex scenes usually include kissing in some capacity, so **kissing sound effects** are worth considering. Subtle noises help boost the realism and physicality of a scene. Like clothing, kisses can be particularly hard to animate – recall the "air-kissing" mentioned in the cutscenes chapter – so combining sound effects with some clever camera tricks can help the illusion become reality for your players. As to what "kissing sounds" entail, that really depends on the intensity of the kiss and the sound. There are often vocalizations from the character – their breathing, a hum of pleasure, etc. – which we'll cover in more detail in the next section. There's also the noise of the lips and mouths themselves, and the various ways they can move. In many cases, the distinctive, quiet "smacking" sound of lips is enough, and you can play with it in all sorts of ways. Is it drawn out and lingered? Butterfly light? Loud and hungry? Just one, or over and over? You can also create "wetter" sounds to imply more sexual, passionate kissing (e.g., with tongue); this usually sounds much more explicitly sexual in nature, and can often be interpreted as lewd. A good rule of thumb for these kinds of sound effects is the wetter the sound, the more explicit it feels. So use your judgment as to whether your scene needs gentle, restrained kissing sounds or wetter, more lustful effects (Figure 22.7).

- Consider as well the sounds of **skin-on-skin contact**. If you brush your hand against the bare skin of your arm – or someone else's arm – it makes a quiet but distinctive noise, a noise that, like clothing rustling, can evoke a very sensual impression. Again, this is the sort of sound effect that can cover for issues on tech, art, and animation. Without having to stress about replicating skin-to-skin contact, sound can be used to reinforce the illusion of caressing or clasping each other's bodies even when the camera tricks hide it.

- Lastly, there are of course **the explicit sounds of sex itself**, sounds that tend to be either "fleshy" (e.g., flesh slapping together rhythmically) or "squishy and wet" (e.g., slurpy oral sex, lubricated activities). These sounds call attention to the full physical reality of sex. While sounds of kissing and skin contact evoke the body as a holistic concept, this deals with very specific body parts (usually genitals but not always), very specific interactions with those body parts, and other extremely explicit and

FIGURE 22.7   You may want your players to "hear" this, even if you don't have the capacity to *show* it. (EWStock/Shutterstock.com.)

specific sexual activities. Sometimes, this is exactly what you want! Pornographic games often lean on this heavily, as might a game with extremely explicit and realistic scenes on the profane/mundane spectrum. However, as with the kissing example above, this is where you'll need to use judgment, as this level of detail may be overkill for a lot of game sex scenes. Without careful setup, these sounds can make players focus more on the body parts smushing together than on the context, emotions, and character reasons for that smushing. If you aren't trying to go for the super-explicit or pornographic mood, or you're less interested in the fleshy body realities of sex and more in the holistic sensual side, then use these sounds with caution, or perhaps avoid them entirely (Figure 22.8).

FIGURE 22.8   "Okay, either these characters are getting REALLY raunchy or a Foley artist is doing something UNSPEAKABLE to an orange." (Harbucks/Shutterstock.com.)

VIVID VOCALIZATIONS

Lastly, let's touch on vocalizations for your characters. Note that this is NOT the same as dialogue from them – we'll be touching on that in the next chapter. Rather, vocalizations are the *sounds* they make as part of the sex, whether they're related to breath or voice. Including these vocalizations is a powerful way to convey your characters' pleasure and emotions – when done correctly.

It should be noted that, like other sound effects, some sex scenes exclude these sounds entirely. Quite a few games will feature visuals of characters moaning or screaming but with no accompanying voice. In some cases, this is either a deliberate artistic choice to enhance the dreaminess of a scene, to create a montage effect, or to focus on the music and visuals. However, in other cases, this is a choice to cover a much more logistical issue – namely, working with actors and their comfort levels about sex scenes.

Unlike the music and sound effects discussed already, creating vocalizations for sex is going to involve your actors, and in this, you may be constrained by what your actors feel comfortable doing. Making sexual noises – particularly sexual noises in the context of a sound booth with sound engineers and directors looking on! – is not something all actors are up for, and even the most seasoned can feel incredibly self-conscious and awkward. Even Doug Cockle, Geralt's voice actor for the *Witcher* games, finds it embarrassing, likening it to "being caught masturbating."[2] So as discussed in an earlier chapter, if you intend to go this route, you need to communicate your intentions for the scene to the actors from the very beginning, ideally back during the casting process, and gauging and respecting their comfort levels appropriately. If you really want erotic, breathy vocalizations, picking an actor who is not just comfortable but gung ho to do it will ensure they bring as enthusiastic a performance to the sex scenes as all the other scenes. But if your ideal actor for a character isn't comfortable with sex scenes – at least, not voice acting them to that degree – then you will have to adjust accordingly.

If you do decide to use vocalizations, you have a lot of opportunity to increase the sensuality and eroticism of the scene, to highlight the subtle emotional and physical shifts of your characters with the catch of a breath or a gasp at the right moment. Vocalizations to consider might include (but not be limited to):

- Moaning

- Gasps

- Soft breaths (inhaling or exhaling)

- Sighs

- Grunts (quiet or loud)

- Laughter

- Panting

- Cooing

- Humming

- Screaming (in pleasure, of course!)

SIDEBAR 22.1 – DIRECTING ACTORS THROUGH SEXY SCENES AND SEXUAL SITUATIONS

By Souha Al-Samkari

In a previous chapter, we talked about preparing your actors for sex scenes, from ensuring they're fully informed as to the content of their scenes to having intimacy coordinators on set/in session. Let's assume you've done all this as your budget allows, and here you are, with actors who are fully ready to help you bring your sensual and sexy scenes to life. As director, you'll be responsible for setting the scene for your actors and helping guide them to where they need to be to get the reads you need. But what if your actor is inexperienced with love scenes? What if they're simply shy? In a case like this, there are a few things you can do.

- Recontextualize it for them. If your actor's moans and sighs are not quite passionate enough, try giving them a completely different scenario (e.g., you've just had a drink of water after walking ten miles through the desert and you've just tasted chocolate for the first time).
- Take a break if needed – sometimes continuing to double down uselessly on a take can stress both you and your actor out. If you have the time, take a few minutes break, or return to it at the end of the session (or another day).
- If your actor is comfortable with this (Please ask first! Some actors hate this!), you can give them an example of what you're looking for with a line read.
- Bring in a pinch hitter – sometimes you may have an actor who is down for everything else but is not willing to do a love scene, which is perfectly valid and acceptable. In this case you can have someone else sub in – just be certain to inform your actor, and credit accordingly (or not – some people prefer to be uncredited for roles of this nature).

What to do if your actor feels uncomfortable in the middle of a scene?

- Stop immediately.
- Take a break if needed.
- Check on your actor – are they ok to continue with the specific scene or in general? If not, make the necessary arrangements. If so, proceed with caution, keeping up your communication. Don't linger too long.
- Do not belabor the point or make too big a deal – it's a delicate balance, but you really don't want to make someone feel guilty on top of having crossed a boundary.
- Wrap up the scene when you've got what you need and keep it moving.

Need to do less with more? Don't underestimate the power of words. Your actor may not be willing to do a love scene with moans and groans and all of that, but certain words and phrases delivered just so can be equally or more devastating than the most explicit sounds you can manage (e.g., "Come here," "good girl").

Spend time with your writing team to come up with alternate words, phrases, or sounds in the event of your actor's discomfort or unavailability. If you're doing a partially voiced game, as in a visual novel or an RPG, giving yourself a library of little sounds or short phrases will go a long way toward making scenes without full voiceover just that much more immersive. Spend time at the end of your session, if you have any time leftover, just doing a few sounds and phrases like this to cover yourself for multiple scenarios.

When it comes to sexual vocalizations, *less can be more*, and that can extend to the amount, volume, and frequency just as much as whether it's there in the first place. One issue with lots of sex scenes is that their vocalization comes in one setting....one obvious, performative, over-the-top and *constant* setting. I'm sure you know the type; a constant stream of aroused moans, occasionally including giggling, cooing, or appreciative hums, never letting up, constantly filling up every second of the sex scene's audio, building louder and higher and more performative until it finally ends in a theatrical scream of ecstasy (Figure 22.9).

FIGURE 22.9   Bad yodeling and sex scene vocalization: two things that involve going OOOH AAA EEE AAAH OHHHH! (Sandra Foyt/Shutterstock.com.)

Now, there's nothing inherently wrong with these vocalizations as sounds or reactions – sometimes people moan in pleasure during sex, or laugh in enjoyment, or hum, or scream, and that's all fine! The problem comes with the consistency and the performative nature of it. When this sort of vocalization keeps up during the whole thing, it becomes less a reflection of what's actually happening and more just erotic filler, a sort of obligatory performance. There's a difference between "character moans because of a particularly pleasurable sensation" vs. "character moans because it's a sex scene and sex scenes involve moaning," or even, "character moans because moaning will arouse the player." It feels like an attitude and performance lifted from pornographic movies, and while there's nothing wrong with those movies, they follow a logic and format that does not apply to (most) games, and as such, it can end up feeling alienating, annoying, or just forced.

Also, let's be frank; that obvious, performative moaning is highly, HIGHLY gendered. There are countless games, from AAA to indie and from porn to romance, that feature long audio sequences of female characters constantly cooing and moaning their way through the vowels (OOOO AAAAA EEEEE, etc.) in ways that clearly mark them more as objects of desire…or the gaze. The number of games that feature similar focus on the erotic vocal performances of the male character is…vanishingly small. Most male game characters remain stoically silent throughout the sex or, at most, offer a few quiet breaths and a low manly grunt. It's basically male gaze, but with audio instead of camera and character design (Figure 22.10).

None of this is to decry sexual vocalizations or dissuade you from using them in your game. In fact, for many players, vocalizations of desire can be some of the most potent erotic content you can offer them, one that engages them both in the characters involved and in the sexual activity that they're seeing – they tune in AND get turned on! In fact, I wish games would use vocalization more! But the trick is to consider different ways to use it, and to properly value how impactful it can be so as to use it the right amount. Think of

FIGURE 22.10 "Sorry, but we can't run the risk of you making any noises that might be arousing… our straight male players would never forgive us!" (ANDRANIK HAKOBYAN/Shutterstock.com.)

it like a seasoning; sometimes adding a little for flavor is better as opposed to dousing the scene liberally with it. So keep in mind:

- **A little can go a long way** – Moaning, sighing, cooing, screaming, grunting – these are all great ways to convey a character's arousal or engagement with sex. But consider that because they are great, sometimes one or two may be all you need. If the point is to depict the kind of sex that provokes constant moaning, or reveal that one of the characters is a constant screamer, that's all well and good. But for a lot of sex scenes, you're better served by using those noises judiciously. Try varying the sounds and letting them *sit* with the player at key moments, allowing them to hang in the air just that little bit longer before the next moan or sigh. Whether the sex is slow and sensual or fast and passionate, using a few vocalizations to set off key moments can often do way more for your scene than simply filling the audio space with rote moaning filler.

- **Consider the breath** – On the other hand, if you *do* want to have constant vocalization for some reason, you know what people *will* be doing constantly during sex, particularly if the sex is good? Breathing. Breathiness is an underrated approach to sex. Some of the most erotic vocalizations are those that affect the breath – rate of breathing, depth of breathing, inhaling vs. exhaling, hesitation and shakiness – and combining it with the voice – huskiness, sighing, gasping. Plus, unlike more vocal outbursts, breathiness can be kept quiet and subtle, a gentle cadence in the background as the scene progresses. You can tell a whole story with a series of subtle breaths – the inhale of air during a kiss, a hitch of breath as bodies meet, a shaky exhale in the aftermath – and that story will probably be really, really hot.

- **Let all genders vocalize their pleasure equally** – Do not assign your actresses hours of moaning and cooing recording sessions if you are not ready to do the same to your actors. Ensure that all characters, regardless of gender, vocalize their arousal or pleasure in ways that make sense with their character. And if you find that all of the male characters are "coincidentally" the stoic and silent type while the female characters are "coincidentally" free with their ecstasy, that may be a sign to step away and rethink how you're approaching your characters in terms of gender stereotypes both in and out of the bedroom.

CONCLUSION

Audio can be one of the most powerful, versatile, and accessible ways to capture and convey the mood of a sex scene, sometimes even outstripping visuals in terms of its arousing content and relatively low bar for entry. To all the audio designers and sound engineers out there, I hope this chapter serves as an inspiration and encouragement for making sex scenes spectacular…and to all the non-audio readers, I hope it serves to provide you with an appreciation for what these disciplines bring to the table and some new ideas about how they can bring it.

WORKSHOP QUESTIONS

Analysis: Take a listen to how the sex scenes in the game you're investigating handle audio.

- What sort of music does it use during the sex? Is it part of the world, or part of the soundtrack?

- What noises do the characters make? Is there moaning, breathing, sighing, etc.? Do both characters make noises, or just one? (and if so, what gender is the character who makes noises?).

- What other sound effects are there in the scene? Is it ambient, or caused by a particular act or moment (e.g., rustling cloth for taking off a shirt)?

- Can you identify any moments where the game uses sound in place of visuals or other techniques?

Creative: Outline the planned audio for the sex scene(s) in your game. Include:

- Proposed music, including the genre and setting, the tempo, and the general mood. Provide musical references if possible.

- A list of requested sound effects for the scene. If possible, indicate which need to be bespoke SFX and which can be used from a sound effect library.

- If your game is voiced, general direction notes for the sort of vocalizations (if any) you want as part of the scene.

- Any other important sound notes – is there ambient noise like crickets or the hum of a ship? Any special filtering that diegetic sound will need (e.g., tinny speakers)?

NOTES

1 Supplement Place, "The World's Favorite Sensual Songs," accessed September 3, 2021, https://www.supplementplace.co.uk/sensual-songs/.

2 R Purchese, Eurogamer, "The voice behind *The Witcher*," January 27, 2017, https://www.eurogamer.net/articles/2017-01-27-the-voice-behind-the-witcher.

CHAPTER 23

Tender Talk and Naughty Narration

Dialogue and Sex

W HILE THERE IS CERTAINLY tons of potential for exploring how sex scenes work in minimalist, text-and-dialogue-free games, a lot of games featuring sex scenes are games with dialogue. In most games, dialogue is part of how the characters become sexually drawn to each other, in terms of how they speak to each other, flirt, etc. And for many sex scenes, the intimacy will begin with dialogue, whether it be a direct invitation, sexually charged banter, or even unrelated conversation broken off by a special moment – a word, a touch – that triggers the deluge of desire and passion.

But…then that's it, right? Once the sex starts, all the talking stops, and it's all about the bodies and the sex. Only when they're all finished is it okay to have your characters talking again. But certainly nobody ever talks DURING sex, right?

For sure, in many sex scenes, a lot of dialogue during the intimate action is going to ruin the mood, or be on the nose, or just be plain awkward. But that doesn't mean dialogue has no place in the height of passion – only that, like most things in this book, it should be used thoughtfully, with an eye for what it's meant to accomplish and whether it's the best tool to use for that end. To that end, let's take some time to look at different ways dialogue can be used in the midst of a sex scene – specifically, when the sex is *actually* happening, not before or after – and the impact it can have on how the scene plays out. For now, we're focusing purely on dialogue that happens *during* the sex itself, both diegetic (i.e., from the sexual partners in the moment) and from other sources such as narration, flashbacks, and crosscuts.

WHY WE THINK TALKING AND SEX DON'T MIX

A lot of people are resistant to the idea of talking during sex, both in real life and in the context of fictional creations like games. The usual complaint is that it either ruins the mood or that the people involved should be beyond coherent speech due to pleasure, shortness of

DOI: 10.1201/9780429356650-27

breath, etc. And usually, the assumption is that the only kind of conversation you're going to have in the middle of sex is going to be either extremely explicit dirty talk out of a porno, or awkward discussions around physical comfort ("Ow, my leg is cramping!"). Any other kind of conversation is going to be seen as out of place, unrealistic, or just plain silly.

The reasons for these beliefs are varied, and of course, tie in a lot with our Western cultural hang-ups about sex in general. As a rule, we are not great about talking frankly and openly about sex at the best of times, and thus it makes sense that the idea of talking AND sex together making people uncomfortable, at least outside the "safe" parameters of "dirty talk." There's also another unspoken but common cultural assumption in play: namely, that "good" sex is something that does not require communication, that both partners should just "know" what to do, when to do it, and what the emotions behind it mean. As such, the idea of talking during the act is considered to "ruin the mood" by "forcing" communication into the mix, that talking about sex while you're having sex – whether it be to request a different position or sex act or just to tell someone what emotions you're feeling – somehow removes "the magic" (Figure 23.1).

There is a grain of truth to be taken here that in the context of a game (as opposed to real life), dialogue during sex can very, very easily be overdone if you're not careful. There is something to be said for the effect of a wordless but passionate tryst, and how adding dialogue can change (if not ruin) that effect. An explicit blow-by-blow commentary of the erotic activity might be expected in pornographic content, but in most games, it's only going to slow down the pacing, come over as self-indulgent or ridiculous, or just feel

FIGURE 23.1 Oh, hadn't you heard? Sex feels like this until someone has the temerity to actually speak, at which point the magic is gone and you fall flat on your ass, apparently. (pathdoc/ Shutterstock.com.)

generally unnecessary. And having too much talking can feel out of keeping with the mood of the scene and the activities of the characters.

But then, many of these considerations are the same ones your writers and designers should be employing for non-sexual dialogue *anyway*. In other words, dialogue during sex isn't somehow a strange anomaly, or a completely aberrant situation that has to be handled *completely* differently than anything else in a game. It's simply another circumstance in which characters speak, albeit with some unique complications and considerations. Getting those wrong can be a little fraught, but getting them *right* can deliver deeply meaningful character moments, or at least some added passion. After all, communication makes good sex *better*, and the right line at the right time can spike the heat levels through the roof or reveal a new side of a character you never knew.

BEST PRACTICES FOR IN-THE-MOMENT DIALOGUE

So if sex scene dialogue is great if done well and bad if done poorly, how do you do it well? As usual, a huge amount depends on the context of the scene and the characters, and there are no set-in-stone best practices. What will be ludicrously awful in one project might be right on the money for another. But in general, here are some useful guidelines to consider:

- **Identify the purpose of the dialogue** – This is actually true of ANY dialogue in a game, not only sex scenes. Like a scene, dialogue should always serve a purpose: advance the plot, reveal something about the characters, provide information, develop a relationship, or build on a mood. That last one allows for some unique headway in sex scene dialogue – for example, the mood can be based around the sexual tension and desire of the characters, and/or it can be tied in with a titillating, arousing mood for the player. While it's best to tread carefully around this – the line between enticingly titillating and boringly self-indulgent is a thin one, and titillation is not enough to build a scene on – this is one place where "because it's hot" can be a valid reason to explore verbalization.

- **Go for quality over quantity** – Again, this is a good rule of thumb for all dialogue, not just sex scenes, but it holds true particularly for sex scenes. In the previous chapter, we talked about avoiding using vocalizations (gasps, moans, etc.) just to fill up dead air, and the same is true for sexual dialogue. Too much, and it ends up feeling bloated. That's not to say that sexual dialogue can't be good, but as with many things, a little can go a very long, very effective way. If your sex scenes ARE getting very chatty, interrogate why, and again, ensure that the volume of dialogue is tied to a particular purpose (e.g., showing how distracted and disengaged your characters are in the moment).

- **Write your characters with less of a "filter" than they may normally have** – If they're in the middle of sex and properly "into" it, there's a good chance that their minds are in an altered state in which they may be less guarded or less careful with their words (though, of course, this is not universal).[1] This doesn't have to be a dramatic shift;

there's no need to have your characters lose their eloquence, start speaking totally differently than normal, or acting drunk! It simply means that if they do speak, they are more likely to speak off-the-cuff and in the moment based on their feelings or what pops into their heads. If nothing else, they may be too distracted by the sex to really consider what they want to say and whether it's a good idea to say it!

- Opinions differ wildly on the inclusion of "poetic" or "flowery" language in sexual dialogue. For some people, it's overwrought, saccharine, and laughable. For others, it's like a sexy narrative catnip that they can't get enough of. Of course, use of poetic dialogue will depend heavily on the characters. Some characters clam up or keep things simple, while others turn into the second coming of Petrarch when they get aroused, or have sex with someone they love, etc. etc. The dialogue will also depend heavily on the setting. Flowery language, metaphors, and pet names may play much better in a fantasy setting than a contemporary modern one, for example.

  - However, one good rule of thumb is that **while poetic phrasing is (or can be) great, *elaborate* phrasing likely isn't**. This ties back in with the previous point that the characters are not going to have the mind state or brainpower to focus on composing a complicated turn of phrase. Poetic language or expressions can still work very well, depending on the character, but more as a reflection about the way they think about sex and the vocabulary they usually use. After all, some people just genuinely DO use florid or antiquated words and metaphors in their daily speech patterns, so naturally, that would play out in their moments of passion when they're scrambling to express themselves. But there's a difference between gasped out sentiments about hearts beating together or flowery references to "depths" or "cores" versus full on iambic pentameter verse with rhyming couplets, complete with double word plays and intricate multi-subject sentence construction. The latter is either going to come off as artificial and unbelievable… or signal that your character is one HELL of a multitasker!

- **Play with back-and-forth dialogue vs. one-sided monologue** – Both have different sorts of effects and impact on the scene and on the dynamic between the characters. If the dialogue is a full conversation, with each responding to the other, this is a way to develop the dynamic and interplay between the characters in question, often in a way that echoes how the sex itself is proceeding. If only one character speaks, however, or if they speak out of sync (e.g., one speaking at the beginning, another saying something at the end), this puts more focus on the characters as individuals, getting snapshots of how that individual is currently thinking and feeling in the current moment.

- **Either work with or subvert the silly** – Let's face it, people CAN sound a little ridiculous during sex. The brain can go to odd or unusual places during sex, and it's not uncommon for people to say incredibly bizarre things in the height of passion, or speak in unusual ways (repetition, baby talk, etc.) And for the people who are having sex, it might only make them hotter (hopefully!), but for a player or viewer (or for the occasional partner taken out of the mood), it might be the most unintentionally funny thing they've heard all day. In these cases, one can either lean into the awkwardness and silly – acknowledge that sex can be weird and funny, particularly when you're not the one having it! – or make the scene more arousing and engaging to the player – so that THEY will be so steamed up that the "silly" things sound just right in the heat of the moment. Or of course, sidestep the silly entirely – no one said dialogue has to always reflect EXACTLY what real life conversation sounds like!

- Lastly, **consider the physical logistics of the sex and how it will affect the voice and the dialogue**. This is something to consider not just on a writing end, but in terms of voice direction. Sex can involve a lot of physical exertion, which can in turn cause shortness of breath, panting, huskiness, etc. If the dialogue and the voice direction lack any of these markers – i.e., the actor delivers the line in a conversational tone without any hint of breathiness or other vocal arousal – then that is going to throw the player out of the scene and the line very quickly and throw a spotlight on the disconnect between "voice actor in a booth" and "character in a sexual embrace." A voice performance that incorporates the signs of exertion and arousal, coupled with a line written with these vocal inflections and physical logistics in mind, helps erase that disconnect. Remember also that some sexual activities will preclude dialogue at all, or at least severely muffle it (e.g., kinky gags, oral sex). And of course, consider the effect of different voice registers and volumes for your characters (and actors) to speak in; there's a big difference in impact between a line screamed in passion vs. whispered huskily in someone's ear (Figure 23.2).

Note that all of these best practices and considerations are specifically for diegetic conversations and lines set in the moment of sex. Dialogue such as dubbed-in narration requires a different approach (which we'll discuss later in the chapter) and does not require incorporating arousal and exertion, at least not in the same way.

FIGURE 23.2 Even the simple act of saying a lover's name can feel emotionally and narratively different in this quieter context, compared to "head thrown back, yelling at top of lungs." (Lipik Stock Media/Shutterstock.com.)

THE OBVIOUS: DIRTY TALK AND ENTHUSIASTIC VERBAL CONSENT

Firstly, let's get this out of the way – yes, dirty talk and aroused discussion of the sex is absolutely something that happens in real life and fiction, and is a valid route to go in your game, as long as it still fulfills a purpose. For erotic games, the purpose can probably be as simple as, "to be hot," while for more mainstream work, the purpose might be to establish a dynamic between your characters in terms of their relationships or even character development. Is one of them domineering and commanding in bed? Needy? Playful? Calm and measured, or heated and desperate? Dirty talk is a great way to capture a quick snapshot of these characters in the moment, talking about exactly what is on their mind, at least in terms of what bits they want touched next.

Dirty talk is often associated with a certain cadence and content of banter consistent with pornographic movies (e.g., repeating fifty times that yes, you do, in fact, want that [BODY PART] in/on/under your [BODY PART], please please please, etc.). Outside of that context, or the context of intense arousal, this kind of dirty talk can be more comedic and sillier than hot (actually, it's arguably silly in the context of porn as well!) But don't let that blind you to the possibilities of what dirty talk can be and how it can work in the context of your game. Believe me, it does not all have to be, "YES, YOU BEAUTIFUL STUD, INSERT YOUR TUMESCENT BODY PART INTO MY EXCITED AND CAREFULLY PREPARED LOADING ZONE!" (Figure 23.3).

Dirty talk is another place where less can be more, and lewdness can come as much from the inference as from what is spelled out. It all comes down to the context. In some cases, a simple three-word command – "part your legs" – can be more erotically charged than the most explicitly filthy blow-by-blow commentary. In other cases, the dirty talk may need to tend to the "obscene" – e.g., swear words, obscene slang, and even consensual verbal degradation – to reflect who the characters are and what headspace they're in as part of the sex.

FIGURE 23.3 But if one of you puts that EXACT line in your game, please let me know because I will almost certainly buy it for the lulz. (siam.pukkato/Shutterstock.com.)

This is also a place where dirty talk and consent can overlap, as discussed earlier. Enthusiastic consent can be far more active, engaged, and explicit than just, "may I touch?" – although for some characters, even that question can be turned into something deliciously filthy. There are countless other ways to seek enthusiastic consent, whether in terms of:

- Intentions open to agreement/refusal ("I'm going to touch you now." "I want to touch you.")

- Instructions and requests ("Show me where you want to be touched.")

- Directed invitations ("Please, touch me!")

- Open-ended invitations ("Tell me what you want.")

Having said all this, again do be aware that, unless handled carefully, dirty talk can come off as redundant or silly to whoever ISN'T in the throes of passion (i.e., your players), so use it cautiously and sparingly. Also, be cautious of it causing your scene to drag out a little. If it goes on for a long time or into a lot of detail, it can bring the larger narrative to a temporary halt to put the full spotlight on the sex scene and what takes place within it. In some cases, this will be exactly what you want, but for many games, the goal is to make the sex scene flow smoothly with the larger narrative. To that end, pacing is important, and too much dirty talk can go from "hot phase of the larger story arc" to "hit the brakes, this is what we're doing now." Just make sure that, if you incorporate dirty talk, it serves a purpose, drives the scene forward, and does not knock the player out of the mind-space you're creating.

THE AWKWARD BUT REAL: BODY LOGISTICS ("OW, MY ELBOW")

Another approach to sex scene dialogue can be that of the less passionate, more "realistic" variety that capture the various awkward physical moments of sex. Sometimes weird things happen to our bodies during sex – we bang our heads on the headboard, or get a cramp in our leg, or get our hair caught in something, or have trouble getting into the right position – and quite often, we verbally communicate this to our partner, whether it's through expressions of pain and discomfort, a request to move or shift in a more comfortable or accessible way, or simply commenting on the situation outside of the erotic side of it (Figure 23.4).

This sort of dialogue is very rare in video game sex scenes, and understandably so. As a general rule, it does not tend to further the plot or the sex scene itself, and like dirty talk, it can go into a little more physical detail than the designers may want for a sex scene ("Great, now we have to animate her hair getting caught under her elbow!"). Plus, let's face it, games tend to embrace a somewhat idealized version of reality, so acknowledging that sex isn't "perfect" – that it is, in fact, awkward, messy, and occasionally uncomfortable, like anything else involving human bodies – is not something most games do. Thus, of all the types of sex scene dialogue, it is probably the least "vital" to include, thus the easiest to skip out on.

FIGURE 23.4 "Honey, I think you're crushing something squishy…and sensitive…" (SuperStock 2018/Shutterstock.com.)

However, don't discount the benefits of including this sort of dialogue in your sex scenes. For one, in terms of the sacred/profane/mundane trifecta, this is one of the fastest, clearest ways to define sex as fully in the "mundane" space, to communicate that your game's vision of sex is realistic and squarely in the context of humans, in all their variety, having normal, imperfect sex…down to the awkward leg strain and the arm going to sleep. Another aspect of including this kind of dialogue is that it vividly establishes a certain relationship dynamic between the sexual partners, one which lends itself to humor and vulnerability. Telling someone in an intimate moment something as "unsexy" or "unromantic" as, "hang on, let me shift my leg so I don't get a cramp" can suggest one of several possibilities:

- An endearing awkwardness about the characters involved and their relationship. This works particularly well for brand-new sexual relationships, where initial confusion and embarrassment can be very common as the characters attempt to work out the best way to fit together in a physical sense.

- A deep level of comfort and trust between the characters, a lack of shame and a willingness to show their imperfect side to each other. The characters feel emotionally safe enough with each other to be silly, vulnerable, and imperfect in the moment.

- A shared sense of humor, and a willingness not to take themselves too seriously. It's hard to come across as a deeply serious savior of the galaxy or elite soldier or noble knight when you're yelling, "oof, hang on, cramp!" Characters can be open about their physical comfort in funny, irreverent ways, and convey them in ways that make their partners laugh to ease the tension. In this, an "awkward" moment is likely to have both parties dissolve into laughter in each other's arms…where it leads from there is up to you!

- If the awkwardness persists and the characters can't negotiate past it, it may be a sign that the characters are actually mismatched, at least at that particular moment in time. Depending on how you play this, it could be a benign moment of, "let's try another time," or a more serious moment of realizing their needs and communication styles aren't compatible (or even that one party isn't interested in the comfort of the other).

Making awkward body-related interjections in the middle of sex – about the body's aches, pains, strains and surprises – is extremely relatable to many in your audience. There will be plenty of players who recognize themselves in the moment or recall their own personal experiences – who among us has not had a leg cramp at the worst possible moment? For some more aspirational, idealized games, that might not be the goal, but definitely consider it if your aim is to reflect the actual sexual experiences that your players (and people other than your players) have in the real world.

THE VULNERABLE: EXPRESSIONS OF EMOTION

While talking about your awkward and messy moments of sex can require a certain level of vulnerability, there are other moments that require even more. On a more "dramatic" note, sex scenes can also be excellent places to have your characters expressing their emotions in honest, open, achingly vulnerable ways. As discussed earlier, the arousal and passion around sex (or, at least, certain kinds of sex) has a way of bringing down emotional walls or reserve. For some people, it can be hard to keep a cap on their feelings when they are at their rawest and most aroused! Thus, characters may be more likely to speak emotionally, or to express their deeper feelings, in the throes of passion, making sex scenes a wonderful opportunity to tap into this vulnerable raw side of them.

Of course, one of the most obvious examples of expressing emotion in a sex scene is a confession of love. It's a classic moment in all kinds of media, not just games – that in a passionate embrace, lost in each other, one character will look deep into the other's eyes, filled with emotion, and whisper, "I love you," for the first time. For some players, this can be a cliché or corny moment, but for others, it can be the emotional high point of the characters' relationship and a beautiful, cathartic moment that blends the physical connection with the emotional connection. It defines the context of the sex scene and the emotions that the sex evokes in the partner(s)…or at least, it defines what the character *interprets* the intense emotions and feelings to be in the moment. And let's face it: some players (this author included) are just suckers for lovemaking when it's connected to romance and true love, and enjoy nothing better than an erotic, passionate declaration of eternal devotion! As long as the foundations of the connection have been built (both in the bedroom and out of it!) and the moment does not feel forced, it's perfectly valid to go for the classic tried-and-true confession in each other's arms (Figure 23.5).

But naturally, emotional expressions during sex do not have to be declarations of love, or indeed have anything to do with love. The most effective verbalizations of emotions simply have to express what the characters are feeling and what they want in a naked (ha ha) raw sense. This is particularly true in the context of sex in which the characters are in different

FIGURE 23.5 The passionate, sexual embrace…the long look into each other's eyes…the confession of true feelings…yeah, this is absolutely going to appeal to many of your players. (Photographee. eu/Shutterstock.com.)

states of mind (e.g., highly aroused, orgasmic, post-orgasmic). In this state, emotional declarations may be unusually blunt and honest, or may come in bits and pieces (e.g., short sentence fragments). As for emotions besides love, the possibilities are endless. Some of the most common are related to seeking comfort from stressful or bad situations, a common context for sex scenes in games. Characters might talk about how much they "need" the connection, or how good things feel, or how much they prefer it to the horrors of the outside world. Other common emotions that might be explored are those relating to the character's sexual partner. Even if they don't love them, that does not mean they may not have deep feelings that they wish to express, even if the deep feelings are, "You make me feel good."

And of course, when it comes to emotional declarations in sex, don't discount negative emotions as well as positive. Sex is a time that can bring out very complicated emotions or be a catharsis for harsher emotions. This can be doubly true in many games where the sex is happening in or after highly stressful or traumatic events. Consider how, in a moment of emotional vulnerability in the context of sex, a character might break down in grief over a recent loss, or might confess their terror and fear about a dangerous mission, or even admit something about themselves that they've been trying to ignore or repress. While these moments can of course happen in other contexts, integrating them with a sex scene adds a certain raw and unrehearsed quality in which the usual filters are removed; the results, when done well, can feel deeper, more honest, and from a totally unrehearsed perspective.

We can see a particularly good example of this kind of vulnerable, emotional sex scene dialogue in the closet sex scene in *Wolfenstein: The New Order*. As discussed in previous chapters, the initial scenario – rough sex in a closet – strikes a somewhat lewd and awkward tone. But the scene is recontextualized when BJ begins to speak, looking into Anya's eyes and saying in a husky voice, "I want this. With you. Like this. Always." Moved, Anya replies breathlessly, "It will happen, William. Believe it." While this is not an explicit confession of love, it clearly carries similar overtones in their shared desire to continue their relationship (particularly the sexual aspect) and to be with each other as much as they can be. It also speaks to BJ's larger emotional state. In a world full of horrors and hate and danger, the moments they make love take on a halcyon, almost holy quality, one of the few times he has peace, and all he can think of in the moment is how he wishes this peace would continue forever. Anya, in turn, is able to express how she shares the same hopes and dreams, as well as showing her steely emotional conviction that such things ARE possible. The clipped, almost broken cadence of their speech patterns (e.g., sentence fragments, short words) conveys the raw, unscripted nature of their declarations; in the context of their passion, exertion, and need, there's no artifice or holding back, and the result is a moment that feels deeply honest, vulnerable, and emotional.

Another good AAA example of vulnerable, emotional dialogue can be seen in *Assassin's Creed Origins*, albeit as a borderline case – technically, the dialogue happens before the sex starts, not in the middle of it, but it shares many of the same qualities as the *Wolfenstein* example, and frankly could have worked just as well in the throes of sexual passion. Reunited after a long and dangerous separation, Bayek and Aya fall into each other's arms, hungry for each other, their mutual love and joy tempered with grief for their dead son and savage relief that he's been avenged. This cocktail of emotions mixes with their mutual sexual desire, building the emotions and tensions of the scene to a fever peak, until Bayek finally breaks away from the kiss, looks into Aya's eyes, and speaks to her. But in his emotional state, overwhelmed with bittersweet love for her, all he can say is a husky, unsteady, "My wife...my wife," before he kisses her again and they fall to the floor together. The line might be a simple one, but it serves as another fantastic example of how dialogue can convey feelings far beyond what is being said. Bayek – a strong, devoted, dedicated man, and the hero we've been following and *being* throughout the game – being so overwhelmed with emotion that he can barely speak, can only breathe out a desperate endearment...all while the music swells and the visuals show him and Aya in a deeply loving, tender gaze. It's a truly striking moment, arguably one of the highlights of Bayek and Aya's entire arc together, and though we may not see the intimate moments immediately after, on some level we have seen Bayek "naked."

THE BORED OR DISCONNECTED: IMPATIENT OR DISTRACTED DIALOGUE

During sex, some people will be completely engaged with the erotic moment, or with the emotions the moment inspires. And some people...won't. These are the kinds of people who will often carry on conversations or make remarks entirely unrelated to the sex or the other character(s) involved in the sex. Examples of this can include the following:

- Sudden distracted reminders or recollections ("Wait, I left the oven on!")

- Unrelated monologues or conversations about other topics entirely (e.g., evil villain monologues about their evil plan)

- Conversations with characters not part of the sex scene at all (e.g., someone taking a phone call about a mission and barking orders over the phone while still continuing to have sex!)

- Overly distracted, bored, or disconnected dialogue (e.g., "Uh huh. Yeah. Sure. Whatever.")

Note that while this may seem similar in vibe to the awkward body chat – i.e., someone being honest with their partner and embracing the mundane details of life – the end effect is quite different. Mundane interjections about cramps or gas or positions or what have you still establish the character as being engaged and present in the moment, even if it's in a slightly awkward or uncomfortable capacity. Your player character might be complaining about his butt aching, but he's at least reacting to whatever he's in the middle of doing with that butt! With these more distracted interjections, however, we see that the character's mind isn't focused on what's happening, but is somewhere else entirely.

Thus, with some major exceptions (which we'll cover in a minute), this sort of dialogue should be used to emphasize a character's extreme disconnect and disinterest in the sex, and moreover, disinterest or disconnect with their sexual partner(s). If a character is either replying in bored monosyllables or having full conversations about entirely unrelated topics, the implication is that they are distracted and much more focused on other things. They are not paying attention to the sex, and they are not focusing on pleasing their partner in the present moment. In fact, in extreme examples of this, they may barely register the partner's presence at all, or even treat them as a mild inconvenience or bother to be put up with. *Grand Theft Auto V* offers some good examples of this, with scenes like the Trevor/Ashley scene or the scene where a "teen" starlet is getting vigorously railed by her co-star while she checks her phone, asks him to hurry up so she can eat, and talks cheerfully about how her age and virgin image is a sham for marketing purposes.

Unsurprisingly, this approach tends to pair with unsympathetic, unlikable, or "villainous" characters, as most players are likely to register the character as selfish, disrespectful to their partner, or just a joyless bore. Most sympathetic or heroic characters are expected to engage more fully with their partner and with the moment. If they ARE likely to be distracted or have other things on their mind, a "good" character would probably just politely decline sex in the first place if they were not in the right mindset, or would stop the sex once they realized they couldn't focus. As such, tread extremely carefully when using this kind of distracted dialogue for heroic characters, unless for certain archetypes and situations (e.g., a "cool" superspy taking a vital mission call in the middle of sex, a particularly likeable but easily distracted character who charges off on random topics). Otherwise, this type of dialogue is best used in the context of driving home an unsympathetic character's disinterest and self-absorption in the context of sex and partnership.

However, as mentioned, there are some major exceptions to this rule when "distracted" dialogue doesn't necessarily drive home a disconnect:

- Sudden realizations/comments around major emergencies or massive realizations. While it is a mood killer to have a character, in the throes of passion, suddenly yell, "Holy shit, I know where the bomb is, we've got to go!" it does not necessarily follow that this means that the character is/was disinterested in the sex and their partner.

- Comedy and slice-of-life material centered around certain aspects of long-term sexual relationships (e.g., discussions between a long-term couple talking about timing for fertility in the middle of sex). These scenes should be approached cautiously as the humor can run the risk of being mean-spirited or upholding negative or incorrect stereotypes (e.g., married couples don't enjoy sex and just talk about the housework while they do it!). But in certain contexts, this can provide light-hearted and sweet comedy, particularly when it's paired with genuine affection and connection between the couple.

- Non-sexual topics that, due to certain fetishes or turn-ons, actually arouse one or more sexual partners. For example, if a character is actively turned on by, say, killing, then it might make sense for them to explicitly describe their murderous plans in the middle of sex as a way to get even MORE hot and bothered. This would actually thus count more as dirty talk, and should be written/approached accordingly. Take another look at the Bayek/Aya roof scene and see how, ah, *excited* Aya gets about Bayek talking about the death of one of their son's killers…

TAKING A STEP BACK: DIALOGUE FROM DIFFERENT SOURCES

Most of the examples of dialogue we've discussed so far are between the characters in the middle of sex. It's diegetic in the sense that it is happening in the moment and in the world. But this is not the only way to incorporate dialogue into a sex scene. There are other sources to consider as well: namely, dialogue of other characters (e.g., in a cutaway scene) and character narration.

These lines of dialogue serve a very different purpose than ones spoken by the sexual partners in the moment, and they should be approached very differently. For one, as they are not being spoken in the throes of passion, a lot of the more erotic considerations – breathiness, arousal, dirty talk, emotional outbursts, etc. – are no longer something to worry about, as the speakers are now in entirely different physical and emotional spaces. In fact, in many cases, the dialogue might not be about sex at all, or not about that particular encounter.

However, that does not mean that the dialogue should not be connected to the scene. In fact, if anything, the connection is even more vital. In this case, the connection between dialogue and scene needs to be *thematic and emotional* – dialogue that either touches on the emotional core of the sex scene and either echoes it or directly subverts it. For example, if the characters are having sex for a particular reason, you might have narration that explores the emotions and ramifications of that reason, or you might have some other characters having a conversation about, "No one hooks up just because of X reason!" to serve as an ironic counterpoint. Or perhaps you could have two characters in each other's arms juxtaposed with other characters talking about why those two characters being together is a great idea, or a terrible mystical world-destroying idea, etc. etc. In all cases, however, the connection between what the player sees (the sex scene) and what they hear (the narration or other dialogue) should be clear and should be doing its part to boost that connection. In other words, this is not a time for deep subtlety. Some of the most successful examples of this kind of narration or dialogue are the most "obvious" you can find…well, as long as you steer clear of "nature documentary" obvious!

SEXY BODIES AND DISEMBODIED VOICES: INTERNAL NARRATION FROM PARTICIPANT

There are two common sources for narration during a sex scene; both tend to involve different narrative goals and foci for the action.

The first is **internal narration from one of the sexual partners** – in other words, a vocalization of their internal thoughts, either in the moment or in a retrospective or detached perspective. Usually, this directly addresses either the sex or the emotions involved. For example, the character might be describing after the fact why they decided to have sex, or describing the emotions they felt/are feeling in the moment, or talk about how they feel about their partner. This sort of dialogue, naturally, can be a little "on the nose," and there is an argument to be made for this approach falling short of communicating the character's feelings in other ways (e.g., body language, actions during the sex scenes, in-the-moment dialogue). However, it's still worth exploring this approach in certain contexts:

- For one, if your game *already* features narration from your characters on a regular basis anyway, it makes sense to have them narrate through something as intimate (or not-intimate!) as sex. Otherwise, if they've narrated their way through everything else then go silent at such a moment, that seems a little out of place!

  - Of course, if you've had no narration apart from this sex scene, that also has potential to seem odd or out of place, so maybe consider matching whatever the narration style (or lack thereof) is for the rest of the game.

  - Also, consider that some genres use narration as a deliberate stylistic device (e.g., detective noir) that is part of the artistic approach of the genre as a whole.

- Narration, as with other dialogue, can also offer greater nuance in terms of the emotions the characters are experiencing, either about the sex or about the partner. While body language can convey overarching feelings such as exhaustion, desire, love, or need for comfort, it can be tricky to get into the details. In other words, using body language to convey "I'm happy," or even "I'm happy because I'm with this character," is usually enough. But if it's something more complicated that you really need to lay out for some reason – "I'm happy because everyone in my life has treated me like crap and then I met this person who, during our first meeting – etc. etc. etc." – you may need to express that level of detail in a way that isn't wrapped up in the immediate sexual encounter. Narration can be a great way to explore this.

- Narration is also a great way to have the characters give their viewpoints on the sex or connection – or even larger, more philosophical thoughts stirred by them – with the benefit of hindsight and distance. For example, in games that are narrated in past tense (i.e., as what already happened), the narrator might be looking back at the sexual encounter in hindsight. This can offer a wildly different perspective than what they may have had at the time, and usually is expressed in much different ways. As discussed above, talking in the middle of sex tends to be fuelled more by the immediate physical and emotional feelings, which lends it a particular perspective. Looking back at something in hindsight, on the other hand, or speaking as an observer rather than a participant, brings a different mood and perspective. Note that neither is "wrong" or "better," only different, and your writers will need to consider which is right for your game.

There is another excellent example of this kind of narration in *Wolfenstein: The New Order* during the train sex scene (yes, this game has a lot of good examples of dialogue in sex in general!) While BJ and Anya have sex through a somewhat blurry and obscuring filter, BJ narrates: "Sometimes Christmas…sometimes birthdays…sometimes mayhem, suffering and death…sometimes you just need to feel…something good." It gives an extremely clear picture of what's going through his head during the scene and why he's embraced the sexual intimacy with Anya – that amid the "mayhem, suffering and death" he's experiencing, he wants to feel "something good" with Anya. As he's narrating from a "distance" as opposed to speaking in the middle of sex, he has room to philosophize, even to apply his reasons on a larger scale – he uses general "you" and speaks more in universal terms than in his own personal experience. His narration could also extend just as strongly to Anya as to him, implying that she is drawn to him and to their lovemaking for similar reasons, that this is something they can share. It's the key theme to their scene, but it would be lost if the line were delivered as dialogue in the middle of sex! It would be unbelievable for BJ to be monologuing in the middle of the act, and since this particular moment needs that kind of larger thematic statement, narration is the best tool to deliver it.

CUT AWAY AND BACK: NARRATION AND DIALOGUE FROM OTHER CHARACTERS

The second kind of narration actually overlaps with a type of diegetic dialogue, and it's monologues or conversation from other characters who are not involved in the sex scene. Here, the line between "narration" and "live dialogue that you cut away from" can be somewhat blurred, as what begins as a conversation between these other characters might *become* a narration track in how it's handled and how it's overlaid over the sex scene. Either way, the dialogue is handled in a much different context than dialogue from the sexual partners; in many examples, the speaking characters are having a conversation about something completely different and may be completely unaware that the other characters are having sex or being intimate.

However, that doesn't lessen the importance of their dialogue connecting with the sex scene; if anything, it heightens it. If they are not commenting on the specific people or sexual encounter, then above all, their dialogue should connect thematically to the sex or to the relationship between the two people having sex. Ideally, the dialogue should help to give context to the sexual encounter, even if it's via an entirely different topic; the speaking characters discussing that topic should be a reflection on what is passing between the two who are having sex.

There are obviously multiple ways you can do this with dialogue from other characters; here are a few variations, from most "general" to more specific:

- The speaking character(s) can be discussing a theme or phenomenon that has nothing to do with sex, love, or the characters having sex, but that still parallels the action and the emotion in some way. This can basically convert whatever the discussion is into a metaphor for the sex. This can be an academic discussion – for example, discussion of the movement of the stars or the collision of solid bodies as juxtaposed with the intimate scene. Or it could be something more emotional or observational – for example, commentary on some aspect of human nature (say, need for connection) that contextualizes the sex.

- The speaking character(s) can be discussing another sexual relationship, romantic relationship, or sex in general, in a way that reflects on the sex that's going on. For example, if the speaking characters are discussing a fairy tale about true love while other characters are having sex, then the implication is that these characters and their lovemaking ALSO share true love.

  - This can also be used in subversion, in which the speaking characters will be discussing attitudes toward sex and/or love that are then immediately disproved by the scene itself. Perhaps the speakers are being cynical about love and connection while juxtaposed with a tender, gentle scene; perhaps the speakers are being romantic or naive about sex while the action cuts away to something raunchy and primal, and so on.

- The speaking character(s) can be discussing the couple in question, or one of them. Rather than overarching themes and story arcs like the previous examples, this approach focuses more on character-building, albeit through the eyes of *other* characters and how their vision matches/contradicts what the player sees in the sex. For example, imagine Character A telling some listeners about how Character B is a cruel, ruthless killer with no interest in human connection, all against Character B engaged in passionate sex. How does it recontextualize both streams of narrative? Is Character A totally wrong about Character B and prejudiced against them? Is this a side that Character B doesn't show or is only just developing? Or is Character A totally right and Character B is about to straight up murder their sexual partner? There's a lot of potential for contrasts and revelations if done correctly.

- Lastly, of course, don't neglect simple dialogue that might touch on the timing and logistics of the sex happening. An easy example of this could be the speaker characters wondering aloud, "Where is Character X?" looking for them, asking around...all intercut with scenes of Character X entwined in a sexual embrace somewhere private. Or perhaps the speaking characters are overhearing, witnessing, or even walking in on the sex! This sort of dialogue is usually humorous in tone and execution, setting up an amusing contrast between the obliviousness or shock of the speakers and the sexual antics of the lovers. However, this can also be used in darker, more urgent contexts like action and horror ("We need to get out of here! Where are A and B?") or more bittersweet and sad moments in the context of the speaking characters ("Have you seen my husband? He was supposed to meet me, but…maybe he was busy…").

The pool sex scene in *The Witcher 2* offers a good example of using this kind of character speech to offset a sex scene. After the initial kiss and disrobing of Geralt and Triss, the action cuts briefly to above ground, where a Scoia'tael party of elves and a dwarf have tracked Geralt to the area. The elves, frustrated with human meddling, exclaim about how the humans have twisted a particular legend about two elven lovers, Eldan and Cymoril, to involve a "handsome human prince" and made it "silly and shallow" in the process. As the action then cuts back to Geralt and Triss making love, the elf then says, "We Aen Seidhe remember how it was…limitless devotion, passion, commitment…and sacrifice." These words then linger over the images of Geralt and Triss in passionate embraces, gasping and sighing in pleasure, eager in their desire. In describing the elven lovers and their passion for each other, the exposition provides deeper context for Geralt and Triss's intimate moment as well, that what they are doing together is also part of "limitless devotion, passion, commitment." It recasts the human couple in the same roles as the elven lovers and gives their sexual intimacy an almost mythic, spiritual quality – certainly, a romantic quality! – that it might not have without that connection and context. This is only heightened by the elf adding more context to the myth: "Legend has it that the lovers' sighs are enchanted within these very stones, though only those in love can hear them." Again, the implication is clear – that this is a place of sacred sex, of lovers sighing erotically in each other's arms, of love and passion so powerful that it is bound into the magic of the very stones…and that this is the same powerful force of love and desire that Geralt and Triss are acting out.

In contrast, the scene ends on an amusing, much more prosaic note of dialogue. The dwarf, unimpressed by this legend, belches and scoffs at the story and at the idea of hearing sighs enchanted into the rocks. But to his surprise, seconds later, he hears feminine moaning and sighing, those he thinks are those of the lovers…but of course, are only Triss's ghostly, echoing moans of pleasure from the underground chambers! It's a humorous moment that fleshes out the dwarf character and brings the sexual discourse back to earth a little, combining the mystical, romantic legend with the simple logistics of "loud sex echoing up a well."

CONCLUSION

Not every sex scene needs dialogue, and some will be better without it. But hopefully, this chapter will have gotten across that dialogue can have a place in sex scenes that is not over-wrought, pointless, or ridiculous. Consider how dialogue, either in the moment or from other sources, can heighten the emotion of your scenes and provide necessary context.

And if nothing else, remember that communication – whether it's verbal communication between lovers or thematic communication to the audience – is one of the most vital ingredients of the best sex scenes.

WORKSHOP QUESTIONS

Analysis: Is there dialogue in the sex scene(s) you've been analyzing – specifically, any dialogue in the middle of sex? If so, what kind of dialogue is it – between the participants, between other characters, or from narration? Using the different models in this chapter, identify the kind of dialogue and its role in the sex scene.

Creative: Consider at least one of the sex scenes or sexual sequences in your game. Do you plan for there to be dialogue as part of the sex? For what purpose, and what will it say? What is the nature of the dialogue? (e.g., narration? Other characters? The sexual partners?). How will you present it and integrate it with gameplay and/or visuals?

If possible, working with your writing team, write a short rough draft of the sort of dialogue you envision for this scene, along with what visuals or gameplay it corresponds with. Don't worry, this isn't the final version and there will be plenty of time to edit and iterate to better reflect the sex scene context; the goal here is to aim for the *kind* of conversation you envision for this scene, to experiment with what dialogue content, presentation, type, etc., will best complement the scene itself and leave the right emotional impression with your players. Consider this as more of a proof of concept than something to go into the final game...though you may find it provides very useful goalposts to aim for as you iterate...

NOTE

1 Which might open up some ideas for spies who use pillow talk to find out information on their enemies...

CHAPTER 24

Sex and Game Design (Part 1)

Branching Choices, Interactivity, and Agency

EARLIER IN THE BOOK, we discussed different ways of approaching branching design, such as choices or dialogue options, in the context of initiating sex as part of the larger narrative. In many cases, particularly in AAA games, this is the only sex-related choice you get – once you have made the decision to have sex, the most common result is a non-interactive cutscene depicting the characters having sex. But this is selling sex scenes and their potential for agency and experience short. By taking more time to develop different options and allowing the player to make meaningful choices in the midst of a sex scene, the developer can offer more direct emotional, erotic, narrative, and ludic control and experience of a scene and give the scene more weight in the larger story and narrative arcs (Figure 24.1).

It's worth noting, of course, that there are legitimate reasons for sticking with a single non-interactive cutscene. If the game handles the majority of its narrative beats through cutscenes – for example, in linear AAA games such as *Uncharted* – then sticking with cutscenes for sex makes sense. Pacing is another aspect to consider. An interactive scene will often be slower paced in terms of play, as the player must take time to make decisions and the outcome of each decision plays out. In contrast, a cutscene can be set to a certain pace and time, which can allow for faster, more streamlined sequences that get back to the regular gameplay more quickly.

However, these are not the only reasons that hold designers and creators back from introducing more interactive elements in sex scenes. The bigger barrier is built from misunderstandings of what interactivity in sex scenes might entail...including sex-negative judgment and fear of being associated with more pornographic works.

When many developers think in terms of "interactive" sex scenes, they usually assume that it's a reference to purely mechanical interaction and choices about sex acts alone. Pornographic games often offer this type of control or choice. A hentai visual novel might

FIGURE 24.1 Or even just give the player more control over their own erotic experience. (Iryna Gyrych/Shutterstock.com.)

allow players to choose what sex acts to do, while a 3D animated sex game might involve more direct control of penetration, movement, and so on. While this sort of interactivity and choice works for pornographic game content – and might have merit in non-pornographic games as well! – the fear of being labeled as "porn" means that many mainstream developers aren't willing to consider interactivity and choice in relation to sex. After all, they might say, we're not making a porn game, so why would we want to have that level of detail and interaction? On top of this, while choosing where to grope or bend or penetrate might be interesting on a purely erotic level – and there's nothing wrong with that! – it isn't always a truly meaningful choice, the sort that the developers want to provide to their audience. Impactful choice, control, and agency in a game sex scene can be much, much more than, "Press A to grab right buttcheek, B for left buttcheek."

Of course, there are some sex scenes and sexual sequences that don't even provide this level of choice – where interactivity is possible, but only in a very limited, linear sense. The most obvious form of this is sex quicktime events, where there is a linear series of button presses to "succeed." For example, the quicktime event sex scene in *Heavy Rain* has an initial choice to begin the sex scene, but then a linear sequence of button presses in order to progress the sex scene. "Failure" simply involves backtracking slightly (e.g., buttoning up a shirt or refastening a bra), and unlike much of the rest of the game, there are no options to do things in a different way, to move the sex to a different place (e.g., the bed instead of the floor) or even to stop the sex in the middle of things. As a result, the interactivity feels constrained and does not add depth or options for player creativity or agency.

We've been driving home the point that sex scenes should be tackled with the same level of detail, respect, and thoughtfulness as any other scene, and this extends to the interactive design just as much – if not more. Sex scenes should not be designed or written by default only as "endings" to more interactive sequences and scenes leading up to them, where the player makes a few choices and is "rewarded" with a sex scene. Nor should the interactivity only be restricted to sexual mechanics and nothing else. Instead, developers should consider the potential of using interactivity as ways to shape player mood, character dynamics, and even larger narrative beats. That means considering choices and interactivity beyond the mechanics of sex, ones that shape the emotions and experiences of sex in a holistic way.

In the next chapter, we'll focus more on holistic game design as it relates to sex, about how to consider new verbs, new mechanics, and new ways of approaching sexual game design. In this chapter, however, we'll be keeping our focus on more traditional narrative game design (e.g., visual novel, RPGs) that uses explicit player choice – of dialogue, of interactions, even of location – as part of gameplay and story. So with this in mind, here are some examples of how branching choices, interactivity, and player control can be incorporated in meaningful ways in sex scenes.

SEXY CONSENT AND PLAYER AGENCY

Yes, I am going to keep hammering this theme home every chance I get: in systems with player choice, players should be given full control of consent, and that means moving beyond the single question of "yes or no?" at the start. Players should be offered more granular options throughout the encounter, allowing them to say yes to certain things and no to others; player choice should be designed around respecting their agency and empowering them to do the things that they (and their partner!) *want* to do!

I won't go into detail again as we had an entire chapter around the possibilities of enthusiastic consent in narrative and game design already. But in the spirit of exploring player choice through the lens of consent, a few refreshers and reminders:

- If possible, offer a more nuanced choice of consent to begin with, beyond "yes/no." Include possibilities for "later," "not yet," "let's just make out for now," and so on.

- Ensure that players/characters can revoke consent at any time, either through branching choices throughout the encounter or through a "stop immediately" UI feature that triggers an in-universe stop to things.

- Embrace enthusiastic consent and "no, but" design where possible. If a character or player isn't ready or interested in a particular act or experience, approach the writing and choice design by letting them express and choose what they ARE ready for and interested in.

- Design and write consent negotiations as a sexy collaboration, rather than a one-sided whining for permission. Make seeking consent into a sexy, seductive act, and design the player choice or NPC response as "HELL YES!" rather than "sure, I guess…"

As you might imagine, designing for consent – and the player agency inherent in consent – has big ramifications for how the scene plays out. In a sense, every choice or player action in a sex scene can be seen through the lens of consent, even if it's just the game offering options to the player. It also opens up a wide range of choice types, from the general

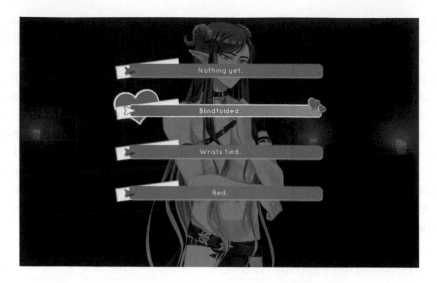

FIGURE 24.2 *Cute Demon Crashers!* marries sexy enthusiastic consent and player choice, allowing the player at all choice points to choose what sexual acts they're willing and eager to try, or to call an end to things (using a safeword in this example). (SugarScript, *Cute Demon Crashers!*, PC/Mac/Linux, partial version published April 7, 2015, full version published August 15, 2015. Screenshot from Haru's Otome Reviews, "[Otome Game Review] Cute Demon Crashers [R-18]," October 25, 2015, http://otoutoreview.blogspot.com/2015/10/otome-game-review-cute-demon-crashers-r.html.)

("Yes, I'm ready,") to the specific ("Please, take my shirt off…") to the very erotically specific ("Yes, please bend me over and spank me with…[player choice] the paddle!") In this sense, designing a game scene with explicit sexual choices is an exercise in consent *anyway* – at least, if it's handled properly! – but by being conscious of consent, and how to integrate it with safe, fun enthusiasm for sex, you can come up with strong narrative and gameplay choices that respect the agency of the player, their character, and the NPCs (Figure 24.2).

But what about less explicit sexual choices?

THE HOWS OF SEX: CHOICES TO SET THE TONE FOR SEX

When people think about choice, agency, and control in sex scenes, they usually think in terms of physical choices, whether they be explicitly sexual ("grab butt") or more situational ("push them onto the bed.") These choices are great, but another approach is offering high-level choice and control as to how the scene itself plays out. In this model, rather than making specific detailed choices about what actions to take, the player choices or actions are focused more on shifting the emotions and context of the encounter or the action, guiding it toward a certain type of feeling or mood. In other words, **rather than designing for sexy or sexual verbs and nouns, there is room to design around erotic adjectives and adverbs.** Even if you are designing around actions in the context of sex, focusing less on "what do you do" and more on "how do you do it" or "why do you do it" can result in greater player agency in terms of what the character emotions and experience of the scene.

A very simple example of this: for many sex scenes, once the decision has been made to kiss someone (vs. not kiss), there is usually a set cutscene or text that happens, and the kiss always happens the same, set way. But what if, before the kiss happens, there was another choice: "kiss softly" vs. "kiss passionately." Both choices might then lead to a very different sort of emotional and erotic beat in terms of the sexual encounter; the former resulting on slow, languorous kissing that takes its time to build to removing clothing, sex, etc., while the latter resulting in an urgent, excited tussle of ripping clothes and panting. Giving the player a choice of *how* they kiss, rather than just sticking with kissing as a binary set experience, allows them to better adjust their experience based on either their own preferences or those of their character, as well as just allowing for more variety for expression and exploration in a scene (Figure 24.3).

Approaching interactive design for sex scenes with allowing broad choice of adjectives and adverbs (vs. choice of verbs) can be surprisingly flexible, in that it can work both for detailed physical interactions and for more abstract treatments of sex. On a high level, there's no reason why something like a visual novel or a branching choice game couldn't have abstract thematic choices like, "make love tenderly" and "rut like animals," the choice determining how the resulting scene plays out. On a moment-by-moment level, even if a scene is designed to have certain "canonical" actions or moments – for example, that the characters will always kiss, or will always get naked – the player has the freedom to choose how they take those actions. Are they romantic or brusque? Slow or frantic? Gentle or rough? Sweet or lustful? Hesitant or confident? Are their hands shaking, or are they smooth and steady? The potential choices for adjectives and adverbs – and how they play out – are almost limitless. These choices are a great way to roleplay a character or experiment with different nuances in their sexual relationships, something that will be covered in the next section. On a meta-level, it also lets players engage in the sorts of scenes they enjoy and offers them replayability value. How *do* things play out differently if you're slow and gentle with a particular character vs. heated and aggressive?

These design principles can be incorporated as part of choice-based game design (e.g., visual novels, BioWare games), but they can also be expressed in direct gameplay design by making the game responsive to how the player goes through these motions. For example, a more nuanced version of the *Heavy Rain* sex scene mentioned earlier in this chapter might

FIGURE 24.3   The moment right before a very interesting player choice…(fizkes/Shutterstock.com.)

reflect different outcomes based on how fast the player does the actions. Quickly nailing the prompts for unhooking a bra might trigger a fast, confident removal that shows the character's eagerness, while doing it slowly might result in the character being slower and more tentative in disrobing their lover. This responsiveness to player input is quite common in many 3D pornographic games, with different feedback and responses from the partner based on how slow/fast or gentle/rough the player makes their motions or grabs certain parts of the body. Still, this doesn't need to be restricted just to extremely explicit sexual actions; even just tracking how a player makes their character linger over a kiss or touch can have lots of potential for different experiences, narrative triggers, and so on. Imagine the intimate possibilities of, say, the player directly controlling their fingers as they "walk" up their partner's body, "Itsy Bitsy Spider" style, during post-coital cuddling…and imagine if their gentleness, speed, or where they linger affected how their partner responds to them!

REVEALING AND SHAPING CHARACTER DYNAMICS THROUGH SEXUAL CHOICE

Regardless of how a sex scene plays out, you can usually bank on at least one constant: that at least one character will be involved! As such, sex scenes are great opportunities for revealing more about the characters involved, both PC and NPC – how they express themselves in sexual situations, how they relate to their partners, how they feel in the moment. Designing player choice with these character dynamics in mind is a great opportunity to allow players to customize and roleplay their own characters while also engaging with NPCs in a more meaningful, fully fleshed out way.

In terms of revealing character dynamics from a player character perspective, almost any choice can allow for this. Whether it's initiating touch vs. waiting passively, being gentle and romantic vs. rough and wild, or missionary in bed vs. swinging from the chandelier, any choice the player character makes in this scene is telling us something about the character, or allowing the player to shape a little bit of who they are…even if it's just in the context of what arouses them. And of course, don't forget about the possibility of choosing a character's kinks!

On top of physical actions, however, there is also room for players to explore and control how their character might *feel* about the encounter, about the person they're engaging with, how they express those feelings – and even develop as characters along these lines. Does being with their lover feel like the first day of the rest of their life, or a desperate grasp for life amidst death, or just something fun between two adults? Do they react to their lover's touch with eagerness, or restraint? Do they let themselves go in the moment, or do they keep the same gruff facade they show in the heat of battle? Do they speak openly about their arousal or their feelings, or express them through facial expressions and body language? And are these choices simply extensions of how the character has behaved so far, or are they moments where the character shifts, grows, and changes? These are all choices that a designer or writer would have to consider for a linear, pre-scripted sex scene…but what if the player was the one who made the choice? Allowing players agency over these choices allows for a subtler, nuanced exploration and creation of who their character is, particularly in cases where the character is fully customizable. It allows them to tell a story both about their character's sexuality and about who they are, both in the bedroom and, occasionally, outside of it too.

On top of being a way to customize and explore the player character, choices also reveal more about the non-player character partners. How they respond to the PC's choices is a way to explore the sexual side that you and your team have developed as part of the character – their turn-ons, preferences, responses, etc. For example, if the player makes that choice about whether they prefer whips-and-chains or a gentle massage, then the game can (and should!) hold space for the NPC's genuine response. If the NPC partner responds to the former with enthusiasm and the latter with derisive laughter and, "that's your idea of foreplay? C'mon, I like it rougher than that!" that tells us some pretty big things about who that character is, at least in the context of sex! This, again, is an extension of enthusiastic consent, where you explore what THEY are enthusiastic about and what they consent to! That can extend to both subtler choices and reactions (e.g., different physical reactions to different kinds of touches) or more dramatic character shifts (e.g., major reactions to players confessing their love in a moment of passion). This approach offers the opportunity to go deeper into your NPCs' desires and emotions in ways that engage your players and even encourage replayability. After all, different players are going to make different choices, and thus potentially learn different things and different aspects of your NPCs – all of which will get your players buzzing online or eager to play again and pick new choices (Figure 24.4).

And of course, player choice can go beyond the characters as individuals and into revealing, expanding, or developing the relationship between them. How the player chooses to interact with their partner(s), and how the partner(s) react to those choices can illuminate their connection or shift it one way or another. Many AAA games boil this down to a post-sex choice to either make the relationship "serious" or keep things casual. This has the benefit of clearly signaling to the player what the lasting relationship consequences of the

FIGURE 24.4 "I can't believe it's taken me this many playthroughs to find the deep secret behind why you're allergic to shirts!" (WAYHOME studio/Shutterstock.com.)

choice will be, but the downside of being highly "on-the-nose" and a little stereotypical. There are so many other choices we could be exploring and experimenting with in terms of exploring or developing relationships! Even some of the "explicit" choices could be the starting point for larger discussions and conversation trees of how the characters feel, how they respond to and treat each other, and what they eventually end up doing about it.

For example, let's keep going with the choice we've been playing with (whips-chains vs. sensual massage) and the NPC's response ("hell yeah" vs. "ugh, too drippy and romantic for me!") This could then spin out a lot of different ways depending on the context of their relationship (particularly how the player has built it up so far) and the subsequent choices that the designers offer for the player to take. As a result, each of those routes can lead to other, relationship-focused options for the player:

- Unlocked conversation choices discussing turn-ons or preferences calling back to previous optional discussions, creating a natural progression from those conversations ("Wait, you're down for whips? But you said you liked romantic stuff!" "Not all the time! Not even from you...")

- Choices to make personal revelations about feelings ("But my feelings for you ARE drippy and romantic!" "Oh...oh, I see.")

- Playful pushback within the bounds of mutual consent ("Aw, but we did the whips and chains LAST time, sweetie! Just one drippy romantic run, for me?" "Ha ha, all right, you sap...")

- "Eject buttons" for the encounter and relationship, including choices that lead to falling outs and negative shifts in the relationship ("Look, clearly we're not looking for the same thing. We're done.").

All of these can then lead to further choices, further responses, and further interactions between the player character and their NPC partner; it's not impossible to start from a place of "yay whips and chains!" and end up five choices later either having a serious conversation about the future or, well, having whip-and-chain sex! And of course, don't discount how some of these relationship developments can be part of the actual sex. Choosing to give a breathless confession or make an unexpected gesture can change not only the tenor of the scene, but the tenor of the relationship, for good or ill. Sex scenes are great places for designers to layer choices and explore nuanced ways for the emotional relationship between the characters to grow and explore outward, as opposed to a single line or a very simple branch. Committing to more of a weblike structure of options can leave every player feeling like THEIR sex scene and THEIR relationship with their NPC sexual partner is unique to them, and that they are able to influence (if not outright control) how that relationship grows in a sexual moment through their dialogue choices and physical actions.

And if all that character and relationship development seems a bit too much to tackle... then don't discount the simple pleasures of getting to decide how your characters have sex!

Of course, the downside of taking this approach is that increasing your web of choices is one of the fastest ways to blow up your budget AND your scope of your project. While players often enjoy more complex, nuanced choices and branching, it can be a lot of extra work to write, create, etc. For some games, however, particularly games that focus on very intricate and nuanced branching, that decision is often worth the extra time. If nothing else, it serves well to "match" the level of branching and choice you have in the rest of the game. If all your other interactions with the NPCs offer tons of investigative choices, options for fun wordplay, and moments that influence or change the course of your relationships…might want to throw at least some of the same sort of content into your sex scenes?

SENSUAL ENVIRONMENT X-PLORATION: CHOOSING SETTING FOR SEX

So far, we've been talking about choices as they relate to the characters, both in terms of physical actions and personal interactions. But even though much of the tone and emotion of sex is set by the two characters and what they do, don't discount the power of *where* it happens. Elsewhere in this book, we've spoken about the general importance of environmental design in sex scenes for heightening and supporting the mood and providing sensual and narrative context, even for non-interactive cutscenes. But these environments can be much more than just pretty backdrops, but places that the player can choose to explore in an erotic context, changing the scene in interesting ways.

Of course, it should be noted that this will depend heavily on buy-in and capacity from your environment designers. If it's a bespoke environment, it's much harder to add on extra interaction points as opposed to just a backdrop for a cutscene. On the other hand, it may be a reused environment from other parts of the game, possibly with interactions already built in – your team may have less work on some fronts, but need to be on the lookout for new bugs or issues caused by sex-specific interactions. Either way, it's worth discussing with your team and getting their reaction; they may be exhausted and disinterested, or they may be excited for their work to get explored in new ways! Consider the possibilities of creating a lush, sexy location and actually allowing the players to get a full experience of it, rather than just seeing a corner of a bed or other restricted section! (Figure 24.5).

FIGURE 24.5 And if you're going to have to spend three weeks rendering the couch AND the bed, may as well let people get freaky on both, right? (fizkes/Shutterstock.com.)

Considering agency and choice in terms of environment design is, again, an element that many pornographic games are already exploring. Many have location-specific animations that can be triggered in different parts of a room or environment (e.g., bending a character over a chair vs. lying down in a bed). In the context of pornography, this does allow for a variety of sexual positions for the purposes of player arousal. But even non-pornographic games can use the environment in sexy and creative ways, particularly when combined with other choices already discussed, such as abstract tone or characterization. Having control over where the characters fall into each other's arms or perform certain acts can have a major impact on what the player takes away from the encounter and what emotions and moods they're left with.

As an example, imagine a penthouse environment like this in a video game (Figures 24.6 and 24.7).

It's a luxurious, fully realized living room, with beautiful views, warm fireplaces, and cozy couches. It's easy to envision characters getting "in the mood" in such a location, so let's explore how environment-based choice could be used in this kind of a space in a branching choice game.

Imagine the scene beginning with a player character and love interest (LI) sitting together on the couch, engaging in branching conversation with each other. Near the end of the conversation, players can choose to initiate a kiss with the love interest, which they reciprocate; not doing so will result on a non-sexual, non-romantic ending to the scene. Kissing then escalates into a little mutual "making out" then triggers another non-environment consent choice, whether to ease off for now or to initiate sex explicitly. Rather

FIGURE 24.6 This penthouse is not that unlike some actual in-game locations, such as penthouses in *Grand Theft Auto* or Shepard's apartment in the *Mass Effect 3 Citadel DLC*. (Kuprynenko Andrii/ Shutterstock.com.)

FIGURE 24.7 This penthouse is not that unlike some actual in-game locations, such as penthouses in *Grand Theft Auto* or Shepard's apartment in the *Mass Effect 3 Citadel DLC*. (Kuprynenko Andrii/ Shutterstock.com.)

than that being the last choice, however, the love interest might ask playfully, "where?" The dialogue could then branch out into three environment-based choices, which in turn affect the tenor, mood, and context of the sex:

- **Continue kissing/having sex on the couch** – if players choose this option, the characters continue "making out" on the couch, but gain more urgency, fumbling with excitement and desire. One partner presses the other back on the seat, pulling their shirt off before diving back in eagerly to kiss and embrace. The rest of the sex proceeds with a similar energy as a couple of horny teenagers having sex on the couch – a little logistically awkward but enthusiastic and eager, as well as showing an active hunger and urgency for each other. The mood is lighthearted and fun, including the aftermath – think panting and silly grins and "wow" (Figure 24.8).

- **Move to the floor in front of the fireplace** – bonus if the floor has a nice big fluffy carpet! Moving the activity here takes on a very different energy, one of romance, sensuality, and lush sexuality. The camerawork might change to reflect this, focusing on the light playing over the lovers' bodies, or shifting to slow motion or artistic close-ups. The character dynamics would be more serious, sentimental, and emotional – this would be the choice with moments like staring into each other's eyes and passionate declarations of eternal love. The aftermath would continue the romantic energy with lingering embraces, soft whispered confessions, etc. (Figure 24.9).

- **Have sex up against the window** – if the couch is "fun teenage fumbling" and the fireplace is "idealized romance novel sex," the window would be "raunchy passionate

FIGURE 24.8　The couch could be giddy and fun…(Dean Drobot/Shutterstock.com.)

FIGURE 24.9　The floor could be emotional and sensual…(Doronin Denis/Shutterstock.com.)

kink." Here, the emotion might be on the thrill of the encounter, both in terms of pseudo-voyeurism ("I wonder if someone could see us!") and illusion of danger ("Could we bang *so hard* that we shatter the window?") The encounter could be rougher, rawer, with elements of kink and consensual power exchange – the player might "order" the LI over to the window (who goes eagerly) as part of dominance play. The blocking could also be particularly intense and sexual, with emphasis on their bodies and lust and physical reactions, until finally the scene climaxes (ha ha) and leaves both exhausted after their exertions (Figure 24.10).

FIGURE 24.10   And the window could be steamy and raunchy! (Zapylaiev Kostiantyn/Shutterstock. com.)

FIGURE 24.11   Er…only if your team is up for it, that is. (Xavier Gallego Morell/Shutterstock.com.)

This kind of design is, of course, just an idea, and it's also just a baseline and beginning; depending on the mechanics of a game, environment-based interactions can be even more granular than a simple three-way choice. Imagine the sexy possibilities that could play out in a 3D or VR game if you pick up a pillow and begin play-fighting with it… (Figure 24.11).

THE CHOICE VS. THE VERB

For the purposes of this chapter, we have been discussing agency and interactivity in sex scenes in the term of "choice" – often in terms of branching choices, or dialogue trees, or something similar. But there is, of course, a wide range of other possibilities out there, of other mechanics and application of game design, of other verbs to use…things that involve direct controller input, or reaction time, or complete control over touch and movement. These mechanics are important enough to warrant their own chapter, which is coming up next, but it's worth noting that they too can be used to influence the narrative in the same ways that a branching choice might. You could have the player choose "touch his cheek," from a menu or a button press to deepen the romantic vibes of the encounter…but what if the player can make the gesture and touch the character's cheek themselves?

Game systems are infinitely varied, and of course, not all of them will allow for this level of physicality, but it's worth considering how the systems you *do* have can allow players to express themselves in intimate moments and influence the narrative, as opposed to just abstract text choices like "kiss him." Just as many games eschew simple branching choices in favor of player-responsive narrative (e.g., walking away from an NPC triggering a voice line, "Hey, where are you going?") consider designing sex scenes around the same concepts of player-responsiveness and recognizing what their physical actions, touches, and interactions are.

CONCLUSION

Not every sex scene needs deep choice to be effective, but it doesn't follow then that choice for sex scenes is meaningless or only related to titillation and sexual satisfaction. While opening up sex scenes for further agency and choice can result in more work in terms of narrative, character, cinematic, and environment design, the results can feel more organic and more nuanced than a simple cutscene. By giving players more freedom and agency over their sexual encounters, game designers can offer more meaningful, more personal, and more erotic sex scenes and choices, as well as allowing them to really roleplay their avatar in the world.

WORKSHOP QUESTIONS

Analysis: Do the sex scenes in the game you're analyzing offer any mid-scene choices to the player?

- If so, what kinds of choices do they offer? Are they primarily dialogue, or actions via branching choice? (e.g., "Kiss him") Are they high-level decisions (e.g., about mood, emotions) or more hands-on (e.g., types of sex acts)? Are they adjective, adverbs, or adverbs? How do they influence the way the scene plays out?

- If not, does the scene work better without it? Is it part of a linear game as a whole (i.e., in a game where the player doesn't make such choices anyway?) Does it use other gameplay verbs (e.g., touching, moving?) If you were to introduce this kind of choice in the middle of the scene, what type of choice would you include?

Creative: Does your game include branching choices as part of its gameplay, and will there be branching choices as part of your sexual content? If not, feel free to skip, but if so:

- Brainstorm at least two separate choice points within the sex scene, NOT including the initial choice to initiate sex.

    - For at least one of those choice points, plot out at least one set of sub-choices per option. For example, if Choice A is a choice between the bed and the couch, then there should be a unique sub-branch for the bed (e.g., position) and another unique one for the couch.

    - Plot out the structure of the choices in the scene as a flowchart. You can have branches reunite (e.g., bed and couch might always come back to the same conversation), or you can have different "routes" or endings (e.g., choosing a certain position on the couch might result in getting a cramp and ending the scene!)

CHAPTER 25

Sex and Game Design (Part 2)

Mechanics and Verbs

Contributor: Sharang Biswas

A S MANY OF YOU eagle-eyed readers and designers have probably noticed long ago, a large majority of this book has been dealing with the idea of sexual game content as heavily narrative focused, more specifically focused on singular story beats and cutscenes with either choice-menu-based interactivity or no interactivity at all. In a shocking twist that surprises no one, a game writer with a love for visual novels and AAA games has Lots of Thoughts About That Sort of Sex In Games, surprise surprise! (Figure 25.1).

But that is absolutely not all there is to sex in games; in fact, it's really only scratching the surface of what games can do. Because games, after all, are not only about watching or choosing, but about doing; they're about verbs, systems, mechanics, and design. And as lovely as characters and dialogue and narrative "moments" are, your game systems are 100% a part of your story. And yes, that goes for sex as much – if not more – than anything else.

FIGURE 25.1 "Wow, that's really shocking that you would come at the topic from that angle. This is my surprised face." (fizkes/Shutterstock.com.)

DOI: 10.1201/9780429356650-29

Tabletop game designer Sharang Biswas has contributed a primer on sexual game design and exploring sexuality through gameplay. His recent book, *Honey and Hot Wax*, co-edited with Lucian Kahn, is an anthology of erotic art games intended for tabletop play. But while tabletop and analogue game design does not always translate fully to digital video game design, many of the same principles overlap or, at the very least, can provide good starting points to branch off from.

Take it away, Sharang!

SIDEBAR 25.1 – SEXUAL GAME DESIGN – BY SHARANG BISWAS

We tell children that sex is something two people share only when they love each other. Few cling to this naïveté as they grow older. Indeed, most of us discover in our teens that sex – and the desire for it – need have nothing to do with love (though many still cleave to the "two people" part until much later).

Like any social interaction, sex is about whatever we want it to be about. Self-exploration, duty, power, fun – these are just a few of the themes stories can explore through depictions of the erotic. Literature knows this. Film revels in this. And games…Games can take advantage of this from a unique vantage point: as an interactive medium, rather than merely showing sex via cutscenes, a game can allow a player to engage in the acts of sex. Long relegated to the field of porn games, playable sex can offer much more than titillation (though titillation as an end is neither blamable nor lamentable). If games are the artform where verbs carry meaning, than we can gain much from carefully considered sex scenes where players are handed the reins.

As game designers, how do we take best advantage of our interactive medium to tell stories about and through sex? Obviously, we can reach no single, definitive answer for such a varied artform as games. But looking at games that have tackled the issue in interesting ways might offer some insight.

Move Beyond Cutscenes

When I refer to "playable sex," I don't simply mean "Press X for a Fingers, Press Y for Tongue." While there's nothing wrong with that model, infinite possibilities exist beyond it.

Take Robert Yang's tiny masterpiece of a videogame *Hurt Me Plenty,* which thrusts the player into the role of a BDSM dominant and offers up the willing rump of a submissive partner in want/need of a spanking (Figure 25.2). Using a mouse or – if you possess the right motion-sensing technology – your hand, you actively strike your partner's butt. You have to watch for your partner's cues and vary the rhythm, speed, and intensity of your strokes in order to keep them satisfied. In fact, if you push your partner too much, if you ignore his signals and his safewords, the game literally locks you out, rendering itself unplayable for days.

Hurt Me Plenty grounds us in the physicality of sex. Through both the physical demands on the player and the simulated bodily reactions of the on-screen

FIGURE 25.2 *Hurt Me Plenty* by Robert Yang allows direct feedback from your mouse or other controller to translate into spanking a submissive partner, complete with speed, intensity, and frequency. Players must listen to the submissive's feedback and adjust accordingly to his comfort. (R. Yang, *Hurt Me Plenty*, published by R. Yang, PC/Mac/Linux, first published December 2, 2014. Screenshot from R. Yang, Radiator Blog, "Radiator 2 as Loud and Quiet," June 16, 2016, https://www.blog.radiator.debacle.us/2016/06/radiator-2-as-loud-and-quiet.html#more.)

submissive, the game reminds us that bodies – soft, moving bodies that can feel pleasure and pain – are part of sex. The game explores the *acts* of sex, not merely the *idea* of it.

Really Move Beyond Cutscenes

In some ways, analogue games have an advantage over their digital counterparts when it comes to interesting explorations of meaningful verbs. The entire meatspace canvas of verbs is available, onto which a game designer can paint whatever metaphors and meanings they choose. Stephen Dewey's *Ten Candles* asks players to snuff out candles to represent the mounting horror of the apocalypse. Hakan Seyalioglu and Kathryn Hymes' *SIGN* forces players to invent and comprehend a new sign language as a way to explore the powerlessness humans feels when they can't communicate. So perhaps we can employ the verbs commonly associated with sexuality in our games?

In my game *The Echo of the Unsaid*, part of the *"Honey & Hot Wax"* anthology of erotic games that I co-edited with Lucian Kahn, I attempt a similar feat. In the larp, I ask two consenting, informed players to perform various sex acts on each other as they play the roles of closeted college dudes navigating difficult feelings. The players repeatedly have sex, but are barred from ever talking about it. They may discuss anything else under the sun – but not the sex they *just* had. They're asked to use the awkwardness they might feel to flesh out their interactions.

Through this game, through the intimate acts with which the players are asked to engage, players are challenged with examining what sex acts *mean*. Do they change the way you think and feel about someone? Do their echoes color future interactions? Can you even play a game, put on a persona, and engage in fiction, while having sex?

Think *Around* Sex

The spectrum of human activity that pertains to "sexuality" is vast and varied and offers fertile inspiration for games. Loren Schmidt and Jimmy Andrews' *Realistic Kissing Simulator* is all about awkward make-out attempts. Robert Yang's *Cobra Club* is about sending consensual dick pics. Yeonsoo Julian Kim's *Pass the Sugar, Please* (also from the *"Honey & Hot Wax"* anthology) is a larp that casts players as new acquaintances at a tea party who just realized that they might have hooked up with each other at a masked, BDSM sex-party the previous night. Players spend the whole game confirming their suspicions and then attempting to euphemistically communicate their feelings through humorous comments about the food in front of them.

These games illustrate just a few ways in which we can dip into the holistic world of human sexuality, to create engaging (and often artistic) play experiences.

Where Do We Go from Here?

Even if you're not making a game "about" romance or sex, it's useful to consider whether touching on the topics would be valuable to the game. If you do decide to include such elements in your work, think *how*; think outside the box. How can players engage with the emotions and acts of sex more fully? What does sexual activity entail?

In your game, what is sex?

Sharang puts forward some great examples of games pushing new verbs and approaches to sex, as well as emphasizing the need to think outside the box. And of course, coming up with those sexual verbs, like *any* kind of game design centered on game verbs and systems, requires iteration, testing, and experimentation. Obviously, only you and your team can find out what verbs work for your game and for your sexual content, so don't be afraid to put down the book now and go start brainstorming on your own!

But if you're looking for a few suggestions or other inspirations for verbs and mechanics to consider for your game, here might be a *few* other good places to start. As always, this is not an exhaustive list, more like a place to start if you're looking to move beyond cutscenes and dialogue and into the systems, mechanics, and verbs of your video game.

YOU'VE GOT THE TOUCH! – TOUCH AS GAME VERB FOR SEX

Touch can include anything from rubbing, caressing, and grabbing to physical gestures like spanking or tugging. This might be done by actual player touch and gesture (e.g., motion controls or smartphone touchscreens), or it can be accomplished by abstraction with other game mechanics (even, as Sharang puts it, "press X for tongue!") Allowing players control over what they touch, where they touch, and in what way they touch can convey a more physical, grounded experience of sex, one that is more immersive and personal to the player. While it may not always be appropriate for every game, they can serve to create truly erotic play, sexiness and game mechanics married together. And of course, it's not like there are no narrative opportunities here either; there's nothing stopping you from connecting those character reveals and mood shifts we discussed in the last chapter to these verbs, rather than just dialogue choices!

Depending on the context, there can be a lot of emotional, narrative, and erotic difference between cupping someone's cheek gently vs. tugging them to you aggressively, or leaning in slowly for a kiss vs. quickly, or groping someone's chest vs. gently stroking a feather touch against them, or even touching with fingers and hands vs. touching with tongues or other appendages. If designers take a step back from assuming these choices are inherently "pornographic" or "meaningless," there's a lot of room to explore how players might express themselves physically in the moment and how that will influence their experience of the story and the gameplay. This is particularly true in games in formats that allow for more direct physical expression, such as touchscreen gaming (which allows for touching, rubbing, etc.) or VR (which allows for much more fidelity for hand movements, head movements, body language, gestures, etc.) (Figure 25.3).

And, of course, don't feel beholden to frameworks of traditional narrative, or even traditional reality! Who needs humans to get tactile, after all? Some of the most interesting touch-based gameplay can be explored through surrealist settings, visuals, or even concepts. One of the best examples of this in motion is the abstract game *Luxuria Superbia*; although it's not "explicitly" about sex, much of its imagery and text lends itself to sexual, or at least sensual, interpretation. The game centers around journeying to the center of a flower, represented by a long, pale tunnel with closed buds on the tunnel walls. As players touch the buds (either with mouse on PC, or with their fingertips on phone), the buds

FIGURE 25.3 "I have traced every single one of this guy's abs, and I can confirm…he is ticklish." (ArtFamily/Shutterstock.com.)

open and the walls flush with color, and the "delight score" goes up. If the player colors the whole flower, the whole thing starts shaking, the camera moves faster, the buds jump up and down "in joy," and suggestive text like "Touch me," and "Ah…" flashes onscreen…but only if the player has driven the delight score high enough. Thus, the core loop is touching the flower's tunnel and petals, edging it closer and closer to a high point of delight, then with one last touch, making it flush with color completely and triggering the final explosion of joy (Figure 25.4.).

FIGURE 25.4 *Luxuria Superbia* is an abstract game about sensuality that encourages the player to touch in a way that causes pleasure. (Tale of Tales, *Luxuria Superbia*, published by Tale of Tales, Android/Windows/Linux/Mac, November 5, 2013. Screenshot taken from game website, http://luxuria-superbia.com/.)

…why yes, it DOES sound extremely suggestive of touching a vulva and masturbating it to orgasm, doesn't it? And if that weren't suggestive enough, there's this text from the game's tips page:

> Your touch will color the flower.
> If the color becomes too intense,
> The flower will finish.
>
> Sometimes that is what you want.
> But most often, be gentle and slow.
> Enjoy!

Luxuria Superbia and games like it prove that there are plenty of ways to explore touch as a game mechanic in ways that are explicitly, implicitly, or abstractly about sex, sensuality, and pleasure, so don't write off the potential for exploring meaningful erotic gameplay just because your game may not involve "story" or "characters" in the traditional sense!

TENSION: THE GAME! – TENSE/CLIMB/BUILD AND RELEASE/FALL/TUMBLE AS GAME VERBS FOR SEX

Earlier chapters discussed tension as part of narrative, such as in relation to rising action and three act structure; we also discussed sexual tension, the buildup of anticipation before the satisfying release. But of course, this is also a cycle that works in the context of game design itself. There are many non-sexual games – particularly horror games or games with a hardcore challenge – that ground their experience in the ratcheting up of gameplay-related tension. The player experiences mounting tension in the form of anxiety, fear, frustration, until finally they find catharsis. In a game like *Ten Candles*, the apocalyptic tragic horror tabletop game that Sharang mentioned, this catharsis can be horror, or sorrow. In other games, that catharsis can be pleasure, almost orgasmic pleasure, even if the game itself isn't sexual. If you don't believe me, take a look at some Let's Plays of *Getting Over It with Bennett Foddy* (a brutally hard climbing game) and check out the reactions of some of the players when they finally reach a "safe" spot, or when they finally finish the game. The game may not be sexual in the least, but it certainly hits a deeply primal pleasure spot (Figure 25.5).

Surely there is room to explore how these similar game loops can be deployed in an explicitly erotic way? After all, when we discuss sex, or write about it in erotic text, we often use the metaphor of pleasure "building" or "climbing" to a peak. Well, if we look around, we can see plenty of games that use building and climbing as actual literal verbs in gameplay. Are there ways we could marry the literal game verbs with the metaphors of sexuality? I'm not suggesting a literal erotic version of *Getting Over It* with the player climbing up a naked body or something,[1] but there are ways to integrate gameplay that rises or climbs with rising sexual tension or arousal. There are also other gameplay loops

FIGURE 25.5 The average Let's Player's reaction to beating *Getting Over It with Bennett Foddy*. (tugol/Shutterstock.com.)

and gameplay verbs that rely on rising tension – endless runner games that keep speeding up as you run, for example, or deck-building games based around pulling The Perfect Card – so there's potential here to see how that rising tension might be made implicitly or explicitly erotic.

On the flip side of the building/climbing gameplay verbs, or the building/climbing tension, there's also the concept of falling or tumbling as release. Again, we see this in lots of erotic writing about sex or sexual relationships – I've used the phrase "fall into each other's arms" more than once in this book, and there's also often "falling" imagery related to orgasm or climax (e.g., "falling over the edge") Can we use literal tumbling and falling as verbs related to sexual release, or even just sexual action in general?

A good tabletop example of how both building and tumbling can be used in sexual contexts can be found in the game *Star Crossed*. The game is for two players, where each plays one half of a couple that really, *really* want to be together (whether romantically or sexually), but for some reason really, *really* shouldn't (e.g., enemies, dark secrets) The gameplay verbs revolve around an unsteady Jenga-like tower of blocks. When one character does something to attract the other, that player takes out a brick and puts it on top. And if the tower of bricks falls before the final scene, the characters "give in" and act on their forbidden attraction. Depending on the players and characters, that could mean kissing, confessing their feelings, or full-on passionate sex. The building of the tower of attraction, the tension of when it will topple, and the release are fantastic metaphors for building sexual tension (specifically, the "I know what will happen but not how" type we talked about earlier), and while the final collapse and surrender doesn't *have* to be sexual in nature, it says something that many user reviews on its website describe it in terms of being "hot" or evoking genuine desire (Figure 25.6). Like many of Sharang's examples, this is a tabletop game, but it may be possible to apply the same mechanics, or similar ones, in the context of digital video games.

FIGURE 25.6 This artwork from *Star Crossed* shows example characters in the context of the gameplay mechanic – the block tower – and in the context of sexual, narrative, AND gameplay tension. When the tower falls, will these characters fall into each other's arms? And what will the consequences be? (A. Roberts, art by J. Fink, *Star Crossed*, published by Bully Pulpit Games, February 14, 2019. Artwork sourced from Bully Pulpit Games, "Star Crossed," accessed September 15, 2021, https://bullypulpitgames.com/games/star-crossed/.)

SEEKING CONEXXXION: CONNECT AND FITTING TOGETHER AS GAME VERB FOR SEX

The last verb we'll discuss here is that of connecting, both literally and metaphorically. Connecting things together is another popular game mechanic, particularly in puzzle games, and the way those connections happen can be varied even just within that genre:

- For example, some puzzle games invite you to literally connect tiles together by drawing a line between matching tiles; once the line is drawn, the tiles are connected, and they vanish, granting you a high score. **Verb: connect**.

- For others, like match 3, the connections come when you bring similar tiles into physical contact with each other; once enough of them are together, they also disappear. Rather than the player literally connecting the tiles, they are moving them, matching them, and pushing them into physical contact in order to trigger the connection. **Verbs: match, push together**.

FIGURE 25.7 Yes, it's the triumphant return of Sexy Tetris! Fit that line piece in! (ace03/ Shutterstock.com.)

- Still other puzzle games, like the classic Tetris, are about taking differently shaped pieces and finding the optimal way to fit them together. The pieces connect as they are put into place, and the newly connected lines disappear. Usually, the better the piece fits, the better the play, and the better the player feels. **Verbs: fit in, fit together, insert** (Figure 25.7).

Sex also involves connection on a human level, whether it's purely physical (the connection of bodies), social (the connection of people), or spiritual (the connection of souls). As such, connection-as-action and connection-as-verb seems like a good match (ha ha) for sex as a theme. If you look at the verbs above, they all work as sexual verbs almost as well as gameplay verbs. Perhaps this is why several adult games, such as *HuniePop*, use match-3 or other puzzle gameplay as the main mechanic in sexually pleasing the love interests, or in triggering sexual scenes or CGs.[2] But the actual gameplay itself doesn't always fully lean into these verbs' sexual potential; matching successfully might score higher "pleasure" or make the NPC moan, but the actual ACT of matching isn't particularly erotic in terms of its tile imagery, its tactileness, or how its tiles meet and connect with each other. More could be done to connect the act of matching, connecting, and fitting pieces together to the way bodies can do the same. Just saying, if you're going to do Sexy Tetris, may as well not pull any punches!

There are, of course, other ways to explore connection as an actual emotional or social action. Verbs you might see in strategy or diplomacy games like negotiate, ally, agree, even trade can be brought into erotic contexts. Or other game mechanics can be brought into play to generate attraction, connection, arousal, or compatibility. We see another good tabletop example of this in Naomi Clark's *Consentacle*. *Consentacle* is a cooperative card game where two players take the role of a human and a tentacled alien trying to have a consensual, mutually satisfying romantic or sexual encounter. This gets expressed in gameplay

FIGURE 25.8   Naomi Clark's *Consentacle* uses cards with sexual gestures and verbs to build a connection of trust and satisfaction between human and alien. Note how the trust tokens in the upper left corner *literally* connect together, emphasizing the notion of trust (and later satisfaction) as something shared and combined. (N. Clark, Consentacle, published December 22, 2018, updated July 15, 2020, https://metasynthie.itch.io/consentacle-print-and-play-edition.)

by having both alien and humans gain their own trust tokens, then pooling and sharing them with their partner, then eventually converting them into Satisfaction tokens by "connecting" them. All of these actions are represented by cards with gestures like "wink," "stroke," "kiss," and "release." Depending on how the players choose to play, all of these actions, negotiations, and token sharing may have to be done through complete nonverbal communication, reflecting the challenge of the human and alien in communicating without language, yet still managing to connect on a sexual level (Figure 25.8). Like *Star Crossed* and Sharang's list of tabletop games, *Consentacle* might be tricky to replicate in a purely digital game, as it relies at least partially on in-person gestures and interaction. But it's still a very useful and inspirational example of how sexual connections, and the verbs that generate those connections, can be done in a measurable and playful way. That leaves plenty of room for designers to explore and create similar dynamics that are tailored for a virtual, video game space.

These are just a few examples of the sorts of verbs, game systems, and mechanics you might consider for sex games or sexual gameplay. But this is only the tip of the iceberg. You may find, as you dig into the sexual imagery or metaphors you want to explore, that other verbs present themselves, verbs you've never even thought of, at least not in a sexual way. Don't be afraid to experiment, and as Sharang says, don't be afraid to think outside the box!

CONCLUSION

Games tell stories as much (if not more) through their systems and mechanics as through their characters and cutscenes. Allowing players to explore sex through gameplay verbs also allows them to create their own meaning, whether it's through a character or persona they're playing or whether it's as themselves. There are so many ways for us to play – and sexual game design should reflect that too.

Having said that, there's no reason gameplay and traditional video game narrative can't coexist! Only you can say whether your game is better served by integrated sexual game mechanics, steamy story cutscenes, or both. At any rate, next chapter, we'll be going back to the narrative cutscene well one last time…

WORKSHOP QUESTIONS

Analysis: Does the game you're analyzing use any gameplay verbs for its presentation of sex, or verbs other than "talk" or "choose menu options?" If so, how do those verbs relate to the platform it's on (e.g., using touch for mobile games)?

Creative: Define at least two gameplay verbs that apply to your sexual content in your game.

- If you are making a straightforward visual novel or similar game, these verbs might be, "pick choices" and "talk," or something similar; however, do not feel you have to limit yourself if you wish to explore other modes of gameplay!

- For other genres, the sky is the limit for your verbs (and feel free to define more than two!) But take the time to consider and indicate how these verbs will be sexual. Are they eroticized? Do they involve directly engaging with the sex (e.g., touching, grabbing, moving), or are they abstracted? What do the systems have to say about sex?

Bonus creative exercise: Take an existing non-sexual game you like with particularly strong basic game mechanics and/or a strong core loop. Consider the verbs used for this game. Then consider: how would you make a game with those verbs/loops/mechanics as "sexual"? Use the original game as a jumping off point, not a restraining influence or a simple answer of, "X game but with more sexiness." For example, if you take a competitive card game like Magic: The Gathering as your base, don't just say, "Magic with more butts"; consider how you might create a competitive card game where the card-to-card combat is replaced by card-to-card intimacy, and how that might affect things like game balance, win states, and game mood. Brainstorm with your team, then write out your "redesign" notes on a page or two (or more, if needed). If you're feeling really daring, see if you can prototype your new game out and playtest it!

NOTES

1 Though now that I write it out…it could be kind of interesting, if done well!
2 HuniePot, *HuniePop*, published by HuniePot, January 19, 2015, https://store.steampowered.com/app/339800/HuniePop/.

CHAPTER 26

The Aftermath of Sex Scenes

I T'S DONE. YOUR CHARACTERS have fallen into each other's arms, the clothes have come off, and a fun time has been had by all (character AND players).

That's all there is to it, right?

Well, not exactly. A gymnast can do the most amazing loop de loop triple flip in the world, but they still need to stick the landing. Similarly, you can have the most amazing, wonderful, emotionally moving sex scene in the world…but if the "dismount" (ha ha) falls flat, your scene may only be half as effective, and the transition back into "regular game" can be jarring. That's why it's important to consider how you depict the aftermath of sex (or even WHETHER to depict it) at least as carefully and thoughtfully as how you depict sex itself. There's a reason why, when one looks up images of the Cullen sex scene in *Dragon Age: Inquisition*, the majority of the image results are of the aftermath, of him naked in bed cupping the Inquisitor's face; the moment captures as much intimacy and physical eroticism as actual sex itself.

As we discussed in the context of narrative structure and falling action, aftermath scenes are not always vital to include. In some cases, cutting straight back to action IS the right call. But as a general rule, they can provide immensely useful moments for character and plot development, as well as an important space for an emotional transition back into the main flow of the game narrative. In many cases, there are threads – of emotion, of action, of story, or character – that are still dangling and need knitting up, or at the very least rearranging and being carefully placed for future consideration. If the sex itself knits them up, ending it there is likely the right call as "sticking around" would just draw things out after they're already resolved…but otherwise, the aftermath scene is required to do that knitting and arranging, or the transition will feel unfinished and rushed.

On top of that, showing the aftermath of sex can be particularly effective in situations where the sex itself is never shown. It's a space in which the developers, designers, and writers can explore the intimacy of sex (including the physical realities of that intimacy like nudity and touching) without the need to be extremely explicit. A fade to black *can* be

DOI: 10.1201/9780429356650-30

as erotic and meaningful as a full blow-by-blow sex scene if the lead-in is properly sexy… and if the lead-OUT feels like a satisfying payoff to the tension and dynamic of the scene.

However, it's worth noting that this is also a place where pacing can be a major consideration, as well as the need to progress the game and story as soon as quickly and efficiently as possible. While some games will benefit from long, languid pillow talk, others need only the briefest of moments – or sometimes, not even that much – before things start dragging and players start getting impatient. Knowing which approach to take with your game requires a strong understanding of your narrative, your characters, your gameplay, and the emotional journey that your players will be on…and when they're ready to make the next step into something new.

Remember that, in general, a scene in a game should always either further the story or the characters (either individually or in terms of relationship). We'll look at how scenes of afterglow, aftermath, and "the morning after" can deliver and develop these…. But first, some thoughts on logistics!

LOGISTICS AND DETAILS

For the purposes of this chapter, we're defining an "aftermath" scene as any scene that takes place in, well, the aftermath of having sex. This usually means a scene that takes place in the same location as the sex, or at least close by (e.g., in a bed, a next-door room) and in a reasonably short period of time from after the sex has finished, at maximum the next day or next morning.

Within those boundaries, the possibilities are almost infinite – pillow talk in the afterglow, getting dressed the next morning, weird dream sequences, explosive interruptions, oversleeping, almost anything you can think of! And in terms of navigating those possibilities, the choices your team makes have a strong impact on the mood and narrative underpinning of the scene. Just like with the sex scenes themselves, this is a place where the nitty-gritty details can be extremely important in how they tell a story. This is doubly true of aftermath scenes that take place after a "fade to black" – this will be a chance to use environment, dialogue, and even lighting to tell a story of what happened during that fade to black.

So, here is a (non-exhaustive!) list of questions and things to consider for scenes dealing with the aftermath of sex.

- Exactly how soon is it after the sex?
  - Are we talking collapsing on the bed, sweaty and panting? Cuddling and pillow talk a few minutes/hours later? Waking up the next morning? All of these will have different impacts on the immediacy and intimacy of the moment, as well as how much of a "continuation" it feels from the sex.
    - If you're showing the sweaty panting seconds after sex, it grounds the scene in the physical and character realities of what's just happened, and prioritizes the characters' exhaustion, satisfaction, and release of tension. This exhausted state can then lead to OTHER emotions bubbling up, e.g., blurting things out in an exhausted haze.

- In contrast, showing the next morning/day means the characters will often be in a very different mindset (since they've had time to sleep, or at least time to think) – the scene therefore is likely to feature more conscious, deliberate actions and conversations, with a more relaxed feel and tone.

- In between these is arguably the most flexible (and most common) approach for an aftermath scene – setting it at an indeterminate but short time later (could be minutes, could be hours), where the characters have had sex but also had time to catch their breath, come to rest, etc. These scenes offer an opportunity for quiet intimacy where the characters are calmer and not out of their minds with either lust or exhaustion, but also basking in the afterglow and close enough to the sexual encounter to still be in a particular headspace, to be dwelling on certain emotions, and potentially be more vulnerable and honest. Also, another minor but fun benefit of this approach – players have space to imagine just how much sex the characters actually had, and how many times! This approach is very common in AAA games (an example that springs to mind is Cora/Ryder in *Mass Effect: Andromeda*), but it happens in many indie games as well.

- What time of day/night is it?

  - This is related to the question of how soon after – after all, change of day is a simple way to convey passage of time – but also has some bearing on mood and ambiance, as Ashley discussed. Having the scene take place at night, for example, features cool colors and has connotations of sleep, secrecy, privacy, etc. In contrast, having the scene during golden light (dusk/dawn) can fill the scene with warmth, a literal afterglow. Connect with your lighting and environment teams as well as your writers and designers to discuss the best time of day to show the characters after the sex.

- Where are the characters (physically, location, etc.)?

  - This, of course, will depend heavily on where the sex was taking place, but spare a thought as to where the characters are in relation to that spot. The most common place we see characters after sex is cuddling in bed, and it's a classic for a reason – beds are handy for both sex and sleep, so it makes sense for the characters to be resting there. But don't discount other possibilities of where these characters could be and what position they're in! Are they still exactly where they began, or have they travelled around the room or space? Have they rolled onto the floor, found another soft surface, or maybe even in a place like a bath or pool? Are they lying down, sitting up, or even standing and walking around? And are both doing different things (e.g., one lying down while the other is getting dressed), and what does that indicate about their different emotional states?

- Are the characters physically close, or distant? Are they touching, and how?

- On a similar note, how close are the characters, and are they still entwined in some way? As a good rule of thumb, the closer the characters are, the more affectionate they will seem and the closer and more romantic their relationship comes off as – although it's absolutely possible to have casual partners cuddling too! Alternatively, if the characters are at opposite sides of the room, this *can* create a sort of distancing effect or reduced intimacy, though again, exceptions definitely exist. It's good to be aware of the undertones that proximity can convey, and either use or subvert them deliberately.

  – Also, consider your player base and what they may want to see in terms of character contact, cuddling, etc. – if you don't feature it, even if you feature plenty of other romantic cues, your players may still feel frustrated. There was a minor incidence of this in *Mass Effect 3*, where Shepard would wake up from a bad dream and see their lover; Liara and all the human love interests are in bed and undressed, cuddling with Shepard, but fan-favorite aliens Garrus and Tali are sitting on a couch on the other side of the room, already dressed. While this was partly for narrative and technical reasons (Tali has to remain suited up; Garrus had no unique "naked" models), and they do eventually cross to the bed and join Shepard, the result does make this scene feel slightly less intimate for those characters.

- What state of dress are they in? (Naked? Clothed? Underwear?)

  - A reasonably straightforward question, albeit potentially muddied by censorship issues (e.g., having to have characters in full underwear as opposed to nude). The answer to the question depends pretty heavily on what you've depicted in the previous sex scene – if you had characters stripping down naked, then suddenly having them reappear with underwear might be jarring! Going from clothes to underwear/naked (e.g., "up against the wall" to a bed) can work, but the scene must flow in a way that makes the passage of time clear. In cases where the sex scene was left ambiguous (e.g., fade to black), it comes down again to what mood and impression you want to leave with players.

  - Nudity or underwear is a much more explicit acknowledgment of what the characters have just done, and it's a state that suggests at least some level of vulnerability and/or comfortable repose.

  - Fully clothed can be a bit trickier, as it is VERY easy to jog a player out of the moment if they think, "wait, did they just do it in full armor?" But that doesn't mean it can't work, particularly if the aftermath scene actually focuses on the act of redressing itself. While having sex in full armor is going to make a lot of players roll their eyes, a scene where the character is donning and adjusting their armor after a night of intimacy has a lot of emotional and symbolic potential (e.g., readjusting their metaphorical armor and shields as well before going out into the world) (Figure 26.1).

FIGURE 26.1 Also, consider the implications of having the characters in different states of dress! This can imply different levels of vulnerability…or just that one of them has to head off to work sooner than the other! (Dusan Petkovic/Shutterstock.com.)

- What state are their surroundings in?

  - That is, environment design, mark 2! Assuming the characters are in the same place that they started having sex in, are there now any visual changes to that space? While it's perfectly legitimate to leave the environment the same as when the characters began having sex, a little extra detail can suggest added context and subtleties about the sexual encounter. For example, newly rumpled bedsheets, broken furniture, or underwear hanging from somewhere implies an extremely enthusiastic encounter; candles burnt low can convey long passage of time and a long, languorous encounter.

- Are the characters at rest/"savoring," or are they active/getting ready?

  - This ties in somewhat closely with how long ago the sex finished – the more recent the sex, the more likely the characters are going to be resting and savoring the afterglow (though again, there are exceptions!) In many ways, this is a good way to set the tone of the scene and the characters; are they in a place where they can bask in pleasure (of the sex, of sensuality, of their romantic bond, etc.), or are they restless and either eager to get back to "the fight" or reluctantly forced to get back to it? The more "active" your characters are in terms of doing things like dressing, equipping, moving around the room, the more you will weight the scene toward "business as normal" and a new phase of the character and/or their relationship… hitting the "play" button, in a sense. In contrast, a restful scene where the characters savor the moment feels more like hitting the "pause" button, allowing the characters to remain in the moment before moving into the next phase of the story.

- Also, again, consider the interesting implications of having the two characters be in different phases or states, and what that says about their characters (e.g., in the first *Mass Effect*, the love interest waking from a deep restful sleep only to see Shepard already awake, dressed, and watching them – the contrast emphasizes Shepard's focus and enthusiasm).

- Is aftercare depicted?

  - Aftercare refers to activities designed to help sexual partners process and calm down after a sexual encounter, as well as seeing to any immediate physical needs. Examples can include bringing food and water, keeping them warm with a blanket, ensuring they have proper circulation (e.g., loosening bonds, rubbing wrists or other constricted areas), reassuring them or talking them through and out of the moment, cuddling them, or alternately, giving them space and not touching them. It's a particularly important component of BDSM and kink practices, particularly those that involve bondage, physical pain, or altered mind-spaces (e.g., sub space), but it should be a part of all healthy sexual encounters, even if it's just a quick "check in" between the partners afterward. Aftercare is different for every person, so this is a good avenue to explore new aspects and sides of your characters in relation to sex. Do they need to be held, or left alone? Do they need time to "drift off" into their own head, or need to be brought back in the moment? Is their preferred aftercare tender and emotional, or do they just want to stretch their legs a bit and have a beer? While aftercare can be an interesting and unique interaction to explore in aftermath scenes, one can still imply it without explicitly depicting it – cutting a scene to "some time later" can allow for the player to infer or imagine their own interpretations of the characters' aftercare, and sometimes even a short line of dialogue (e.g., "You okay?") can work as an implication that one or both characters has had to process and go through an aftercare phase (Figure 26.2).

- Is there dialogue, or is the scene silent?

  - They call it pillow talk for a reason! These scenes can absolutely be fantastic scenes of dialogue and conversation between characters, either through linear cutscenes or through player-chosen branching dialogues. Depending on the context of the aftermath scene (e.g., afterglow, altered states of consciousness), there is great potential for some really honest, vulnerable conversations between the characters.

  - However, don't discount the potential of a partially or completely silent scene! If you have the tech to execute it well (e.g., show facial expressions or subtle body language), you could possibly have an even more effective moment of communicating the characters' thoughts, feelings, and personal arcs. A verbal confession of love can be absolutely lovely, but sometimes, what you need is just one character touching the other's cheek and looking meaningfully into their eyes. Don't neglect the potential of your visual storytelling, and be ready to consider if an aftermath scene NEEDS dialogue…

FIGURE 26.2 *Cute Demon Crashers!* uses text and visuals to depict aftercare after the sexual encounters with the demons, particularly with the one who practices BDSM. In that scene, the player is made comfortable, has some tea to drink, and is able to decompress. (SugarScript, *Cute Demon Crashers!,* PC/Mac/Linux, partial version published April 7, 2015, full version published August 15, 2015. Screenshot from VNS NOW, "CDC Orias End," May 13, 2016, http://vnsnow.com/cdc-orias-end/.)

- Do the characters have sex again (or at least implied sex or intimacy)? How does the scene end?

  - A common trope for many romantic aftermath scenes is to have the characters kiss as the scene ends, with a heavy implication that they may be going to have sex again. "Round 2" can be a good cap for an aftermath scene, and usually does not require the same focus or attention as the first sex scene (in fact, focusing on it can throw off the pacing). Of course, if it's just a kiss, the player can also assume they just snuggled and went to sleep. An open-ended suggestion of intimacy like this is a good "default" to aim for in that it is so open to player interpretation.

  - But there are other ways to end a scene that should be considered, endings that may have more definitive emotional beats. For example, if your character has mentioned that they don't sleep well, then having a scene end with your character falling asleep in someone's arms is a major step! Similarly, if their ship just arrived at the crucial mission destination and time is of the essence, it makes more sense to see the characters getting up and preparing to tackle the job as opposed to going for a second round.

- Do other characters appear? How much of an "eyeful" do they get?

  - Consider the involvement (if any) of other characters (i.e., not the lovers) in this scene. It's possible to have serious, subtle nods to them – for example, a radio message from a crewmate reporting that something has happened or that they've arrived at the mission site. Of course, there's also the comedy approach, where other characters walk in on this aftermath and react accordingly. Adding more characters usually reduces the intimate, romantic aspect of a scene – naturally, since there are more people milling around – but can also provide a lightening of the tone and some genuinely funny moments, particularly if they get "an eyeful" or become aware that sex has happened. One of the most famous examples of this, of course, is the Iron Bull scene in *Dragon Age: Inquisition*, but there's plenty of potential for other amusing (or serious!) approaches.

- What about dream sequences?

  - The aftermath of sex scenes is often a very useful place to put dream sequences – the logic being that the character(s) are tired, sleep is likely to happen, and thus dreaming is likely to occur. Most games feature dream sequences that tie back into the plot (e.g., a prophetic dream, a nightmare of the villain winning). But don't discount the potential for more intimate, emotional dreams, whether about the dreamer or their lover. Dream sequences can follow quite a different kind of narrative logic than other elements of aftermath scenes – of course, they're dreams! – and they can be interspaced with more conventional afterglow or morning after sequences (e.g., sex scene -> dream sequence -> waking up cuddling with sexual partner, at which point pillow talk happens). Of course, there is a risk of dream sequence storytelling coming off as either clumsy or heavy-handed, much like in non-sexual contexts, so use with caution.

Now that we've talked a bit about the details and logistics of a sex scene's aftermath, let's discuss how they can be used and the sorts of narrative transitions and purposes they can play.

PILLOW TALK AND PRIVATE CONFESSIONS: EXPLORING RELATIONSHIP AND CHARACTERS

The most common context and purpose of scenes that deal with the aftermath of sex is to explore character dynamics, both individually and in terms of relationship, particularly as they've been affected and influenced by the sex itself. We've talked about the common trope of pillow talk, where the characters will have a relaxed, intimate conversation, usually with heavy emphasis on bonding, honesty, and trust, while basking in the afterglow of sex. This is a great context for characters to have honest conversations or confessions about their feelings for each other, or how they want the relationship to progress. A large number of games go in this direction – popular AAA examples can be found in the *Dragon Age* series, *Mass Effect 3* and *Andromeda*, and *The Witcher 3*, along with plenty of others. These scenes are often fan favorites, offering them a moment that both explicitly defines the nature of beloved characters' relationships and focuses on intimacy, connection, and pleasure (or the afterglow of it). It can also be a relatively "cheap" place, in terms of narrative footprint and development, to set up or imply a future for these characters, whether short term or long term. Your game may not be set up for showing "happily ever after" at the end, but having the lovers discuss what they will do after everything is "done" – and whether they will do it together – can be a touching and effective substitute. Beyond dialogue, there's also great potential for symbolic dreamscapes – dreams of chasing one's lover and then either finding them or losing them can add important context to the dreamer's feelings after they've had sexual intimacy. And in the waking world, don't discount physical gestures of intimacy, love, or affection either. While honest and vulnerable discussions are great to have, they can sometimes be had without words at all, and sometimes a quiet moment of cuddling in the afterglow can hit your players harder and better than any full dialogue scene.

Note, of course, that "honest and vulnerable discussions of relationships" can be an amazingly broad and open-ended topic. All kinds of interesting conversations can be had, and not all of them are necessarily cozy or deeply emotional. For example, several of the aforementioned game examples offer the player a dialogue option during the pillow talk where they can either choose to make their relationship serious...or assert clearly that they see it as just a casual fling. How the NPCs respond depends heavily on their characterization, as well as to a certain extent the larger intent of the game. For example, if the game does not want players to feel "punished" or "bad" for pursuing casual relationships, they may respond positively, even if they may have hoped for something more serious, but if the game wants to explore more complicated, realistic, and sometimes messy dynamics, the characters may feel hurt or angry or used. Other possibilities could include more aggressive dynamics such as arguments, either about the sex itself or about a non-sexual element of their relationship (e.g., "How could you risk your life like that?") Others may find themselves wanting to pull away (e.g., in *Dragon Age II*, Fenris is overwhelmed by the experience of sex and ends up pulling away from Hawke). This should be done carefully; ask yourself if a "sour" moment after the sex runs the risk of "spoiling" the pleasure the players will get from the previous sexual or intimate moment. Still, there are absolutely examples where it makes logical sense, from a characterization and narrative perspective, for things to play out a little less positively (Figure 26.3).

FIGURE 26.3 Not every conversation after sex is going to be a positive one. (Motortion Films/ Shutterstock.com.)

Lastly, while we've been discussing aftermath scenes as a way to explore relationship dynamics between characters, they can also be ways to explore the mindset or the arc of a specific character. Given that pillow talk, afterglow, and aftermath scenes are often highlighted by their emphasis on honesty and vulnerability, it makes sense that those would extend to characters on a personal level, whether it's forcing them to confront their hopes and fears or simply making them contemplative about themselves and the journey they have been on. Given the high-stakes nature of many video games, this is often tinged with fears or worries about how "the battle" is going to go, but you can theoretically explore any aspect of a character where some time to rest and connect with someone would make them thoughtful, regretful, or hopeful. These character moments can be depicted through dialogue, silent body language (e.g., a scene where the character quietly slumps in worry) or even a dream sequence about their hopes/fears/etc.

There are excellent examples of this character-focused aftermath dynamic in several games, but *Mass Effect 3* offers a particularly good example of both dream use and dialogue for establishing Shepard's character state after sex.

- Shepard and crew are on their way to one of the final climactic battles of the game, with the fate of the galaxy and billions of lives at stake. In the wait before arriving at their destination, Shepard spends time with their love interest (if there is one present) and can initiate sexual intimacy, which triggers either a short intimate scene (Liara, Kaiden, Ashley) or a fade to black (other romance options).

- Immediately after the scene, Shepard has a short dream sequence – part of a recurring set of dreams – where they seek a mysterious child (who looks like a real-life child they failed to save at the start of the game). When they find him, he's in the arms of another Shepard, and they are both calmly consumed by flames. While the dream's meaning is not made explicit, Shepard is clearly disturbed by the dream, and it can be interpreted as an expression of their fears of dying, of failure, of feeling responsible, etc.

- Shepard wakes up next to their lover in bed (except Garrus/Tali, who sit elsewhere), and has a moment of silent body language (slumping, looking exhausted, etc.) that conveys their emotional state, as well as the fact they feel honest and vulnerable enough to show that state around their lover

- Sure enough, their lover questions them, and the player can choose dialogue options to convey Shepard's honest emotional state (e.g., "I think we can win," "It's hopeless," "It's too much responsibility"), in which Shepard will go into some detail over the extent of their hopes and fears. While this honesty is partly due to exhaustion, it also ties into the trust and intimacy already established by the sexual scene prior.

- Shepard's lover reassures them of their strength and that they are trying their best. Their sincere support transitions easily to an affirmation of their shared romantic relationship and bond (including, in some routes, some hints at a future together), while also providing a framework and support for Shepard's emotional journey.

- After a kiss or other intimate gesture, Shepard gets up, ready to face whatever comes.

This weaving of dream symbolism, post-sex vulnerability, and romantic support takes a small, intimate moment after sex and turns it into a major snapshot and insight into who Shepard is, where they are in their journey, and the emotions they're dealing with before the end. While it's arguably true that these could also be conveyed in a non-sexual version of the scene, the gentle intimacy and context of the scene gives it a different sort of weight, as well as making good use of emotional beats for Shepard AND their relationships (as well as fulfilling player expectations for some intimate moments after the sex!).

Before moving on, a few best practices for doing character or relationship-centric scenes in the immediate aftermath of sex:

- While it's certainly possible to do them "the next day," particularly right after waking up, it should be noted that setting this scene "too long" after the sex can result in some of the post-orgasmic relaxation and intimacy having faded, resulting in a slightly different feel. If your goal is "afterglow," featuring it soon afterward (before the characters go to sleep, for example) is your best bet.

- Similarly, if the goal is to depict the characters in a vulnerable state of emotions, it can often be easier to convey that when paired with visual vulnerability of being naked, in underwear, or in some sort of intimate or private clothing like special nightwear.

- In general, keep the mood low-key and quiet for these scenes – these are usually moments to be savored or carefully worked through, not rushed.

Okay, but what about when you, the developer/writer/etc., ARE in a rush?

THE MISSION-ARY POSITION: FURTHERING THE PLOT

Space and time can be at a premium in games, and in general, the sooner the player can return to gameplay and interactivity, the better (well, depending on the game!). While some games and genres lend themselves well to long, quiet, intimate scenes which take their time to explore characters and dynamics, other games want to get back to the shooting, climbing, etc....or at least, want to get back to the storyline directly related to that gameplay! So in these cases, if there is an aftermath of a sex scene, it might be the best call to use this scene to actually further the plot and push the player onto the next stage of the game. If done correctly, this can be a way to both further the plot of your game without sacrificing the intimacy and bonding between your characters.

There are several ways this can be done. The first is about as direct as you can get: **have the plot interrupt the sex or aftermath.** The classic version of this is to have the lovers cuddling or sleeping together...only for the wall to suddenly EXPLODE as they fall under attack! This is a useful trick as it allows you to still incorporate elements of a slower, more intimate scene while also moving quickly back into the action – in other words, you can hint at a more meaningful character or relationship moment that is tragically (or comically!) snatched away by circumstances and the violence that the characters have to deal with. Also, if the interruption is urgent in nature and relates directly to gameplay (e.g., enemies attacking), it's a fantastic way to get RIGHT back into the gameplay in a way that isn't jarring – or, at least, is deliberately jarring (for characters AND players) as opposed to negatively jarring. Other interruptions besides explosions and attacks could include phone calls, other characters bursting in, visuals that the characters notice ("Wait, how long was that black pyramid in the sky outside?"), a vehicle/train/ship arriving at a destination, or even news broadcasts on the radio or alarm clock.

Another approach is to have **a plot realization from the character(s)** as part of the intimate aftermath scene. In other words, after the sex, something about the context of the scene allows one of the characters to realize something vital about the story that will move the plot forward, either having a mental breakthrough or having some external influence or inspiration that triggers the realization. In some settings, a good example of this would be sleeping after sex and then having a prophetic dream which gives the character the clue they need to solve the mystery, progress their quest, or so on. Other examples could be where something about the sex or the connection they had inspires them to make a connection they normally wouldn't – perhaps some pillow talk in the context of intimacy ("This is about connecting…") could spark a realization ("Connecting…wait, that's it! We need to use the X to make a connection to Y!"). Regardless of what triggers it, and whether it's from the sex/intimacy/aftermath directly or not, the point is to further the plot and set up the next mission via the character's sudden realization.

Lastly, there is the approach where **the characters discuss and set up the next mission/ quest** as part of their "pillow talk" in the aftermath of sex. The characters can still be in an intimate situation (e.g., cuddling), but rather than discussing intimate subjects, they're focusing on and talking about what the player character needs to do next. This can be addressing an existing mission, or setting up a brand-new one based on the character(s) goals or stated concerns (e.g., saying they're worried about a particular threat -> a mission to neutralize that threat.) In a sense, the structure functions as a sort of intimate mission table – like a mission table, the player character receives instructions on their next moves, just with more nakedness involved.

Some examples of this structure in motion:

- After the train sex scene in *Wolfenstein: The New Order*, the action cuts to BJ (as first person POV) and Anya, both naked and close, waking up in their train car as the train announces the next stop at Berlin. Anya immediately tells BJ that she knows where to go for their mission to infiltrate a prison – a hotel that's on the same street as secret police headquarters. She gets out of bed (with a glancing touch from BJ) and opens the window, triggering a time jump cut to much later that day, at the hotel in question, with her giving BJ further details about the mission, then at last sending him off with a tender but brief kiss on the temple as a nod to their earlier intimacy. The player then engages in the mission, following the details Anya laid out.

- In *Assassins' Creed Origins*, after killing the last of the men responsible for the death of their son (at least, as far as they know), Bayek and Aya initiate romantic sex on a rooftop, after which the action cuts briefly to modern day. When it comes back to the couple, they're cuddling in a state of undress on the roof, but Bayek is troubled and distracted; what if they weren't the only ones, and there are more of them? Aya tries to reassure Bayek, but when he remains distracted and troubled, she suggests talking to Apollodorus, but to find "his man" at the Hippodrome first. The scene ends with some playful intimacy (a gentle tug, a passionate kiss) before Aya goes to report their latest kills to her contact. Gameplay resumes, and players can seek out Apollodorus' man at the Hippodrome as the next step in the crit path mission.

While both of these scenes do their job at progressing the story, their differing levels of effectiveness do highlight the difficult balance of revealing plot vs. intimacy, and how too much of one can unbalance or lessen another. In the *Wolfenstein* example, the scene works because whatever intimacy they may have shared (such as cuddling) is interrupted by the train arrival and by the urgency of their mission. The time jump to several hours later "softens" the sudden loss of intimate contact, and the scene as a result feels like it stands alone. It also doesn't "mix" the intimacy and the mission in extreme ways – the characters aren't discussing plans while canoodling naked, and the intimate gestures and moments are sweet but fleeting, as per the urgency of the mission. In *Origins*, however, while there is still clearly intimacy and romantic/sexual affection between Bayek and Aya, and the visuals support this, the scene is so laser-focused on setting up the next story beat as quickly as possible that their bond and sexual connection loses focus, at least slightly. As a result, players who want to savor the romantic connection between the couple may end up mildly frustrated and wanting more, even if it's just a few lines of emotional confession. Contrast, for example, the earlier scene with the characters in the cave, where they express their pleasure about being able to touch each other *before* launching into discussion of their mission. In some ways, the state of undress and physical intimacy makes the gap more noticeable, as players are visually primed for pillow talk and instead get The Next Mission. While the scene still generally works, it's a good idea to figure out if your scene is structured in a way where intimacy will be lessened by plot (or vice versa), and if so, where you want to hit that balance, and how you want to mix the two, if at all.

Some other suggestions and best practices:

- While pillow talk and character/relationship scenes can benefit from being set immediately after sex – in terms of time of day, state of dress, etc. – these scenes can sometimes benefit from being a little further along, such as when the characters are dressed or getting ready. This works as a good visual AND narrative transition back to missions and gameplay, i.e., "the intimate quiet moment is over, back to work!" Also, without nudity/beds/nighttime/etc., there's less visual priming for players to expect quiet bedroom intimacy and be frustrated when they don't get it.

- Having said that, it is 100% possible to integrate a more emotional or interior scene with a plot scene – for example, having one character talk about what they need to do the next day, then having an emotional moment where they discuss what it might mean. The sweet spot is going to be different for every game, so test early and often.

- Tone here can be quite varied, anything from OH CRAP WE'RE UNDER ATTACK to stern professionalism and focus to even comedic interludes (e.g., characters waltzing in at awkward moments to announce plot points)

- In general, the next actual gameplay beat should be somewhat soon after this scene, ideally immediately after the scene ends – after all, the point of this approach is to get back to the core game crit path quickly, so take advantage of that.

But of course, there's a way to get back to gameplay, or to other trains of story and plot, even faster than this…

DONE WITH PASSION, BACK TO THE ACTION: CUTTING TO BRAND-NEW SCENE

Scenes that deal with the afterglow or aftermath of sex can be meaningful and engaging, but as mentioned at the start of the chapter, they are not ALWAYS necessary. In some cases, the right call may actually be to cut away from the sex to a completely different scene, often a different time and place a while after the sex is done. The most common variant of this is to show player character with their partner – either in a fade to black or a full sex scene – then transition straight to the preparation for the next mission (e.g., mission table, preparing in a troop transport, arriving at the target destination). Unlike the examples in the previous section – where a mission or next plot beat is set up in the context of a scene of post-intimacy – this is a complete transition away from the sex and intimacy in favor of something different. There may be a brief mention or nod to it (e.g., the lovers showing up late and flustered, other characters making a joking comment, or even just a subtle gesture like making eye contact or holding hands), but beyond that, any sexual narrative beats end at the scene cut, and the next story beat begins immediately (Figure 26.4).

This approach CAN be done effectively, and in fact in some cases may be the better call, even over a post-coital mission discussion. It gets the player back in the flow of the game

FIGURE 26.4 "Glad you three could join us. Now, we've got intel on our next mission…" (Gorodenkoff/Shutterstock.com.)

very quickly and draws a neat line under the conclusion of the previous scene as opposed to drawing it out. *Mass Effect 2* manages this cut expertly, concluding its endgame sex scenes in a satisfying way while making an immediate transition to a pre-mission debrief with the Illusive Man. The *Wolfenstein* series also features a few quick transitions and cuts away (Anya/BJ in the cupboard and Bombate/Sigrun in the sub both feature immediate jumps to later scenes). These play out as more cinematic cuts that reflect the slightly comedic lines and beats each sex scene end on.

However, in cases where a cut away isn't done properly – or isn't the right transition for the scenes in question – the effect can be either jarring or dissatisfying. The former is often a result of shifting emotional gears too quickly without guiding the player out of the mood of the previous scene. Players CAN transition from a scene of gentle, sweet intimacy into explosions, danger, and excitement, but only if that transition has a deliberate tonal switch and setup (e.g., a surprise attack meant to jolt them out of the afterglow). Without that intentional shift, making the emotional jump is much harder. As for player dissatisfaction, this can often arise from simple disappointment over not getting MORE of a sexual relationship that the players have been invested in. If players have been rooting for the two characters to get together for the entire game, then finally have their wish come true, they need to have enough of a satisfying payoff for that patience…and if the camera and action cuts away too quickly, they may feel cheated.

In general, a good rule of thumb for cutting away directly from sex scenes and skipping an "aftermath" scene depends on two key points.

Firstly, ensure that the new scene you're cutting to is a somewhat close match in *energy* to the sex scene you're cutting from. Note that this does not mean a match in tone (the tone can be wildly different), nor does the energy and tension have to be an exact match, but they should be close enough that the step down (or step up) feels like a natural, easy transition to make. Transitioning to a terrifying death-defying action beat from a calm, sweet love scene can be too much of a jump, but transitioning to a serious but calm discussion of the mission feels like much less of a lurching shift.

- The game examples mentioned above follow this pattern:
  - *Mass Effect 2* features relatively calm, quiet, tender sex scenes for all love interests and then follows up with a conversation with the Illusive Man. The conversation is certainly not tender, trading it in for steely determination from both characters, but the scene itself is still relatively calm and quiet, and the tension is only ratcheted a few rungs higher from the previous scene, making it an easy transition.

  - The *Wolfenstein* examples, in contrast, feature rather quick, frantic, and somewhat tense sex scenes, then cut away to equally tense scenes – slightly LESS frantic (e.g., preparing for a mission or sneaking into an area), but still an energy match from what the player just witnessed.

- One exception to the rule to consider: transitioning from a frantic, tense sex scene to a calmer, less tense non-sex scene can be effective as a release of tension; in a sense, such a scene can function as a sort of "afterglow" in its own right, where the player has a chance to take a breath and gain their bearings.

Secondly, truly and honestly ask yourself whether the sex scene, as it stands, has an emotional conclusion that satisfies and stands alone, particularly in its last visual or moment, AND ask whether it has *fully* wrapped up and concluded any and all narrative, emotional, and plot threads related to that particular sexual encounter. This is vital to ask yourself EVERY time you create a sex scene, from both angles:

- If the answer is no, then there may need to be scenes that explore and develop the last moments of the sex scene and the emotional journey the characters have gone on. Without those scenes or conversations, the arc may feel "abandoned" at a critical moment, and players will feel frustrated that they're left hanging and wondering what happened next between the characters.

- If the answer is yes, but you put in "aftermath" scenes anyway, then you run the risk of over-elaborating or repeating on the characters' emotional journey, dragging the pace of the narrative down, and just generally contributing to narrative bloat. Sometimes the last beat of a sex scene is strong enough that the player doesn't NEED to know what happens immediately after – that they might be interested in imagining it for themselves – and adding it in unnecessarily just bores or frustrates them

To be clear, there is no right or wrong answer to this question, or any sense that one approach is better or worse than the other. Just because a sex scene does not end on a "strong enough" note (heavy quotation use here!) to make the scene stand alone does not mean it's a weak sex scene! All it means is that the sex is a part of the emotional arc of the scene, but not the *final* part; you need to fill in what that final part is before flying off to the next beat in the story.

CONCLUSION

Depicting the intimate aftermath of sex can be, in its own way, as thematically and emotionally meaningful as anything that comes before it. It is, after all, the last moment you leave the player with before returning to high-flying adventures, somber gritty conflict, or just the daily life of your protagonist. Make sure that final moment is a good one, and you may well find that it's the part that your players will remember most fondly.

WORKSHOP QUESTIONS

Analysis: What is the aftermath of the sex scene(s) or sexual content in the game you're analyzing? Does the game hop immediately back into "battle," or does it have some transitional scenes? If so, would you describe these as establishing a mood, exploring characters and relationships, or furthering the story? Does it leave you at a "good" place for the sex scene, or is more of a resolution needed?

Creative: For the sex scene(s) and content you're planning for your game, outline your plans for the scene immediately following. Make note of:

- Whether it's a continuation of the sex, a transitional scene (e.g., getting dressed), or a completely unrelated scene.

- What the dominant tone of the scene is (e.g., tender, quiet, tense, shocking, business-like) and whether you would describe it as high or low on energy.

- What are the character interactions and relationships like in the scene? What, if anything, do the characters talk about?

- What are the key points (either emotional or plotwise) that the scene has to convey to the players?

- How quickly do players return to regular gameplay? Is there a chance they may get impatient, and if so, how will you adjust?

- Are all the plot threads and rising tensions resolved or at least paused satisfactorily by the sex? By the subsequent scene? Can you identify any negative tension points the player may experience? (i.e., "Wait, that's IT? But I wanted to see…").

If you foresee this section including dialogue, it may be worth working with your writing team and experimenting with some sample conversations; like the earlier chapter, these don't have to be kept in the final game, but they may give a guideline for general mood, content, and feel for the final version.

Afterword

A
s this book comes to a close, I find myself thinking of all the topics there still are to cover. For every chapter in this book, as important as they are, I can think of at least two more that I would have loved to cover, but ran out of time or space. There's still so much more to say about sex in video games! What about kink, or polyamory in romance and sex? What about sex involving non-human characters like aliens…even the non-humanoid kind? What about magic and how it can be used for erotic purposes? What about foreplay; surely there's much more to be said about that in the context of game sex! What about creating sex scenes around player characters of customizable genders or bodies, or a chapter about the importance of creating sexual or erotic content for all five senses, or discussions of haptics in sexual game design, or the future of VR, or how to market games with sex in them, or or or…

But I keep in mind something from the first chapter in the book: this book is intended as a starting point, a foundation to build off as readers start thinking about video game sex in new ways and with new lenses. The same is true for me as much as my readers; this might not be a comprehensive book that covers everything, but hey, it's a pretty good place to start!

I hope that is true for you too. Most of all, I hope that this book will be helpful in your future projects, or at least enlightening as you play other games with sex in them. I want the game industry to start talking more about sex in games, and not just in generalities of "we need mature storytelling," but in terms of what makes sexual content work and how to make that content that appeals to all kinds of players. If this book has helped even a few developers start thinking in those terms, then I'm absolutely thrilled. And if it's helped those developers actually *make* games with some of the ideas in this book in mind, then I'm beyond ecstatic.

This is a start, not an end. There will be more discussions, more questions, and more books about sex in games to come, I'm sure – if not from me, then from other amazing developers and academics. And hopefully, there will be more games with interesting, compelling sex…maybe made by *you*, dear reader.

Believe me when I say that I cannot *wait* to play them.

Michelle Clough
September 18, 2021

Bibliography

Abernathy, Tom, and Richard Rouse III. "Death to the Three Act Structure! Toward a Unique Structure for Game Narratives," *GDC Vault*, accessed August 23, 2021, https://www.gdcvault.com/play/1020050/Death-to-the-Three-Act.

Atlus, *Catherine*, published by Atlus, PC/PS3/Xbox 360, February 17, 2011.

Aviles, Gwen. "'Fifty Shades of Grey' Was the Best-Selling Book of the Decade," *NBC News*, December 20, 2019, https://www.nbcnews.com/pop-culture/books/fifty-shades-grey-was-best-selling-book-decade-n1105731.

Blizzard Entertainment, *World of Warcraft*, published by Blizzard Entertainment, PC/Mac, November 23, 2004.

Blizzard Entertainment, *World of Warcraft: The Burning Crusade*, published by Blizzard Entertainment, PC/Mac, January 16, 2007.

Blizzard Entertainment, *World of Warcraft: Legion*, published by Blizzard Entertainment, PC/Mac, August 30, 2016.

BioWare, *Dragon Age: Origins*, published by Electronic Arts, PC/Mac/PS3/Xbox 360, November 3, 2009.

BioWare, *Dragon Age II*, published by Electronic Arts, PC/Mac/PS3/Xbox 360, March 8, 2011.

BioWare, *Dragon Age: Inquisition*, published by Electronic Arts, PC/PS3/PS4/Xbox 360/Xbox One, November 18, 2014.

BioWare, *Mass Effect*, published by Microsoft Game Studios and Electronic Arts, PC/PS3/Xbox 360, November 20, 2007.

BioWare, *Mass Effect 2*, published by Electronic Arts, PC/PS3/Xbox 360, January 26, 2010.

BioWare, *Mass Effect 3*, published by Electronic Arts, PC/PS3/Xbox 360, March 6, 2012.

BioWare, *Mass Effect: Andromeda*, published by Electronic Arts, PC/PS4/Xbox One, March 21, 2017.

BioWare, *Mass Effect Legendary Edition*, published by Electronic Arts, PC/PS4/Xbox One, May 14, 2021.

BioWare, *Star Wars: The Old Republic*, published by Electronic Arts, PC, December 20, 2011.

Biswas, Sharang, and Lucian Kahn. *Honey and Hot Wax*, London: Pelgrane Press, April 1, 2020, https://storytelling.pelgranepress.com/190-2/.

Bunting, Joe. "Freytag's Pyramid: Definition, Examples, and How to Use this Dramatic Structure in Your Writing," *The Write Practice*, accessed August 23, 2021, https://thewritepractice.com/freytags-pyramid/.

Castleman, Michael. "This Is Why Many Women Watch Porn," *Psychology Today*, June 1, 2020, https://www.psychologytoday.com/ca/blog/all-about-sex/202006/is-why-many-women-watch-porn.

Castlevania. Created by Warren Ellis, Adi Shankar, and Samuel Deats, Powerhouse Animation / Netflix, 2017–2021.

CD Projekt Red, *The Witcher 2: Assassins of Kings*, published by CD Projekt, PC/Mac/Linux/Xbox 360, May 17, 2011.

CD Projekt Red, *The Witcher 3: Wild Hunt*, published by CD Projekt, PC/PS4/PS5/Xbox One/Xbox Series X/S/Nintendo Switch, May 19, 2015.

Clark, Naomi. *Consentacle*, published December 22, 2018, updated July 15, 2020.

Clement, Jessica. "Distribution of Video Gamers in the United States in 2020, by Age Group," *Statista*, accessed August 8, 2021, https://www.statista.com/statistics/189582/age-of-us-video-game-players-since-2010/.

Clement, Jessica. "Distribution of Game Developers Worldwide from 2014 to 2021, by Gender," *Statista*, August 19, 2021, https://www.statista.com/statistics/453634/game-developer-gender-distribution-worldwide/.

Clement, Jessica. "Distribution of Video Gamers in the United States from 2006 to 2021, by Gender," *Statista*, August 20, 2021, https://www.statista.com/statistics/232383/gender-split-of-us-computer-and-video-gamers/.

Dalke, Rachel. "The Business of Romance Novels in the U.S. and the World," accessed August 8, 2021, https://cpb-us-w2.wpmucdn.com/u.osu.edu/dist/6/17036/files/2016/04/The-Business-of-Romance-Novels-Presentation-1t534ld.pdf.

Epler, John. Twitter Post, October 8th, 2019, 7:17 PM, https://twitter.com/eplerjc/status/1181755624599646209.

Entertainment Software Rating Board, "Ratings Guide," accessed September 19, 2021, https://www.esrb.org/ratings-guide/.

FindLaw, "Movie Day at the Supreme Court or 'I Know It When I See It': A History of the Definition of Obscenity," April 26, 2016, https://corporate.findlaw.com/litigation-disputes/movie-day-at-the-supreme-court-or-i-know-it-when-i-see-it-a.html.

Foddy, Bennet. *Getting Over It With Bennett Foddy*, published by Bennett Foddy, PC/Mac/Linux/iOS/Android, December 6, 2017.

Game of Thrones. Created by David Benioff and D. B. Weiss, HBO Entertainment, 2011–2019.

Hsu, Jeremy. "Why 'Uncanny Valley' Human Look-Alikes Put Us on Edge," *Scientific American,* April 3, 2012, https://www.scientificamerican.com/article/why-uncanny-valley-human-look-alikes-put-us-on-edge/.

Human Rights Watch, "No Support: Russia's 'Gay Propaganda' Law Imperils LGBT Youth," December 11, 2018, https://www.hrw.org/report/2018/12/11/no-support/russias-gay-propaganda-law-imperils-lgbt-youth.

HuniePot, *HuniePop*, published by HuniePot, January 19, 2015, https://store.steampowered.com/app/339800/HuniePop/.

Lanouette, Jennine. "A History of Three-Act Structure," *Screentakes*, December 24th, 2012 (originally published December 1999), https://www.screentakes.com/an-evolutionary-study-of-the-three-act-structure-model-in-drama/.

Leach, Samantha. "Romance Is a Billion-Dollar Literary Industry. So Why Is It Still So Overlooked?" *Glamour*, December 2, 2019, https://www.glamour.com/story/romance-is-a-billion-dollar-industry.

Lin, Brittney. "Diversity in Gaming Report: An Analysis of Diversity in Video Game Characters," *Diamond Lobby*, August 9, 2021, https://diamondlobby.com/geeky-stuff/diversity-in-gaming/.

Love Conquers All Games. *Ladykiller in a Bind*, published by Love Conquers All Games, PC/Mac/Linux, October 10, 2016.

Lunaris Games, *When the Night Comes*, published by Lunaris Games, PC, September 4, 2018.

Lunaris Games, *Errant Kingdom*, published by Lunaris Games, PC, January 24, 2020.

Lunaris Games, *Call Me Under*, published by Lunaris Games, PC/Nintendo Switch, release planned for late 2021.

MachineGames, *Wolfenstein: The New Order*, published by Bethesda Softworks, PC/PS3/PS4/Xbox 360/Xbox One, May 20, 2014.

MachineGames, *Wolfenstein II: The New Colossus*, published by Bethesda Softworks, PC/PS4/Xbox One, October 27, 2017.

Malcolm, Jeremy. "Payment Processors are Still Policing Your Sex Life, and the Latest Victim is FetLife," *Electronic Frontier Foundation*, March 15, 2017, https://www.eff.org/deeplinks/2017/03/payment-processors-are-still-policing-your-sex-life.

Morris, Sarah. "Video Game Age Ratings around the World: A Look at How Countries Rate Their Games," *Outcyders*, October 15, 2016, https://www.outcyders.net/article/video-game-age-ratings-around-world-a-look-at-how-countries-rate-their-games.

Mustanski, Brian. "How Often Do Men and Women Think About Sex?" *Psychology Today*, December 6, 2011, https://www.psychologytoday.com/ca/blog/the-sexual-continuum/201112/how-often-do-men-and-women-think-about-sex.

Mulvey, Laura. "*Visual Pleasure and Narrative Cinema*," scanned PDF, originally published in Screen, Volume 16, Issue 3, October 1, 1975, https://www.amherst.edu/system/files/media/1021/Laura%20Mulvey,%20Visual%20Pleasure.pdf.

Nededog, Jethro. "5 Reasons So Many Moms Are Obsessed with Starz's Sexy New Historical Fantasy Show 'Outlander,'" *Business Insider*, May 7, 2015, https://www.businessinsider.com/starzs-outlander-mom-audience-2015-5.

Nooney, Laine. "The Odd History of the First Erotic Computer Game," *The Atlantic*, December 2, 2014, https://www.theatlantic.com/technology/archive/2014/12/the-odd-history-of-the-first-erotic-computer-game/383114/.

Obscurasoft, *Coming Out On Top*, published by Obscurasoft, PC/Mac/Linux, December 10, 2014.

Pan European Game Information, "What do the labels mean?" accessed September 19, 2021, https://pegi.info/what-do-the-labels-mean.

Purchese, Robert. "The Voice behind The Witcher," *Eurogamer*, January 27th, 2017, https://www.eurogamer.net/articles/2017-01-27-the-voice-behind-the-witcher.

Quantic Dream, *Fahrenheit* (aka *Indigo Prophecy*), published by Atari, PC/PS2/Xbox, September 16, 2005.

Quantic Dream, *Heavy Rain*, published by Sony Computer Entertainment and Quantic Dream, PC/PS3/PS4, February 23, 2010.

Ready at Dawn, *God of War: Chains of Olympus*, published by Sony Computer Entertainment, PlayStation Portable, March 4, 2008.

Ready at Dawn, *God of War: Ghost of Sparta*, published by Sony Computer Entertainment, PlayStation Portable, November 2, 2010.

Reid, Graeme. "China's Pornography Laws Are a Backdoor for Censorship," *Human Rights Watch*, November 29, 2018, https://www.hrw.org/news/2018/11/29/chinas-pornography-laws-are-backdoor-censorship.

Roberts, Alex, art by Jess Fink. *Star Crossed*, published by Bully Pulpit Games, March 1, 2019.

Robertson, Adi. "Apple Is Using Itch.io's 'Offensive and Sexualized' Games as a Cudgel Against Epic," *The Verge*, May 7, 2021, https://www.theverge.com/2021/5/7/22425759/epic-apple-trial-app-store-itch-io-offensive-sexualized-unspeakable-games-day-5.

Rockstar North, *Grand Theft Auto V*, published by Rockstar Games, PC/PS3/PS4/PS5/Xbox360/Xbox One/Xbox Series X/S, September 17, 2013.

Santa Monica Studios, *God of War*, published by Sony Computer Entertainment, PlayStation 2, March 22, 2005.

Santa Monica Studios, *God of War II*, published by Sony Computer Entertainment, PlayStation 2, March 13, 2007.

Santa Monica Studios, *God of War III*, published by Sony Computer Entertainment, PS3/PS4, March 16, 2010.

Scott, Aubrey Jane. "Genderf*ck 2077," *GDC Vault*, accessed September 4, 2021, https://www.gdcvault.com/play/1027180/Genderf-ck.

Stuart, Keith. "The Writing of The Witcher 3," *Eurogamer*, October 15, 2019, https://www.eurogamer.net/articles/2019-10-15-the-writing-of-witcher-3.

Sucker Punch Productions, *inFAMOUS Second Son*, published by Sony Computer Entertainment, PlayStation 4, March 21, 2014.

SugarScript, *Cute Demon Crashers!*, PC/Mac/Linux, partial version published April 7, 2015, full version published August 15, 2015.

Supplement Place, "The World's Favorite Sensual Songs," accessed September 3, 2021, https://www.supplementplace.co.uk/sensual-songs/.

Tale of Tales, *Luxuria Superbia*, published by Tale of Tales, PC/Android, November 5, 2013.

tsweeney79, "FOX NEWS Mass Effect Sex Debate," YouTube video, 6:45, Jan 21, 2008, https://www.youtube.com/watch?v=PKzF173GqTU.

TV Tropes, "Establishing Character Moment," accessed August 12 2021, https://tvtropes.org/pmwiki/pmwiki.php/Main/EstablishingCharacterMoment.

Twitch, "Nudity, Pornography, and Other Sexual Content," accessed August 14, 2021, https://www.twitch.tv/p/en/legal/community-guidelines/sexualcontent/.

Ubisoft Montreal, *Prince of Persia: The Sands of Time*, published by Ubisoft, PC/PS2/Xbox/Gamecube, October 28, 2003.

Ubisoft Montreal, *Assassin's Creed II*, published by Ubisoft, PC/Mac/PS3/PS4/Xbox 360/Xbox One, November 17, 2009.

Ubisoft Montreal, *Assassin's Creed Brotherhood*, published by Ubisoft, PC/Mac/PS3/PS4/Xbox 360/Xbox One, November 16, 2010.

Ubisoft Montreal, *Far Cry 3*, published by Ubisoft, PC/PS3/Xbox 360/PS4/Xbox One, November 29, 2012.

Ubisoft Montreal, *Assassin's Creed Origins*, published by Ubisoft, PC/PS4/Xbox One/Stadia, October 27, 2017.

Ubisoft Montreal, *Assassin's Creed Odyssey*, published by Ubisoft, PC/PS4/Xbox One/Stadia/Nintendo Switch, October 5, 2018.

Valens, Ana. "Queer Developer Blasts Steam over 'Backwards' Adult Filter Review," *Daily Dot*, published January 16, 2020, updated May 19, 2021, https://www.dailydot.com/irl/steam-adult-content-queer-developer/.

Vimeo, "Vimeo Acceptable Use Community Guidelines," April 15, 2021, https://vimeo.com/help/guidelines.

Volition, *Saints Row IV*, published by Deep Silver, PC/Linux/PS3/PS4/Xbox 360/Xbox One/Nintendo Switch, August 20, 2013.

Watercutter, Angela. "Yes, Women Really Do Like Game of Thrones (We Have Proof)," *Wired*, June 3, 2013, https://www.wired.com/2013/06/women-game-of-thrones/.

Wikipedia, "Asexuality," accessed August 8, 2021, https://en.wikipedia.org/wiki/Asexuality.

Wikipedia, "Gaze," accessed September 5, 2021, https://en.wikipedia.org/wiki/Gaze.

Wikipedia, "Sex-Positive Movement." Last modified July 19, 2021. https://en.wikipedia.org/wiki/Sex-positive_movement.

Wood, Olivia. VideoBrains Event, "*Sex: it's complicated*" YouTube video, 18:01, May 17, 2016, https://www.youtube.com/watch?v=jZle4c1wFWk.

Yang, Robert. *Hurt Me Plenty*, PC/Mac/Linux, published by Robert Yang, first published December 2, 2014.

Yang, Robert. "On My Games Being Twice Banned by Twitch," September 24, 2015, https://www.blog.radiator.debacle.us/2015/09/on-my-games-being-twice-banned-by-twitch.html.

YouTube, "Nudity & Sexual Content Policies," accessed August 14, 2021, https://support.google.com/youtube/answer/2802002#zippy=%2Ceducational-content.

Index

Note: **Bold** page numbers refer to tables; *italic* page numbers refer to figures.